THE INVESTMENT TRUSTS HANDBOOK

Every owner of a physical copy of this edition of

can download the eBook for free direct from us at
Harriman House, in a DRM-free format that can be read on any eReader,
tablet or smartphone.

Simply head to:

ebooks.harriman–house.com/itshandbook18

to get your copy now.

THE
INVESTMENT
TRUSTS

HANDBOOK

2018

The latest thinking, opinion, research &
information on investment trusts

EDITED BY
JONATHAN DAVIS

HARRIMAN HOUSE LTD
18 College Street
Petersfield
Hampshire
GU31 4AD
GREAT BRITAIN
Tel: +44 (0)1730 233870

Email: enquiries@harriman-house.com
Website: www.harriman-house.com

First published in Great Britain in 2017.
Copyright © Harriman House Ltd.
Original chapter text and photographs remain copyright © of individual authors or firms.

The right of the authors to be identified as the Authors has been asserted in accordance with the Copyright, Design and Patents Act 1988.

Hardcover ISBN: 978-0-85719-669-9
eBook ISBN: 978-0-85719-670-5

British Library Cataloguing in Publication Data
A CIP catalogue record for this book can be obtained from the British Library.

Hh Harriman House

CONTENTS

INTRODUCTION

O VER THEIR 150 years of history investment trusts have proved themselves to be one of the great innovations in the financial world and rightly command loyalty and admiration among those who have taken the trouble to understand how and why they operate.

They remain, however, if not the best kept secret in the City, as was once said about them, still relatively little known and used by far fewer investors than they deserve to be. In an age when increasing numbers of individuals have shown themselves able and willing to take more responsibility for their own investment decisions, and the internet makes researching and monitoring investments greatly easier than in the past, anything that can shed a brighter light on the potential of the investment trust business is, I trust, to be welcomed.

The Investment Trusts Handbook you are looking at now is the first edition of a new publication. The idea behind the *Handbook* is to combine a detailed data-driven snapshot of the sector as it is today with a range of features, analysis and useful information that illuminates the opportunities trusts create for new and experienced investors alike. It is a reference work to keep and consult throughout the coming 12 months. The next edition will be published in November 2018.

As a longstanding investor in trusts, as well as a non-executive director, I am conscious that boards of directors need to keep pressing for improvement – keeping costs down, performance under review and portfolio managers on their toes. A flourishing trust sector is a force for good and it is important that more investors are kept aware of its potential to provide – as, in the right hands, a great number of trusts already do – a rewarding investment experience. We hope that this *Handbook* will contribute to that process.

* * *

Of course, some readers may say, what is the point of producing an annual handbook when so much information can be readily found in real-time on the internet? It is a fair question, but I don't think it is that hard to answer. One reason is that while basic information about investment trusts is indeed widely available on a range of websites, and many accessible for free, the context and analytical approach you need to take full advantage of that information is not. Interpretation of data is just as important as content.

A second reason is that some of the best research on investment trusts has long come from broker analysts, but it is becoming ever more difficult for individual investors to access; indeed, from 1 January 2018, thanks to a complex piece of European legislation known as MiFID II, it will become even harder than before. With the best analysts having already effectively been prevented from distributing research directly to anybody other than professional clients, the new legislation requires that all broker research be paid for directly for by those who use it.

One consequence of these new arrangements, almost certainly, is that the number of analysts following investment trusts in the City, and with it the amount of published research, will contract. At the last count there were 14 broking firms working in the sector, and not enough fee-paying business in the coming environment to justify the cost of the research that they collectively produce. As the number covering trusts declines, it creates a gap that other publishers and research providers such as ours will seek to fill.

A third reason is that not everyone wants to spend their time using the web to do research – in my experience, even as a professional investor, it can be tedious and time-consuming to collect all the relevant information you want in one place, even when you know where to go to find it. Not every website is able to provide all the information you need – numbers, charts, links – in the form that you want it.

One particular thing that I know would help me is a convenient calendar that gives me notice well in advance of when the investment trusts that I follow are likely to produce their interim and annual results. I also appreciate having advance warning of when annual general meetings are coming up. A calendar of just that sort is one of the features you will find in this *Handbook*, along with a directory of all the largest trusts currently listed in the London market.

Another important function that handbooks can play is to provide understanding and perspective. There was a time when cricket fans simply had to buy *Wisden* if they wanted to study and compare scorecards and averages across a whole season. Today online cricket databases, like those for many other sports, are wondrous things full of arcane facts and the most extraordinary minutiae.

The scores and averages, however, were never the sole, or even the primary reason, to rush out and buy the latest *Wisden*, as many used to do. It also included some excellent features by and about the best cricket writers and players. The handbook format similarly lends itself to picking and reproducing interesting commentary on the investment trust sector.

This inaugural edition includes contributions from some of the most highly-experienced and well-qualified investment trust professionals around, including Peter Spiller, Robin Angus, John Baron and James Burns. Mark Dampier, the head of research at the UK's largest retail broking firm, Hargreaves Lansdown (which is doing an increasing amount of business in investment trusts), also chips in with his observations about the sector.

We also have three in-depth interviews with prominent fund managers from different sectors, some additional insights on venture capital trusts, and a section that offers broad guidance on how to analyse trusts. We are looking forward to coming up with more features for next year's edition. All suggestions for improvements will be gratefully received. The problem, I suspect, will be to decide what to leave out as much as it is what to include.

* * *

How stands the investment trust business as we head into 2018?

At the time of writing these notes the short answer, I would say, is: in a pretty good place. Global equity markets are buoyant, which always helps, interest rates are still very low and the bond market has yet to reverse course decisively enough for us to be able to call the final turning point in the 35-year-old cycle of falling bond yields.

As a result of these positive market tailwinds and the broader use of discount controls by trust boards, the average discount across the sector – always a good indicator of its health – continues to narrow. At the end of the third quarter of 2017, the average discount on mainstream trusts was around its lowest level since the great financial crisis, while the average alternative asset trust, the fastest growing part of the IT universe, was trading at a premium to net asset value.

Investment trust discounts over the past ten years vs the ten-year average

Market-cap-weighted average discount for all investment trusts with an equity mandate
Source: Numis Securities, Morningstar

The emergence of a flourishing sector of alternative asset trusts, a broad grouping that extends from private equity to renewable energy, and from warehouses to mortgages and aircraft leasing, has been the most striking feature of the last few years in trust-land. The common feature that binds most of these disparate types of trust together – private equity being the major exception – is their ability to generate income for shareholders.

Alternative asset investment trusts – premiums/discounts over the past ten years

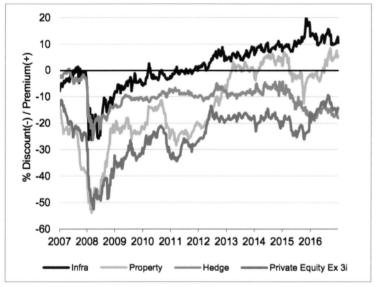

Based on market-cap-weighted averages
Source: Numis Securities

This in turn has spawned a steady stream of new trusts coming to the market and finding ready buyers, particularly among the wealth management and financial advisor communities, which are now the largest institutional buyers of investment trusts. Although it is not strictly true, it feels as if almost any new entity that can offer a headline yield of more than 5% will find a buyer, so great is the demand for anything with an income attached.

Trusts with what can broadly be described as an alternative asset mandate now account for around a third of the trusts in the Association of Investment Companies classification. Headline yields are not always what they appear to be, however. Trusts have a range of ways to enhance or pad out their income-generating capacity, now including the ability to draw on capital as well as revenue reserves, and you would do well to heed the advice from our contributors that it pays to look very carefully under the bonnet at how real and sustainable those yields may be.

* * *

How long the fashion for income and the persistence of premiums for these newcomers continues is one of the things that observers will be watching closely as we move into 2018. The greater diversity that you can now find in the trust universe as it has evolved today is, however, undoubtedly a source of strength. The ability of the investment trust sector to regenerate itself at periodic intervals has always been one of its defining characteristics.

History tells us, of course, that it is exactly at times like this, when all seems set fair, that a crisis may be just around the corner. The only predictable thing about stock markets, as J. P. Morgan observed many years ago, is that they will fluctuate. The cycle of boom and bust will persist as long as markets exist. Financial markets generally, however, are notable at the moment for their placidity. Volatility is at its lowest level for many years.

Experienced investors have noticed this and the prudent ones are making preparations for at least a temporary interruption in this benign picture – not because they necessarily can see the causes of the next downturn, merely that they know one will come eventually, as it always has done. Anyone who doubts as much would be well advised to study the history of the first and oldest investment trust of them all, Foreign & Colonial (F&C), which in 2018 marks the 150th anniversary of its formation.

As historian John Newlands reminds us in his essay on the subject, F&C was set up by three enterprising Victorian professionals to offer those with means the opportunity to invest in a well-diversified portfolio of high-yield bonds issued by what were then the emerging markets of their day. (A good quiz question, the answer to which you can find in John's piece, is to ask which government amongst the 19 original issuers in its initial portfolio was the first to default?)

While F&C was the pioneer in creating a listed investment vehicle of this kind, and rightly deserves the celebrations which are to be held to commemorate the fact over the course of 2018, it has had to endure many turbulent moments in its history since. So too has the whole investment trust sector, which over the years been buffeted by two world wars and market collapses, as well as occasional scandals.

F&C owes its continued survival and prosperity in part to its willingness to take big contrarian bets at times of market weakness, as it did in 1974 and 1987. An opportunity to do so again will undoubtedly emerge in due course. Whatever the trigger, the next bear market is sure to test the resolve of existing shareholders, but it will also – just as certainly – provide an opportunity for savvy trust connoisseurs to pick up bargains as discounts widen once more. For the forearmed investor, a crisis is an opportunity, not just a threat.

*   *   *

In the 1930s, just as investment trusts were starting to recover from the trauma of the 1929 market crash, a new and potent competitor to the investment trust appeared in the shape of the first open-ended fund. The unit trust, as it was known, being easier to run and market, and with the huge advantage of being able to offer sales incentives to financial advisors, has continued to outsell its older closed-end counterpart more or less ever since. The investment trust has survived that threat only by its ability – admittedly sometimes only under duress – to generate superior performance and higher standards of governance.

Scroll forward 80 years and it is possible to see new – and not dissimilar – threats emerging in the competitive landscape. One is the relentless rise of passive investment, which has seen ultra-cheap index funds and more recently exchange-traded funds (ETFs) challenge the traditional dominance of actively managed funds, into which category effectively all investment trusts fall. Tracker funds and ETFs offer a direct challenge to two of the investment trust's fundamental competitive advantages – low running costs and a commitment to effective active management.

The second threat comes from the ever-increasing burden of compliance with regulation. Ironically the Financial Conduct Authority, the financial services regulator, shows little sign of either understanding or caring much about investment trusts – in its recent Asset Management Review, it only mentioned the trust sector once by name (and that was in a footnote on p.94!). Some of the regulator's policies, such as the banning of sales commission to financial advisors for recommending funds and the drive for greater transparency on fees, have been positive for investors. Nevertheless the overall impact of a heavier-handed and more intrusive regime is clearly bearing down in a number of ways on the ability of the investment trust sector to operate profitably and grow.

Aside from the loss of competitive advantage of lower costs, one particularly important side effect of the new regulatory regime is that it has led to considerable consolidation in firms that traditionally have managed private client portfolios and remain the trust sector's biggest source of institutional support. That in turn has made it much harder for new trusts in the conventional equity fund mould to come to the market. Some private client firms now say they will only support the launch of a new trust if it is capable and likely of reaching at least £200m in assets.

Unless you are a particularly highly regarded star fund manager, such as Neil Woodford or Terry Smith, that is a disincentive and a tough hurdle for firms contemplating a trust launch to overcome. Only trusts with a clearly differentiated active management strategy and investment team are able to make it to the IPO stage. Were it not for the popularity of the all-conquering high-yielding newcomers in the alternative asset space, and the resilience and longevity of the bull market, you might perhaps be hearing questions raised about investment trusts' continuing relevance and survival.

*   *   *

Such questions are nothing new. Investment trusts have regularly had to demonstrate the ability to adapt or shrink and will doubtless do so again. It helps that the quality of board director, it seems to be widely accepted, has improved, as has their willingness to take a more active role in obtaining terms from their investment managers. The last couple of years have seen more trusts negotiating lower annual management charges and/or reviewing – and often eliminating altogether – the use of performance fees.

Trusts such as Scottish Mortgage have shown it is possible to use economies of scale to bring down their fees without apparent difficulty; its ongoing charge ratio of 44 basis points

(0.44% per annum) for an actively managed global equity fund is certainly competitive with the cheapest index fund alternative. The most successful trusts remain profitable for fund management firms, so I suspect there is room for margins to be squeezed further. For many smaller trusts, however, given the cost of their legal and reporting requirements as listed companies, and the competitive and regulatory challenges now emerging, it is going to remain an uphill struggle to keep costs down and some will probably fall by the wayside.

A somewhat different challenge faces those whose job is to analyse and value trusts. Putting a value on a trust that invests in renewable energy, or in infrastructure projects, or peer-to-peer lending, requires a different set of skills and techniques. Trusts in a new specialist sector such as renewable energy all use different discount rates and inflation assumptions, making valid comparisons more difficult. When index-linked gilts first appeared in the 1980s, it took a few years for the market to work out how to price them correctly. Something similar may be happening now in these new sectors. Analysts too, therefore, are also having to raise their game.

*   *   *

Such issues aside, investment trusts are in good order. They remain the investment vehicle of choice for many of the smartest investors I know. Performance of the best ones has been good and their traditional strengths – high-quality active management, effective use of gearing, the ability to follow a conviction approach – continue to stand them in good stead. They offer investors plenty of choice and diversification potential. That is why we look forward to continuing the task of chronicling their progress in the interesting times that undoubtedly lie ahead.

JONATHAN DAVIS
Oxford, 2017

JONATHAN DAVIS MA, MSc, MCSI is one of the UK's leading stock market authors and commentators. A qualified professional investor and member of the Chartered Institute for Securities and Investment, he is a senior advisor to Saunderson House and a non-executive director of the Jupiter UK Growth Trust. His books include *Money Makers, Investing With Anthony Bolton* and *Templeton's Way With Money*. After writing columns for *The Independent* and *Financial Times* for many years, he now contributes regularly to *The Spectator* and records a weekly interview with leading professional investors for the *Money Makers* podcast channel.

www.independent-investor.com
www.money-makers.co

ACKNOWLEDGEMENTS

Compiling the *The Investment Trusts Handbook 2018* has been an intensive and collective effort. Thanks are due to all those who have helped to bring it to fruition, whether as contributors or handmaidens to the production process.

At Harriman House: Stephen Eckett, Myles Hunt, Chris Parker, Sally Tickner and Tracy Bundey.

At the publishing partners: Alex Denny, Alex Wright and Dale Nicholls (Fidelity), Derek Stuart, Simon Edelsten and Billy Aitken (Artemis), Jo Oliver, Stuart Lewis and Dan D'Souza (Octopus).

Contributors: Robin Angus, John Baron, James Burns, Geoffrey Challinor, Sandy Cross, Mark Dampier, Max King, John Newlands, Peter Spiller.

Research: Charles Cade, Simon Elliott, Christopher Smith, Alan Brierley, Annabel Brodie Smith, Neil Shah, Robert Murphy, David Elliott.

TRUST BASICS

INVESTMENT TRUST BASICS

For first-time investors in trusts, here is an overview of investment trusts – what they are and how they invest – from editor JONATHAN DAVIS.

What is an investment trust?

INVESTMENT TRUSTS, ALSO known as investment companies, are a type of collective investment fund. All types of fund pool the money of a large number of different investors and delegate the investment of their pooled assets, typically to a professional fund manager. The idea is that this enables shareholders in the trust to spread their risks and benefit from the professional skills and economies of scale available to an investment management firm.

Collective funds have been a simple and popular way for individual investors to invest their savings for many years, and investment trusts have shared in that success. Today more than £170bn of savers' assets are invested in investment trusts. The first investment trust was launched as long ago as 1868, so they have a long history. Sales of open-ended funds (unit trusts and OEICs) have grown faster, but investment trust performance has generally been superior.

How do investment trusts differ from unit trusts and open-ended funds?

There are several differences. The most important ones are that shares in investment companies are traded on a stock exchange and are overseen by an independent board of directors, like any other listed company. Shareholders have the right to vote at annual general meetings (AGMs) and vote on the re-election of the directors. Trusts can also, unlike open-ended funds, borrow money in order to enhance returns. Whereas the size of unit trusts rises and falls from day to day, the capital base of an investment trust remains fixed.

What are discounts?

Because shares in investment trusts are traded on a stock exchange, the share price will fluctuate from day to day in response to supply and demand. Sometimes the shares will change hands for less than the net asset value of the company. At other times they will change hands for more than the NAV. The difference between the share price and the

NAV is calculated as a percentage of the NAV and is called a discount if the share price is below the NAV and a premium if it is above the NAV.

What is gearing?

In investment gearing refers to the ability of an investor to borrow money in an attempt to enhance the returns that flow from his or her investment decisions. If investments rise more rapidly than the cost of the borrowing, this has the effect of producing higher returns. The reverse is also true. Investment trusts typically borrow around 10%–20% of their assets, although this figure varies widely from one trust to another.

What are the main advantages of investing in an investment trust?

Because the capital is largely fixed, the managers of an investment trust can buy and sell the trust's investments when they wish to – instead of having to buy and sell simply because money is flowing in or out of the fund, as unit trust managers are required to do. The ability to gear, or use borrowed money, can also potentially produce better returns. The fact that the board of an investment trust is accountable to the shareholders can also be an advantage.

Another advantage is that investment companies can invest in a much wider range of investments than other types of fund. In fact, they can invest in almost anything. Although many of the largest trusts invest in listed stocks and bonds, more specialist sectors, such as renewable energy projects, debt securities, aircraft leasing and infrastructure projects such as schools, have also become much more popular in recent years. Investment trusts offer fund investors a broader choice, in other words.

And what are the disadvantages?

The two main disadvantages are share price volatility and potential loss of liquidity. Because investment trusts can trade at a discount to the value of their assets, an investor who sells at the wrong moment may not receive the full asset value for his shares at that point. The day-to-day value of the investment can also fluctuate more than an equivalent open-ended fund. In the case of more specialist trusts, it may not always be possible to buy or sell shares in a trust at a good price because of a lack of liquidity in the market. Investors need to make sure they understand these features before investing.

How many trusts are there?

According to the industry trade body, the Association of Investment Companies, there are currently 390 investment trusts with more than £170bn in assets (as at the end of August 2017). They are split between a number of different sectors. The largest trust has approximately £5bn in assets. 96% of the assets in investment companies are in conventional trusts with another 2% in venture capital trusts and 2% in split capital trusts.

How are they regulated?

All investment companies are regulated by the Financial Conduct Authority. So too are the managers the board appoints to manage the trust's investments. Investment trusts are also subject to the Listing Rules of the stock exchange on which they are listed. The board of directors is accountable to shareholders and regulators for the performance of the trust and the appointment of the manager.

How do I invest in an investment trust?

There are a number of different ways. You can buy them directly through a stockbroker, or via an online platform. Some larger investment trusts also have monthly savings schemes where you can transfer a fixed sum every month to the company, which then invests it into its shares on your behalf. If you have a financial adviser, or a portfolio manager, they can arrange the investment for you.

What do investment trusts cost?

As with any share, investors in investment trusts will need to pay brokerage commission when buying or selling shares in an investment trust, and also stamp duty on purchases. The managers appointed by the trust's directors to make its investments charge an annual management fee which is paid automatically, together with dealing and administration costs, out of the trust's assets. These management fees typically range from as little as 0.3% to 2.0% or more of the trust's assets.

What are tax wrappers?

Tax wrappers are schemes which allow individual investors, if they comply with the rules set by the government, to avoid tax on part or all of their investments. The two most important tax wrappers are the Individual Savings Account (or ISA) and the Self-Invested Personal Pension (SIPP). The majority of investment trusts can be held in an ISA or SIPP. There are annual limits on the amounts that can be invested each year (currently £20,000 for an ISA). Venture Capital Trusts (VCTs) are a specialist type of investment trust which also have a number of tax advantages, reflecting their higher risk.

Where can I find more information?

The best place to start is with the website of the Association of Investment Companies (AIC), which has a lot of basic information, as well as performance and other data. The *Money Makers* website has detailed interactive tables summarising the main features of all the most important trusts. Most online broker platforms, such as Hargreaves Lansdown, Fidelity Funds Network, The Share Centre and Alliance Trust, provide factsheets, performance data, charts and other information. Most trusts now have their own websites too.

Independent research sites, such as FE Trustnet, Interactive Investor, Citywire, DigitalLook, Morningstar and periodicals such as the *Financial Times*, *Money Week*, *Money Observer* and *Investors Chronicle* also regularly provide updates and recommendations on investment trusts. Citywire has a dedicated online investment trust newsletter. *Investment Trusts* is an independent subscription-only newsletter.

SOME USEFUL SOURCES OF INFORMATION

Industry information

The Association of Investment Companies | www.theaic.co.uk

Data, news and research

Morningstar | www.morningstar.co.uk

FE Trustnet | www.trustnet.co.uk

Citywire | www. citywire.co.uk

DigitalLook | www.digitallook.com

Financial Times | www.ft.com

Platforms

Interactive Investor | www.iii.co.uk

Hargreaves Lansdown | www.hl.co.uk

The Share Centre | www.share.com

Fidelity International | www.fidelity.co.uk

Alliance Trust Savings | www.alliancetrustsavings.co.uk

Sponsored research

Edison | www.edisoninvestmentresearch.com

QuotedData | www.quoteddata.com

Trust Intelligence (Kepler Partners) | www.trustintelligence.co.uk

Specialist publications

Investment Trust Newsletter (McHattie Group) | www.tipsheets.co.uk

Investment Trust Insider (Citywire) | www.citywire.co.uk

Money Observer (regular supplements) | www.moneyobserver.com

Publications that regularly feature investment trusts

Financial Times | www.ft.com

Investors Chronicle | www.investorschronicle.co.uk

MoneyWeek | www.moneyweek.com

TAKING THE PLUNGE

Considerations for the DIY investor

Investment trust expert MAX KING *offers advice to private investors on how to benefit from closed-end funds.*

A SIGNIFICANT PROPORTION OF the financial service sector operates on the assumption that savers are neither capable nor willing of looking after their own investments and so need help from the 'experts'. Inevitably this help and all the regulatory encumbrances that accompany it are costly, eating into investment returns. There is often a strong bias towards sacrificing returns for what the professionals regard as lower risk, but which is, in reality, only a reduction in short-term price volatility.

People are accustomed to taking significant financial decisions such as buying a property or a car without paying for advice so why do they not take the same view of their investments? Taking the DIY plunge requires confidence and nerve, but it soon becomes much easier. The greatest dangers lie in getting carried away by success or despondent about disappointment, in letting personal emotions get in the way of sensible decisions and in being influenced by people whose job it is to entertain, scare or impress you, but not to make you money.

The best advice for all would-be investors was carved on the lintel of the doorway to the temple of the Delphic oracle thousands of years ago: "know yourself". What works in investment varies from person to person. It takes time, experience and some uncomfortable mistakes to learn the rules which you are best suited to follow.

Long ago I realised that I was happier investing my own money in funds rather than directly in stocks, bonds or private companies, despite the tax advantages. Many investors successfully combine all three, but investment funds have some distinct advantages so should form at least a significant part of most portfolios.

Firstly, they encompass a broad spread of underlying investments making them less vulnerable to individual stock disasters. Secondly, they are managed by professionals who are better able to keep abreast of corporate developments, their markets and the broader economy. Finally, with the professional manager taking the individual stock decisions, the investor in the fund can leave well alone, just monitoring its performance and keeping an eye out for signs of trouble.

Inevitably, there are costs attached to this, which means that if you pay a wealth manager to invest in funds for you, you are paying twice over. There is little more satisfying than picking a stock market winner based on an insight the professionals have missed and few more salutary lessons, on the other hand, than seeing the value of an investment wiped out.

Having decided to invest in funds, your decision to go for investment trusts or other closed-end investment companies rather than unit trusts (now called open-ended investment companies or OEICs) is an easy one. Numerous studies have shown that over all time periods, closed-end funds nearly always outperform comparable open-ended funds in each sub-sector of the market, even when the funds are run side by side by the same manager.

There are several reasons for this: firstly, closed-end funds tend to have lower costs. Secondly, their managers can take advantage of gearing, borrowing for investment when the opportunities are attractive and raising cash when they are not. Thirdly, fund managers find it easier to manage a fixed pool of money than a variable one so when an open-ended fund is doing well, new money floods in, forcing the manager to invest even though prices may be unsustainably high. When the market drops, money floods out and managers have to sell into falling prices. The risk of this also constrains the manager's ability to invest in less liquid but perhaps highly attractive opportunities.

Another major advantage is that closed-end funds are governed by a board of non-executive directors who are independent of the management company. The management company may be more interested in growing funds under management and in keeping fees high than in performance, but the directors won't be. If the performance is poor, they can negotiate for a fee reduction, a change of manager or a move to another investment company. They will issue new shares only if it is to the advantage of all investors but can also buy in shares if they are cheaply priced. Finally, they scrutinise performance, cross-examine the managers and keep them on their toes far more effectively than happens under the internal governance of OEICs.

Of course, there are some excellent open-ended funds while some interesting segments of financial markets are poorly or not at all served by closed-end funds. On the other hand, there are some areas of the market where open-ended funds with daily liquidity simply don't work because the underlying assets are too illiquid. Examples include funds investing in private equity, property and the fast-growing area of alternative assets.

Alternative assets encompass funds investing in infrastructure, loans, aircraft, alternative energy and a growing list of other tangible or intangible assets. These funds generally offer a high yield, moderate dividend growth and the prospect of some capital appreciation. This makes them attractive relative to cash, corporate or government bonds and their consequent popularity has led to a flood of new issuance in recent years.

New issuance is likely to hit a new record in 2017 but little of it is in the conventional equity space. Investors need to be wary of stock issuance whether for new or established funds as it is often opportunistic, driven by current investor fashion and of more benefit to the sponsors and managers than the investors. But wariness should not extend to a full aversion; I can remember as many new funds I later regretted not buying at the start as ones I was glad I had avoided.

Fund flows are far from being one way; in fact, more money left the closed-end sector in the second quarter of 2017 than was raised. Funds reach the end of their pre-determined lives, continuation votes are voted down, boards decide that the investment thesis no longer works and so wind up the company or boards, whether of their own volition or at the instigation of activist shareholders, return capital to investors. In closed-end funds, disappointing performance usually leads to action but in open-ended funds, it often leads only to stagnation.

A key indicator of disappointing performance, or merely that the fund's investment focus is out of fashion, is the appearance of a discount to net asset value in the share price. Clearly, this cannot happen in an open-ended fund but in a closed-end fund it reflects an excess of sellers over buyers and it makes the share price somewhat more volatile than the net asset value.

For existing investors, a widening discount is a problem, at least in the short term, as it constitutes a drag on the share price. For boards, it may represent an opportunity to enhance performance by buying in shares cheaply and for new investors, an opportunity to buy the shares cheaply. However, investors should regard a sizable discount as enhancing the case for purchase but not the main reason for purchase.

Maybe the fund, the sector or the market is out of fashion and will soon bounce back, with the discount disappearing again, but maybe the discount reflects structural issues which cannot be easily addressed. Many good investment trusts habitually trade at a premium but are still worth buying while discounts will not necessarily narrow if performance is good. That said, there is a long-term trend towards narrowing discounts so that the sector average is now only 2%.

Getting access to information and good research is becoming less of a problem for private investors. Reports and accounts, interim reports and monthly fact sheets are usually available on websites and these contain details of past performance. Click the professional investor/financial adviser tab on the website rather than the private individual one as the latter gives access to much less information.

Comparative information on investment companies is available on the AIC website together with helpful information on them generally and links to research notes. These have usually been sponsored and paid for by the companies so are not independent but they are a good source of information and it's in nobody's interest for the writers of them to be less than honest.

Many funds and management companies go to considerable length and expense in marketing, providing updates from the manager, podcasts, links to media coverage and easy access to statutory information. There is some very good coverage in the financial press – including, I hope, my own modest contributions. Finally, it is definitely worth turning up to annual general meetings, even if you can't vote in person. These almost invariably include a presentation by the manager and an opportunity to ask questions either in public or face-to-face afterwards.

Time, however, is not necessarily on the investor's side. Opportunities can be fleeting so there is little time for homework. Waiting for a setback in the share price or the market or for any discount to asset value to widen is nearly always a mug's game. Remember the response of Nathan Rothschild when asked the secret of his success: "I never buy at the low and I always sell too soon." Expect the share price to dip after your purchase and be pleasantly surprised if it doesn't.

As important as picking good funds is putting together a coherent portfolio. This should include core generalist funds as well as specialist thematic funds. It makes sense to invest in technology, smaller companies, emerging markets and so on but not to have too much in any one niche. It's good to have a reasonable level of income but this usually involves some sacrifice of total return. A bird in the hand is more highly valued than two in the bush but you may prefer the latter.

Investing in cheap trusts on wide discounts or in unpopular, undervalued areas of the market can be lucrative but be careful; "reassuringly expensive" trusts often perform much better than ones that are visibly cheap. Everyone loves a bargain but real value is reflected in long-term prospects while wide discounts reflect serious trouble as often as investor short-sightedness.

The most difficult question of all is when to sell. As Warren Buffett said, "My favourite holding period is forever." You don't need to sell or take some profit in good investments unless you need the cash. I still hold the shares I bought on the flotation of Worldwide Healthcare Trust at launch in 1995, and have only added to the holding along the way. I was sorely tempted to sell out of BlackRock World Mining a couple of years ago but the share price doubled in the next year. I missed selling out of Polar Capital Technology in 2003, but can't be sure I would have bought it back lower down.

Many investment sages point out that nobody ever went bust taking a profit. True; they went bust selling winners and reinvesting in losers. Sell if the investment thesis changes or you have made a mistake but don't assume that the departure of a good manager is your cue for an exit. The directors are not fools and will be rigorously looking for a worthy replacement.

But isn't the stock market heading for another meltdown? Isn't this the time to hold cash and wait for the bargains that litter the bottom of a bear market? At the time of writing (September 2017) share prices have more than doubled in dollar terms since early 2009 (and nearly quadrupled in the US), but the signs of euphoria and complacency which normally mark market peaks are conspicuously absent. Valuations are not stretched by historic standards and look cheap relative to cash or government bonds. The first decade of the new millennium saw two of the four worst equity bear markets in 100 years, so caution and nervousness prevail. Yet growth is steady, inflation is low, corporate profits are rising and the signs of economic over-heating which usually precede a recession remain absent.

Geopolitical concerns abound but their impact on markets is highly uncertain. The long bull market in government bonds will surely be over soon, but the constraints on banks that prevent another credit boom and consequent bust look unlikely to be lifted. Market wobbles and setbacks are inevitable but should prove only temporary. Waiting for a better long-term buying opportunity could mean missing years of steady returns with no bank interest to compensate.

Nick Train, manager of Finsbury Growth Trust, likes to tell investors each year that he is bullish; he points out that markets rise in three years out of four so that is the smart way to bet. Even if next year turns out to be the one in four, don't panic. Buying at the high is not the biggest mistake an investor can make – selling at the low is. In time, markets recover and setbacks become barely visible interruptions of the long trend upwards.

MAX KING was an investment manager and strategist at Finsbury Asset Management, J O Hambro and Investec Asset Management. He is now an independent writer, with a regular column in *MoneyWeek*, and an adviser with a special interest in investment companies. He is a non-executive director of two trusts.

INVESTMENT TRUSTS AND DIY INVESTORS

MARK DAMPIER, *Research Director at Hargreaves Lansdown, the UK's largest and most influential online platform, says that investment trusts can make good choices for self-directed private investors.*

ALTHOUGH I ONLY own one or two myself, investment trusts are in some respects an ideal investment vehicle for the DIY investor. Many of the principles of investing in unit trusts and OEICs apply equally to investment trusts, but it is undeniable that they are slightly more complicated and harder to explain, which can be a deterrent.

How investment trusts differ from unit trusts is that they are (a) closed-ended and (b) trade on the stock exchange. This means that to start life they need to raise money through a public offering of shares (an IPO, in technical jargon) and this gives them a fixed amount of starting capital. Unlike unit trusts, which create or cancel units at will, they can't grow or reduce their capital anything like as easily as a unit trust can, although it has become easier to do so in recent years.* The net asset value of an investment trust generally rises and falls in line with the market and the expertise of the fund manager. Consequently, whereas the price of a unit in an open-ended fund should nearly always track its net asset value very closely, this is not so with investment trusts, whose share price is influenced by supply and demand.

If the trust is in fashion, or performance is stonkingly good, the shares may stand at a premium to net asset value. If you buy shares in the trust in these circumstances, you will be paying more than its current assets are worth. If on the other hand demand is poor or non-existent, and performance has been indifferent or worse, the trust's shares may well slip to a discount. The share price will then stand below the net asset value of the

---

* What they can do is issue more shares from time to time, either by buying them in and reissuing them, or making what is called a C-share issue. It is still a more cumbersome process.

trust; now when you buy the shares, you will be paying less than the underlying value of its assets.

Got that? I can assure you that it isn't as complicated as it sounds. In simple terms, buying shares in an investment trust when they are at a discount is broadly a good idea – akin to something being in the January sales. Buying at a premium, however, certainly if it is more than say 3% to 5%, is usually a poor idea in the long run. There are some nuances behind this simple formula however!

It depends a lot on why the discount has come about. If it is because the fund manager is no good and the trust's performance reflects that, the case for buying is weak, even if the price is a bargain basement one. But if it is because the whole sector is unfashionable and unloved, it can often be an indication of genuine value and you should investigate it as a potentially contrarian buying opportunity. Even in the first case, it may be worth keeping an eye on the trust as the board of directors always have the power to change the fund manager for someone better. If this happens, you will tend to see the discount start to narrow, though rarely immediately, which may still give you time to get on board.

When a trust is trading at a very large premium, it may be because the fund manager is exceptionally good, or more often it is an indication that the sector the trust invests in has become highly fashionable and therefore at risk of a sudden or dramatic change in sentiment. When a trust is trading at a premium of over 10%, it strongly suggests to me that you should not be buying it. It really has to go some in order to justify that kind of fancy rating. Even top-quality fund managers can see shares in their trust go from a premium to a discount. In those cases, however, they can often go back to a premium again, so keeping a watching brief on the share price and discount can be worthwhile, since from time to time it can throw up attractive opportunities.

One of the best examples of that phenomenon over the last decade has to be the case of Fidelity China Special Situations. The story includes one of the UK's best fund managers, a sector that has drifted dramatically in and out of favour, and the impact of huge media exposure. The trust was born when Anthony Bolton, who had successfully run unit and investment trusts for Fidelity for more than 25 years, decided after a brief retirement that he wanted to move to Hong Kong in order to run a China fund for his old firm.

Given his track record and high profile in the industry, coupled with the popularity of China as an investment theme, the launch of his new investment trust attracted a record amount of money, more than £500m. Initially the fund performed well, and before long was trading at a premium of more than 15% to net asset value – a classic example of a warning bell sounding. What happened next was that the Chinese stock market started to perform less well, and a couple of Mr Bolton's core stock selections turned out badly (one of his companies being accused of fraudulent accounting practices). Given his high profile, these problems inevitably hit the headlines in a big way.

The fund slipped from a premium to a discount and, worse still, the share price fell as far as 70p, well below the issue price of 100p. The media was full of stories that Mr Bolton was unable to transfer his skills from the UK to China. Some gave the impression that he was over the hill and had lost his way. Many private investors expressed their disappointment by selling their holdings at between 70p and 90p a share.

By the time Mr Bolton retired from running the fund in 2013, the media was still largely hostile, some going so far as to imply that his time at the helm had been a failure. Although performance had already improved, the shares at that point were still trading on a discount of 14% to net asset value. Yet the reality was that he had beaten the fund's Chinese benchmark while he was in charge, which hardly justifies being called a failure. More to the point, he had already laid the seeds of a high-return stock portfolio.

Since then the portfolio has blossomed under Dale Nicholls, its new manager. Seven years after launch, shares in the fund stand at around 230p, more than treble its price at the earlier low point. Those who sold out after the initial disappointing performance missed out on a chance to make a superb gain.

This neatly illustrates the fact that you shouldn't believe everything you read in the media. A little time spent in research would have suggested that the move to a big discount was actually a classic buying opportunity, not a sell signal. Given that any equity investment should be seen as a long-term project, it was a mistake for investors to sell after just two years of experience, however disappointing the ride had been. The other point is that the Fidelity China Special Situations story illustrates how investing in investment trusts can be both more hazardous and more rewarding than investing in an equivalent unit trust, precisely because of the discount/premium cycle. It takes more work and more courage to invest this way – whether that is for you is a matter only you can decide.

Another important difference between investment trusts and unit trusts is that investment trusts can 'gear' their returns in a way that unit trusts cannot. What this means is that, if the board of directors agree, the trust can borrow money in order to boost the amount of capital that they have to invest. If the fund manager can make a greater return with this extra capital than it costs to borrow the money, the trust and its shareholders will be better off. (To continue the driving analogy, they have moved up a gear or two.) The scope for gearing is another factor that makes analysing investment trusts more complicated as the decision to gear or not can make a significant difference to investment performance. It also adds to the risk of share price volatility.

Each trust makes its own decision, adding to the diversity of returns. Some investment trusts never gear, believing that their portfolio is already risky enough. Gearing can work both ways. When interest rates were much higher than they are today, many trusts mistakenly geared up by borrowing at a fixed rate, in some cases locking into permanently high borrowing costs. With the march of time this problem has gradually unwound. In a world of very low interest rates, as we have today, gearing does appear to make more sense. The effect of gearing means that investment trusts in general outperform their unit trust equivalents when prices are rising in a bull market, but are certain to suffer disproportionately the next time the stock market takes a tumble. Care therefore needs to be taken when comparing unit trusts and investment trusts. In the main, the last few years have been good to investment trusts, as they have had the double benefit of narrowing discounts and gearing. It will not always be so.

Should you be put off by the greater complexity of investment trusts? I don't think so, although it does obviously depend on how much time for research you have at your disposal. Potentially investment trusts are a rich feeding ground for the self-directed investor. There are plenty of pricing anomalies you may be able to exploit. One reason is that professional investment institutions, which once were big buyers of investment trusts, have steadily divested their holdings over the years in favour of managing their investments directly. In a market dominated by individual investors, pricing anomalies do not always disappear as quickly as they would do in the professional institutional market.

In my view their complexity means that investment trusts will never be mass market investment vehicles in the same way as unit trusts were designed to be. That is actually a good thing. If they were to become more broadly owned, it would remove most of the advantages that private investors enjoy with them today. The very first investment trust, Foreign & Colonial, was formed as long ago as 1868. Despite its long illustrious history, after more than 150 years it is still only capitalised at £2.5bn. By contrast, in the few months after Neil Woodford launched his CF Woodford Equity Income unit trust in 2015, it had attracted more than £6bn of investors' money. Now that is what I call a mass-market product – simple, easy-to-own and simple to monitor. Investment trusts will never be that, but they do have other advantages instead.

You will see in the media that financial firms are often criticised for not recommending investment trusts more frequently. There is a simple reason for this. Many investment trusts are quite small and that makes it difficult for firms with large numbers of execution-only clients to suggest them. The reason is that buying and selling shares in many investment trusts in size is difficult. The top 20 largest trusts rarely trade more than £2m in a day. This won't matter to a DIY investor who is looking to buy or sell between £1,000 and £10,000 of trust shares, or to advisors who can spread client orders over a period of time. But for a firm like ours with thousands of clients, recommending an investment trust could suddenly swamp the market with buy orders, something that could never happen with a unit trust.

Just suppose we recommended an investment trust through our newsletter. What might happen? The market makers, the professional firms that take and implement buy and sell orders, would see the recommendation and mark up the price of the trust before the orders came through. Buy orders on any significant scale could not all be fulfilled, leaving clients frustrated. Worse still, the clients might want compensation for failing to have their orders fulfilled, particularly if that price continues to move up. If our advice was to sell, then the problem would be even more acute. This is why platforms offering execution-only services are wary of investment trusts and is why I also think they are generally unsuitable for the mass market.

That does not mean they might not be right for you. If you can get to grips with understanding how investment trusts work, they can be an attractive way to invest. They can still help you even if most of your money is going into open-ended funds. I own shares in RIT Capital, in part because there is no open-ended alternative. The premium or discount at which investment trusts trade can also be extremely useful in seeing how investor sentiment is moving. It can be a good indicator of whether a particular sector or market is on the cheap or expensive side. If many more trusts are trading at premiums, it may be flagging up that we are near to a market top, while large discounts across a number of sectors suggest the opposite.

MARK DAMPIER has been head of research at Hargreaves Lansdown, the UK's largest independent stockbroking firm, since 1998. He has been in the financial services industry for 32 years, initially working as an advisor helping individual clients to invest their money. He holds a BA Honours degree in Law. He has become one of the best-known and most widely quoted figures in the fund management industry. He wrote a regular column in the *Independent* on funds and markets for many years, and regularly comments in the national press and on broadcast media. *Effective Investing* (Harriman House, 2015) was his first book (and, he swears, definitely his last!). In his spare time, depending on the season, you will find him shooting, skiing, sailing or fishing.

INSIGHTS OF AN INVESTMENT TRUST EXPERT

JOHN BARON

ECOGNISING WHEN SENTIMENT and fundamentals diverge is the essence of a good investment decision. This is no easy task but it can be doubly rewarding when it comes to investment trusts. Their particular characteristics, including their closed-ended structure, ability to gear and lower cost – all of which help to account for their superior performance over unit trusts – present a wealth of opportunities to informed investors.

* * *

However, the prerequisite for any successful investment journey is clarity regarding financial goals and risk tolerances.

1. Determine your goals.

Equities produce better returns than bonds and cash over the long term. But the path is rarely a smooth one. Market corrections are part of the investment cycle, which is one reason it is important to adopt a long-term investment approach.

It is also why it is important, at the outset, to ensure that portfolio construction truly reflects investment objectives, risk tolerances and time horizons. Other factors to consider can include currency exposure and income requirements.

Choosing the appropriate benchmark and timescale to monitor a portfolio's performance can also help in attaining financial goals. However, never let benchmarks dictate how a portfolio is constructed – they cannot be beaten if they are simply copied.

Furthermore, in pursuing a long-term approach, it should be remembered any meaningful performance comparisons therefore require a minimum five-year period. At best, over the short term, benchmarks should be seen as a reference point for monitoring a portfolio's progress.

* * *

Clarity about investment objectives, risk tolerances and required timescales can then be complemented by the application of tried-and-tested investment principles.

2. Time in the market is better than market timing.

Once invested, it is important to remain so provided such an approach continues to reflect investment objectives and risk profiles. Many investors try to time the markets, and a few are successful. But for most long-term investors it is better to remain invested.

The evidence certainly suggests that the longer one is invested, the more likely a positive return will result. Recent research from Fidelity has shown that over the period 1980–2012, investing in global equities for 12 years or more produced no negative returns. By comparison, five-year periods produced a 16% chance of a negative return.

Furthermore, a few years ago Fidelity also showed that missing out on just the ten best trading days of the MSCI World Index over a ten-year period from 31 December 2002 would have resulted in negative returns of -4.6%. Had an investor missed the best 20 days then the negative return would have extended to -32.1%.

Bad luck aside, evidence further suggests some investors have a tendency to buy after markets have risen, and to sell when they have fallen – and then to remain in cash for too long, and so exacerbate the original mistake at additional cost. This is easy to criticise with the benefit of hindsight, but difficult to counter at the time.

Yet it is precisely at such times that markets tend to bounce – when the bad news is in the price. The single best trading day during the past 10–15 years was on 24 November 2008 when, in the middle of the financial fallout from a ballooning credit crisis, the UK equity market rose 9.2%.

Barclays has also highlighted that investors who tried to time the market from 1992 to 2009 were down 20% compared to those who had simply stuck with it. So ignore the noise and chatter. The evidence suggests that time in the market is better than market timing.

3. Do not spend your dividends unless you have to.

There is another reason to stay invested – to enable the full harvesting of dividends, which account for the vast majority of market returns over time. Legendary investor Jeremy Siegel calculated in 2005 that, over the previous 130 years, 97% of the total return from stocks came from re-invested dividends. $1,000 invested in 1871 would have been worth $243,386 by 2003. Had dividends been reinvested, the figure rises to $7,947,930!

The message is clear: do not spend your dividends unless you have to. Re-investing dividends is the best way of growing wealth over time – and to fully access these dividends, investors must stay invested.

However, there is a downside to this rule: the longer in the market, the greater the chance of a market setback. This can be particularly galling if one is about to realise financial objectives

– especially after a long investment journey. A couple of strategies, pursued together, can help to mitigate the effect of such an event: diversification and regular rebalancing.

4. Diversify to reduce portfolio risk.

The aim of diversification is to reduce portfolio risk by investing in 'uncorrelated' assets – asset classes that tend not to move in the same direction over the same period.

Equities, bonds, commercial property, renewable energy, commodities, infrastructure, 'real assets' (such as gold, vintage cars, rare stamps or fine wine) and cash are, to varying degrees, examples. Whilst few investments will escape a major market correction unscathed, adequate diversification away from equities will help to reduce losses.

This important investment discipline is often overlooked – especially in rising markets. There are no fixed rules as to the pace and extent of diversification. An investor's risk profile, time horizon, income requirement and investment objectives are key factors. But there are some general principles which can be helpful.

The four 'seasonal' portfolios (Spring, Summer, Autumn and Winter) covered on the investment trust website www.johnbaronportfolios.co.uk reflect an investment journey over time and, as such, best illustrate how we gradually increase diversification as time unfolds.

When starting, it makes sense to focus on equities because of their history of superior returns – so the Spring portfolio consists only of equity holdings, as longer time horizons usually allow greater tolerance when it comes to volatility. However, as time passes, the portfolios become increasingly diversified.

One of the key asset classes employed is bonds – mostly corporate, as the portfolios are wary of government debt. Bonds usually act as a good counterweight to equities. Each is driven by different economic forces – as such, when one rises in price, the other usually falls. The weightings in the Summer, Autumn and Winter portfolios gradually build in ranges of 5–10%, 15–20% and 25–30% respectively.

Other less-correlated assets also become increasingly evident as the journey unfolds including commercial property, renewable energy, infrastructure and commodities. The website's Rationale and Diversification pages have more details.

How many asset classes should one employ? The answer, as with investment generally, is to keep it simple – four or five asset classes usually suffice. As Warren Buffett once said: "Wide diversification is only used when investors do not understand what they are doing." Too much diversification also increases costs.

Meanwhile, in addition to greater diversification, a further objective as time passes is for the website's portfolios to produce a higher and, importantly, still growing income. Commercial property, infrastructure, renewable energy, together with a greater focus on higher-yielding equities within the portfolios' declining equity weightings, all help to achieve this goal.

Accordingly, the Autumn and Winter portfolios currently yield 4.4% and 5.9% respectively. Such asset classes also help the Dividend portfolio achieve a yield of 4.9%. It should, of course, be remembered that whilst income levels should rise with time, yields are also a function of portfolio value and so can vary as portfolio values change.

5. Rebalance — but not too frequently.

Rebalancing is one of the first principles of investing, and yet it is often overlooked. The concept is simple. A 60/40 equity/bond split may, because equities perform well, turn into a 70/30 split. Evidence suggests it pays to rebalance provided one's risk profile and investment objectives remain in sync.

Forbes has shown that $10,000 invested by way of a 60/40 split in the US in 1985, and rebalanced annually, would have been worth $97,000 in 2010 – whereas an unbalanced portfolio would have been worth $89,000. However, again, do not rebalance too frequently. Keep it simple and dealing costs low – for most investors, an annual rebalance is usually sufficient depending on how markets have performed.

Furthermore, it is sometimes forgotten that as much attention should be given to the process of liquidation, as investment timelines approach, as to the running of the portfolio. A gradual and balanced liquidation as the finishing line approaches is one method. There are others. Peace of mind should never be underestimated, particularly at the end of a long investment journey!

*   *   *

In addition to tried-and-tested investment principles, insights borne of experience often assist when managing a portfolio.

6. Be prepared to be a contrarian.

Sir John Templeton once said: "It is impossible to produce superior performance unless you do something different from the majority." As touched on previously, a successful investor must be prepared to be a contrarian. A benchmark can only be beaten when deviating from it – and it should be remembered this may involve periods of underperformance.

However, it should also be remembered that remaining committed to an over-arching strategy over time can be rewarding. Whilst acknowledging that a portfolio can contain a blend of strategies and preferences at any point in time, the overall objective of the portfolios run by the website www.johnbaronportfolios.co.uk is to search for and hold companies which are adding value and creating wealth – often by solving problems.

This company-specific approach has more than outpaced the general advance of markets over time. And by remaining focused on such an approach, investors can better see volatility as an opportunity – and capitalise from it.

7. Seize the advantage!

Some have suggested it can be difficult for private investors to compete with the professional fund managers – the pension funds, banks, investment houses and wealth managers. Yet the private investor has many advantages – the most important being time.

Many professional fund managers are trapped into a three-monthly cycle of trustee or actuary meetings, which encourages the shadowing of benchmarks. Private investors are free of this restraint. They can afford to take a longer-term view, and therefore stand a better chance of recognising mispricing and being able to capitalise from it.

To benefit from this natural advantage, patience is a virtue. Unloved assets can take time to come right, but then more than make up for lost time when they do. Warren Buffett once said: "The stock market is a device for transferring money from the impatient to the patient."

8. Keep it simple.

Meanwhile, it is important investors remember that investment is best kept simple to succeed. Complexity usually adds cost, risks confusion and hinders performance. When diversifying a portfolio, do not use too many different asset classes – the simpler, the better. But perhaps more importantly, investors should avoid overly complicated investments – especially if they are difficult to understand.

Accordingly, the website portfolios avoid hedge funds, absolute return funds, structured products, multi-manager funds and any other investment vehicle or approach which have high costs and poor transparency. Many tend not to live up to expectations.

In keeping investment simple, investors are also keeping costs down. Picking complicated or expensive products can easily cost a further 1.5% a year in fees – this may not sound a lot, but it can materially affect the final sum achieved. A £100-a-month investment producing a 5% annual return will be worth £150,000 after 40 years. But if a further 1.5% in annual costs is deducted, the final portfolio value will fall to just £105,000. This is a significant difference.

9. Be sceptical of 'expert' forecasts.

At the very least, question consensus forecasts. The renowned economist J. K. Galbraith once said: "Pundits forecast not because they know, but because they are asked." Successful investors tend to be sceptical – after all, one of the prerequisites of being a contrarian is to question the consensus.

In doing so, such investors are asking what could go wrong – their default position is not to own a stock. This contrasts with those fund managers who are more focused on short-term relative performance for fear of being left behind by their peers – scepticism takes a back seat as non-ownership is less of a possibility.

10. Harness Einstein's eighth wonder.

One should never ignore the magic of compounding – allegedly described by Einstein as the eighth wonder of the world. Compounding is the regular reinvesting of interest or dividends to the original sum invested, with the effect of creating higher total returns (capital plus income) over time. Time and a decent rate of return allow the concept to fully bloom.

£100 a month invested over 20 years and producing a 3% annual total return (the dividends/interest are not withdrawn) will produce a final portfolio value of £32,912. If the rate increases to 7.5% (the average long-term return for US equities) then the final figure rises to £135,587. The challenge is to achieve the higher rate of return. Again, the message is clear – start early, be patient and try not to interrupt the magic of compounding.

* * *

Having acknowledged the importance of investment principles and insights, most portfolios would benefit from using investment trusts when seeking stock market gains.

11. Harness the potential of investment trusts.

Investment trusts are ideally suited to help the private investor. Despite being less well known, investment trusts have a superior performance record when compared to their better-known cousins – unit trusts and OEICs. They have on average beaten most of the global investment benchmarks whether delineated by region or country – unlike unit trusts and OEICs. Part of the reason is they have charged lower fees.

Another reason is because of their structure. Investment trusts are 'closed-ended', in that they have a fixed number of shares like other public companies such as M&S or BP. But instead of specialising in the management of clothes or oil, they specialise in the management of financial assets – usually other public companies. And as with other public companies, the share price does not always reflect the value of the assets – and usually stands at a discount.

This allows investors to take advantage of movements in the discount, which is often influenced by swings in sentiment towards the investment and/or underlying portfolio. Indeed, the market will usually present opportunities and risks that are often exaggerated by the fluctuation of discounts. Therein lies the investor's opportunity.

As a first step for those new to investment trusts, the ideal purchase is when a trust, run by a fund manager with a good long-term track record, stands at a wider-than-average discount – possibly because of a market wobble or the sector and/or manager is out of favour. It is usually wise to ignore the short-term noise and focus on the long term. Should sentiment improve, the investor benefits from both the underlying assets rising in price and the discount narrowing.

The ideal sale is when the discount has narrowed considerably from its average and factors may suggest caution, such as a change in manager or outlook for the underlying markets. Should a portfolio's assets fall in price, investors can further suffer from a widening of the discount. Needless to say, there are many nuances to such trades.

A further consequence of the closed-ended structure is that, like other closed-ended companies, investment trusts can borrow to buy more assets. Historically, this has benefitted share prices because markets have tended to rise and such gearing has also enhanced the returns from good fund management. But gearing can make for a volatile share price which is another reason to monitor the discount, as well as the level, cost and duration of the debt, and to see investment trusts as a long-term endeavour.

Other factors to take into account when judging the value of an investment trust include the reputation of the manager and the investment house, the underlying strategy, the outlook for the sector or region, the valuation of both the trust relative to its peer group and the portfolio relative to its universe, the level of management and any performance fees, and whether the portfolio's income is covering the trust's dividend and the extent of its revenue reserves (particularly if investing for income).

Changes regarding most of these factors can, to varying degrees, influence swings in sentiment. Capitalising on such swings can be profitable in the short term. However, it should be remembered that such an approach is best employed when initiating a long-term holding. Choosing and sticking with a trust which has a good track record often results in better long-term performance than constantly dealing in an attempt to capture short-term price movements.

WEBSITE PORTFOLIOS

Words and theories can only be tested when put into action. The website www.johnbaronportfolios.co.uk reports on the progress of seven real and benchmarked investment trust portfolios, including same-day details of trades, new portfolio weightings and yields. Members are informed by email whenever the website is updated. The portfolios pursue a range of strategies and income profiles, whilst adhering to the investment principles and insights touched upon previously.

Four of the portfolios reflect an investment journey over time and so are named after the seasons. Spring's objective is capital growth courtesy of a portfolio comprised entirely of equities. Over time, the bond and 'other' less correlated elements increase to both generate a higher income and to help diversify holdings and so protect past gains. The Winter portfolio finishes with a yield of 5.9% at time of writing.

The three remaining equity portfolios pursue distinct objectives. The LISA portfolio helps smaller portfolios capitalise on the Government's Lifetime ISA (LISA) proposals – and therefore could be seen as a precursor to the four 'seasonal' portfolios. The Thematic portfolio focuses exclusively on special situations. Meanwhile, the Dividend portfolio seeks a high and rising income and yields 4.9%.

Whilst never complacent, the portfolios are performing well relative to their respective benchmarks – the website's Performance page has more details. Meanwhile, both the Rationale and Diversification pages have a statistic summary of the portfolios and overview of the other portfolio pages, whilst the Subscription page gives details of the seven-day trial allowing free access to the website's closed pages.

JOHN BARON is one of the UK's leading experts on investment trusts, a regular columnist and speaker at investment seminars, and author of *The Financial Times Guide to Investment Trusts*.

He is a director of Equi Ltd which owns the investment trust website www.johnbaronportfolios.co.uk. The website reports on the progress of seven real investment trust portfolios, including same-day details of trades, new portfolio weightings and yields. The portfolios pursue a range of strategies and income objectives, and enjoy an enviable track record relative to their benchmarks.

Since 2009, John has also reported on two of these portfolios in his popular monthly column in the *Investors Chronicle* – fees are donated to charity.

John has used investment trusts in a private and professional capacity for over 35 years. After university and the Army, he ran a broad range of investment portfolios as a director of both Henderson Private Clients and then Rothschild Asset Management. Since leaving the City, he has also helped charities monitor their fund managers.

THE FIRST INVESTMENT TRUST

2018 marks the 150th anniversary of the formation of the UK's oldest investment trust, Foreign & Colonial. Historian JOHN NEWLANDS *describes how this first pioneering example of an enduring new type of investment vehicle came into being.*

ARCH 19TH 1868 is the date on which Foreign & Colonial (F&C) launched what is generally regarded as the first investment trust. It did so into a world that was still in the process of coming to terms, politically, socially and financially, with the consequences of the Industrial Revolution. While there were railways, steamships and telegraphic cables, there were also 50,000 horses on the ill-lit streets of London, creating a 900-ton pollution problem every day. The telephone, the motor car, wireless communication, and the light bulb had yet to be invented; the Suez Canal was not yet in use. The opening of the London Underground in 1863 had been greatly lauded, until it was realised that steam locomotives running in tunnels created a real danger of travellers choking to death between stations. On the other side of the Atlantic, Colonel George A. Custer's defeat at the Battle of the Little Bighorn, at the hands of Sitting Bull and Crazy Horse, was still eight years away. In short, the Industrial Revolution had produced a thin veneer of modernity, but the so-called 'developed' world was a long way off.

The small investor could be forgiven for thinking that the same was true of the financial markets. The world was full of opportunities and risk. Some early financial disasters, such as the South Sea Bubble, were so severe that it took decades, if not generations, to restore the confidence of investors. The first half of the 19th century had seen several speculative boom/bust cycles, in commodities, in railway stocks and even in foreign loans. In the 1820s foreign loans boom, it proved possible to issue gullible investors with bonds for an imaginary country, called Poyais, mysteriously located "somewhere in Central America". Fraud was common, usually involving false accounting and the issue of bogus shares. There were three major fraud trials in the 1850s alone. Until 1855, investors had faced unlimited liability in the event of a company's failure, but even after limited liability was introduced, the rash of company formations – 4,859 between 1856 and 1865 – produced many new failures, frequently through mismanagement or fraud. Then in 1866 the Overend & Gurney bank collapsed, creating what a later historian described as "the greatest financial strain the City had experienced, in time of peace". Little wonder, then, that Victorian novelists were moved to denounce the financial world in print: "so common were references to frauds, swindles, and bankruptcies in literature that … only a peculiar variation on the theme could guarantee a response".

The solution for the rich investor, one who could afford the best professional advice, was to build up enormously broad portfolios [that combined holdings of government stock with] scores of high-yielding but individually risky overseas stocks. These portfolios were akin to investment trusts in miniature. One or two failures would not sink the ship, and, even if such failures occurred, the average yield would still be better than that available on safe investments at home. The following list, taken from a real private portfolio of the time gives a flavour of the kind of securities that a rich man would be likely to own in the late 19th century:

Abbontiakoon Mines Ltd.

Anglo Argentine Tramways Co.

Atchison, Topeka & Santa Fe Railroad Co.

Chicago, Milwaukee & St Paul Railroad Co Ltd
(Wisconsin Valley Division).

Consolidated Gold Fields of South Africa Ltd.

Hokkaido Colliery & Railway Co Ltd.

Imperial Russian Government Loan, 5%.

Imperial Japanese Loan, 6%.

Kansas City Electric Light Co.

Lobitos Oilfields.

Matador Land & Cattle Company.

Mexican National Railroad Co.

Tanganyika Concessions Ltd.

Wyoming Cattle Ranch Co Ltd.

Ural Caspian Oil Corporation Limited.

The small investor could not hope to spread his risk in this way. It is essential to realise that investment, until the turn of the 20th century, was all about income rather than capital growth. Interest rates were low and inflation, once the Napoleonic Wars had finished, was negligible. In any case, investment in ordinary shares was often reserved for a company's proprietors, and was regarded as far too risky for all but the wealthiest. Other investors had very few options. They could invest in Consols – safe but unrewarding UK government stocks, which, staggeringly, yielded more than 3.5% only twice between 1830 and 1914. Banks offered no more than 4.5%, and "the enormous accumulations of the insurance companies have hitherto been managed on the footing that anything beyond 4% is unsafe".

Overseas government stocks were yielding double, or three or more times, the return on Consols and justifiably so, because of their higher risk. Diversification could, however, reduce the risks. If it is true that the simplest ideas are often the best, then a pooled and managed investment scheme that owned a wide range of such stocks – carefully chosen, naturally – certainly meets the description. That is why Philip Rose, Samuel Laing and James Thompson Mackenzie, the three founders of what became Foreign & Colonial, went to work on creating a new vehicle to do just that and how, in the process, investment trusts were invented.

Philip (later Sir Philip) Rose was an accomplished City lawyer. He had a meteoric rise to fame and fortune during the 1840s railways boom and became financial advisor to Benjamin Disraeli. By the 1860s, Rose had become a specialist both in arranging and investing in overseas loans. Samuel Laing was a wealthy financier and politician. A former Minister in India, Laing was a qualified barrister, and a member of the founding family of stockbrokers Laing & Cruikshank. James Thompson Mackenzie was described in the prospectus as "Deputy Chairman of the East Bengal Railway". He was Laing's business partner, and a shrewd entrepreneur. Both Mackenzie and Laing had already made a good deal of money in the railway boom. The three men had, by 1868, worked together for five years, forming and managing the General Credit & Finance Company (GCFC). The GCFC, to all intents and purposes, was effectively a trial run for the Foreign & Colonial Government Trust and many valuable lessons were learnt from it.

The three men already made a strong team and they were determined that their new venture would be presented as the very epitome of trustworthiness, reliability and integrity. The trustees were selected with this aim in mind. For the trust's chairman, Rose, Laing and Mackenzie went to the top. Lord Westbury was "the most brilliant barrister of his generation … a man who was as respected for his integrity as he was feared for his intellect". Formerly Richard Bethell, QC, he had held the positions of Solicitor General, Attorney General and Lord Chancellor. He was also a Member of Parliament and a Privy Councillor. Yet his was a far from privileged background. When he was six, his father, Dr Richard Bethell, lost his life's savings through investing in an unlimited liability clothing company which collapsed. For a time, the family were deeply in debt and Dr Bethell almost ended up in a debtors' prison. The event had a profound effect on the young man.

Richard Bethell's abilities had, to say the least, been recognised early. At 14, he was accepted by Wadham College, Oxford. By the age of 17, he had broken a number of records by simultaneously taking a first in classics and a second in mathematics. By his early 20s, he had become a Fellow of Wadham, and at 23 he left academia for the Middle Temple and the Bar. Bethell's wit, turn of phrase and cutting satire soon became a legend. News of his ability to demolish opponents with such phrases as, "What he pleases to call his mind" soon spread, gaining him many admirers, and not a few enemies.

In Parliament, the prospect of listening to his verbal exchanges with Gladstone ensured a full house. He could be especially scathing about judges and the clergy. On one occasion, when asked why Lord Cranborne always sat with the Lord Justices, he replied, "I take it from a childish indisposition to be left alone in the dark!" When Bishop Wilberforce proved to be a tougher opponent than he had anticipated, Lord Westbury ventured that he "had never met a clergyman, with the exception of your Lordship, who had a mind". Westbury's professional income in the 1860s approached £30,000 – an astronomical sum in those days. Despite this, he could be an exceedingly frugal man, who put tuppenny pieces aside to use as tips.

The most important of the other trustees was Lord Eustace Cecil MP, who brought with him "the most distinguished lineage, and his own achievements as a prominent Member of Parliament". Lord Eustace Cecil was to be involved with the Foreign & Colonial for 51 years, including 32 years as Chairman. The two final trustees, apart from Philip Rose himself, were George Sandiford, who was another prominent MP, and George Woodhouse Currie, a well-known banker. The team, as a whole, had a formidable breadth of expertise and influence, as well as, in Rose's personal relationship with Benjamin Disraeli, access to a man who had just become Prime Minister for the first time a month before the launch. Few ventures can have been so well-founded.

The trust's initial 'Schedule' of investments

THE SCHEDULE.

Referred to in the Agreement dated the 19th March, 1868.

Description of Stock.	Amount of Stock. £ s. d.	Proportion of Stock to Total Investment.	Market Price of Stock.	Price at which Stock Sold to the Trust.	Amount of Purchase Money. £ s. d.
Argentine 6 per Cents.	52,900	Eight two-hundredths	73	75½	39,939 10 0
Austrian 5 per Cents.	88,200	Twelve two hundredths	65½	68	59,976 0 0
Brazilian 5 per Cents., 1865	46,800	Seven two-hundredths	72¾	74¾	34,983 0 0
Chilian 6 per Cents.	54,600	Ten two hundredths	89	91½	49,959 0 0
Chilian 7 per Cents.	50,200	Ten two-hundredths	97	99½	49,949 0 0
Danubian 8 per Cents.	83,200	Twelve two-hundredths	69½	72	59,904 0 0
Egyptian 7 per Cents., 1864	55,400	Ten two-hundredths	87½	90¼	49,998 10 0
Egyptian Railway Loan, 7 per Cent. ...	53,300	Ten Two-hundredths	91½	94	49,968 15 0
Italian 5 per Cents., 1861...	201,000	Twenty two-hundredths	47½	49¾	99,997 10 0
New South Wales 5 per Cents.	15,100	Three two-hundredths	96½	99	14,949 0 0
Nova Scotia 6 per Cents	34,700	Seven two-hundredths	99½	102¼	35,480 15 0
Peruvian 5 per Cents.	124,200	Twenty-two two-hundredths	78	80½	99,981 0 0
Portuguese 3 per Cents.	119,700	Ten two-hundredths	39¼	41¾	49,974 15 0
Russian Anglo Dutch Bonds Fl. 1,070,000	90,682	Sixteen two-hundredths	85¾	88¼	80,027 6 2
Spanish New 3 per Cents...	259,590	Twenty two-hundredths	36	38½	99,942 3 0
Turkish 5 per Cents.	166,000	Twelve two-hundredths	33⅞	36⅛	59,967 10 0
Turkish 6 per Cents.	69,200	Eight two hundredths	55¼	57¾	39,963 0 0
United States 10/40 Bonds	36,225	Five two-hundredths	66⅞	68⅞	24,949 19 5
Total	£1,600,997	Two hundred two-hundredths			£999,910 13 7

The prospectus for the new vehicle, though aimed at those of modest means, could not be described as a light read, running to a daunting 76 pages. The Foreign & Colonial Government Trust – the word 'Government' would be removed from the name in 1891 – was structured initially with a fixed 'Schedule', or portfolio, of investments. All the stocks purchased were to be deposited, for safety, with bankers Glyn, Mills, Currie and Co. Changes in the portfolio were not expected to be a regular feature: "...a power of sale, under special circumstances, will be vested in the Trustees and a committee of five certificate holders, to be chosen at general meetings, held annually for this purpose, and for receiving a report and accounts from the Trustees".

The trust was initially planned to have a fixed life of 24 years. The offer was in the form of £100 certificates at £85, repayable at par, giving an expected yield of 7% on a forecast dividend of 6%. Detailed estimates of future income and capital prospects were given, having been checked by Mr C. Jellicoe, former President of the Institute of Actuaries. Mr Jellicoe calculated that the actual return on the portfolio, assuming there were no defaults, would be 8%. The surplus funds thus generated would allow the creation of a "sinking fund", which would be used for "repaying certificates at par by annual drawings". As the Schedule shows, the launch sought to raise just over £1m for a fund investing in a spread of 18 foreign government bonds or fixed interest stocks.

Although the coupons of these bonds varied from 3 to 8%, they were nearly all bought at well below par. The actual yields, therefore, were higher, and varied from 5.05% (New South Wales 5 per cents stock – clearly very creditworthy) to 13.69% (Turkish 5 per cents – credit rating not so good). Italian 'five per cents' were purchased for £49¾, so the initial yield was just over double the 'five per cents' coupon, at 10.11%. Nova Scotia 6%, on the other hand, clearly had a much higher credit rating, and was bought for £102¾. The yield was in this case 5.84% – slightly less than the coupon.

Every one of these overseas stocks looked tempting on a yield basis. Consols, comfortingly secured on the massive assets of the Bank of England, were in 1868 yielding a mere 3.3%. Future prospects therefore depended on how safe the foreign loans really were. Foreign securities were often regarded, with good reason, as high-risk vehicles in dubious emerging markets, including the United States. There had been several defaults on foreign bonds before 1868, some producing a total loss for investors. There was, therefore, bound to be a degree of scepticism in some quarters about the F&C's likelihood of success.

"To provide the investor of moderate means the same advantage as the large capitalist in diminishing risk in Foreign and Colonial stocks by spreading the investment over a number of stocks."

STATED OBJECTIVE OF THE FOREIGN & COLONIAL
GOVERNMENT TRUST, 1868

Initially the new trust scarcely received any publicity. On the launch day itself, a small paragraph, well down the 'Money Market and City Intelligence' column of *The Times* mentioned that: "It is understood that a new company for the investment of capital in all the principal dividend-paying foreign securities is about to be brought forward, so as to enable persons to employ money in this manner without incurring the entire risk incidental to any one particular stock. As a rule, foreign securities have produced a good average return, while there have been some deplorable instances of individual loss".

No more details were provided, not even the new company's name. It was a subdued start to what was to become a great financial institution and far from newsworthy. Over the next few days, advertisements for the Foreign & Colonial Government Trust were published, and coverage in the financial columns increased. *The Times* was an early supporter: "The scheme in its principle supplies a want that has long been felt". *The Scotsman*, however, was more sceptical: "A prospectus has appeared of a Foreign & Colonial Loan Trust scheme for £1,000,000, based on the principle of average risks. Investments in low-priced foreign securities look very tempting on paper, but recent experience should induce caution before adopting new speculative projects."

The Economist noted the originality of the new venture, saying "…the shape is very peculiar; it is not a company, and yet it is to do things like a company; it promises great gains without risk; the exact idea upon which it starts has never been used before. In our judgment, the idea is very good". It was more sceptical about some of the forecasts made in the prospectus. It did not care for the intention to put over a quarter of the trust's funds into Danubian, Egyptian and Turkish stocks, or what it called "loans to semi-civilised states … which will go on borrowing as long as they can, and when they cease to borrow, they will also cease to pay interest." Some of the promises, in fact, were "far too sanguine to ever be performed".

The Economist's point about the Foreign & Colonial being like a company, but not a company, is an important one. Rose, Laing, Mackenzie and Westbury used their unique combination of experience and talents to 'invent' the investment trust. The fact that the Foreign & Colonial exists to this day, and flourishes, is a tribute to their ingenuity. On the other hand, all modern-day investment trusts, as we colloquially describe them, are really investment trust companies. In the legal sense, they are not trusts at all. The Foreign & Colonial, however, *was* a trust and not a company until 1879. (Having been registered as an unregistered common law trust, it changed to a corporate form in 1879, following a court judgement, later reversed on appeal, that investment trusts were illegal, being "associations of more than 20 persons for the acquisition of gain".) This was at least partly for marketing reasons. In the financial panic of 1866, many shareholders and creditors had lost everything, and companies had, not for the first time in history, gained a bad reputation. As *The Economist* went on to observe, the trust form was "an evident attempt to avoid the now unpopular name of company".

The stock market in late March 1868 was variously described as idle, dull and inanimate. There were also fears of an early general election. It did not help that the newspapers were still full of articles reviewing the Overend & Gurney collapse and losses incurred in the latest railway mania. At first, the rate of applications for the new trust was slow, but, as a more favourable press developed, subscriptions picked up. The *Standard* suggested that "in consequence of the manner in which this proposal has been received, it is said that other trusts will be formed for general securities, with a view to paying average dividends on invested capital". How right it was!

By the end of the subscription period, just over half of the £1,176,500 stock offered had been taken up. It was a slow start, but the concept of a professionally managed trust, smoothing out the investor's risk and enhancing his rewards, rapidly found favour. Within eight years, 17 other investment trusts had been launched and were quoted on the Stock Exchange. The Foreign & Colonial Government Trust itself made five separate issues of trust certificates, raising the total subscribed to £3,500,000, and in 1873 the F&C's managers also launched a second trust, the American Investment Trust, specialising in US railway stocks.

Having started life perceived as a high-risk venture, the Foreign & Colonial Investment Trust has long since proved its staying power and vindicated the vision and investment philosophy of its founders. It remains today, 150 years later, one of the largest UK investment trusts, with total assets of over £3.5bn and a highly creditable and consistent long-term performance record. As far as *The Economist*'s "semi-civilised states" were concerned, only one of the original 18 government stocks defaulted, namely the Spanish New, 3 per cents. The stock missed its coupon payment in 1875, reducing the trust's income for the year by £4,099. In the finest tradition of a soundly managed investment trust, the deficiency was by then so well-covered by reserves, and by the success of other stocks, that the investors could be forgiven for not having noticed.

JOHN NEWLANDS is the author of *Put Not Your Trust in Money*, a history of the investment trust industry from 1868 to the present.

THE WEALTH MANAGER'S VIEW

JAMES BURNS, *a partner at Smith & Williamson, explains why investment trusts remain popular with firms that manage private client portfolios.*

How long have you been following investment trusts?

Since January 2001, or about 16 years in all. I joined what was NCL Investments in 1999, did a year and a bit in the back office. There was no official graduate trainee role but as and when slots appeared on the investment floor, you were asked if you were interested in the role. At some stage I was asked if I wanted to join the bonds desk, but I declined that one. Then I was asked to help with the firm's fund of investment trusts. I did not know a lot back then, but it opened up a whole new world of investment choices to me.

Why are investment trusts popular with wealth managers?

Investment trusts have always been popular with wealth managers, and become more so in recent years as more and more asset classes have opened up as options in the investment company space. As the sector has morphed from being mainly conventional UK registered companies to moving into a much broader investment company space, we have become equally big supporters, and an early call for brokers promoting all the new launches.

The sector has changed a lot since the financial crisis. Up until then it was primarily equity trusts. There was a very small fixed income sector and we had a big boom in property investment companies leading up to the financial crisis. Hedge funds also came in for a while. But since the financial crisis there has been a massive explosion in different asset classes to access. The easy explanation is that the banks have come out, or at least had to retreat, from this part of the market. So now we have things like commercial property lending, aircraft leasing and more specialist property sectors, such as student and healthcare property. There have been a few more private equity launches too.

So overall there are far more different asset classes to play with now. The financial crisis has been good for the sector in that respect because the investment company structure is an absolutely ideal vehicle for these less liquid pools of capital. At the same time, the investment company sector has really benefited from wealth managers looking to build more diversified multi-asset class portfolios, an approach which is becoming much more common.

How do you use investment trusts within the firm?

One is as a core building block for a portfolio. Conventional equity investment trusts such as Monks and Scottish Mortgage have good management teams and are very attractively priced these days. The sector offers good income vehicles with revenue reserves and good historic payout ratios. With trusts whose managers have the ability to invest in smaller and less liquid shares than they are allowed to do in their open-ended funds, you are hopefully getting their best ideas as they can afford to take a longer term view.

The second attraction is the ability to access multi-asset trusts which give you diversification away from conventional equity and bonds, whether that is in the form of commercial property lending, renewable energy or whatever. I always look at the sector in these two ways. The key thing for me is that natural selection works in the investment company sector. If you are not performing, or the management house is not performing, shareholders and boards are much more active now. Poorly performing vehicles will die out. Dead wood gets kicked out relatively quickly.

Do you expect fees to continue coming down?

Yes. There is certainly a long list of funds that have cut performance fees in the last few years. I think that boards of trusts now realise that they are able to assert their strength in negotiations with management houses over fees. Their argument is that as investment companies have the advantage of permanent or semi-permanent capital, so their fees should be coming down. Trusts like Monks and Scottish Mortgage are now charging incredibly attractive fees for active management.

Are trusts doing too much or too little by way of using gearing?

On the whole I think the use of gearing has been pretty good. There are different approaches. Some boards are involved in every gearing decision. Others give managers leeway up to a certain level. Some trusts say that as we have a long-term view, we are going to be geared pretty much all of the time. Other managers look to reduce gearing when they think that valuations are looking potentially stretched. We have seen very few increasing their gearing recently.

What about the added volatility that shares in investment companies have?

You can't dispute that trusts will be more volatile than open-ended funds in terms of price because of the supply and demand dynamic and also potentially because of gearing. We always say that, if it is part of a sensibly constructed portfolio and if you are happy with the level of volatility, then investment companies make absolute sense. A lot of people use the sector for income and as long as that income is being paid, that is the key thing. In 2008 in the equity income sector, only one trust cut its dividend. Every other trust in the sector held its dividend while open-ended were cutting. That is important for clients because they want to know that their income will keep on growing and they can afford to hold for the longer time.

Are the regulators doing enough to promote investment companies as an alternative?

The Financial Conduct Authority has probably been showing a bit more interest lately. The AIC has been lobbying hard to make sure that investment companies are not classified as complex investments under the latest European legislation. The truth is that investment companies are slightly more complicated investments, but it is really just a case of having a few more moving parts to look at. You have to do a bit more research. The good thing about investment companies that needs to be emphasized is that in this post-RDR, governance-driven world there is a board of directors there to protect shareholders' interest, which is a big positive.

But has the quality of investment trust boards improved? They were the butt of many jokes not so long ago…

Over the last decade boards have been showing far more independence over fees and moving management contracts around. We have seen more examples of directors taking their responsibilities more seriously than they were. There is definitely still room for more improvement. I can think of a couple of cases recently where boards have failed to bite the bullet and move the management contract when they should have done.

Are you in favour of more boards introducing discount controls?

I am actually quite relaxed. I am still of the view that there are few things more fun for me than buying a really good investment trust that is trading on a discount because of some short-term wobble in the market. What I don't like to see are boards turning to cash registers at the wrong time, purely because they have put something in the sand and they end up shrinking the trust to a point which may not be in the interest of everyone. That said, what you don't want are no controls at all and boards adopting a laissez faire approach, with a discount staying at 20% forever. I quite like the fixed life idea, giving us the ability to get out after a few years. While the discount may move out a bit in the short term, you know that on a three or four year view you can exit at Net Asset Value.

Is there a limit on how large a trust has to be for you to invest in at IPO?

Ideally we are looking for investment companies with £100m in assets, but we won't say no if it is less than that, particularly if we think it has the potential to grow, and will be able to raise more money. There is no absolute limit. £100m is our unofficial limit. At some other houses it is £250m. I can understand why they do it, but it also means that there are trusts in the area that they don't consider at all, so they are missing out on some very good vehicles in that space. We monitor our holdings but we do allow exceptions. We think our approach is more flexible.

What has been the driving force behind the wave of recent launches?

Yield has been a big driver of new issues and that makes sense. Things like Real Estate Credit Investments we really like because you are getting attractive income yields from the lending and still have an equity cushion above you. If you buy Land Securities, by comparison, you are just taking the equity risk, so if you can get 6% yield on real estate lending, that is attractive. The search for income has been a particularly big factor behind all the new issues in the alternative asset space. At the moment nearly all IPOs have an income story behind them. Pershing Square was a big launch that wasn't particularly successful.

Are you not worried that income-based IPOs are becoming too much of a fashion thing?

Yes. I am becoming a little concerned. The investment company market does have a tendency to get quite excited about certain asset classes. Some of the issues recently have become very niche-specific, particularly in the REIT (Real Estate Investment Trust) space.

JAMES BURNS is a partner in Smith & Williamson and responsible for leading the firm's research into investment trusts. He also manages three multi-manager funds that invest in investment trusts and a number of private client and discretionary management portfolios.

USING INVESTMENT TRUSTS TO DIVERSIFY

Fidelity's investment trust specialist ALEX DENNY *underlines the importance of spreading risk across different markets and trusts.*

WHEN IT COMES to investing, the benefits of diversification are clearly significant. Most investors will likely be well familiar with how spreading your investments across a range of areas can reduce your exposure to single-asset risk. Putting all investment eggs in one basket can offer extraordinary returns (think Apple in 2003), but it can also lead to catastrophic losses (Northern Rock in 2007).

As a general rule, the majority of investors will therefore look to build a core portfolio of investments and savings, split across the three broad areas: cash, bonds and equities. This core portfolio will be held through bank accounts and, probably, funds. The allocation or balance between these different assets will vary between different people and are clearly dependent on individual objectives and circumstances – what you are saving for, your age, appetite for risk and capacity for loss.

These core asset classes are exactly that – core. They form a central component of how our financial systems and markets work, but as such, they may all suffer from related setbacks. For example, an equity investor may feel confident that holding a range of index trackers provides sufficient diversification. However, in today's global economy, major inflexion points can occur simultaneously across all markets – just see returns over the second half of 2008 or mid-2015 for a painful reminder.

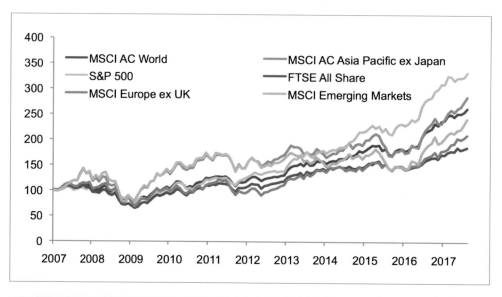

	AUG 12–AUG 13	AUG 13–AUG 14	AUG 14–AUG 15	AUG 15–AUG 16	AUG 16–AUG 17
MSCI AC World	19.2%	13.3%	1.7%	26.7%	19.7%
S&P 500	21.9%	16.7%	8.5%	32.2%	18.1%
MSCI Europe ex UK	27.0%	10.5%	1.9%	15.2%	25.4%
MSCI AC Asia Pacific ex Japan	10.2%	13.0%	-12.1%	33.5%	25.5%
FTSE All Share	18.9%	10.3%	-2.3%	11.7%	14.3%
MSCI Emerging Markets	3.6%	12.1%	-16.5%	31.8%	27.0%

Source: Datasteam, 31 August 2017. Index performance based on total return in GBP. Past performance is not a guide to the future.

INVESTMENT TRUSTS AND AVOIDING SYSTEMATIC RISK

There are lots of reasons why global equity markets can follow each other; markets are not rational in the short-term. Driven by sentiment, a sell-off in one market can often trigger a downturn in another. The trick to avoiding this sort of risk – and achieve genuine diversification – is to access parts of the market which are not well-covered or represented in an existing core portfolio.

Investment trusts are nearly all actively managed and have structural advantages which allow them to avoid these systemic risk pitfalls. Their capital structure – with a fixed number of shares and no flows of cash in or out from investors – allows them to invest in much smaller, illiquid companies which fall outside of mainstream indices (or have negligible correlation to them).

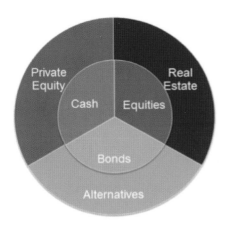

Source: Fidelity International, 31 August 2017

They also have the ability to invest in companies before they are even listed, as well as alternative areas like real estate or long-term infrastructure projects which aren't well represented in mainstream funds due to liquidity issues.

There are investment trusts which specialise and focus on investing in these kinds of areas – smaller companies trusts, private equity and venture capital trusts, real estate investment trusts – as well as trusts which follow relatively mainstream markets from the core of your portfolio while adding these non-core elements as well.

Take Fidelity China Special Situations PLC, an actively-managed investment trust which focuses on the growth of China's domestic economy. The trust's portfolio has exposure to some of China's largest and most significant companies, as well as holding a significant proportion of its assets in unlisted and micro-cap stocks which do not form part of the index. Importantly, these types of companies tend to be more exposed to the domestic drivers of the Chinese economy and are less sensitive to external political and economic events than other larger companies in China or the rest of Asia.

Elsewhere and closer to home, Woodford Patient Capital – the actively managed UK-focused investment trust focused on small and micro-cap stocks – has limited overlap with mainstream UK indices. Whether you're looking to gain exposure to specific alternative asset classes, or you are attracted to the ability to invest in small or unlisted companies, these examples highlight to good effect the benefits that investment trusts can offer when held as part of a well-diversified portfolio.

ALEX DENNY is the head of Fidelity's investment trust business.

AN IN-DEPTH LOOK AT VCTS

GEOFFREY CHALLINOR *of wealth management firm Saunderson House explains the pros and cons of investing in venture capital trusts.*

INTRODUCTION

HIGH EARNERS AND wealthy individuals can be subject to high income tax and capital gains tax liabilities. There are a number of government-backed investment initiatives which enable individuals to save tax efficiently but are often overlooked. Venture capital trusts (VCTs) are an important feature in this landscape.

The UK government has made a number of tax reforms in recent years to increase tax revenue and reduce the fiscal deficit. Most notable among these are changes to pension legislation, with people earning more than £150,000 a year (including their employer pension contribution) seeing their pension annual allowance drop to £10,000 per year and, unless they hold one of the forms of Lifetime Allowance Protection, their lifetime allowance fall to £1m. Individual Savings Accounts (ISAs) remain an attractive investment vehicle, although with annual contributions restricted to £20,000 they only provide a limited tax shelter.

Buy-to-let investing has been a successful strategy for some, providing a steady level of income in retirement and, in many areas, strong capital growth. However, increases in stamp duty on buy-to-let properties (and second homes) and restrictions to landlords' mortgage interest relief now make this less appealing. Finally, with asset prices having risen sharply since the 'nil rate band' was fixed at £325,000 in April 2009 (where it will remain until at least 2020/21), family members and beneficiaries of wills are increasingly left with inheritance tax bills to pay.

This changing landscape is driving investors to look at other tax-efficient investment schemes, namely Venture Capital Trusts (VCTs), Enterprise Investment Schemes (EISs) and Business Property Relief (BPR). An overview of the tax reliefs for each scheme is shown in the following table. Here we cover the different types of VCT and their performance over the last 10 years, before commenting on VCT fundraising and related considerations for investors. We then list some of the risks and drawbacks of investing in a VCT and finally, present a case study of a generic VCT investor. It is important to note that VCTs will not suit everyone and they are not substitutes to more conventional tax shelters such as pensions, ISAs, CGT allowances and dividend allowances. However, they can be effective when used appropriately and, for high earners and wealthy individuals, should be included in wider financial planning discussions.

Overview of tax reliefs

	MAXIMUM INVESTMENT	INCOME TAX RELIEF	CGT RELIEF / DEFERRAL	TAX–FREE DIVIDENDS	TAX–FREE GROWTH	IHT FREE	LOSS RELIEF
VCT	£200,000	30%	No	Yes	Yes	No	No
EIS	£1,000,000	30% + carry back	Deferral	No	Yes	2 years	Yes
BPR	Unlimited	No	No	If in ISA	If in ISA	2 years	No

Source: HMRC

VCTs were introduced in 1995 to encourage investment into small UK companies. They are closed-ended investment companies listed on the London Stock Exchange. They pool investors' money and employ a professional manager to make investments in unquoted companies or companies whose shares are traded on the Alternative Investment Market (AIM) and PLUS Markets. These companies must carry out a qualifying trade and, at the point of investment, be less than seven years old (with certain exceptions), have no more than 250 employees and have assets of less than £15m. To retain government approval as a VCT, it must invest at least 70% of raised money in qualifying investments within three years. The balance of 30% can remain in other 'non-qualifying' investments.

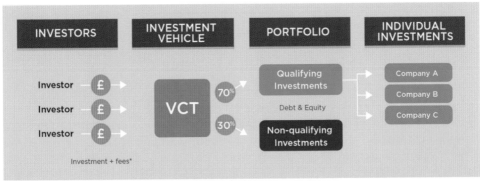

*The investment will be subject to initial fees and annual management charges, while performance fees are common

VCTs may raise money either for new share pools or existing ones. Established VCTs will typically raise money for an existing share pool, providing access to a portfolio of maturing investments which has the benefit of immediate diversification and, in most instances, is already paying dividends (since holdings are closer to being realised and a number will be generating income from interest on loans and dividends from companies they have lent to or invested in).

TAX BENEFITS

There are three main tax benefits available on investments of up to £200,000 per tax year:

- Income tax relief at 30% on the purchase of newly issued VCT shares (received upfront), allowing investors to reduce their income tax liability in that tax year.
- Tax-free dividends, providing the potential for a regular stream of tax-free income.
- Tax-free capital gains, meaning investors have no tax to pay on gains when shares are sold.

VCTs are therefore among the most tax-efficient investment vehicles available and can be a useful option for investors looking to complement their pension plans or other long-term investments, such as ISAs. It is worth adding that investing in small UK businesses offers the potential for significant long-term growth if the companies in the VCT are successful. They may also bring extra diversification to an investor's portfolio.

TYPES OF VCT

Whilst all VCT managers must follow the same qualifying investment criteria, each has a slightly different objective and investment focus, and will employ a different investment strategy in order to achieve their goals. The different types of VCT fall into one of three broad categories:

- **Generalist VCTs** invest in a wide range of (predominantly) unquoted companies across different sectors. They are 'evergreen' in nature – i.e. they don't have predetermined wind-up dates – and tend to focus on high growth, high risk investments. They aim to deliver tax-free income and/or capital growth, with the bulk of an investor's return likely to come from the former (paid from the sale of portfolio holdings as well as income produced within the portfolio).
- **AIM VCTs** invest in companies whose shares are traded on AIM. Like Generalist VCTs, they are diversified across different sectors, focus on rapidly growing businesses, are evergreen in nature and aim to deliver tax-free income and/or capital growth.
- **Specialist VCTs** concentrate on just one sector, such as media or technology. Their risk profile is determined by the sector that they invest in and, related to this, the business models of investee companies. Those at the lower risk end are sometimes branded 'planned exit' or 'limited life' VCTs, both sharing the same objective of returning the invested capital at a modest profit at a predetermined date, typically as soon as possible after the company has passed its five-year qualifying period.

The VCT market has total assets of £3.5bn[*], which is spread across 96 VCTs (including different share pools) and 26 different managers (note that some managers run more than

---

[*]   Figures from The Association of Investment Companies, as at 15 September 2017.

one type of VCT). Generalist VCTs are the most common type, representing 70% of assets across 59 VCTs and 14 managers. AIM VCTs represent 22% of assets across 11 VCTs and 7 managers, while Specialist VCTs represent 8% of assets across 26 VCTs and 9 managers. The largest VCT, with £419m of assets, is Octopus Titan VCT (a generalist), while the smallest VCT, with £0.5m of assets, is Downing Four VCT 2011 Structured Shares.

PERFORMANCE

The track records of VCTs vary widely, with some performing very well and others very badly. Of course, the year in which an investor purchases VCT shares will influence the returns that they experience, although more important for long-term investors is the manager that they select. Investors should undertake (or seek an adviser that undertakes) thorough due diligence to understand the manager's investment strategy and evaluate the likelihood of their successfully executing it.

According to research by the Association of Investment Companies (AIC), over the ten years to 31 December 2016, the VCT sector as a whole is up 82% on a share price total return basis. This does not include tax reliefs. By comparison, the FTSE All-Share index of companies listed on the UK's Main Market is up 72% (on a total return basis). The AIC's figures show that the top 20 performing VCTs are up an average 141% over the period, which includes average dividend payments of 87p per share. Looking at the performance of different strategies, 17 out of the top 20 were generalist, one was AIM and two were specialist.

FUND RAISING

VCTs have traditionally launched share offers shortly before the tax year-end, with fund raisings in recent years filling up quickly as demand for the strongest-performing VCTs has outstripped supply. However, concerns within the VCT industry that the UK government will revise VCT tax reliefs in the Autumn Budget 2017 prompted a change in fundraising plans for the current (2017–18) tax year.

In November 2016, the Prime Minister announced that HM Treasury would carry out a consultation titled 'Patient Capital Review' aimed at identifying and tackling factors affecting the supply of 'patient capital'. The Treasury defines patient capital as "long-term investment in innovative firms led by ambitious entrepreneurs who want to build large scale businesses". One of the key objectives of the consultation is to assess what changes in government policy, if any, are needed to support the expansion of patient capital.

Since tax advantaged investment schemes such as VCTs were introduced for this very reason, their effectiveness is part of the review. Whilst there are no proposals in the paper to change VCT tax reliefs, they have been adjusted in the past (upfront income tax relief ranging from 20% to 40%, currently 30%) and may be considered an effective tool for redistributing state aid into new avenues for growth. That said, changes could come in various other forms, for instance targeting the investment strategies employed, and it is noteworthy that the paper lists 'capital preservation' strategies as an area where the cost effectiveness of current tax reliefs could be improved.

Should VCT tax reliefs become less favourable, this would clearly impair the attractiveness of the scheme with a likely consequence being a fall in demand for VCTs. One could argue that this goes against what the consultation is trying to achieve and is therefore unlikely. However, the VCT industry is sufficiently concerned that this year's fundraising activity is launching earlier than usual; crucially ahead of the Budget. Moreover, the amounts being sought are larger than normal (at least in absolute terms). The near-term implications for investors are:

1. There will be a wider range of VCT offers to choose from.
2. VCT offers that have only had capacity for existing shareholders in recent years may also have capacity for new shareholders this year.

However:

3. Investors will need to be **ready to make their subscriptions in the coming weeks/months**.
4. Investors should **not expect another opportunity later in the tax year** (i.e. just before the tax-year end) to make a subscription for this tax year.
5. Investors should **expect fewer and smaller offerings next tax year** (i.e. 2018/19) irrespective of there being changes to the tax reliefs this year, as VCT managers will already have capital to deploy (since they'll be raising more than they normally would this tax year).

Any longer-term implications for investors will become more apparent after the Budget.

RISKS AND DRAWBACKS

VCTs have a higher risk profile than an investment in larger companies. Businesses in the early stages of their development have a higher failure rate than more established businesses and can change value more quickly and more significantly than larger companies. Investors therefore have greater risk of losing their capital and dividends can be reduced or suspended altogether.

Although VCTs are listed on the London Stock Exchange and in theory can be bought and sold at any time, as only newly issued shares qualify for income tax relief, the secondary market is illiquid. This means that even if a buyer can be found, many VCT shares trade at substantial discounts to their respective net asset values (NAVs). Further, as the price of shares bought on the secondary market is determined by supply and demand, should these not align (as is often the case), the difference between the buying and selling price (the spread) may be wide. Disposing of a VCT holding in the secondary market may therefore only be possible at a price significantly below the NAV of the shares. A large number of VCT managers do, however, offer share buy-back schemes, which they typically undertake at a 5%–15% discount to NAV.

It is important to note that income tax relief is clawed back if the shares are not held for at least five years. Investors should be prepared to invest for at least this long and a longer time frame is advisable. It is worth adding that how much an individual benefits from the tax reliefs will depend on their particular circumstances and HMRC may change the rules at any time. Investors should also note that the ongoing charges associated with VCTs are typically higher than those for mainstream collective investments, while it is common for them to have a performance fee.

WHO MIGHT CONSIDER BUYING VCT SHARES?

VCTs are most suitable for individuals with a balanced or adventurous attitude to risk, with surplus cash available to invest for the long term and a large income tax liability. Pension and ISA allowances should already have been fully utilised, as well as any tax-free growth available using dividends allowances and annual capital gains tax exemptions.

Case study

David is a high earner and comfortable taking a higher level of investment risk. He makes full pension and ISA contributions, although is looking at other tax-efficient ways to supplement his income in retirement. He plans to work for another five years and will have considerable surplus income over that period.

After meeting with his financial adviser, David agrees to invest £50,000 per year for the next five years into a range of Generalist and AIM VCTs. For this example, for the sake of simplicity it is assumed that the VCTs have an average target dividend yield of 5%, which is achieved every year in perpetuity, and there is no movement in capital values.

When David enters his first year of retirement, he has a VCT portfolio of £250,000 at a net cost of £175,000 (after 30% income tax relief). He has received £37,500 in tax-free dividends (5% on the sum invested over five years) and stands to receive a further £12,500 in tax-free dividends each year thereafter. The tax-equivalent yield of £12,500 in dividends to an additional rate taxpayer on a net investment of £175,000 is 13.0%. David must remain invested for five years into retirement to keep all of the tax breaks provided (as the income tax for each contribution invested for less than five years would otherwise be repayable), so this should be seen as part of a long-term holding and capital to which he does not need access. The VCT holdings could be sold if required, although David understands that this would be at a discount to NAV.

For a well-managed Generalist or AIM VCT, a 5% dividend yield together with some uplift in capital value over the long term is a reasonable expectation. However, dividends may be higher or lower in any single year depending on market conditions and the level of realisations, while portfolio values are also likely to fluctuate.

CONCLUSION

In recent years it has become more difficult for high earners and wealthy people to shelter their income and capital from the taxman. VCTs help investors to mitigate future tax liabilities and receive tax-free income and gains by making long-term investments in risky start up and growing businesses. The scheme is well-established and we anticipate growth in this area as investors look for additional financial planning options given restrictions to more conventional tax shelters. However, it should be noted that HMRC has changed the rules governing the schemes in the past and may do so again in the future.

It is important to recognise that VCTs are not suitable for all individuals and investors must understand and be comfortable with the level of investment risk inherent in the offerings. Their high-risk nature should not automatically be viewed as a negative, since the track records of some managers show strong investment returns even before the tax reliefs are factored in. We recommend that interested investors seek information and advice from specialist financial professionals before making a subscription.

GEOFFREY CHALLINOR CFA is an investment analyst at Saunderson House.

EXPERT VIEWS

WHEN CONTRARIAN THINKING IS KEY

Fidelity Special Values portfolio manager ALEX WRIGHT *explains why it is important to avoid doing what most other investors are doing.*

To be a contrarian investor means to focus your attention on stocks and sectors that have fallen out of fashion in the market and trade on cheap prices due to a lack of demand. The chief advantage to this approach is that, if done well, it improves the balance of risks and rewards by limiting your downside and maximising potential upside.

This is because companies that are out of favour have probably disappointed investors in the past, meaning current expectations are low and therefore, the chances of further disappointment leading to steep falls in share prices are lower. On the other hand, if things improve, the share price can rise significantly as the market responds to this better than expected news.

This philosophy and approach has underpinned the management of Fidelity Special Values PLC since it was launched back in 1994. Since then, the economic, political and investment landscape across the UK has changed significantly. We've seen five prime ministers and more than ten managers of the England football team, yet the trust has had only three portfolio managers – each employing a contrarian, bottom-up approach to managing a well-diversified portfolio of shares in mainly UK-listed companies.

Investing against the tide is a psychologically difficult thing to do. Humans are social animals, and behave socially when making investment decisions. It takes a particular mindset and a highly disciplined approach to execute a contrarian investment process successfully.

Fidelity Special Values PLC past performance – hypothetical growth of £10,000 invested at launch

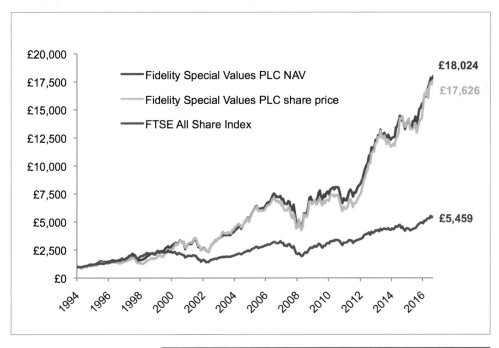

	JUL 12–JUL 13	JUL 13–JUL 14	JUL 14–JUL 15	JUL 15–JUL 16	JUL 16–JUL 17
Fidelity Special Values PLC net asset value	53.3%	7.4%	14.3%	0.1%	25.7%
Fidelity Special Values PLC share price	67.2%	6.8%	21.1%	-6.7%	31.0%
FTSE All Share Index	24.3%	5.6%	5.4%	3.8%	14.9%

Past performance is not a guide to the future.

Source: © 2017 Morningstar, Inc. All Rights Reserved. Fidelity International, 31 July 2017. On a bid-to-bid basis with income reinvested in GBP terms. Launch date: 17 November 1994. Holdings can vary from those in the index quoted. For this reason the comparison index is used for reference only.

Central to the long-term success of our approach has been company research and making full use of the insight and expertise of our large team of analysts. Fidelity's philosophy is to base investment decisions on company fundamentals such as competitive position, management strength, growth opportunities, valuation and so on. Overarching trends in the economy (top-down factors) play a supplementary rather than a primary role in our investment decisions.

Our investment team spends many thousands of hours meeting company management, speaking to suppliers, competitors and customers in order to build up a picture of the true state of a company's fundamentals. It is this work that allows us to form a view of the company's future profitability and ultimately whether we consider it an attractive investment for our shareholders.

THE BENEFITS OF A CLOSED-END STRUCTURE

In many ways, an investment trust is naturally sympathetic to the rhythms of contrarian investing. As the trust has a fixed number of shares – so every buyer needs a seller – I do not have to manage the daily inflows and outflows that occur in open-ended funds as a result of investors buying or redeeming units.

The major consequence of this is that I'm able to position the portfolio to fully and directly express my investment views, rather than be forced into trading decisions by client activity, which can sometimes result in being forced to sell holdings into unloved markets or vice versa. This means we can spend more time on company research and stock selection rather than cash flow management.

This characteristic is also particularly advantageous in the context of our investments in smaller companies, where liquidity can often be a constraining factor. The trust has a structural bias towards small and medium-sized firms – as this segment is less widely covered by mainstream analysts it tends to create more opportunities to identify positive change that others are overlooking or underappreciating.

The closed-end structure of the trust also provides enhanced investment powers and the ability to use gearing to amplify the portfolio's market exposure. This can increase overall portfolio volatility, but if implemented effectively it has the potential to improve long-term performance and provides the flexibility to deliver returns across a wide range of market conditions.

The trust's net gearing is actively managed; so when valuations are depressed and I'm finding a large number of investment ideas, the portfolio's net exposure is likely to increase. Conversely, when the broader market rallies strongly, the level of gearing would generally tend to reduce as aggregate valuations rise.

Fidelity Special Values PLC — net exposure vs market over Alex Wright's tenure

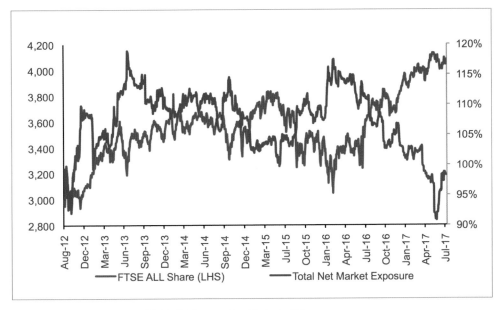

Source: Fidelity International, 31 July 2017. Alex Wright tenure since 1 September 2012.

This is highlighted to good effect in the above chart. For example, as the FTSE All Share has rallied strongly since the summer months of 2016, the trust's net gearing (ie. its overall market exposure) has trended downwards. This is in contrast to how we managed the portfolio between July 2015 and April 2016 where net gearing increased as the broader market fell.

Such periods of market volatility often create a favourable environment for contrarian stockpicking. This is worth highlighting today given the looming political and economic uncertainty as the UK prepares to leave the European Union. Among Warren Buffett's many pearls of wisdom, "be fearful when others are greedy, and greedy when others are fearful" remains as pertinent today as it ever has been.

ALEX WRIGHT has been manager of Fidelity Special Values since 2012.

THE CASE FOR CHOOSING ACTIVE MANAGEMENT

Private client manager SANDY CROSS *has six pieces of advice for anyone looking to put money into investment trusts.*

I AM A GREAT believer in active fund management. I see the attraction of passive funds: getting more or less average performance for a bargain basement price isn't a bad thing. However, my colleagues and I remain convinced that when it comes to investing man (or woman) can do better than machine. We are sure that there are genuinely talented managers operating in the market and that we can use them to diversify our clients' holdings while also making them better returns than if we simply tracked the wider market indices. Below are a few thoughts on how we find the funds run by those talented managers.

1. Look for the fund managers who enjoy macro stories, but mostly ignore them.

Everyone loves a story. And if that story manages to make something complicated and inherently unpredictable look like it might be both straightforward and pretty predictable, all the better. So children read fairy tales (from which they get the idea that morality somehow only comes in black and white) and investors devour market research (from which they get the idea that the complexity of markets can somehow be tidied up via a pertinent chart or two). But just as fairy tales are an unsatisfactory preparation for real life, so investment stories tend to turn out to be a dubious basis on which to invest.

That's largely because most macro forecasts – on the direction of markets and of economies – are wrong. Consider the efforts of the US Federal Reserve. It is well-resourced and packed to the gunwales with very intelligent people. There have been eight recessions in the last 60 years. Those people have forecast none of them. It's just too hard. Far better, we find, to skip the fallacy of precise macroeconomic forecasting in favour of assuming that there is always a range of outcomes possible and look to build portfolios that will be resilient to them.

2. Remember that investing is about companies.

The bright side of forecasting failure is that it doesn't matter nearly as much as you think it does to long-term investors. Investing, whether you do it through funds as we do in our business, or you own individual equities directly, is about companies – their products, their cash flows, their profits, their management's expertise and their cultures. And while identifying the trends in these isn't easy it comes with many fewer variables than forecasting the direction of global interest rates. Better to focus on what is useful and possible than what is usually impossible and not necessarily useful (forecasting a macroeconomic trend correctly doesn't mean you will have any luck predicting its effect on the sales of the actual investment in question).

3. Invest with managers who have some sense of stock market history.

The past is easier to grasp than the future. It can also help us to minimise the mistakes of the future. I strongly recommend that new investors visit the Library of Mistakes in Edinburgh. There (as is also the case in the libraries of many a business school) you can find shelves groaning with research that comes to one key conclusion: about three quarters of M&A is a complete failure for shareholders. I can therefore tell you with some certainty that shares in companies engaged in M&A (beyond small infill acquisitions) are less likely to be good investments than those that stick to organic growth. I can also tell you that any deal described as 'transformational' is to be avoided like the plague. If your manager loves an acquisitive company, acquire holdings in someone else's fund.

History teaches us similar lessons about leverage. We always want to be ready for a crisis (there is almost always one on the way). And we know that it is the companies with the most debt that come a cropper the fastest in a crisis. Having debt to pay back and banks to keep happy reduces their flexibility and their autonomy – both things managers really need when the chips are down. Long-term investors are far better off accepting lower annual returns in return for a greater degree of financial resilience – and a greater chance of long-term survival. So check your manager's top ten holdings list – if there are too many highly-leveraged firms you may be better off avoiding the fund.

4. Be in it together.

You want to see a manager investing in their own fund. If it isn't good enough for his own money, why should it be good enough for yours? Check their holdings before you give them yours. There are all sorts of definitions of risk around in the financial world. The only one that should matter to most investors is the risk of permanent loss of capital. If a manager isn't investing in his own fund you might wonder why he reckons his own capital isn't safe there.

5. Make sure your manager isn't overworking himself: less trading is generally better.

A big difference between a successful asset manager and an unsuccessful asset manager is often turnover. Low turnover means lower costs (which are a helpful predictor of long-term performance). But it also suggests a higher level of conviction. You want a manager who has a clear strategy which brings him good ideas and who then gives those ideas time to play out. All too many managers get swayed by the short-term direction of the market: it takes only the smallest of worries that their own strategy might mean they underperform the market in the short term for them to adopt someone else's. We're looking for the small number of managers in the market with a bit more stamina than most. The ones who have a (good) plan and stick to it regardless of what everyone else is up to.

6. Investment trusts – an old but successful idea.

If you want to invest for the long term, you could well be best off in an investment trust. These are effectively companies, the purpose of which is to invest in other companies. But their key virtue is that their pool of capital is fixed. Investors can sell their shares, of course, but they can't actually pull capital from the fund. This means that the trusts can hold investments for the very long term and that they can invest in the kind of illiquid assets that other funds would see as too risky (on the basis that they couldn't be sold in a hurry rather than that they are inherently dangerous).

So you can use an investment trust to buy into the kind of things you may want for diversification these days – smaller companies or property, for example. And if it goes wrong you will find that unlike with most investment products there is someone obvious to complain to. As listed companies, trusts have independent boards. If you don't like the way they are investing your money, just turn up to the AGM and tell them so.

SANDY CROSS FCSI is an investment manager and director at Rossie House Investment Management in Edinburgh (rossiehouse.com), where he specialises in managing private client portfolios. He is a graduate of the University of Edinburgh and also has an MBA from Imperial College.

TEN GREAT MISCONCEPTIONS

ROBIN ANGUS *is a director of Personal Assets Trust, a great favourite with risk-averse private clients, who like its focus on absolute returns (capital preservation first, make money second). In a letter to shareholders he lists what he claims are ten of the greatest investment misconceptions.*

1. The point of investing is to beat an index.

IF YOU SPENT all your time reading investment company reports you might be forgiven for thinking that the point of investing was to beat an index. Nearly every investment fund has a benchmark or comparator (even Personal Assets, although we'd be happy not to) and funds' own reports often focus on performance relative to their benchmark.

But to quote Bobby White, formerly Chairman of Personal Assets, "Good relative performance does not necessarily buy the groceries." If a fund sets out to preserve the value of capital and then, if possible, to make it grow, an investor would have every excuse for being as sick as the proverbial parrot if the All-Share fell by 30% and the fund's net asset value fell by only 25%. It should have been able to protect its shareholders' funds better than that even from the investment equivalent of Hurricane Irma.

The all-important criterion for judging the performance of an investment fund is whether it does what it says on the tin. Read the writing on the tin first, and if it accords with what you're aiming to do, then that's a reason for buying it. Thereafter, judge it on the extent to which it keeps its promises.

Even good performance in the absolute (as opposed to against a benchmark) doesn't excuse everything. If I entrusted some of my 'sacred savings' to an investment adviser who promised to invest it conservatively but instead put it on a horse which romped home at 50-1 in the 3.30 at Chepstow, I might buy him a case of champagne to celebrate but I'd still give him the sack as my financial adviser, because he hadn't done what he had promised. Never forget that a result by itself tells us nothing about how it was achieved. It might have been through careful, steady investment or wild, reckless plunges. As well as knowing where we are we also must understand how we got there.

2. The point of investing is to beat your competitors.

The second of my great investment lies is closely related to the first. The competitive spirit is in all of us, and we easily fall into the language of sport (indeed, I've just done so). My toes still curl when I remember how, nearly 30 years ago, I hypothesised in an investment trust annual about a 'Management Olympics' for investment managers. So forget all those metaphors about races. If an investment fund does what it says on the tin, that's what matters. If it delivers more than it promises, then that's fine – but not if the fund, in attempting to over-deliver, takes more risks than it said it would.

3. The point of investing is to make your money grow as much as possible.

No, it isn't. Risk comes into it too. Every investor has a different degree of tolerance of risk, and a level of risk which one investor would be happy to accept would be much too great for another.

To investors who value stability and try to reduce worry to a minimum, Personal Assets offers low price volatility. Every year in our Report & Accounts we show a chart of share price performance against share price volatility. This shows investors not only how our share price has performed, but also how smooth a ride it has been. We may not be among the trusts which travel the farthest, but we do (we believe) offer a less bumpy ride.

4. Total return is the only fair way of measuring performance.

Total return is one valid way of measuring performance, but it's less useful to private investors than to institutional investors. Private investors are not homogeneous. They have very different aims, tolerances of risk and tax positions. Therefore the total return I get from a particular investment may be different from the total return you receive from exactly the same investment, or I would receive if I held the investment in an ISA.

Let's say I hold the investment in an ISA because I want to accumulate capital by reinvesting dividends free of tax. Total return in those circumstances is a useful measure. But suppose that I hold an investment because I want to live off the income from it without touching the capital. Total return is of no interest to me then. What I want to know is how big, safe and fast-growing the stream of dividends is. Total return would be the universally best measure of performance only if all investors held their investments for exactly the same reasons. But they don't.

5. Past performance is no guide to the future.

To adapt the old chestnut, there are three great lies in life: the cheque is in the post; I'm from the government and I'm here to help you; and past performance is no guide to the future. A moment's thought shows you how silly the last statement is. Were it true, we could abolish examinations, references and almost every other means of distinguishing between the options open to us.

Past performance is not a perfect guide to the future, but it's the only one we've got and it can give us useful information. Do we want to invest in small companies? Then we go for proven small company managers. Do we want yield? Then we go for income managers with good track records. And so on.

6. The unforgivable risk for an equity investor is to be out of the market.

While there are circumstances in which this is true (fund managers who promise to be fully invested in equities at all times have a fiduciary duty to keep that promise), equity fund managers not compelled to be 100% in equities at all times can and should use their discretion. This is what they are paid for, and they shouldn't hide behind a non-existent policy restriction.

7. To hold cash is an admission of failure.

Our industry hates holding cash, especially now that it's all but impossible to earn any interest on it. It's regarded as a failure of imagination and a waste of fees. But at times it's right to hold cash, for without it we couldn't do what we hope eventually to be able to do – buy bargains when at last these appear. We hold cash not only to reduce risk but also to ensure that it'll be there when we need it.

8. Never be forced to pay Capital Gains Tax.

A major advantage of investment trust status is that investment trusts are exempt from CGT on gains realised within their portfolios. This is more tax-efficient than if a private investor managed the same portfolio in the same way. (Gains realised on the disposal of investment trust shares are of course subject to CGT at the normal rate.)

While CGT may not be as grim a levy as it was between 1988 and 2008, when a higher rate taxpayer was liable to pay it at the rate of 40%, even paying it at the current rate of 20% for higher rate taxpayers still goes against the grain. Sometimes, however, it's better to pay it and sacrifice a portion of your capital gain in order to secure the rest. Purely tax-driven investment decisions are best avoided.

9. Gold, being sterile, is not a proper investment.

Ian Rushbrook, when he was managing Personal Assets, would never hold gold, for this very reason. And he wasn't alone. Lots of able investment managers I have known held the same view, even if a few of them may have accumulated Krugerrands on the sly. Yes, gold is sterile. It pays no dividends but costs money to keep safe, and – in short – it's easy to see why it's been called a 'barbarous relic'. But we don't see it that way. Gold can do a job for us, and as long as it does we're prepared to hold it.

10. Capital is capital, and income is income, and never the twain shall meet.

Is this a great investment misconception? You'd think that someone who regularly questions the usefulness of the total return approach to measuring investment performance would deplore any blurring of the lines between capital and income.

Far from it. Sometimes it makes good sense. As a recent example, we began temporarily 'borrowing' from capital to maintain the level of our dividend. Our reason for so doing is that it's more conservative to realise a small portion of high-quality investment profit than to switch into lower quality, higher-yielding stocks. Counter-intuitive though it may be, sometimes being prepared to dip into capital for living expenses rather than reduce portfolio quality can be what true total return investing means.

ROBIN ANGUS has been an executive director of Personal Assets since 1984 and for many years was part of the No 1 rated team of stockbroker investment trust analysts.

A WORD FROM THE WISE

PETER SPILLER, *founder and guiding light of Capital Gearing Trust, has been analyzing and managing investment trusts for nearly four decades. He offers some guidance on what he has learnt over the years.*

1. Funds are a tax haven.

ALONG-TERM PORTFOLIO IN a tax-paying account should invest in a fund if possible. The reason is that any capital gains tax is deferred until the investment is realised, or extinguished if held to death, rather than charged each year on realised gains. The difference over long periods can be startling.

I have been running Capital Gearing Trust for 35 years. Assuming an average 25% capital gains tax rate, an annual turnover of 20% (probably conservative) and an annual return of 15% (the actual rate achieved by the trust over the period), an investment of £1,000 in a discrete portfolio would have produced, after tax, cash proceeds of £51,298.

Inside the fund, the actual return, even after paying a terminal capital gains tax of 25% to make the comparison fair, would be just over £100,000, and that is after all fees, which were ignored for the direct portfolio. That leads to the final advantage of a fund over a direct portfolio: namely that the fees are deducted before distributions, so that they are in effect tax-deductible. Of course, these advantages are less the lower the tax rate, the fees and the return, but they are always positive.

2. Asset allocation should respond to values.

It is well-established that asset allocation should reflect the time frame of the investor. Those close to retirement cannot afford the risk of having to sell assets at the bottom of a bear market, whereas a young worker can tolerate much greater volatility and illiquidity in her pension fund. Academic institutions have an even longer, essentially unlimited time frame.

But that does not mean that those with a long horizon would always hold only equities, the asset class that has the best record of long-term returns and the highest volatility. That is because the balance of risk against returns is determined by the price of the asset.

Far better for long-term investors is to shift the duration of their portfolio to reflect the prospective returns of each asset class.

Fundamentally, the valuation of most assets reflects the long-term real risk-free interest rate. When real interest rates are high, valuations will be low and prospective returns good. The key point is that attractive prospective returns should be locked in for as long as possible; since equities are broadly speaking the longest duration asset, the asset allocation should heavily overweight them.

Similarly, bond portfolios should have long duration. By contrast, when risk-free returns are low, duration on the portfolio should be as short as possible. That means short-dated bonds and low allocation to equities and probably property. Of course, relative values play a large role in all asset allocation. But the main point is that markets can be timed if the horizon is far enough away. It is only the short term that is random.

3. Beware of ETFs.

Exchange-traded funds (ETFs) are growing in popularity and often with very good reason. Few looking at the track record of active fund management in the S&P 500 in the US would conclude that the extra costs of an active fund are money well spent. Unfortunately, the great insight of index-tracking – that in well-researched liquid markets, prices are sufficiently efficient that the winners will be those with the lowest cost rather than the brightest mind – is not applicable to all markets.

The less efficient and the less liquid a market, the less appropriate it is to invest through ETFs. That is true even of quite large asset classes like corporate bonds and smaller company equities. In both cases, ETFs purport to offer daily liquidity in an asset class that is of limited liquidity. In ordinary times, sales of underlying stock either by the ETF or the Authorised Participant (AP), with whom investors actually trade, are easily absorbed. But in the event of sustained redemptions, those APs will not be willing to finance large inventories, not least because regulatory charge has raised their cost of capital. They will simply lower their bid for the shares in the ETF, perhaps to a significant discount to the NAV or enough at least to show a profit after accepting discounted prices themselves to place the above normal market size of the individual assets.

Effectively, investors will be unable to realise their assets at close to their 'real value'. If investors hold on until markets have stabilised, they should not suffer too much harm – but it is easy to see how downward momentum could gather in difficult markets. Given the size of ETFs, their problems could powerfully effect the valuation of the asset class. Put another way, the change in nature of the ownership of illiquid assets could make the dynamics of the next bear market in various assets quite different from those of the past. And the consequences for the real world are important. If the primary market for junk bonds, for instance, dries up, then companies may have difficulty in refinancing maturing debt.

4. Corporate governance matters.

In the world of investment trusts, the board of directors is critical to the long-term success of an investment. The two critical variables are the total investment return, which is down to the manager, and the relationship of the share price to the net assets. Where those assets are liquid, there is no real excuse for a large discount; all discounts are voluntary. Unfortunately, not all directors understand that.

Often they are appointed with little experience of investment trusts, though usually a record of success in something else. So that if, for instance, a trust is controlled by a manager who is indifferent to the interests of shareholders, it should be the job of the directors to make sure that the other shareholders, whom one might call the oppressed minority, do not have to accept a large discount if they wish to sell their shares. Sadly, on occasion, directors fail to exercise that responsibility, whether through inertia, ignorance or lack of gumption.

Less extremely, powerful management houses sometimes give the impression of putting the size of their own funds under management ahead of the interests of shareholders. Once again, it is the role of directors to assert the interest of the latter, particularly where commitments made by the board are broken, e.g. the discount will never exceed x%. The lesson for investors is to avoid such trusts. The apparent attraction of a significant discount now can turn into the nightmare of a much wider discount in a bear market. Far better to buy on little or no discount where corporate governance is good and particularly where a zero discount mechanism is in place.

5. Don't trust votes in investment trusts.

Wind-up votes were introduced by imaginative investment bankers so that they could launch new trusts in a world where discounts were widespread. The concept was that new investors could relax about discounts in the short term because the vote, typically five or seven years later, would ensure a tight discount, or none at the point of the vote. A wide discount would always lead to a vote to liquidate the trust. Turkeys don't vote for Christmas and shareholders would always vote in their own interest.

In practice, that did not turn out to be true. Trusts on large discounts and sometimes dreadful performance have sailed through wind-up votes. The reasons are too numerous and on occasion ignoble to go into here, but the lesson is clear. Investors should buy such trusts only with deep knowledge both of the board and their fellow shareholders.

6. Turnover is the enemy of performance.

It has become fashionable to note the importance of fees as a determinant of future returns. But fees are merely a subset of total costs and the impact of turnover can be substantial; think of commissions, dealing spreads and, for UK equities, stamp duty.

Furthermore, since the short-term direction of markets is more or less random, with a slight bias to momentum, there is usually little advantage to high turnover. Much better to buy good value for the long term and simply ride out short-term fluctuations. That helps to avoid the final trap: trying to be too clever.

PETER SPILLER founded CG Asset Management (cgasset.com) in 2000 and has been the lead manager of Capital Gearing Trust since 1982. He was previously a partner at Cazenove & Co Capital Management.

INTERVIEWS

GLOBAL EQUITIES THE "SAFEST PLACE TO BE"

Global equities specialist SIMON EDELSTEN, *lead manager of the Mid Wynd International Investment Trust, gives a manager's perspective on how he is handling today's market conditions.*

How did you come to be managing this trust?

To start at the beginning, I got to know Nils Taube [a legendary equity investor] in the '80s when I was a stockbroker. I was one of his firm Taube Hodson Stonex's closer stockbrokers. I'd talked to Nils about leaving broking and moving into fund management quite frequently in the 1990s, and then, in 2000, it seemed like a good time to do that, and so I joined in 2001.

I think you'll find most of the way in which we run money will remind you of the global, growth-oriented and thematic approach that Nils' funds tended to have. I think that we have added some enhancements, particularly, about risk management, use of data, and use of modern technology, which has moved us a bit away from his more artisanal style. We use more data and structure, and less of a call on experience, because we have less experience!

In 2004, Cazenove rang us up and asked us whether we'd be interested in sorting out an investment trust called Electric & General, which was the rump of the litter in the Henderson stable, and we took over this fund, which had a 200 stock portfolio, a little bit of this, a bit of that. Nils had been on the board for a while, but it had rather lost its brand, nobody quite knew what it was there for, it had been used as an in-house vehicle by Henderson to pay people in shares to avoid tax, and of course, it was surrounded by other funds like Witan and Bankers which, for various reasons, had a higher profile and higher priority. Henderson's marketing department couldn't sell five trusts which were all in the same sector.

The takeover worked pretty well. We tightened the list up. We gave the trust our own rationale for trying to increase people's real wealth patiently. We probably made it more capital-protective than the other Henderson trusts. We ran net cash positions, where the other trusts were structurally geared.

After Nils passed away, and John Hodson wanted to leave, I decided I wanted to go for a much more structured and disciplined approach to running money, less artisanal if you like. I felt it was time for me to move on.

Fortunately, I only had to move a few floors in the building, as Artermis, which was another firm I'd known from my time in broking, worked in the same building. The Scottish clients were on my patch when I was at Phillips & Drew, so I'd known John Dodd particularly and Adrian Frost very well from my years in broking. They had just bought out the business from ABN and it was very UK-oriented, they had ambitions to grow the business again because they had a new funding partner and they knew that I could bring them a disciplined, sensible approach to global equity fund management.

From my point of view, it was also another partnership and could underwrite my building a business without there being much time pressure. The lack of timetable pressure – wanting to know when you were going to be profitable and so on and so forth – allows you to run money the way in which you want to run the money rather than take on a higher risk profile in your early years because you've got to get that critical mass to attract retail attention.

We launched the unit trust here six and a half years ago now, called Global Select Fund. Then, lo and behold, a couple of years after that, in 2014, Cazenove again rang up and said we've found this Baillie Gifford fund which is a bit overshadowed by other Baillie Gifford funds, and the board and the family, with a big shareholding in the fund, feel that it won't get the attention and profile of the other funds. I think 27 firms pitched for it. The shortlist included the incumbent, a shortlist of five – and the chairman of the board who set that ball rolling, by the way, was Richard Burns, the ex-senior partner at Baillie Gifford, which surprised me and other people even more.

As you can imagine, our proposition was to move it to a much more capital-protective structure, with a more focused portfolio. But that did not involve us having to sell the large number of internet stocks in there, which have done terribly well, so the reorganisation wasn't that vigorous. The number of stocks in it went down to about a third of what it was. Mike McPhee [the previous manager] always had a section of the fund he called "get rich slowly but surely", I seem to remember, and that is a bigger part of what we do than what he did, but he always did that.

The trust started life as a family trust, you said?

Yes, and there are a number of family members on the board. The Mid Wynd International Investment Trust is the family trust of jute mill owners in Dundee. It came to the market very late compared with some others, so it was floated in 1981, and Richard Burns was the first fund manager of it when Baillie Gifford was quite a small firm and very dependent on its investment trust client base. It was before the heady uplands that they've headed into since. Richard sorted the fund out, taking it on himself, and Mike McPhee was the only other fund manager that they've had.

The whole extended family probably owns about 13% or 14% now, because we have expanded the trust quite significantly since we took it over. When we took it over, it was just over £70m of assets. It's now about £145m, so that's a combination of performance, the market going up and net share issuance. I think it's found a niche here in the global equity universe as being targeted to be a bit more capital-protective than the others.

How do you manage the trust with your team?

There are three of us doing the job: I've had my THS background; Alex Illingworth ran very similar funds at Rothschild and Insight; and Rosanna Burcheri comes from a European background and worked for M&G and Shell. We've got three experienced fund managers. It's a bit like the old THS style of having three grumpy old people who argue endlessly until, finally, somebody shuts up. But that keeps your standard and quality up. The hurdle to get in the fund is set really very high. But it also means, even though there are very few of us, we know a lot of stocks, and what we're looking for is pretty consistent and we agree on the quality that we're prepared to go down to.

What is different about your approach to managing a global equities fund?

There are some very good trusts out there in the investment trust universe, with excellent performance, but because it's 10 years now since the financial crisis, many have forgotten how badly some of the global equity funds did at that time. Structural gearing works in both directions! This is an ungeared trust basically. Although we do have a credit facility, we don't often use it, whereas for most of the trusts which have outperformed us, the contribution from their structural debt is quite significant. Some of them have also picked stocks better than us, but generally we are pretty solidly in the pack on the stockpicking, if you de-gear the performance figures.

When I look at the universe, what surprises me is how unbalanced some of the other portfolios are becoming because they allow successful holdings to keep going up and they don't trim them. We are the other end of that policy. We take more active bets and are more valuation-sensitive. When we took over the trust, we had as many internet stocks as other people, we had consumer staple stocks like other people, which were the right things to own, but as valuations have carried on going up we started selling our consumer staples 18 months ago, because we felt that paying over 30 times earnings for Nestle when it's only growing, top line, at 3% per annum is just not very good value for money. As we have quite a broad view of interesting stocks around the world, we generally think we can find something more interesting to do.

Can you give an example of how the profile of the fund has changed?

This year, we sold our biggest holding, which is Amazon, when they did the Whole Foods acquisition. We have no criticism of that. We understand what they're trying to do, but it's just a valuation issue. If it means that they're becoming more capital-intensive than the other internet companies, then they shouldn't be on a rating as if they are very low capital intensity. As the market moves on, and particularly in the last couple of years, our portfolio – which was quite like other global growth-oriented managers when we took the fund over – is becoming less and less like them. We are trying to find decent quality growth themes that are on more modest ratings.

We've also sold our Facebook recently, as we think some of the internet stocks are now quite pricey. We've built up a new theme recently in automation stocks, which seem to be having a boom and which has led us back to Japan. You won't be surprised that the average multiple of cash flow of the stocks we're buying is a fraction of the internet stocks, however you analyse them. The growth rate will not be quite as heady, but some of the robot companies are seeing 20% or 30% increases in order books. One of them saw a 100% increase in order books this year.

Again, I think this is very like the way we managed money at THS. You never know that you've got a new theme coming along, but if you find that you're starting to get a bit uncomfortable with one part of your portfolio, that it seems to be a bit too fashionable, and the multiples really seem to have gone through the limit of where you think things should be, you always have other themes and new ideas you have been working on in the background to fall back on. There's generally something out there which allows you to recycle money gently over time into a new idea which is less fashionable and certainly more modestly rated and yet keeps the fund reasonably fully invested.

You also have a sizeable personal stake in the trust?

Yes. I always have been an investor in my funds. When I turned up to THS, I put as much money into that as my mortgage would allow me. Personally I happen to think that my fund is the best way to make real returns for savers out there! I back it up personally in quite a lot of size. While I'm open to ideas, I really can't think of anything better. It's an enormous privilege being allowed to buy little bits of other people's hard work globally, and currently, with no exchange controls, the investment trust allows me to invest in an efficient manner round the world, keep my money outside the UK, which is not a currency I particularly want to invest in, not that I have terribly strong currency views, and to invest in growth where I can find it round the world.

It is important for investors to know that the fund manager has a similar attitude to risk, is it not?

Yes. If I lost all my money now, I haven't got time to make it back again, and we're quite a long way into a massive bull market, which was, to be blunt, one of the other reasons that I left THS. In 2009, I thought this is the best opportunity to invest I've ever seen and probably the best I will ever see, and so I was, I think the correct term would be, "aggressively bullish". You have got to take these opportunities. Does that mean that I think it's now time to sell equities? No. I don't think you make that decision on the basis of whether you've made a lot of money out of the bull market. You make it on the basis of whether the valuations are telling you that there's a problem, or whether the macro is telling you that there are imbalances you need to worry about.

But I prefer to own the equity of the stocks that we own in this fund than have my money in anything else. Gold? I've never met anyone who comes up with a sensible view of what the price of gold should be – people have very strong views on which direction the price of gold should go in, by and large always up, and it's always the same people – but if I can't value something, I don't want to own it. And any bond I look at in the world either is what Buffett calls "reward-free risk", as far as I can see.

So what I spend my time worrying about for the fund is of course informed by my own caution and desire for capital protection, and it is: can I find assets in global equities which will balance the fund if things go wrong? The main thing that could go wrong is that inflation goes from massively subdued and much lower than people expected to something different. It has undershot everyone's expectations in major economies for the last seven years.

Are you as surprised by that as many economists seem to be?

No. When I went to college in 1980, it was all about monetarism, and quite clearly Milton Friedman's proposition that, if you expand money supply this much, you will get inflation, is wrong. It is interesting that there are still global equity managers who try to run money using economic theory when it clearly is of no practical use at all while secondly, the central banks are also listened to with enormous awe and wonder, when, quite clearly, they haven't the faintest idea what's been going on at all! It is much easier having a stockpicking approach to have confidence about the future.

My confidence in the future of my savings is principally down to the 20 big holdings that we have in the fund, which are fine companies, which I meet every now and again and seem to me to know how to run capital much better than anyone else I meet. They are also diversified. We have half the money in America, but we also own Chinese banks and many other quite different things. If you look at the THS long-term record and the unit trust record, you'll see that, over the whole piece, including big bear markets, we've been chugging along at 11% per annum in real terms.

I'm not confident that I'm going to carry on doing that, but even if I miss that by quite a bit I can afford to have a couple of bear markets. And where else are you going to put your money? What on earth is the argument to put some money in an infrastructure fund or something like that if equities generally deliver that kind of return for the patient investor? That's the key thing: you've still got to be patient. We do say to anyone considering investing in the fund, what I used to say at THS as well, which is this is for people who can afford to wait.

If you're serious about trying to deliver an equity product for investors, it is worthwhile giving up quite a lot of the last bit of the bull market to put that insurance in place so that people don't panic. Even people who don't need the money panic in bear markets. The best work we did at THS was making sure that none of the clients were panicking in 2003, at the bottom of the bear market. That wasn't the worst bear market I've sat through, it was nothing like '87 in terms of panic, but goodness me, people were still ringing up saying, "Oh, should we sell everything and buy bonds?" and all sorts of nonsense went on. We also kept people in successfully in 2008 and 2009.

I think that our policy is quite a distinct policy compared to others and as long as you've got that mindset, the tools you use to bring it about are quite technical: they are concentrating on valuation, trying to make sure your fund is diversified by stock, theme and country, trying to make sure that currencies and interest rates don't hit you too hard. This is where I think I've tried to improve the use of data compared with the THS approach, which was quite artisanal.

What does that mean?

I set rather stricter limits on how much money we can have in any one theme, any one stock. The portfolio is built around eight or nine investment themes, which is the same as it was before, but we take the stocks we have in each of those themes and then we analyse the historic correlations between those themes. You can't have an oil theme and an emerging markets theme and call them two separate themes without spotting that they go up and down completely together and they're both very volatile. If you want to have those two themes, that's fine, but you need to limit the total amount of capital you have between the two themes. What we want here is to have eight or nine themes which are properly diversified, at least in terms of their historic correlation. It does not guarantee that they will not prove to be correlated in the future, but at least you're trying.

Just like at THS, we have an emerging market consumer theme – much smaller than it was because that tailwind is less vigorous than it was. Some of these countries are getting to have an aging population issue rather than a youthful population advantage. That emerging market consumer theme clearly has a correlation with another theme we had at THS, which is called tourism here, but was called ports and airports there. As tourism is now dominated, 15 years on, by Chinese tourism, in terms of the heady growth rates, there will clearly be more correlation now than there was 15 years ago.

Of course 15 years ago, media and technology stocks were very highly correlated, but now, as you may have noticed, the media sector is seen as complete trash and nobody wants to have anything to do it with it while the internet is going to dominate everything. The two are completely uncorrelated. It is a great thing to have seen through cycles in markets. I remember Nils always saying every year that he hoped he might get it right this year and eventually he would get enough experience! But you can also be wedded to some mythology you've built up for yourself, believing that you know what a defensive stock is and how to make the fund cautious, while actually markets move on, and sectors that were defensive prove not to be defensive the next time round.

So, consumer staples might be a good example of that?

Well, one of the things that I personally think makes a stock enormously undefensive is being on completely the wrong valuation. And yet I sat through a lecture the other week from the biggest endowment in the country, where they said, "Because we have such long duration, it doesn't matter if we're paying huge multiples for Unilever and Nestle because we know that they'll be around forever, so we're not taking a risk". If you're paying 38 times earnings for something and it goes down to 20 times, it may not be permanent loss of capital, which is bankruptcy, but Vodafone at £2 today compared with £4.75 in 2000 is a pretty substantial temporary loss of capital! It's certainly more temporary loss of capital than I'm prepared to put up with.

Now, I'm not saying that the valuation of Amazon or whatever is as stretched as the valuation of Vodafone was in 2000, but I am saying that some of the same mindset is creeping in, that it's more important to have the right stocks in your fund than to worry about the valuations. That's not what we think active fund management is all about. As long as people are trying to do the valuation, if they want to put in very low discount rate and say that they've done a valuation, that's fine, but you will find some people who are saying "we just think this is a great stock and we won't do the valuation".

How do you prepare for the next market downturn?

My view of active fund management is that you apply common sense and are always on the lookout for getting carried away. I do these old-fashioned thought experiments like pretending that we had an 1987 moment and I walked in and the market was 25% lower, and there was no liquidity, no opportunity to trade, and then you sit there and you look at your list of stocks and you think: which of these stocks would I really regret having in the portfolio if that had happened? Not which stock would have gone down the most, in a way, I don't care about that. It's which stock would I just say, "What on earth did I buy that for?"

And are there any stocks where I think I'd get no liquidity? Obviously the great advantage of a closed-end fund is that you don't have to trade in a bear market, but it still matters if you're in an emerging market whether they suspend the currency or whatever. I think some of those differences in mindset do come about by having some money in the fund. I just think it makes life easier. It does help being a global equity manager if you think global equities are the best way to make real returns! I'm very glad that I didn't end up as an expert in say Algerian small caps because then I'd feel very reluctant to have all my money in the fund. Having your own personal greed and fear instincts totally aligned with your job and your friends' savings and endowments that you care about, I think that just makes life quite easy. It really does make making decisions terribly simple.

Can you give me an example?

When Trump got voted in, for example, we had half a day to make decisions before Wall Street opened. We looked at all these American banks we bought last year, and saw that they were all going to get marked up a lot because everyone would get terribly excited about the reflation trade, but we basically also thought this man Trump is a bit odd. Our thinking was along the lines that this was a bit of a windfall that we hadn't been expecting. I'm very pleased we've made this much money much more quickly than we expected to, but we bought these bank stocks expecting Hillary Clinton to have got in, and Elizabeth Warren too, but they're not that good! They're still banks.

There's this big growing sector of the savings market who have chosen to find their own way to invest, and we've seen that on the shareholder list here – it is one of the reasons we're issuing stock very consistently. People are finding their way to the fund despite it having had a very low profile under Baillie Gifford. People are finding it and I think are just picking up that we're offering, hopefully, a smoothed version of the market cycle. They may not understand the maths that means you end up with a better return over a number of cycles. That ratchet effect hasn't been apparent for the last eight years, and that's quite a long bull market. But I think people coming to the market now looking for a way to get more of their savings outside the UK appreciate the point of giving up money to a fund manager who is taking a relatively cautious view on valuation, and yet keeping fairly fully invested most of the time.

The board are keen to grow the trust, however…

Well, it would be nice to get it up to £250m-odd because you're running this losing battle at the moment where the large wealth managers keep getting bigger, and they keep saying the smallest fund we'll look at is £250m, or whatever. Do we need them to pay attention to it? I don't care that much. I'm perfectly happy to spend my time talking to the medium-sized wealth managers who are interesting and care and it's not as if this fund is really in competition with anything. It's a solution for a particular sort of client. Most wealth managers, the old stockbrokers, have got plenty of people this fund suits, and we probably couldn't accommodate those who have rules that say it's not big enough.

My experience is that managing global equity portfolios is not easy and successful fund managers in that space are quite few in number.

We won't really know which of the global managers who've done well this decade understand all the tricks of it until we've seen a proper correction. When we saw a little bit of the correction back in 2015, people noticed that suddenly we went right to the top of the pops, and a lot of the funds which people felt very warmly towards, or were putting fresh money with after the market had gone up a lot, had a dreadful time because their portfolios were very lumpy. There are people who say "you should buy and hold these consumer staple stocks forever because they never go down". Well, it's not that long ago that Unilever was the lowest rated stock in the market! I got shouted at the other week by a 32-year-old discretionary manager, who told me that I was talking nonsense about Unilever and it should never be sold.

That's the kind of idiotic remark you look for, anecdotally, as a sign that things are getting a bit silly.

Yes, but I wouldn't go over the top on this. I think Amazon is on the wrong valuation. Nestle was the main stock we sold 18 months ago, but we recycle the money and we put in the fund a company called Daifuku recently, which, as I'm sure you know, is the world's leading maker of automated warehouses, which is having a boom with e-commerce, but, being Japanese, that stock was on about 15 times earnings when we bought it, cash on the balance sheet, orders up 30% year on year. So there are bits of the market where I'm worried about valuation, but not too many, and then there are bits of the economy where I'm worried about debt. The level of debt in private equity seems to have got very high, moving so much into infrastructure funds and that sort of thing.

My list of 60 stocks has enormously stronger balance sheets than average so why wouldn't I want my money anywhere other than large, listed, profitable, successful businesses? These businesses may trade on a slightly higher multiple of earnings or cash flow than we were used to in the past, but their margins are fat. On top of that, they're incredibly financially strong. When I worry about a recession turning up in America, or a big interest rate cycle or whatever, these stocks aren't going to be that troubled by it. One or two of them will have a worse time than others, but most of them will sail through that pretty well.

So, your point there is: where is all this debt going then if it's not going into these places?

Well, the debt must be somewhere else. Another fascinating thing at the moment to me is that most of the M&A in the world is happening in private equity and not in public companies. It is extraordinary that all these big businesses, with good credit ratings, strong P&Ls, are not tempted to go and buy anything cheap, even when all the investment bankers of the world are running around, knocking on the doors, saying if you buy anything, I can issue you a bond to make it earnings-enhancing in week two. And yet the level of discipline being shown out there by chief executives of large companies is unusual to say the least!

The last big deal we saw was Bayer buying Monsanto and that was debt-funded, weirdly enough, by Germany's second highest credit-rated company. Why did they buy it? Because they could afford it. I mean, there's not much strategic value, but they are buying quality. Nobody is buying anything because it's cheap. I think that's one of the reasons why the value trade isn't working very well. There's not much mean reversion going on. People don't want assets at a discount. They want decent businesses with new products which are fully invested. The fact that there's very little of that going on is quite a healthy sign. It certainly doesn't feel end of cycle-y. We may well get there because that's one of the things I worry about. But there's no sign of it at the moment.

I am sure that when the next crisis happens, everybody will say, "Of course, we should have seen that coming..."

Well, also, I think back to retail pressures. It's hard for young fund managers to make heavy counter-cyclical calls. People are quite comfortable sitting there waiting for something to go wrong and then saying, "Oh, how on earth could I be expected to tell?"! Take Brexit. I did a presentation that week, and there were three UK fund managers, me and a bond bloke, and the three UK fund managers all said, "Oh, we work in big houses and we know that we're going to stay in, so we've positioned our fund for Brexit". I said, "Well, I do global, and I think politics is unpredictable, so I've taken all my money out of sterling for the week because it's easy." For me, it's not a very big decision. There's a big old world out there. You were saying that you thought global equity management is hard. In some ways, I think it's easy because the number of options you've got is always quite high, and so the hurdle to move on to something less troublesome is quite low. You've always got choices.

Yes. I take that point.

When Trump came in, we sold the American banks because it was easy and we had other things we could do. You could just afford to take some money out, take your profits, move on to the next thing, sit back. Being able to duck political issues is a great advantage. It's a shame that politics is mattering more in the market than it has for most of the rest of my career. I would make one caveat on that, which is that I think people are worrying about politics more than they should. I try to stick to listening to companies and trusting them to get through the political cycle. On the other hand, you can move money around from place to place easily enough, in order to step back from the politics.

SIMON EDELSTEN is a partner in Artemis and has been managing the Mid Wynd International Investment Trust with his colleagues Alex Illingworth and Rosanna Burcheri since 2014.

Q&A ON CHINA

DALE NICHOLLS *had never managed a closed-end fund before being appointed manager of the Fidelity China Special Situations investment trust in 2013. He followed one of Fidelity's most successful fund managers, Anthony Bolton, whose original idea it was to launch a trust specialising in China-related equities. After four years at the helm, which has seen the value of the trust's shares more than double, he reflects on what he has learnt so far and the prospects of investors in China.*

How did you work with Anthony before you took over this job?

When he was in Europe, he was spending a lot of time looking at China. I was managing Asian equities in my open-ended fund. We would spend time talking about different ideas. We'd find ourselves ending up in the same meetings, being in the same company, and I think we just developed a pretty good dialogue about our thoughts on different stocks. The relationship was really just sharing ideas and thoughts.

Then when the decision was made, I think it was a well planned transition. It was announced, I think, a year before. We were working really closely together ahead of that. And in the last quarter, before the actual changeover happened, we agreed that we'd agree on all trades. So we were pretty well aligned. There wasn't a huge amount of trading that we needed to do upon the actual handover.

How would you describe your style compared to his? Was there more in common than differences?

I think definitely more in common. I think that's why we found ourselves in the same meetings, looking at similar types of companies, and definitely in terms of looking at the small and mid ends of the market – more off the beaten track in terms of the types of names that we're looking at. In terms of background, obviously his being in Europe and me being in Asia, we're influenced by that. I spend a lot of time in Japan so was probably a little bit more familiar with things like the tech areas. It's hard to say.

In retrospect, it looks like you took over at a pretty good time. Is it fair to say you've always been bullish about the opportunities in Chinese and China-related equities?

I think so. China has been a great stockpicking market from a number of perspectives. As an individual stockpicker I try to let the stockpicking drive portfolio construction. It's a big market and a very diverse market, and a big and diverse economy. You've got great variances between different parts of the economy. There's a great amount of structural change.

We're talking about a market where there's been a lot of macro concerns, some of them pretty well justified – most obviously, the concern about slowing growth and the build-up in credit. But from a bottom-up stockpicking perspective, if you're selective, you're benefiting from those macro concerns bringing down valuations and you can focus on the companies that are benefiting from structural change. There has also been a huge amount of fear and negative sentiment. For a bottom-up stock picker, that's a pretty good environment.

I think that general sentiment is starting to adjust somewhat. The collapse that a lot of people have been predicting hasn't happened. Don't get me wrong, some of the concerns are valid. The build-up in credit is clearly a concern, but as far as the people that were thinking that it could lead to a Lehman-style financial crisis are concerned, I have always found it really hard to understand how that would actually play out in China.

What are your reasons for saying that?

There has been a very rapid expansion in credit over the last 17 years. Since the global financial crisis, credit per GDP has increased a lot. History teaches us that you're going to have credit issues as a result of that. I have no doubt that China has those problems as well. It's part of the reason why I continue to own none of the Chinese banks. Amazingly, the top banks are reporting non-performing loans of just 1.8%. I suspect the real number is higher and needs to be going higher.

But then, when we talk about financial crisis, what really defines a financial crisis? One thing that tends to define it, based on the work that I've done, is a lack of liquidity. When you think about what happened during the global financial crisis, you had the banks stopping lending to corporates and also stopping lending to other banks. That's when you have real liquidity problems. In the China context, first of all, for better or worse, the banks all have one big shareholder – the government – who's shown that it is quite willing to drive lending when it needs to, but you've also got good deposit support in the system. The fact that you've got a very strong consumer base and a high savings rate has been what has driven high levels of bank deposits.

So when we think of loan to deposit ratios, you need to think about it in a broader context, not just the formal banking system but the informal banking system. A lot of credit has grown off the balance sheets of the banks. Even when we bring that back onto bank balance sheets, we still get a loan-deposit ratio of below 100%. Compare that to where you've had real problems in the past, where you generally have pretty highly wholesale-funded banking systems in which credit can disappear quickly. In China you've got this deposit support in the system.

So a real liquidity driven financial crisis I find hard to imagine. What concerns me more is a Japan-type scenario where you've got bad loans that just sit on the balance sheets of the banks and that doesn't get worked out. Then you get poor allocation of capital and that can affect growth. That's why I spend more time focused on how fast the non-performing loans are being dealt with. I think progress is being made there; but it could be faster.

I'm also more encouraged, particularly in the last six months, by the rhetoric that I hear from the government. At the very top, there's more awareness of the risks and less of a focus on growth, which I think is positive and shows that things are moving in the right direction. I think there will be less of a focus on growth and more focus on the quality of growth.

Growth definitely will slow. I think that's natural and necessary. Why? Mainly because you have so much investment-driven growth funded by credit. There's a real awareness that there needs to be a shift in the structure of the economy towards consumption and away from investment. It's happening. Consumption is the key thrust of the portfolio. Regardless of what the final GDP number is, whether it's 6.5%, 6.25% or even 5.0%, you know that consumption is going to be growing faster.

I'd be pretty disappointed as a bottom-up stockpicker if I couldn't find some decent ideas in an economy that's undergoing a lot of structural change and has still got a decent consumption growth story. It's always good when you're investing in China to think about what the government wants to achieve. You generally want to be aligned with that. The broader growth driver is really just the natural development of a middle class. Across a range of sectors, people want their appliances and their cars, there's real aspiration. That just seems like a really strong theme that you can invest in, on a five-, ten-, fifteen-year basis.

How much of the portfolio is driven by the Chinese domestic economy?

The majority of the portfolio is about the domestic economy in China. Obviously, I am concerned about trade policy and that sort of thing going forward. If you look at the revenue exposure of the companies that I've invested in, you're looking at over 90% in Greater China. You can invest in that theme across a range of different exchanges and different countries. So I have holdings in Singapore, Taiwan, the US through ADRs (American Depositary Receipts) – these companies that may be listed in different markets, but their prime exposure is China.

Has that percentage changed at all over your tenure?

Only marginally. The proportion of US-listed companies has definitely increased, with the listing of companies like Alibaba and the fact that the ADRs are now coming into the index. The other big change is A-share exposure. There was a lot of negative sentiment around the A-share market when I took over. In many cases the dual-listed companies were trading at a discount to the H-shares. So I shifted a fair bit of exposure into the A-shares. In the last 12 months the market has become more rational. The exposure to the A-share is still relatively high at 10% of the portfolio now, but it's come down, though it is still above where we started.

More institutional flows, I imagine, are inevitable now that China has been included for the first time in the MSCI world index?

I invest on fundamentals, but when you step back and think about the dynamics around flows, China represents a percentage of global GDP which is in the teens, compared to its share of global markets which is less than 3%. I think that gap is going to close over time. Obviously, MSCI inclusion is clearly a movement in that direction. A lot of global investors could afford to ignore China in the past, but that's going to become that much harder for them to do.

The A-share market is a fascinating market. For me, it's one of the most inefficient markets that I've seen. It's not a great surprise when you think that the majority of traders are retail. You have a lot of small, fast-growing companies that are trading on huge multiples, and larger caps – generally pretty good businesses generating strong cash flows – that are largely ignored and really cheap. That structure is clearly going to change over time. You've got greater foreign participation in the market and that will increase.

Before you took on this job, did you have any experience with closed-end funds?

No. I was completely from an open-ended background, so this is a new departure for me. It's definitely been positive. It allows me to reflect the opportunities I see in the market. When things are looking really cheap, when sentiment is negative, or when I am feeling more bullish about the holdings of the portfolio, it is a time to increase gearing, and vice-versa. When we talk about gearing, we should probably distinguish between gross and net gearing. The structure of the trust gives me the ability to go short as well. I can make bets against companies. That obviously gets included in the gross gearing, but is deducted when calculating net exposure. I focus more on net exposure.

Is this a decision that you make? Does the Board delegate that to you?

They're obviously kept informed about everything that I'm doing, but it's really my decision within the parameters that I operate in. On a formal basis, every quarter I explain how I'm looking at things, but also on an informal basis as well, I let them know pretty regularly how I'm looking at things and roughly where the gearing is running at.

What other advantages have you found in the closed-end structure?

Not having to worry about flows is a huge positive for me. I have a mid to small-cap bias in the trust, so liquidity [how easily shares can be bought and sold in size] is always something that's at the back of my mind. Not having to worry about flows gives me more freedom. When there were discussions about my taking over the trust, that was a very positive factor for me.

How much overlap is there between the trust and the Fidelity Pacific fund you also run?

Significant. Obviously, China being a sub-set of the Pacific region, I definitely wouldn't own a Chinese stock in my Pacific fund and not own it in China Special Situations. So, everything that's in China, in Pacific, is part of China Special Situations. The overlap is pretty significant. With the trust, again I just get a little bit more flexibility, particularly around liquidity, and probably more exposure in the small-cap space.

The discount widened steadily for quite a period and then started to reverse. How much of that do you think is due to the share buybacks and how much to improving sentiment?

I think it's improving sentiment, to be honest. It's quite hard to control the discount. Part of the recent closing of the discount is just a recognition that the doomsday scenario that some people were predicting for China just hasn't played out and now doesn't seem likely to play out. I think it's also a recognition that there's actually just some great companies in China – the likes of Tencent, Alibaba – which continue to execute and have really strong management teams.

Corporate governance is not always a great strength of emerging markets. You get a lot of semi-state-owned or family-controlled businesses that aren't particularly shareholder friendly. How does China fit into that category?

As you said, corporate governance is a challenge in any emerging market. It just takes time for the systems to develop. China's no exception. It's a challenge for a lot of companies. We've spent a lot of time doing as deep research as we can, building relationships with management and building a conviction over time about the management teams. There's still a pretty significant proportion of state-owned companies.

I don't ignore the state-owned companies, but the focus for me really is on the private companies. I think that's where so much of the growth is coming in the economy. And obviously, they're the biggest investors, the biggest employers, particularly from a growth perspective.

Looking at any company, management is a big factor in how they're incentivised and the fact is there are a lot of state-owned companies whose goals are not necessarily aligned with ours as minority shareholders. The way the banks have grown since the crisis, obviously there's government policy behind that. When I think about the big energy companies, I could come into the office tomorrow and there's been an acquisition made somewhere in the world which may be more about energy security than economics. So, that's something that's in the back of your mind all the time.

The state-owned companies I focus on are the ones that have really good assets. I'm a pretty big investor in the airports in China, for example. I think that really fits in with the consumption theme. The growth in travel in China just continues to march along at a good rate – double-digit growth both overseas and domestically. I look at something like Shanghai Airport, which has hub status. Shanghai Disneyland is being built as well, which will continue to drive traffic. You've got pretty good expansion prospects.

There are good opportunities to improve the returns on those assets as well. I don't know if you've been through Pudong Airport, but it's not the most exciting retail offering that you've ever seen. If you benchmark against the likes of Heathrow, there's pretty good potential for even better returns. Valuations also compare well globally.

Looking at the risks as well, what do you think are the major risks that you face in having this big exposure to the Chinese economy?

The development of the middle class is a very strong trend that's hard to see reversing. When we think about the goals of the government, they want to see that trend happen, they want to see full employment, they want to build welfare, healthcare, and so on. That's something that's definitely a strong underlying driver.

In terms of the risks, I'm somewhat concerned at the margin. From a political perspective, you think about censorship and that sort of thing. I don't think that's a problem in the short term but if you think about things in the mid-term, obviously as people get richer, I think they're going to want to have more of a voice. They're travelling more, they see things that are happening overseas. And so there's potential for people wanting to have more of a voice over time.

The government at the same time is very focused on that. I don't think it's something that we need to worry about in the next five years. But if you think on a longer term basis, I would like to see things politically moving more towards a freer approach. Obviously we need to think about geopolitical risks as well, things that are happening in North Korea now. That's a risk as well.

From a policy perspective, when you think about the direction the government has set, it's pretty positive in terms of the way they want to transform the economy. When you think about the predictability of policy, we're talking about a government that has a five-year plan that's extremely detailed about what they want to achieve and has a pretty good track record of hitting it.

When I compare that to policy predictability in some of the Western economies, from a policy perspective you know what the government in China is trying to achieve and the direction that's been set. Yet China has lagged and continues to lag in terms of valuation.

It's closed some of the gap versus the Western markets, but it's still a pretty big gap. And at some stage that might start to get reflected in valuations for the markets.

You haven't mentioned currency so far. How do you manage the trust from a currency perspective?

I think purely in local currency terms. I'm thinking about companies that are trying to grow their business as much as they can in local currency. I'm not overly concerned about the Chinese currency. I think there was probably some concern 12 to 18 months ago when the US was hiking interest rates and other markets were cutting. You saw that reflected in some pretty significant capital outflows out of China. That's clearly changed now. It's under control and the reserves are building again. I don't think you'll see any significant rate cuts in China. Obviously, the government keeps a pretty firm hand over rates. That will change over time. The clear goal is to free up the capital accounts over time. But it's going to be a slow process, I think.

How do you see the trust developing?

We're really committed to China, we continue to build the research team and we're out there focused on the best ideas. We've been looking at the A-share market for quite some time. I think a lot of our competitors were late in getting to look in depth at a lot of the A-shares. I think the commitment that we've made to building research is crucial. The fact that we can invest in unlisted companies as well gives us exposure to a broader part of the economy in China. There's so much happening in the unlisted private space. There's a great amount of entrepreneurial activity there. It takes a fair bit of time in terms of looking at the companies but it's really valuable as well. You can find some great ideas and it gives you a sense of what's coming down the road as well, in terms of companies when they do list.

How much value have the unlisted holdings added?

Pretty significant. Obviously, it's hugely biased by our investment in Alibaba. But if I look across the other holdings as well, we've had pretty significant uplift post our initial investment. We've got four holdings now, we've had uplifts across three of those. The biggest holding in the unlisted now is Didi, which is effectively the Uber of China. They're delivering more rides in China than Uber does globally, to give you a sense. This is what I was trying to get to earlier about the pace of structural change. In a lot of industries, it just happens to be faster in China. The penetration of e-commerce has already surpassed the West, surpassed the US. You don't have legacy retail bricks and mortar investment in third and fourth tier cities. So it makes sense that the transition happens faster.

The Chinese stock market has always looked cheap compared to other markets. Where do you think Chinese equities should trade relative to the US amd other markets?

The growth prospects are clearly stronger. As an emerging market, it still trades at a discount, but when we're looking at the price to earnings, when the US is close to double

China, I think that gap should be closer, particularly when you think about the structural change that's happened. Now that you've got the likes of Alibaba and Tencent – which I think are definitely comparable to the big internet names, your Facebooks, Amazons etc. of the world – with those representing 25% of the index, I think that gap should definitely close. I think you can argue that the growth prospects are at least as good as the US-listed peers for better valuations.

As I said earlier, I think China is going to become harder to ignore. The fact that we're seeing some great companies coming through, really delivering on their strategies, it's going to become more of a mainstream market. We have some big investors who like the fact that the trust is big and liquid, unlike a lot of the other options out there. If you put those things together, I think there's pretty good potential for the discount to close over time and for us to bring in new investors, and as you said, more institutional money.

Q&A ON VENTURE CAPITAL TRUSTS

JO OLIVER, *investment director at Octopus Ventures, which manages the UK's largest generalist VCT, Octopus Titan, explains how they operate.*

The issue of how best to finance early-stage and growing companies has been around for a long time and governments obviously aren't very good at doing it. How successful do you think the VCT model has been?

I think it's been really successful investing billions of pounds into companies that have created tens if not hundreds of thousands of jobs since inception. So, in terms of payback from the industry as a whole, I think it's been very positive. That said, it is fair to say that the VCT industry has changed significantly over the last 30 years. Historically at least a proportion of the VCT industry has been focused on downside protection and lower-risk, lower-return asset-backed investments.

There have been some very significant rule changes, particularly in the last two years, which mean that the VCT industry as a whole is now much more targeted at areas that the government wants to address – filling the equity gap, driving innovation and helping to scale up British businesses. The industry is having to evolve and become much more focused on those objectives, though we expect Titan VCT to be largely unaffected as it has always invested in early-stage, fast-growth, innovative and disruptive UK companies.

Titan VCT has a portfolio of approximately 50 companies which in 2016 grew their aggregate revenues by £91m and created 700 new jobs. A great example of a VCT success story is Zoopla, which Titan VCT first invested into in 2009 when its valuation was just a few million pounds and it had only £100,000 of revenues. Zoopla floated three years ago and now has a market cap of £1.5bn. It employs hundreds of people and pays millions of pounds in taxes as it's very profitable.

Another Titan VCT success story is SwiftKey, which develops predictive text on smartphones. Two young ex-Cambridge graduates came to us in 2009, when we made a very small investment to start off with, which we followed through with a series of subsequent investments. Without our investment, SwiftKey would probably have struggled to raise capital. The team grew the business to over 100 employees and it was bought by Microsoft for $250m in 2016 when the SwiftKey product was on over 200m smartphones around the world. It has really helped establish the UK as a continued leader in technology, particularly in artificial intelligence.

Octopus is the largest VCT still doing pure early-stage investing. Was that a conscious decision to go down that route?

Yes, it was. A company called Katalyst was set up in the early 2000s by a few individuals. One of them, Alex MacPherson, now heads the Octopus Ventures team here. Katalyst was effectively an angel investor network. In some respects, it pre-dated crowdfunding. The model that they had was for the Katalyst team to source deal flow, some of which was introduced by the investor group of about 100 individuals, agree the investment terms and then it would be offered out for investment to the rest of the investor group – the crowd, if you like. The group of investors was typically quite broad in terms of background and so as well as providing capital to invest and deal flow, it was also a validation and due diligence network.

Katalyst was bought by Octopus Investments in 2007, and became Octopus Ventures, raising the first Titan VCT fund in 2007–2008. At that stage, a lot of people in the industry said: "You're not going to succeed." They recognised that early-stage investing is tough, as you need sufficient weight of capital to diversify the risk of early-stage investments and provide follow-through on funding.

I think we were fortunate in the sense that we managed to achieve a few exits early on – including Evi to Amazon and graze.com – which proved the ability to generate positive returns and enabled us to continue fund raising to support the existing companies and make further new investments. Some of the first investments were sourced from the relationships that had been build up over the previous years by the Katalyst team, which in some ways gave Titan VCT a head start.

One of the things we're very proud of is that we've got a number of serial entrepreneurs whom we have backed multiple times over. For example, Katalyst invested into a business called ScreenSelect, which consolidated with a number of other businesses to become LoveFilm, and LoveFilm was bought by Amazon a number of years ago. It was not an amazing investment for Katalyst investors, but it was still a huge success for us because the team that had set up ScreenSelect subsequently came back to what was now Octopus Ventures when they had set up their next businesses and said, "We enjoyed working with you. You see things through a similar lens. Can you invest into our new business?" These relationships have spawned numerous Titan VCT investments including Zoopla, graze.com and Secret Escapes, which are some of our most successful investments.

They come from the network, is what you're saying, based on the contacts you've had previously?

Yes. Venture capital is about investing in people. If you have worked with them before, particularly if you worked with them successfully, then that's a massive de-risker. The fund's reputation really matters as we live on our deal flow. As we have had more and more success with exits, it has attracted better and better deal flow – which means that we should be making better and better investments, which results in getting enhanced returns and that positive feedback loop continues.

You describe yourself as primarily technology-based. Why is that? Is it because that's where you think the potential for getting your best returns is going to come from? Or is it that you just love technology and you think that's the place you want to be?

I think it's a combination of factors. We're generalists. There are certain areas that we won't invest in – gaming, for example, as we don't really understand it. Biotech also is too capital-intensive, the cycles are way too long. But generally we are open to investing into early-stage, huge-potential tech and tech-enabled businesses that meet the VCT investment criteria and are led by talented teams with ambitions to build global businesses. The way we look at it, you need to embrace technology to optimise a business model and generate a sustainable competitive advantage.

The pace of technological change means that you can now build a very valuable business multiple times faster – maybe multiple magnitudes faster – and cheaper than you could have done even ten years ago. In simple terms, it's the ability to grow, differentiate, take away business from incumbents, go international and create significant value over a relatively short period of time on a relatively capital efficient model – those are the reasons why we focus on tech and tech-enabled businesses.

You're based in the UK and most of your ideas are generated in the UK. How would you assess how the UK is doing in this field?

I think we're doing well. Since 2010, of the 57 companies that have grown to a value of more than $1bn in Europe, 22 of them are British. On the funding side of things, I think the UK, led in part by the government, is in a much healthier place than it was even five years ago. Additionally, we've now got serial entrepreneurs who are reinvesting their money – and, more importantly, their time and experience – back into business, sharing all of the lessons, good and bad, that they've learnt. The UK is also incredibly strong in certain sectors, driven by a combination of factors, including a world-class academic resource and a very open multicultural and multinational society. It remains a global leader in artificial intelligence, fintech and, in many respects, e-commerce too.

One of the questions that is always asked is, "Is the UK ever going to produce a Google or an Apple? Are people selling out too early?" Well, in some respects they have had to, because there hasn't been the capital or the confidence to enable businesses to continue to build beyond a certain size, albeit that we've seen some exits recently for tens of billions from the UK. I think that's going to change over the course of the next few years, in part because it's a confidence thing. Someone like Alex Chesterman, CEO and founder of Zoopla, is a good example. He had already had some success prior to Zoopla and so had the confidence, capability and ambition to build Zoopla into a £1.5 bn business.

Another good example is Stan Boland, who's had two very successful exits. He has recently founded an autonomous driving business called FiveAI. We're not investors in it, but his ambition is to build a leading global autonomous driving technology business. It's not without its challenges, but it's British, it's British-based and its vision is to be a global dominator. That confidence has come out of his previous success, which should enable him to attract the capital and talent needed to maximise his chances of delivering this huge ambition.

What can you say about the kind of people who start businesses that you back, other than that they're slightly crazy?

I admire everyone that has the bravery to set up a business. It takes courage, ambition, resilience, perseverance, and vision. It has moments of incredible success and joy, but also lots of tough periods when things aren't going your way and everything rests on your shoulders. The best entrepreneurs are geniuses, which I don't say flippantly.

If I was oversimplifying I would say that there are two types of brilliant entrepreneurs. There are those that just keep running through walls regardless and have that titanium head guard so that they can keep doing that. They're a force of nature and if you're in their way, you're in their way. It doesn't matter, you're going to get run over. There are others who are more emotionally intelligent, generally more mature, and they'll recognise that there is a smarter and more enduring way of getting there. They'll bring talent in alongside them to make sure they complement their weaknesses and achieve their objectives as smartly and with as little clash or damage as they possibly can.

Uber's ex-CEO Travis Kalanick is a good example of the former. He created something very special, but is now paying the consequences for some of the collateral damage that he caused along the way. The other type of entrepreneurs tend to build longer, more sustainable businesses or are able to stay in those businesses for longer periods of time. Of course, in reality, it takes all sorts, but typically the best ones share the characteristics that I mentioned earlier, have the ability to make good decisions most of the time (and learn from the bad ones) and the magnetic ability to attract the best talent to work with them.

Do you think that Dragons' Den *and* The Apprentice *and those kinds of television programme are helpful in encouraging entrepreneurs?*

I think on balance they are helpful. They raise awareness of entrepreneurship. A lot of people identify with the idea that, 'This is what real business is about. This is what drives job creation. This is what drives GDP growth'. It is something to be admired when people have the get-up-and-go and say, "I'm going to put myself all in here and try and build a business." I think the credit crunch changed a lot of people's mindsets about what was important. One of the reasons I left the City and was attracted to venture capital is because I stepped back and asked, "What am I actually doing here? I am an analyst and a cog in a big financial wheel. But out there, somewhere, something tangible is being created. Some good is being done. But I'm currently just being part of a cog that's moving money around."

The way that *Dragons' Den* is set up and the way they behave there is obviously not reflective of how it works in the venture capital world. But I think the awareness and exposure is really positive. It's something that we tap into when we go out and talk about Titan to potential individual investors. They want to hear about the companies. "If I put my 20 grand into Titan I can say, 'I'm part owner of Zoopla.' Or 'That's one of mine', when Secret Escapes comes up on telly." I think people really like being associated with success stories. It helps to attract capital into the VCT sector.

Where does the money you raise and invest come from? Is it from people who want to be involved in armchair investing, or is it from wealth managers recycling the funds of their clients in your direction?

We've got about 11,500 investors in Titan. They're individuals. The median investment is about £15,000. So these are not just well-heeled high-net-worth individuals. This is a very generalist product, spread across literally thousands of investors, who typically remain invested in Titan for well over five years, which is the minimum holding period to retain all of the VCT tax reliefs. In terms of democratising and achieving what the government wants to do, filling the equity gap from a broad capital base, I think it's fantastically successful.

So it's not just people who are trying to cut their tax bills?

Well, I think there's an element of that. How do you separate the tax advantages from the pure investment returns? It's interesting that whenever we speak to an investor, they don't talk about, "I am only investing 70p in the pound in this." They want and expect a return on their gross investment. I think that people are also enthused about smaller company investing in a way that they perhaps they weren't 30 years ago. The rise of the AIM market, which launched at a similar time to VCTs, has done a lot to attract people to that.

If you've invested in early-stage companies, you're thinking of big capital gains. But in practice, with a VCT your return comes in the form of dividends rather than capital gains. Why has it worked out that way?

The VCT structure means that while the returns may nearly all be capital gains, they still get distributed as a tax-free dividend. That's just the most tax-efficient way of doing it. Typically we try to keep the NAV at a stable 90–100p, but make sure we're paying out excess returns, particularly if they've been realised, as tax-free dividends. Equally, on the downside, we're not distributing more capital than we need to.

There is a secondary market where investors can sell their shares but it's illiquid and not that attractive because of the discount that you get. So, Titan VCT operates a share buyback, as most VCTs do, in order to provide liquidity. In Titan, the policy is to target a 5% discount to the prevailing NAV. What's interesting is that the redemption rate is very low. Investors are holding their investments on a medium- to long-term basis. The redemption rate is only 2–3% per annum.

What then do you think the government's Patient Capital Review is all about? Is it a positive or negative? What's driving it?

The raft of measures that the government introduced around 1995 – the AIM market, EIS, VCTs – we think have been phenomenally successful. The industry's really active and off the back of the capital that has been raised, you see ecosystems flourish and thrive, with incubators and accelerators coming up everywhere. The Patient Capital Review noted that the UK is third in the OECD as a place to start a business. So the early-stage start-up scene is working really well.

Where there are still challenges is when companies outgrow those current interventions. How do those companies get access to capital to scale up further to become even bigger companies? What we see is that some of them have had to take their foot off the accelerator because they can't get capital. Some of them will be sold to US companies with deep pockets – the Microsofts, the Googles, the Amazons. Some might just go to the deep pockets of US venture capital. That's what we think the genesis of the Patient Capital Review is all about. How do we continue to support those companies as they scale up?

So you don't think there is any risk to you from the Review?

There shouldn't be any risk, based on what the government has been trying to achieve. If you look at the Titan portfolio, over the last three years over 2,300 new jobs have been created and the success of high-growth small businesses is increasingly recognised as being the engine of the economy. If you look through the Patient Capital Review to see what they define as good vehicles for deployment of patient capital, they basically describe a VCT in all but name.

Remember that one of the key attractions of VCTs – and this is very relevant in the context of the Patient Capital Review – is their evergreen, long-term nature. From an effectiveness and efficiency of capital perspective, that is very positive for the government because when you sell businesses, the cash can go back into the fund. You may distribute some of the profits, but you can also reinvest that cash into another investment. That way you get multiple uses out of every £1 that is invested. You get a compounding effect over time.

From the entrepreneur's perspective, one of the key attractions is that we can say to them, "We're going to be around for a long period of time. We can fund raise significantly every year if we want to. We can continue to support your journey all the way through." With most venture capital funds, which are our typical competitors, they only have a limited life. Even if they raise a new fund, they may not be allowed to invest in an earlier portfolio company. So on all sides I think that VCTs are very powerful entities. It is a really good mechanism for deploying patient capital.

You have managed to raise proportionally bigger amounts of money every year. At what point does that become indigestion?

That is a good question. We debate that a lot, both internally and also with the Titan board, which is made up of a majority of independent directors. The strategy has been to make a relatively small investment to start off with. If the businesses are doing well then we will look to deploy more cash into them and build a bigger stake. If they're doing less well then we'll try to limit our exposure.

In a portfolio of 50 companies, we've got really good visibility on our follow-on pipeline. We know that we've got the ability to invest so many millions over the next one to two years. Titan has grown proportionally to meet the needs of the growing portfolio and their ambitions. We have achieved two large fund raises over the last two years and we are targeting another large fund raise in this tax year as well. We know that at least 70% of the fund raising is going into follow-on investments in portfolio companies.

We have always made in the region of eight to ten new investments each year. In the current environment, due to the quality and quantity of the deal flow that we receive, and our ability to build world-class companies, we can see an opportunity to double that new investment rate over the course of the next one to two years. The opportunity out there is extremely attractive at the moment.

Suppose I was an investment banker and said that you could generate higher returns for your investors by doing other things such as targeting a higher annualised return, possibly using gearing, what would you say to that?

We look at this as a long-term asset play. When you speak to our investors, they want visibility and a certain yield. We target a dividend of 5p on a NAV of 93p. So it's slightly more than a 5% yield. For a higher tax-rate payer, that is nearly 8%. Then we pay our special dividends. When we get big exits, or we generate excessive profits, then we'll look to distribute those as well. If you can keep doing that, we'll have lots of very happy investors. That's the equation that we're always balancing the whole time and one of the things we look at very carefully when we're raising large amounts of money.

Would you not expect returns from your kinds of business to be higher than a quoted smaller companies fund? But they're not. Why is that?

Our underlying return, the rate of return in our portfolio, is in excess of 20% per annum, but there's a trade-off here between short-, medium- and long-term returns. We raise a lot of cash. In a fund of £435m, we had cash of £175m at the end of April, around two-thirds portfolio, one-third cash roughly. The cash sitting there is not earning very much at all and that is depressing the overall return.

The way that I square it in my mind is that the portfolio is going to continue to generate returns into the future. If we didn't raise any cash at all and we didn't invest further into our portfolio, you'd remove the dilutive effect of the cash but you would probably run out the fund before too long. You would have higher returns in the short term, but then you'd have a cliff edge because the assets were all sold and you wouldn't be able to reinvest them.

Instead, we are using the cash that is raised today to maximise the return of our best current investments in the future and to also make new investments so that we can continue to deliver our investors' required returns over the medium to long term, remembering that the investments that we make today may not be sold for another seven to ten years.

We're not a passive manager, we're not even an active manager – instead we are a step beyond this and are properly hands-on with our portfolio. We're helping entrepreneurs build big businesses. If we're good at what we do, we get good performance. 68% in the last five years, with positive performance every year, is a pretty good return.

There are two common questions you hear about VCTs. One is why don't you publish more regular valuations? And two, aren't the fees too high?

We publish the NAV on a regular basis as required. But valuing early-stage, private companies is not an exact science and so it would be disingenuous and impractical to publish a NAV on a very regular basis – it's not like quoted companies, which have a real-time price. We disclose the valuations for the top ten holdings, which is about 43% of the investment portfolio.

We stopped disclosing the latest valuations across the whole of the portfolio about two years ago. The reason was that we were finding it was proving counter-productive for the companies and for Titan investors. Normally, private company valuations are private and when you are looking to do a funding round, or when a business is being looked at to be acquired, they don't have that pricing information. We had a number of examples where we found out that because we'd disclosed the latest valuations, the company was getting worse terms on the follow-on funding, or it was getting a much lower price as an acquisition.

So we took the pretty hard decision to go down the road of less disclosure. We thought it was much more important to help maximise returns for investors. We had this debate with a couple of the commentators. The board totally buy in to this. We made that trade-off because we feel that it's in all of our shareholders' interests for that information not to be in the public domain. As for the valuation process we go through, we've got an independent board, we've got the auditors that sign-off our valuations, there's a lot of governance around our valuations which will hopefully provide most investors and commentators comfort that the valuations are appropriate.

And what about fees?

Our total expense ratio is about 2.5%. You're looking at an asset class which is very active in terms of engagement – not just the deal sourcing, which itself is clearly much harder than deciding, 'Today I want to go and buy Vodafone shares', but also much more resource-intensive after you have made the investment. We've reinvested a lot of our fees in the team. So, we've gone from five investment professionals in 2010 to 15 investment professionals now and a total team of nearly 30. It's one of the largest VC teams in Europe. We've set up a US office, which is solely to the benefit of our portfolio. We've got three full-time employees over there. We don't make any investments in the US. It is all about helping our businesses expand into the US as best they can.

When you look at the cost of managing the portfolios, it's very different from a passive investor. It slightly confuses me when people say, "VCTs are really expensive." Compared to what? The VC industry is all funded by institutions, and institutions are smart and hate paying away fees. Yet typical management fees in the VC industry are similar to those of Titan VCT and can be as high as 4%. Even with admin and other expenses, we are at the lower end of that range.

The extra piece that people struggle to get their heads around is that we don't benefit from economies of scale. If you think about Woodford's income fund, which typically holds 70 companies, but in a £7–9bn fund. As VCTs we can only put £5m into each company each year and £20m into a company over its lifetime. If we want to scale the fund, we have to scale a number of portfolio companies. That means more board seats, more people. When you put all that in context, we think it is pretty reasonably priced.

In terms of risks, we haven't had a recession for several years. How badly will the next one affect you and your investments?

Historically, the best returns from venture capital investing and smaller company investing generally come out of uncertain economic times. Titan VCT has some of its best returns from investments made in the last recession, including Zoopla, graze.com and SwiftKey. There are several reasons. Firstly, there is normally a scarcity of capital so prices go down – we make investments at lower valuations. Secondly, times of uncertainty create more opportunities for young businesses than for slower moving businesses. I don't wish for a massive recession. Don't get me wrong. It'll be tough, but I think that through the cycle we'll do really well out of it.

The worst thing that could happen for Titan VCT is if we run out of cash on an unplanned basis. We want to make sure that we've got sufficient cash to fund our forward investment requirements. In the credit crunch, you saw perfectly good businesses going under because they didn't have access to capital. If you've got access to capital to plough through those periods of opportunity/uncertainty, you stand in good stead to come out all guns blazing. We manage Titan to make sure that we're not going to run out of cash.

So they will not be too worried about Brexit then?

There is a significant challenge around talent retention – given the multinational nature of the UK and the teams of earlier-stage companies, in particular – but generally they're going, "Game on, when the going gets tough, this is where we win."

Of course, we still don't know what Brexit means – so I think it will take time for it to fully play out. But over the last year or so that we've been aware of it, a combination of things has happened. Firstly, sterling has significantly depreciated, which has meant for our international businesses that their revenues have grown in sterling terms. They tend to be funded in the UK and have revenues internationally. So, from an asset to liability perspective, it's been very favourable for them.

The second thing is that it's made UK assets much cheaper. That makes inward capital investment more attractive, whether that's the £24bn acquisition of ARM or VC investing more broadly. Capital inflows are good for our portfolio companies and the venture capital landscape more broadly.

As just mentioned, the largest concern that we have – and all of the rhetoric coming out of the government is positive so far, but until we know the outcome, we won't know – is the attraction and retention of talent. A lot of early-stage tech and tech-enabled businesses are multinational in terms of their employee base. The most important ask that we have of the UK government is to make sure that the borders remain open for this talent and that the friction of attracting and retaining that talent is minimised as much as possible.

You've said you always wanted to get into this field. What appealed to you about this business? Is it because of your experience in public markets, or despite that?

I've always been fascinated by young businesses, those with ambition and the vision to try to do something different and do it better than anyone else. From a purely financial perspective, the appeal is obvious as there is undoubtedly potential to deliver very significant returns from investments that we make. No day is the same. I sit on the board of four companies at the moment. They all have their challenges and it's never an easy ride but when the companies get through those bumps you realise the extraordinary potential the UK has to build truly world-class businesses.

ANALYSING INVESTMENT TRUSTS

UNDERSTANDING INVESTMENT TRUSTS

KEY TERMS EXPLAINED

INVESTMENT TRUSTS (AKA investment companies) pool the money of individual and professional investors and invest it for them in order to generate capital gains, or dividend income, or both. These are the most important factors that determine how good an investment they are:

SHARE PRICE
The price (typically in pence) you will be asked to pay to buy or sell shares in any investment company. You want it to go up, not down.

SPREAD
The difference between the price per share you will need to pay if you want to buy and that you will be offered if you wish to sell – can be anything from 0% (good) to 5% (bad).

MARKET CAPITALISATION
The aggregate current value of all the shares a trust has issued – in essence, therefore, what the market in its wisdom thinks the investment company is worth today.*

NET ASSET VALUE (NAV)
The value of the company's investments less running costs at the most recent valuation point – typically (and ideally) that will be yesterday's quoted market price, but for some types of investment trust it might be one or more months ago.

NET ASSET VALUE PER SHARE
This is calculated, not surprisingly, by dividing the NAV (see above) by the number of shares in issue. You can compare it directly with the share price to find the discount.

DISCOUNT/PREMIUM
When the share price is below the investment company's net asset value per share it is said to be trading 'at a discount'; if it trades above the NAV per share, then the trust is selling 'at a premium'.

---

* The market is not always wise and would be a duller and less interesting place if it were.

DIVIDEND YIELD

How much a trust pays out as income each year to its shareholders, expressed as a percentage of its share price.

THE FUND MANAGER

The person (or team) responsible for choosing and managing the investment trust's capital. Will typically be professionally qualified and highly paid. How much value he or she really adds is hotly debated.

THE BOARD

Investment companies are listed companies, so they must comply with stock exchange rules and appoint a board of independent directors who are legally responsible for overseeing the company and protecting the interests of its shareholders, which ultimately means replacing the manager or closing down the trust if results are no good.

GEARING

A fancy word for borrowing money in order to try and boost the performance of a company's shares – a case of more risk for potentially more reward.

FEES AND CHARGES

What it costs to own shares in an investment trust – a figure that (confusingly) can be calculated in several different ways. More important than it sounds on first hearing.

SECTORS

Investment trusts come in many shapes and sizes, so for convenience are categorised into one of a number of different sectors, based on the kind of things that they invest in.

PERFORMANCE

A popular and over-used term which tells you how much money an investment trust has made for its shareholders over any given period of time – by definition, a backward-looking measurement.

TOTAL RETURN

A way of combining the income a trust pays with the capital gains it also generates (you hope) over time, so as to allow fair comparisons with other trusts and funds.

RISK AND RETURN

Riskier investments tend to produce higher returns over time, typically at the cost of doing less well when market conditions are unfavourable and better when they are more helpful. Risk comes in many (dis)guises, however – some more visible than others.

IS THERE ANY DIFFERENCE BETWEEN AN INVESTMENT COMPANY AND INVESTMENT TRUST?

Basically no. Strictly speaking, investment trusts are investment companies but not all investment companies are investment trusts. Feel free to use either term interchangeably, without fear of embarrassment.

CLOSED-END FUNDS

Investment trusts are an example of what is called a closed-end fund, meaning that its capital base is intended to be fixed and permanent (unlike unit trusts and OEICs, which take in and return money to investors on a daily basis and are therefore called open-ended). The distinction is no longer quite as important as it was, as it has become somewhat easier for investment companies to raise new money through share issues.

INVESTMENT TRUST SECTORS

There are no fixed rules for what an investment trust can invest in. The trust's strategy does, however, have to be outlined in a prospectus and approved by shareholders if, as does happen, the board wishes to change that objective at a later date.

For convenience, and to help comparative analysis, trusts are grouped into a number of different sectors, based on their investment focus. New trusts appear on a regular, if cyclical, basis. Certain periods are characterised by a spurt of new issues in a particular segment of the market.

Property trusts and hedge funds, for example, were popular in the run up to the financial crisis in 2008. Income-generating trusts have been particularly popular since then. There have also been some large new trusts launched by big name fund managers in the last few years, including Anthony Bolton (Fidelity China Special Situations), Terry Smith (Fundsmith Emerging Equities) and Neil Woodford (Woodford Patient Capital).

At the same time there are regular departures from the investment trust universe, as funds either close down or return capital to shareholders, typically (though not invariably) as a result of indifferent performance or where the trust has a predetermined wind-up date. The way the universe of listed trusts looks can therefore change significantly from decade to decade.

The majority of the £1.7bn of assets in investment companies, however, remains in traditional equity and multi-asset funds, as the following table, using the categories adopted by the Association of Investment Companies (AIC), shows. (Other research providers, it should be noted, don't always follow the AIC classification, using their own categories instead.)

The sectors are ranked by number of trusts and two measures of size – total assets and market capitalisation (both in £m). The two figures differ for two reasons:

1. the first includes assets funded by debt, whereas the second measures only the value of the shareholders' interest, as determined by the market

2. the impact of discounts – a discount reduces the market capitalisation relative to the asset value.

A breakdown of the trust sector is shown here:[*]

---

[*] Excludes the small number of split capital trusts.

A breakdown of investment trusts by type

TYPE OF TRUST	TOTAL ASSETS (£M)	MARKET CAP (£M)	NO OF COMPANIES	AVERAGE TOTAL ASSETS (£M)	AVG MARKET CAP (£M)	SHARE OF COMPANIES (%)	SHARE OF TOTAL ASSETS (%)
Conventional	113,401	100,634	204	556	493	53.8%	67.6%
Specialist	32,413	32,241	72	450	448	19.0%	19.3%
Property	18,048	13,558	34	531	399	9.0%	10.8%
VCTs	3,855	3,498	69	56	51	18.2%	2.3%
Total	**167,717**	**149,931**	**379**	**443**	**396**	100%	100%

Source: AIC statistics as at 31 August 2017

A breakdown of investment trusts: specialist sectors

SPECIALIST SECTORS	TOTAL ASSETS (£M)	MARKET CAP (£M)	NO OF COMPANIES	AVG TOTAL ASSETS (£M)	AVG MARKET CAP (£M)
Sector Specialist: Debt	7,891	7,812	27	292	289
Sector Specialist: Commodities & Natural Resources	2,466	1,965	9	274	218
Sector Specialist: Infrastructure	9,677	10,719	7	1,382	1,531
Sector Specialist: Infrastructure – Renewable Energy	4,033	4,113	7	576	588
Sector Specialist: Biotechnology & Healthcare	2,370	2,183	4	593	546
Sector Specialist: Environmental	629	527	3	210	176
Sector Specialist: Leasing	1,259	1,353	3	420	451
Sector Specialist: Financials	379	358	2	189	179
Sector Specialist: Forestry & Timber	379	181	2	190	90
Sector Specialist: Insurance & Reinsurance Strategies	510	447	2	255	224
Sector Specialist: Tech, Media & Telecomm	1,706	1,665	2	853	832
Sector Specialist: Utilities	159	132	2	79	66
Sector Specialist: Liquidity Funds	11	11	1	11	11
Sector Specialist: Small Media Comms & IT	944	776	1	944	776
Total	**32,413**	**32,241**	**72**	**450**	**448**

Source: AIC statistics as at 31 August 2017

A breakdown of investment trusts: property sectors

PROPERTY SECTORS	TOTAL ASSETS (£M)	MARKET CAP (£M)	NO OF COMPANIES	AVG TOTAL ASSETS (£M)	AVG MARKET CAP (£M)
Property Direct – UK	6,186	5,217	13	476	401
Property Specialist	5,740	4,986	11	522	453
Property Direct – Europe	3,902	1,839	5	780	368
Property Direct – Asia Pacific	804	364	4	201	91
Property Securities	1,416	1,152	1	1,416	1,152
Total	**18,048**	**13,558**	**34**	**531**	**399**

Source: AIC statistics as at 31 August 2017

A breakdown of investment trusts: VCT sectors

VCT SECTORS	TOTAL ASSETS (£M)	MARKET CAP (£M)	NO OF COMPANIES	AVG TOTAL ASSETS (£M)	AVG MARKET CAP (£M)
VCT Generalist	2,742	2,541	41	67	62
VCT AIM Quoted	653	596	10	65	60
VCT Specialist: Environmental	178	164	7	25	23
VCT Specialist: Technology	16	11	4	4	3
VCT Generalist Pre Qualifying	213	156	3	71	52
VCT Specialist: Media, Leisure & Events	47	26	3	16	9
VCT Specialist: Healthcare & Biotechnology	5	4	1	5	4
Total	**3,855**	**3,498**	**69**	**56**	**51**

Source: AIC statistics as at 31 August 2017

The ten largest sectors – 164 trusts, accounting for 61% of total assets – were as in the following table. A notable feature of the table is that only around 13% of mainstream trusts have the UK as their primary investment focus. Investment trusts from the very earliest days have always had a bias towards investment outside the UK and their external focus remains one of their key attractions.

Twelve largest investment trust sectors

CONVENTIONAL SECTORS	TOTAL ASSETS (£M)	MARKET CAP (£M)	NO OF COMPANIES	AVG TOTAL ASSETS (£M)	AVG MARKET CAP (£M)
Global	26,160	22,941	22	1,189	1,043
UK Equity Income	11,553	9,882	21	550	471
Private Equity	14,744	16,074	20	737	804
UK Smaller Companies	5,319	4,337	18	296	241
Asia Pacific – Excluding Japan	6,208	5,363	15	414	358

CONVENTIONAL SECTORS	TOTAL ASSETS (£M)	MARKET CAP (£M)	NO OF COMPANIES	AVG TOTAL ASSETS (£M)	AVG MARKET CAP (£M)
UK All Companies	5,879	4,758	15	392	317
Flexible Investment	7,918	7,376	12	660	615
Global Emerging Markets	6,873	5,889	11	625	535
Hedge Funds	5,414	4,360	9	602	484
Country Specialists: Asia Pacific	5,113	4,065	8	639	508
Europe	3,885	3,307	7	555	472
Global Equity Income	3,396	3,104	6	566	517

Source: AIC statistics as at 31 August 2017

A full list of the AIC categories is given at the beginning of the *Handbook*'s trust directory. It includes a more detailed breakdown of the specialist, property and VCT sectors. The specialist sector is worth looking at as it gives a flavour of the wide range of investment strategies which are available.

The majority of the sector categories are self-explanatory. It is worth noting, however, that individual trusts within each broad sector category will often have somewhat different investment objectives and benchmarks. The 'flexible investment' sector is a recently added one that includes a number of trusts which invest across a broad range of asset classes.

INDUSTRY STRUCTURE

While some investment trusts are managed directly by their board of directors, the great majority delegate the management of their portfolios to specialist fund managers, employed on annual or multi-year management contracts with a mandate to meet the trust's investment objectives.

These range from large investment management firms to small specialist boutiques. In the case of the big firms, they will typically launch and market their own trusts to investors as well as providing portfolio management and carrying out administrative functions, often centralising them. The smaller firms, especially those managing specialist trusts, by contrast may only have one or more funds that they look after.

Largest management groups

MANAGEMENT GROUP	TOTAL ASSETS (£M)	MARKET CAP (£M)	NO OF COMPANIES	AVG ASSETS (£M)	AVG MARKET CAP (£M)	SHARE OF TOTAL ASSETS (%)
Total all investment companies	**173,723**	**155,311**	**393**	**442**	**395**	**100.0%**
J.P. Morgan Asset Management	11,413	9,466	21	543	451	6.6%
Baillie Gifford	10,320	9,465	7	1,474	1,352	5.9%
F&C Management	9,241	8,007	10	924	801	5.3%
Aberdeen Asset Managers	7,589	6,302	19	399	332	4.4%
Janus Henderson Investors	6,689	5,977	13	515	460	3.9%
3i Group	6,134	9,429	1	6,134	9,429	3.5%
FIL Investments International	4,263	3,262	5	853	652	2.5%
Invesco Asset Management	4,240	3,532	9	471	392	2.4%
InfraRed Capital Partners	3,585	3,927	2	1,792	1,964	2.1%
Frostrow Capital	3,488	3,230	5	698	646	2.0%
BlackRock Investment Management (UK)	3,462	2,745	10	346	274	2.0%

Source: AIC, as at 31 August 2017

The management groups with the most trust mandates are listed here. The ten largest groups manage around 40% of total industry assets. Only five firms out of more than 400 in total manage more than ten trusts. The average trust has £440m in assets, although the largest individual trusts manage many multiples of that.

20 largest individual trusts

TRUST	MANAGEMENT GROUP	AIC SECTOR	TOTAL ASSETS (£M)	MARKET CAP (£M)
Scottish Mortgage	Baillie Gifford	Global	6,514	6,046
3i Group	3i Group	Private Equity	6,134	9,429
Foreign & Colonial Investment Trust	F&C Management	Global	3,841	3,358
Kennedy Wilson Europe Real Estate	KW Investment Management	Property Direct – Europe	3,290	1,415
RIT Capital Partners	RIT Capital Partners	Flexible Investment	3,266	3,025
Pershing Square Holdings	Pershing Square Capital Management	Hedge Funds	3,157	2,491

TRUST	MANAGEMENT GROUP	AIC SECTOR	TOTAL ASSETS (£M)	MARKET CAP (£M)
Alliance Trust	Willis Towers Watson	Global	2,959	2,536
HICL Infrastructure	InfraRed Capital Partners	Sector Specialist: Infrastructure	2,645	2,904
Templeton Emerging Markets	Franklin Templeton Investments	Global Emerging Markets	2,539	2,129
Witan	Witan Investment Services	Global	2,210	1,863
Tritax Big Box REIT	Tritax Management	Property Specialist	2,160	1,948
Mercantile	J.P. Morgan Asset Management	UK All Companies	2,128	1,665
International Public Partnerships	Amber Infrastructure Group	Sector Specialist: Infrastructure	1,922	2,187
Caledonia	Caledonia Investments	Global	1,851	1,525
Murray International	Aberdeen Asset Managers	Global Equity Income	1,804	1,654
3i Infrastructure	3i Investments	Sector Specialist: Infrastructure	1,774	2,023
Fidelity China Special Situations	FIL Investments International	Country Specialists: Asia Pacific	1,766	1,247
Edinburgh Investment	Invesco Asset Management	UK Equity Income	1,707	1,393
Monks	Baillie Gifford	Global	1,668	1,528
City of London	Janus Henderson Investors	UK Equity Income	1,560	1,461

The trust with the highest total assets, Scottish Mortgage, accounted for around 3.7% of the industry total as at 31 August 2017. The 20 largest trusts on this measure accounted for 31% of total industry assets while 48 trusts accounted for 50% of total industry assets. In contrast, more than 100 trusts had less than £50m in assets, although this figure includes a large number of venture capital trusts, which are invariably much smaller on average.

The main takeaway for investors is that the investment trust sector is a genuinely diverse one, which offers a range of different kinds of opportunities. Looking at the range of sectors and the kind of trusts in them is a useful place to start getting familiar with the universe.

OLD WINE AND NEW BOTTLES

The first investment trust, Foreign & Colonial, was formed in 1868 and continues in existence today. A number of other investment companies have also been around for many years.

This is a list of some of the oldest vintage trusts which are also still in existence. There is no obvious correlation between age and size or quality of trust, although the mere fact of having survived for so long indicates that a trust has successfully established a niche in the market.

A number of these trusts were started by wealthy or successful families looking to invest their fortunes in a tax-efficient manner but have since expanded to include outside investors as well. "Longevity," notes market commentator Ian Cowie, "is no guarantee of success but investment trusts that have stood the test of time – such as surviving two world wars and the great depression – can offer some comfort to investors alarmed by the historic events we are living through today."[*]

Vintage investment trusts

TRUST	LAUNCH DATE	TICKER	PREMIUM(+) DISCOUNT(-) %	MARKET CAP £M	NET ASSETS £M	GROSS ASSETS £M	BID/OFFER SPREAD %	YIELD %
Foreign & Colonial IT	1868	FRCL	-6.6	3,305	3,540	3,792	0.1	1.6
Scottish American	1873	SCAM	5.1	486	462	562	0.5	3.0
JPMorgan American	1881	JAM	-5.3	907	958	1,068	0.2	1.3
Scottish IT	1887	SCIN	-9.1	684	752	864	0.3	1.7
JPMorgan Global Growth & Income	1887	JPGI	0.7	392	389	415	0.5	4.9
Alliance Trust	1888	ATST	-5.6	2,552	2,704	2,954	0.1	1.9
Law Debenture	1889	LWDB	-6.7	726	777	921	0.6	2.8
F&C Global Smaller Cos	1889	FCS	1.3	770	760	811	0.7	0.9
Edinburgh IT	1889	EDIN	-5.0	1,466	1,542	1,786	0.1	3.4
Merchants	1889	MRCH	-6.2	528	562	700	0.4	5.0
City of London	1891	CTY	1.8	1,480	1,453	1,547	0.1	3.9
Aberdeen Diversified Inc & Gwth	1898	ADIG	-6.5	392	419	501	0.7	4.4
British Empire	1905	BTEM	-10.2	832	926	1,005	0.2	2.0
Bankers	1905	BNKR	-2.5	1,013	1,039	1,108	0.3	2.2

[*] Citywire Investment Trust Insider, 17 September 2017.

TRUST	LAUNCH DATE	TICKER	PREMIUM(+) DISCOUNT(-) %	MARKET CAP £M	NET ASSETS £M	GROSS ASSETS £M	BID/OFFER SPREAD %	YIELD %
Scottish Mortgage	1905	SMT	2.7	5,958	5,800	6,403	0.1	0.7
Witan	1905	WTAN	-2.1	1,865	1,906	2,112	0.2	1.9
Brunner	1905	BUT	-12.6	310	354	414	0.7	2.2
JPMorgan European – Growth	1905	JETG	-11.7	235	267	311	1.6	2.2
Henderson Far East Income	1905	HFEL	1.9	446	438	458	0.6	5.4
TR Property	1905	TRY	-6.6	1,150	1,231	1,454	0.2	2.9
Murray International	1907	MYI	2.7	1,630	1,588	1,774	0.2	3.8
Murray Income	1923	MUT	-7.7	540	585	620	0.6	4.0
Finsbury Growth & Income	1926	FGT	-0.1	1,166	1,167	1,204	0.2	1.8
Temple Bar	1926	TMPL	-5.5	869	920	1,043	0.3	3.1
Dunedin Smaller Cos	1927	DNDL	-19.2	116	144	149	1.7	2.5
JPMorgan Japanese	1927	JFJ	-12.5	600	686	790	0.9	1.0
Shires Income	1929	SHRS	-8.4	78	85	104	0.9	4.9
3i Group	1945	III	48.2	9,252	6,243	7,313	0.1	2.8
Keystone IT	1954	KIT	-10.3	241	268	309	0.7	3.0
Caledonia	1960	CLDN	-11.8	1,606	1,822	1,826	0.3	1.9
Capital Gearing	1963	CGT	1.5	188	185	185	0.6	0.5

Source: Numis Securities and other sources

Some individual trusts are also notable for having long-serving managers who have been running the trust's investments for many years. In some cases the managers also have significant personal shareholdings in the trust (see also 'Skin in the game' on page 142).

Here is a selection:

Long-serving managers

TRUST	MANAGEMENT GROUP	MANAGERS	SINCE
Value and Income	OLIM	Matthew Oakeshott, Angela Lascelles	Jul-81
Capital Gearing	CG Asset Management	Peter Spiller, Alastair Laing	Jan-82
Northern Investors	NVM Private Equity	Alastair Conn	Oct-84

TRUST	MANAGEMENT GROUP	MANAGERS	SINCE
RIT Capital Partners	J Rothschild Capital Mgmt	Jacob Rothschild, Francesco Goedhuis	Jun-88
Aberdeen New Dawn	Aberdeen AM	Hugh Young	May-89
Pantheon International	Pantheon	Andrew Lebus	May-89
HgCapital Trust	HgCapital	Nic Humphries	Dec-89
Aberdeen New Thai	Aberdeen AM	Adithep Vanabriksha	Dec-89
Lowland	Janus Henderson	James Henderson, Laura Foll	Jan-90
Aberforth Smaller Cos	Aberforth Partners	Six Managers	Dec-90
Baillie Gifford Japan	Baillie Gifford	Sarah Whitley	Jan-91
City of London	Janus Henderson	Job Curtis	Jan-91
Henderson Eurotrust	Janus Henderson	Tim Stevenson	Oct-92
BB Biotech	Bellevue AM	Daniel Koller	Nov-93
North Atlantic SmCos	Harwood Capital	Chris Mills	Jan-94
Herald	Herald IM	Katie Potts	Feb-94
JPMorgan Emerging Markets	JPMorgan AM	Austin Forey	Jun-94
JPMorgan European Smaller Cos	JPMorgan AM	Francesco Conte, Jim Campbell	Feb-95
Oryx International Growth	Harwood Capital	Chris Mills	Mar-95
Worldwide Healthcare	Frostrow Capital	Sam Isaly, Sven Borho	Apr-95
Athelney Trust	Self-Managed	Robin Boyle	Jun-95
Vietnam Enterprise Investments	Dragon Capital	Dominic Scriven, Vu Huu Dien	Jul-95
Aberdeen Asian Smaller Cos	Aberdeen AM	Hugh Young	Oct-95
Schroder AsiaPacific	Schroder IM	Matthew Dobbs	Nov-95
British American	British & American Trust Fd Mgmt	Jonathan Woolf	Dec-95
Primary Health Properties	Nexus PHP	Harry Hyman	Jan-96
Lazard World Trust Fund	Lazard AM	Kun Deng	1997
F&C Capital & Income	F&C Investments	Julian Cane	Mar-97
North American Income	Aberdeen AM	Ralph Bassett, Fran Radano	Jun-97

TRUST	MANAGEMENT GROUP	MANAGERS	SINCE
GIMV	Self-Managed	Koen Dejonckheere	Jun-97
JPMorgan European – Growth	JPMorgan AM	Stephen Macklow-Smith	Sep-97
Manchester & London	Midas IM	Mark Sheppard	Dec-97
Aberdeen Emerging Markets	Aberdeen Emerging Capital	Andrew Lister, Bernard Moody	Jun-98
JZ Capital Partners	Jordan-Zalaznick Advisors	David Zalaznick	Jun-98
Castle Private Equity	LGT Private Equity Advisers	Hans Markvoort	Sep-98
Blue Planet IT	Blue Planet IM	Ken Murray	Mar-99
Chelverton Small Companies Dividend	Chelverton	David Horner, David Taylor	May-99
Perpetual Income & Growth	Invesco Perpetual	Mark Barnett	Jul-99

Source: Numis Securities, various others
Correct at the time of compilation.

COMPARISONS WITH OPEN-ENDED FUNDS

It is not uncommon for the investment managers of trusts to manage other funds outside the investment trust sector at the same time. In fact, a number of managers start their careers managing different kinds of fund (typically unit trusts and OEICs, though also hedge funds) and if successful are encouraged to take over or start an investment trust with the broadly similar investment objective.

Adding an investment trust to their responsibilities gives successful fund managers the opportunity to take advantage of the benefits of the investment trust structure. These include being able to use gearing (borrowing) to enhance returns and take a longer-term view, thanks to the permanent (or semi-permanent) nature of investment trust capital. They can also use derivative securities such as futures and options for investment purposes.

These advantages show up regularly in comparisons between the long-term performance of investment trusts and that of open-ended funds with either the same manager or the same investment objective. Where trusts and similar funds can be directly compared, trusts typically show up with superior performance records.

The following chart summarises the difference in the recent performance of directly comparable trusts and open-ended equivalents. It is fair to point out that such comparisons could be criticised by statisticians on the grounds that the two samples are very different in size and also may display what is called survivorship bias.

Investment trusts vs open-ended in key sectors

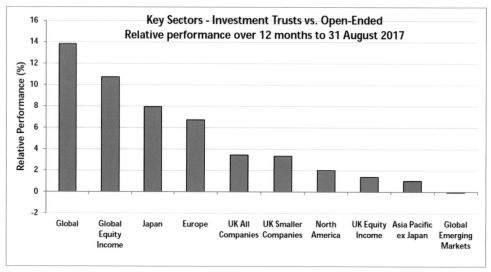

Source: Winterfloods Research Q3 2017 review

Such comparisons do, however, capture an important truth about investment trusts. Where a trust and an open-ended fund with the same mandate are managed by the same individual, it is very rare for the trust not to do better over the longer term. The degree to which comparable trusts outperform varies markedly from sector to sector. In the 12 months to August 2017, for example, it was most marked in the global sector and least marked in global emerging markets.

Performance of closed-end funds vs open-ended funds (equity and property mandates)

	NAV total returns (annualised) Open-Ended funds			NAV total returns (annualised) Investment Cos			Price total returns (annualised) Investment Cos		
	1 yr	5 yr	10 yr	1y	5y	10y	1y	5y	10y
UK - Equity Income	11.0	11.0	6.2	11.4	12.1	7.3	10.7	11.1	7.7
UK - All Companies	13.8	11.4	6.5	14.8	13.8	8.4	13.8	14.7	8.5
UK - Smaller Company	25.4	17.8	10.4	27.0	17.4	10.7	27.8	18.4	11.4
UK - Equity & Bond Income	7.7	9.3	5.8	8.3	11.0	6.3	9.4	10.8	6.5
US - General	14.4	16.9	10.4	17.3	16.1	11.0	15.2	15.0	11.2
US - Smaller Company	15.3	17.3	12.1	13.6	16.3	12.0	19.4	15.3	12.3
Global - Equity	14.7	13.7	7.8	20.7	15.6	8.3	24.7	17.6	9.2
Global - Equity Income	12.5	12.4	7.6	14.6	11.4	8.9	17.8	11.1	9.9
Europe - General	21.7	15.1	6.8	21.4	15.8	8.0	26.3	16.7	8.1
Europe - Smaller Company	24.0	19.7	9.6	26.8	23.4	9.9	37.0	26.0	10.5
Asia Pacific - Ex Japan	15.6	11.0	7.4	17.8	11.9	8.2	21.4	12.8	8.6
Japan - General	13.1	16.0	7.2	13.4	19.4	7.9	20.6	21.7	8.7
Japan - Smaller Company	17.2	21.9	12.6	20.6	22.6	8.5	26.1	23.7	8.9
Emerging - Global	17.6	8.4	5.8	17.8	8.5	6.6	20.3	8.0	6.7
Technology	19.4	17.8	11.5	26.8	19.6	13.9	32.1	20.3	14.3
Property - UK	2.8	8.9	3.2	8.2	11.9	3.5	17.1	14.1	6.6

Note: Data to 30 September 2017. Blue shading indicates outperformance by ICs relative to open-ended funds.
Source: Morningstar, Numis Securities Research

PERFORMANCE ANALYSIS

As with all investment funds, the performance of investment trusts turns on four main things:

- how much money the trust has made
- the way in which those returns are obtained
- how those returns are delivered – as income or capital
- the risk that is being taken to achieve the results.

The distinctive feature of analysing investment trusts stems from the fact that performance can be measured in two distinct ways:

- the rate at which the net assets of the trust grow
- the rate at which the share price of the trust grows.

As a broad generalisation, net asset value growth is an indication of how well the manager is doing the job of managing the investments. The change in the share price reflects how well or how little the market likes what the manager is doing.

Because most trusts invest in shares and bonds that are listed on a stock exchange, both the net asset value and the trust's share price can change from minute to minute as deals go through the stock market. Around half the universe of trusts consequently report their net asset value on a daily or weekly basis.

Trusts that invest in less liquid types of asset, such as property or private equity, report less frequently – monthly, quarterly or six-monthly. The share price of the trust may still change on a daily basis, however, reflecting supply and demand for the shares.

Valuation reporting – NAV reporting frequency

Daily	186
Weekly	33
Fortnightly	1
Monthly	72
Quarterly	23
Six-monthly	76
Annual	1
TOTAL	**392**

Source: Numis Securities
Some trusts report different holdings at different intervals – e.g. listed holdings weekly and unlisted monthly.

The only sensible way to measure how well a trust is performing is to look at the behaviour of its net asset value and share price over longer periods of time. In the digital age, this kind of performance data – along with a host of other useful facts about each trust - is widely available for free on the internet.

It is relatively straightforward to sort this performance data into rankings as well. The AIC's statistics section is a good example of the kind of information that is available. This is a snapshot of the core information that is provided about each trust (here in alphabetical order):

A screenshot of AIC's online statistics section

Company		AIC sector	Share type	Traded currency	Total assets (m)	Price (last close)	NAV	Discount/ premium (%)	Gearing (%)	Share price total return (%)			AIC ongoing charge (%)	AIC ongoing charge plus perf fee (%)	5yr dividend growth (%) p.a.
										1yr	5yr	10yr			
Industry average ex 3i		N/A	N/A	N/A	N/A	N/A	N/A	-3.6	6	17.9	112.3	153.2	1.16	1.28	3.4
Industry average ex VCTs ex 3i		N/A	N/A	N/A	N/A	N/A	N/A	-2.9	6	18.1	113.4	154.9	1.12	1.23	3.4
3i		Private Equity	Ordinary	GBX	6,126.6	945.00	649.82	45.4	3	45.9	429.9	44.2	2.15	2.15	26.8
3i Infrastructure		Sector Specialist: Infrastructure	Ordinary	GBX	1,743.8	198.00	169.87	16.6	0	7.5	94.5	199.9	1.29	1.51	1.7
Aberdeen Asian Income		Asia Pacific - Excluding Japan	Ordinary	GBX	469.1	220.00	235.69	-6.7	7	11.1	31.7	195.5	1.19	1.19	4.7
Aberdeen Asian Smaller Companies		Asia Pacific - Excluding Japan	Ordinary	GBX	478.7	1,065.00	1,257.20	-15.3	10	9.9	31.0	283.3	1.76	1.98	1.0
Aberdeen Diversified Income & Growth		Flexible Investment	Ordinary	GBX	493.3	120.50	125.57	-4.0	10	14.6	28.5	37.4	0.62	0.62	-3.5

Source: AIC – generic example

By clicking on individual columns in the table it is possible to filter and rank the data in various ways – for example:

- 2nd column: clicking this column groups the data by trust sector
- 5th column: clicking here ranks trusts by size (total assets)
- 10th to 12th column: clicking here ranks trusts by how their share prices have performed over three different periods – one, three and five years.

You can also analyse and rank trusts on several other important metrics, such as:

- the discount or premium at which the shares currently trade
- the level of gearing each trust employs (and the allowable range which the board has set)
- the costs of owning the trust (the 'ongoing charge'), expressed as percentage of the share price
- the current dividend yield and the annualised rate at which dividends have grown over the previous five years.

For example, you may wish to see how trusts in the popular UK Equity Income sector have performed over the last five years. By using the filters this would produce a table that looks like the following (only the ten trusts with the highest return over five years are shown, out of 26 companies in the sector).

A screenshot showing filters in use on AIC's online statistics section

Company	AIC sector	Share type	Traded currency	Total assets (m)	Price (last close)	NAV	Discount/ premium (%)	Gearing (%)	Share price total return (%)			AIC ongoing charge (%)	AIC ongoing charge plus perf fee (%)	5yr dividend growth (%) p.a.	Dividend yield (%)	Gearing Range	
									1yr	5yr	10yr					From	To
Sector average	UK Equity Income	N/A	N/A	N/A	N/A	N/A	-4.3	7	12.7	76.6	118.1	0.69	0.69	4.1	3.6	N/A	N/A
Chelverton Small Companies Dividend	UK Equity Income	Ord Income	GBX	58.9	266.25	266.82	-0.2	17	39.6	242.6	147.5	N/A	N/A	5.1	3.2	N/A	N/A
Finsbury Growth & Income	UK Equity Income	Ordinary	GBX	1,238.2	759.00	754.33	0.6	2	14.6	122.4	214.1	0.74	0.74	7.4	2.0	0	25
Diverse Income Trust	UK Equity Income	Ordinary	GBX	391.0	101.38	101.95	-0.6	0	17.3	112.9	N/A	1.17	1.17	8.8	3.2	N/A	N/A
JPMorgan Income & Capital	UK Equity Income	Ord Income	GBX	157.5	94.75	102.65	-7.7	97	22.4	107.3	N/A	N/A	N/A	7.0	8.4	N/A	N/A
JPMorgan Claverhouse	UK Equity Income	Ordinary	GBX	492.3	701.50	762.74	-8.0	11	23.0	96.3	86.2	0.79	0.79	5.4	3.5	0	20
Standard Life Equity Income	UK Equity Income	Ordinary	GBX	265.6	469.25	485.38	-3.3	11	19.4	90.7	122.8	0.96	0.96	5.8	3.8	0	15
Investment Company	UK Equity Income	Ordinary	GBX	17.5	342.50	366.72	-6.6	0	2.3	88.7	117.6	2.54	2.54	20.9	6.0	N/A	N/A
Value and Income	UK Equity Income	Ordinary	GBX	214.4	273.50	336.48	-18.7	29	12.7	79.9	82.0	1.42	1.42	6.4	4.1	N/A	N/A
Lowland	UK Equity Income	Ordinary	GBX	483.2	1,527.50	1,637.52	-6.7	6	19.3	78.5	99.0	0.64	0.64	9.3	3.5	0	30
BlackRock Income & Growth	UK Equity Income	Ordinary	GBX	53.7	206.00	210.04	-1.9	2	11.4	78.1	56.0	1.02	1.02	3.7	3.1	0	20

Source: AIC – illustrative only

Some of these different elements are described further below. A separate section on the AIC website enables you to compare specific individual trusts in greater detail, based on a range of specific criteria that you have set yourself. All the results you obtain can be downloaded into an Excel spreadsheet.

Equally important is that for each individual trust the AIC website provides links to the company's annual report and accounts, its half-yearly results and its latest factsheet. Nobody should invest in any trust without having looked at all these documents.

The annual report, in particular, is a must-read source of information. Company law requires the directors to provide a comprehensive report on the trust's performance and its financial results have to be audited by an independent firm of auditors and approved by shareholders at the annual general meeting. The report also discloses such things as directors' fees and shareholdings, management contract details and a full listing of the trust's investments.

INTERPRETING PERFORMANCE

There is a reason why the regulators insist that every piece of marketing literature issued by any kind of fund provider includes the phrase "past performance is no guarantee of future performance". The reason is that it is true.

While performance data gives you useful information about an investment trust's track record, and the way that it has been investing your money, that information in isolation is insufficient to tell you whether you should buy or continue to own that trust.

There are several reasons for that. They include:

• markets move in cycles and are unpredictable

• styles of investing come in and out of fashion

• superior performance in one period often does not repeat in the next

- managers of trusts can be and often are changed, making direct comparisons with earlier periods difficult

- unexpected events, such as political shocks and natural disasters, may throw a hitherto successful strategy off course.

What the regulators are keen to ensure is that less-sophisticated investors are not misled into thinking that a trust which has done particularly well in the past will continue to do so in the future. Their perspective is underpinned by many academic studies.

However, that is not the same as saying that past performance information has no value at all. Clearly it is essential for any investor to understand how a trust has performed in the past and to seek to establish why it has the track record it does.

At the very least it is important to understand the following:

- whether (and if so why) the trust's investment manager has changed over the track record period being looked at

- how far the performance of the trust has been affected by gearing (explained further below)

- how the trust performed during periods when markets were rising and when they were falling – it may be very different

- whether or not the trust has done better than a suitable benchmark, including the one chosen by the board

- how much risk the trust is taking relative to other comparable trusts and the markets in which it is investing.

DIFFERENCES BETWEEN SECTORS

Different sectors have very different characteristics, reflecting the different kinds of asset in which they invest. You can see this by looking at some of the key metrics for the broadest sector groupings.

Key metrics of broadest sector groupings

	YIELD	GEARING	OCR (EX PERF FEE)	OCR (INC PERF FEE)	DISCOUNT (AVG)
Asia Pacific	1.5%	5	1.25%	1.46%	-11.1
Debt	6.6%	0	1.17%	1.78%	6.8
Emerging Markets	2.2%	1	1.35%	1.59%	-14.7
Europe	1.9%	3	0.97%	1.19%	-9.0
Global	1.8%	3	0.80%	0.88%	-5.4
Hedge Funds	0.7%	12	1.94%	2.17%	-16.0
Infrastructure	4.9%	5	1.28%	1.32%	11.2

	YIELD	GEARING	OCR (EX PERF FEE)	OCR (INC PERF FEE)	DISCOUNT (AVG)
Japan	0.5%	13	1.02%	1.02%	-6.0
North America	1.7%	7	0.87%	0.87%	-6.1
Private Equity	2.6%	0	1.90%	2.10%	8.3
Property	3.1%	23	1.48%	1.90%	-0.7
Sector Specialist	2.1%	2	1.24%	1.99%	-6.3
UK	3.5%	5	0.74%	0.79%	-6.8

So, for example, the debt and infrastructure sectors on average have the highest yields but make relatively little use of gearing. The property, Japan and infrastructure sectors have the highest gearing currently. UK sector trusts have the lowest management charges, and hedge funds and private equity the highest. The level of discount also varies considerably.

These metrics can be usefully compared to the performance figures for the sectors, as follows, ranked by NAV performance over the past ten years.

NAV growth

	1Y (%)	3Y (%)	5Y (%)	10Y (%)
Sector Specialist	24.9	56.5	117.8	245.4
North America	18.2	57.5	109.1	194.9
Infrastructure	13.0	41.1	74.0	159.1
Asia Pacific	25.1	62.5	120.4	158.2
Europe	27.2	65.5	137.2	140.4
Global	22.0	52.6	102.0	133.0
Japan	26.0	81.8	159.8	123.5
UK	16.7	34.8	93.5	119.0
Emerging Markets	19.3	33.2	50.9	92.4
Hedge Funds	3.3	12.6	26.3	67.7
Private Equity	19.5	67.1	99.1	60.7
Property	11.3	36.5	66.8	13.2
Debt	8.5	16.3	42.4	-45.7

Source: Numis Securities

This table highlights the fact that some sectors with the highest yields on average have among the the lowest returns (though this not true of infrastructure), and those with low yields tend to have performed better in NAV terms, though again the correlation is not precise.

Just as striking is the fact that the five-year returns from some sectors (notably property and debt) are higher than their ten-year returns. This is because they were the sectors worst hit by the global financial crisis of 2007–09, which period is included in the ten-year figures, but not in the five-year figures.

This underlines the fact that certain types of asset do better in different market conditions. This can also be seen by looking at which sectors have performed the best in share price terms over different periods. (The disparity from year to year would be even greater if the rankings were done on a calendar year basis.)

Share price performance

1Y	3Y	5Y	10Y
Private Equity	Private Equity	Private Equity	Sector Specialist
Europe	Japan	Japan	North America
Sector Specialist	Europe	Europe	Infrastructure
Japan	Sector Specialist	Sector Specialist	Asia Pacific
Asia Pacific	Asia Pacific	Property	Global
Global	Global	Asia Pacific	Europe
Property	North America	Global	Japan
Emerging Markets	Property	North America	UK
North America	Infrastructure	UK	Emerging Markets
UK	UK	Infrastructure	Property
Debt	Emerging Markets	Emerging Markets	Private Equity
Infrastructure	Debt	Debt	Hedge Funds
Hedge Funds	Hedge Funds	Hedge Funds	Debt

By tracking how different sectors – and the trusts within them – have performed over different periods, it is possible to build up a more detailed picture of the way they perform in different conditions.

ANALYSING INDIVIDUAL TRUSTS

As should be clear from the example of UK equity income funds, there can be considerable differences between trusts in the same sector. Different sources of information may well give different levels of detail. Many trusts are happy to publish some of this data in a standardised format on their own websites, along with other company literature.

The returns that investment trusts make can be broken down into two key elements:

* income, which in practice means dividend payments

- capital gains and losses, arising from share price movements

Once a dividend has been paid, the money used to pay it is obviously no longer available to the trust to invest. The net asset value of the trust therefore falls by the amount that it costs to pay the dividend to all the shareholders. If the investor decides to reinvest the dividend payment back into the trust, however, it will continue to rise or fall in value in line with the movement in the share price from the date of reinvestment onwards.

In practice, most investors keep the dividend payments (which are potentially liable to income tax) and wait to see how the share price of the trust performs over time.

Income returns are analysed in the next section. However, most data sources, including the AIC, use what are called total share price returns, which assume that the dividend is reinvested. This has the advantage of making it possible to directly compare the overall performance of different trusts — otherwise trusts that pay a higher rate of dividend would appear to have performed less well in share price terms than ones which paid little or nothing as income. However, for anyone who does need the dividends as income, it is important to remember that a total return figure includes the reinvested dividends.

Capital gains and losses from holding shares in investment trusts are relatively straightforward to track. The two most important numbers are the share price return and the net asset value return. The difference between the two is primarily determined by the level of discount and the level of gearing.

When an investor sells shares for more than was paid for them, the gain is potentially liable to capital gains tax. There is an annual capital gains tax allowance which allows capital gains up to an annual limit (£11,300 per annum in the 2017–18 financial year) to be exempt from tax. Gains thereafter are paid at a rate of either 18 or 28% (2017–18 rates, which are liable to change in the Budget each year).

Gains made by investments held in an ISA or SIPP are, however, exempt from capital gains tax, although in the case of a SIPP they may become taxable if the money is taken out as income. It is the combination of income and capital gain (or loss) that determines the total return that an investor will make over time. Up to £20,000 can be invested into an ISA each year, a very valuable allowance.

It is just as important to look at past return figures of individual trusts in the same detailed way as was suggested when analysing sector performance. Key factors to analyse include:

- the contribution from gearing
- the movement in the discount
- the variation from calendar year to calendar year
- the volatility of the share price and net asset value
- the fund manager's track record and experience
- performance against relevant benchmarks and peer group

- board policies on discounts and share buybacks
- the history and sustainability of dividends.

INCOME INVESTING

MANY INVESTORS TURN to investment companies to provide them with investment income. It is an area where the closed-end structure has distinct advantages over open-ended equivalents. However, it is also important to look very carefully at how a trust is generating its income, because not everything is always as it seems.

As with all companies, the way that income is distributed by investment trusts is in the form of dividends. These can be paid quarterly, twice a year or annually. In exceptional cases, trusts may also have an opportunity to pay 'special dividends' in addition to their normal regular distributions.

Dividends are set by the board of directors of trusts and typically announced at the time of its half-year and annual results. They will set the day the payments to shareholders will be made (the payment date) and also the date (the record date) on which shareholders will need to own the shares in order to qualify for that payment. Payments are typically paid a few months after the end of the accounting period to which they relate.

Example

On 7 March 2017 Foreign & Colonial announced that it would pay a final dividend of 2.70p to all the shareholders on its register at the close of business on 30 March 2017. The dividend, it said, would be paid on 2 May 2017. Having earlier announced three quarterly interim dividends of 2.30p, that produced a total dividend payment in respect of the 12 months to 31 December 2016 of 9.60p.

The following table summarises the recent history of dividend payments made by Foreign & Colonial Investment Trust. Until 2012 F&C paid dividends twice a year. Now it pays four times a year. You can see the progression of the annual payment over time from 8.5p in 2012 to 9.85p in 2016.

Recent dividend payments by Foreign & Colonial Investment Trust

Year ending:	31/12/2017	31/12/2016	31/12/2015	31/12/2014	31/12/2013	31/12/2012
Dividend payments						
Final:	-	2.70p	2.70p	2.70p	2.70p	2.50p
3rd interim:	-	2.45p	2.30p	2.20p	2.10p	-
2nd interim:	2.50p*	2.35p	2.30p	2.20p	2.10p	2.00p
1st interim:	2.50p	2.35p	2.30p	2.20p	-	-
Interim:	-	-	-	-	2.10p	4.00p
Total dividend for year:	-	**9.85p**	**9.60p**	**9.30p**	**9.00p**	**8.50p**
Dividend metrics						
Dividend growth:	n/a	2.60%	3.23%	3.33%	5.88%	19.72%

Source: Hargreaves Lansdown

You may also notice that the first two interim payments declared in 2017 amount to 5.0p, higher than the equivalent payments in 2016. This suggests that in the absence of surprises the overall dividend this year will add up to more than 2016's 9.85p when the third interim and final payments have been made. Maintaining and ideally growing the annual dividend over time is a priority for many boards.

Because dividends are paid at regular intervals, shareholders in trusts with secure dividends can look ahead to see when the next payment is due. The table below shows the payments that Foreign & Colonial expects to make over the remainder of 2017. Further interim dividends of 2.5p, the first of four dividends for the calendar year 2017 will be paid on 6 July and 1 November 2017.

Foreign & Colonial expected dividend payments over 2017

Interim dividend payment date	01 November 2017
Interim ex-dividend date	28 September 2017
Interim dividend payment date	01 August 2017
Interim results	27 July 2017
Interim ex-dividend date	06 July 2017
Final dividend payment date	02 May 2017
AGM	25 April 2017
Final ex-dividend date	30 March 2017
Annual report	16 March 2017
Final results	07 March 2017

TAXATION OF DIVIDENDS

Investment trust dividends are liable to income tax, unless held inside an ISA (Individual Savings Account) or SIPP (Self-Invested Personal Pension), where no tax is payable and the income does not need to be declared on your tax return. Dividends from venture capital trusts are a special case and not liable to income tax at all if the holding is held for five years or more. The first £5,000 a year of dividend income is free of tax in 2017–18, but this allowance is set to fall to £2,000 a year in 2018–19, unless the allowance is altered by the Chancellor in the Autumn 2017 Budget.

DIVIDEND YIELDS

The dividend-paying capacity of an investment company is typically described as a yield. So a trust that pays an annual dividend of 5p to each shareholder and whose shares are trading at 100p is said to have a yield of 5.0%. That is the income you will get if you buy the shares at that price.

When reading about the yields on different trusts, investors need to distinguish between different ways of presenting the figure. Yields are shown before any deduction of tax and in these examples assume a share price of 100p.

HISTORIC YIELD

Historic yield is based on the total amount of dividend that was paid in respect of the previous financial year. So if trust X has paid an interim dividend of 2.0p per share and a final dividend of 3.0p per share, it will have a total dividend of 5.0p per share. The yield is therefore 5.0%.

PROSPECTIVE YIELD

Prospective yield is based on the total amount of dividend that is expected to be paid in the current financial year, but has not yet been declared. This will typically be an estimate derived from either the company's public statements or from a broker's estimate. Say trust X is expected to pay a dividend this year of 6.0p; its prospective yield will be 6.0%.

TRAILING 12-MONTH YIELD

You may sometimes see a figure of this kind, which is based on combining the most recent dividends paid. If trust X paid a final dividend for 2016 of 3.0p and has paid an interim dividend of 2.5p for 2017 (but not yet declared its final dividend), it will have a trailing 12-month yield of 5.5%.

It is also possible to express the dividends a trust pays as a percentage of its net asset value per share, not its share price. This will produce a different yield figure, depending on whether the share price is higher or lower than the net asset value per share.

PORTFOLIO YIELD

Portfolio yield measures how much income (net of costs) is generated by the investment portfolio of the trust and can be compared to the amount of income that is being paid to shareholders.

A distinguishing feature of investment trusts is that they are required to pay out a minimum of 85% of the income from their investments as a dividend to their shareholders. They need to do this in order to preserve their investment trust status for tax purposes. This in turn allows them to buy and sell investments without having to pay capital gains tax on any profits.

Unlike open-ended funds, which have to pay out all their distributable income each year, they can, however, hold back up to 15% of their income each year as a 'revenue reserve'. In effect they can put aside some of the investment income they have received as a rainy day fund to pay future dividends in years when their investment portfolio has lost money or done less well.

Many investment trusts have taken advantage of this privilege to sustain and grow their dividends consistently over time, drawing on revenue reserves in bad markets and replenishing them in good times. Shareholders benefit in this way from having a steady dividend stream they can rely on.

More recently, new rules have allowed trusts to pay dividends out of their capital reserves, not just their revenue reserves. This is a more contentious practice as it means that the dividends are being paid at the expense of capital gains that have been accumulated over time. They are not strictly income payments at all.

The key point to note is that the portfolio yield of a trust and its dividend yield can be – and often are – very different figures. This can be for a number of different reasons.

1. The portfolio yield is expressed as a percentage of the trust's net assets, not of its share price.

2. The trust may not pay out all its revenues in the form of dividends. It may hold some back as a revenue reserve.

3. The trust may, alternatively, choose to pay more out as dividends than it has earned, either by using accumulated revenue reserves or paying dividends from capital.

4. Trusts also differ in how much of their costs are paid out of income and how much out of capital.

DIVIDEND HEROES

A number of investment trusts, through careful management, are sometimes known as 'dividend heroes', having been able to raise their dividends every year for more than 20 years. This is the current list, according to the the Association of Investment Companies, as at July 2017.*

---

* Some of these trusts, including City of London, have already announced a further dividend increase since the table was drawn up.

Dividend heroes

TRUST	AIC SECTOR	NO OF CONSECUTIVE YEARS DIV INCREASED	DIV YIELD (%) AT 30 JUNE 2017
City of London Investment Trust	UK Equity Income	50	3.9
Bankers Investment Trust	Global	50	2.2
Alliance Trust	Global	50	1.8
Caledonia Investments	Global	50	1.9
F&C Global Smaller Companies	Global	47	0.9
Foreign & Colonial Investment Trust	Global	46	1.7
Brunner Investment Trust	Global	45	2.3
JPMorgan Claverhouse Investment Trust	UK Equity Income	44	3.7
Murray Income	UK Equity Income	43	4.1
Witan Investment Trust	Global	42	1.9
Scottish American	Global Equity Income	37	3.1
Merchants Trust	UK Equity Income	35	5.1
Scottish Mortgage Investment Trust	Global	33	2.8
Temple Bar	UK Equity Income	33	3.3
Value & Income	UK Equity Income	29	4.0
F&C Capital & Income	UK Equity Income	23	3.3
British & American	UK Equity Income	22	8.8
Schroder Income Growth	UK Equity Income	21	7.9
Invesco Income Growth	UK Equity Income	20	3.5

Source: AIC statistics mid-2017

ASSESSING THE YIELD

It is probably clear by now that a whole number of factors need to be taken into account when looking at the yield of a trust you are interested in. A 5p dividend payment will always give you an income return of 5% if you buy a trust for 100p.

The yield figure (as a percentage) will, however, change as the share price goes up and down. If your trust's share price rises from 100p to 200p, but the dividend stays the same, the yield on that trust will halve from 5.0% to 2.5%. If it falls to 50p the yield will rise to 10%.

That is one reason why it is important to look at the total return of your investment – the combination of dividends received and capital gains (or losses) made.

Equally important is to form a view as to how well-supported and sustainable the dividend rate is.

- How much in the way of revenue reserves does a trust have – is the buffer good enough to keep the dividend going if the trust has a bad year?
- Is the dividend being paid partly or wholly out of capital? If so, what you receive as a dividend will be matched an equivalent decline in the NAV per share.
- Trusts that use gearing to increase their returns may also be overstating a trust's ability to pay their dividend on a consistent basis.
- Analysing how a trust allocates its costs will also help to reveal what the true dividend capacity of a trust is.
- Special dividends are by definition meant to be exceptional and probably won't be paid again in future years.

Here are two common metrics that are used to assess the value of particular trust's yield:

- **Dividend growth:** The rate at which a dividend is growing can be compared to the performance of the trust. If it is growing too fast, that is a warning sign.
- **Dividend cover:** A ratio that measures the extent to which a trust has generated enough income to pay its dividend in any given year. A figure of more than 1.0 means that trust has more than earned its dividend. A figure below 1.0 means that the dividend cost more to pay than the trust has earned.

Look at the example of Foreign & Colonial again:

A screenshot of Foreign & Colonial dividends

Year ending:	31/12/2017	31/12/2016	31/12/2015	31/12/2014	31/12/2013	31/12/2012
Total dividend for year:	-	9.85p	9.60p	9.30p	9.00p	8.50p
Dividend metrics						
Dividend growth:	n/a	2.60%	3.23%	3.33%	5.88%	19.72%
Dividend yield:	n/a	1.80%	2.10%	2.20%	2.40%	2.70%
Dividend cover:	n/a	1.07	0.88	0.72	0.85	0.83

* Dividend has not yet been paid but has been declared by Foreign & Colonial Investment Trust plc.

All dividend metrics data is calculated excluding any special dividends. Historical dividends may be adjusted to reflect any subsequent rights issues and corporate actions.

Source: Hargreaves Lansdown

Foreign & Colonial's dividend has been growing at a relatively modest rate of 2–3% per annum over the last three years, having been increased more sharply in 2012 and 2013. The dividend yield (see below) has fallen below 2%. It was not fully covered by earnings in four of the five years, although the cover ratio is not so low as to cause alarm.

A recent report by analysts at Numis Securities* looking at the UK Equity Income and Global Equity Income sectors highlighted how many trusts have been using the flexibility they have over the allocation of costs and the use of revenue and capital reserves in order to enhance their dividend payments. It underlines again that careful analysis is therefore needed to be sure that the yields they offer are sustainable.

KEY THINGS TO REMEMBER ABOUT INCOME INVESTING:

- Investment companies have some unique advantages over other funds when it comes to delivering income.

- They can invest in a wider range of income-producing assets.

- They can smooth dividends over time, and even pay dividends out of their capital profits.

- They can use gearing to boost dividends as well.

- Investment companies can grow income over time to offset some of the impact of inflation.

They are intended as long-term investments and you should therefore be prepared to invest for at least five years, and preferably ten or longer. Your income, and capital, are at risk, and can fall as well as rise, and so they are not a substitute for deposit type investments and annuities. You should not invest in investment companies if you need a guaranteed income or if you cannot afford to lose your capital.

Source: AIC

GEARING

G EARING IS A fancy investment term for using borrowed money to enhance returns. This is something that investment trusts are allowed to do, but open-ended funds (unit trusts and OEICs) are not. It is therefore one of the ways in which investors in trusts can hope to obtain superior returns over time.

In essence, the mathematics of gearing are very simple.

- If a trust can obtain a higher rate of return from its invested capital than the cost of the money it has borrowed, shareholders will benefit from additional gains.

- If the returns are less than the cost of borrowing, however, the shareholders will suffer a greater loss (or make a smaller gain) than would otherwise be the case.

Example

Trust A has £100m of shareholders money (equity capital) to invest.

---

*   3 July 2017, A Blurring of Capital and Income.

The board decides to borrow an additional £20m at 5% per annum interest for a ten-year term. That means it has to pay the lender £1m each year in interest and repay the loan after ten years. At the outset, with the borrowed money, it now has £120m, instead of £100m, to invest.

The charts show how the net asset value will look after ten years on two different, hypothetical outcomes.* In one case the investments return a constant 15% p.a.: in the other they lose a constant 10% p.a. (In reality, of course, the returns will be much lumpier than this.)

The results are shown in the following two charts. In the first case, the NAV of the geared trust grows from £120m to £537m, while that of the ungeared trust also grows – but only to £405m. The gearing has paid off. It has produced an additional 32% (£132m) of return.

In the second case the ungeared trust falls to £35m after 10 years, but the geared trust finds itself with assets worth less than its debt – it would become insolvent. (In practice, no doubt, the trust would have taken remedial action before reaching this point.) The gearing has wiped out 100% of the shareholders' equity. The ungeared trust would have made big losses, too, but would at least still be in business.

Impact of gearing over ten years (return 15% p.a.; interest rate 5% p.a.)

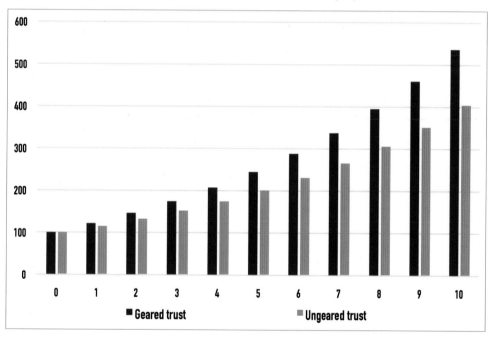

_____

* The example uses simplified assumptions about the timing of returns, investment and interest rate payments.

Impact of gearing over ten years (return of minus 10% p.a.: cost of debt 5% p.a.)

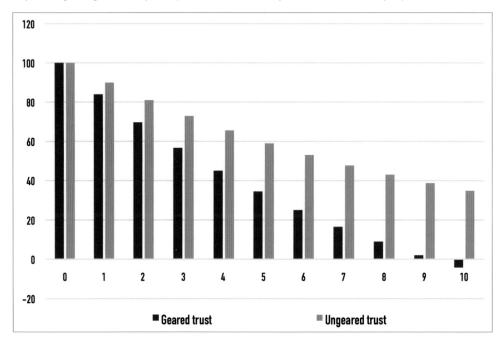

Another way of expressing the impact of gearing is to say that it amplifies the gains or losses that a trust stands to make. It follows that an investment trust with gearing is potentially more volatile and risky than an ungeared one, but with commensurate rewards if the investments produce a higher return than the cost of debt financing.

TYPES OF BORROWING

Trusts can borrow money in a number of different ways – as variable short-term borrowing (akin to an overdraft facility) or a fixed loan over a longer fixed term (more like a mortgage). The interest rate can also be a variable one or fixed in advance.

Interest rates have fallen sharply in the last 30 years and both short- and long-term borrowing has become cheaper and easier to obtain. The recent history of the Witan Investment Trust provides a good case in point.

• In 1986 it borrowed £44.6m in the form of a 30-year debenture. The interest rate it agreed back then was 8.5% per annum. The loan was repaid 30 years later in October 2016.

• In August 2017, Witan borrowed £30m at a rate of 2.74% fixed for 37 years. The 37-year term was believed to be a record for an investment trust in terms of time to maturity.*

---

* James Carthew, *Citywire Investment Trust Insider*, 17 August 2017.

- In 2016 it issued a £12m, 20-year loan at an interest rate of 3.29% and in 2015 it took out a £54m, 30-year loan at 3.47% per annum.

In effect, by the time the debenture was repaid Witan was paying more than 5% p.a. over and above current interest rates. Shareholders would have missed out on another 5% p.a. return had the trust had been able to borrow at current rather than historic rates.

The total return Witan delivered over the 30-year term of its 1986 debenture was approximately 9% p.a. Given that the debenture cost 8.6% per annum, in this case the borrowing added little or nothing to shareholder returns.

On a more positive note, investment companies with long-term debt often publish an NAV with debt at par value and with debt at fair value. The debt at par is based on the face value, whereas the fair value adjusts the value of the debt to reflect the moves in market interest rates since the debt was taken out. For example, consider the historic debt of the Edinburgh Investment Trust, which has debentures paying an interest rate of 7.75% maturing in 2022. This would be highly attractive to a debt holder given current market interest rates. As a result, the fair value of the debt is higher than its par value, resulting in the NAV with debt at fair value being lower (769.19p at 23-Oct) compared to the NAV with debt at par (783.13p).

Looking ahead, the low cost at which many investment trusts have been able to borrow recently might suggest that shareholders can look forward to much more impressive returns from gearing in future.

But interest rates are low for a reason. They have already helped to drive prices of most financial assets to much higher levels, and the implication is that future investment returns may also be much lower than in the past. If so, then gearing will have less effect and – if markets were to fall – add some downside risk, notwithstanding the low interest rates.

GEARING IN PRACTICE

In practice, gearing tends to be used sparingly across most of the investment trust sector. The main exceptions are trusts which invest in property, an asset class which lends itself more readily to the use of borrowing. The more secure and long-term a trust's investments are, the less the risk that comes from using borrowed money to enhance those returns.

Amongst mainstream equity trusts, some trusts use borrowed money as a near-permanent feature of their activities. Other trusts never use gearing at all, while a third group look to vary how much gearing they are employing in the light of market conditions and the terms on which borrowing is available.

An analysis of the gearing employed across the entire trust sector (approximately 600 trusts in total) shows that 88 were employing gearing of 20% or more in mid-2017. The standard way to express gearing is to measure the amount a trust has borrowed as a percentage of its net assets or capital employed.

A trust with £100m of equity and £20m of debt would therefore have potential gearing of 20%. The amount of cash (uninvested funds) that a trust holds is also important. The effect of cash is to reduce the level of gearing. So a trust with borrowing equivalent to 15% of its assets will have effective gearing of 5% (15% minus 10%) if it also holds 10% of its assets in cash.

The four most highly-geared trusts were specialist Guernsey-listed funds engaged in aircraft leasing, an activity once mainly carried out by banks. Nine of the 20 most heavily geared trusts were in the direct property sector (with gearing of between 59% and 119% gearing, against an average for the property sector of 24%).

Most of the trusts investing in listed equities had gearing of between zero and 20%. More than half the trusts in the analysis were not employing any gearing at all. Most boards of trusts, while often delegating tactical decisions on timing, set limits on the maximum amount of borrowing that can be employed by the manager of the trust.

Investors looking for income are often drawn to trusts that offer relatively high dividend yields. However, dividend payments may not always as secure as they look. Trusts that use gearing or other ways to enhance their yields require particularly close scrutiny. A high level of gearing can be a red flag in these cases that the yield may not be sustainable.

Some highly-geared trusts (minimum market cap of £100m)

	GROSS ASSETS	NET ASSETS	GEARING	YIELD
Specialist				
Doric Nimrod Air Two	£659m	£379m	210%	8.2%
Direct property				
Primary Health Properties	£1,275m	£546m	119%	4.5%
Listed equity				
Value and Income	£214m	£152m	31%	1.7%
Fidelity China Special Situations	£1,741m	£1,414m	24%	1.1%

Source: Numis Securities
As at 31 August 2017

WHAT IS NEGATIVE GEARING?

In August 2017 HgCapital, a private equity firm, had an £80m borrowing facility, but this had not been called upon. Its gearing was therefore zero. Only borrowings that have been used count. It also had 24% of its net assets in cash, so the effective gearing was negative (minus 24%). Because it earns little or no return, cash can act as a drag on future performance if it is not either invested or returned to shareholders. During market downturns, however, a high level of cash (negative gearing) can help to protect shareholders against losses.

DISCOUNT CONTROLS

MANY INVESTMENT COMPANIES have measures in place with which they attempt to control the discount and/or reduce discount volatility. Some trusts give a specific discount target, a level at which they promise to take remedial action. Others content themselves with a more modest statement of intent to keep the discount in mind.

Examples of discount control measures include:

BUYING BACK SHARES

If trusts buy back their own shares in the market at a discounted price, the effect will be to bolster the NAV per remaining share, leading to a lower discount. However, it means the fund's costs as a proportion of total assets will increase. Buybacks are not always a practical option for smaller trusts or those investing in illiquid assets (e.g. property).

RESTRUCTURING

If a trust's investment strategy has performed badly, a change of manager or the adoption of a new investment strategy may restore investor confidence in future performance.

MAKING A TENDER OFFER

A tender offer involves offering investors a chance to surrender their shares in return for cash, up to a certain aggregate number of shares in total (say 15% of the issued share capital). The objective is to remove unhappy shareholders from the register in one go.

HOLDING A CONTINUATION VOTE

This involves giving shareholders a vote at a predetermined date in the future on whether the trust should continue. If a continuation vote is lost, the trust's assets will be liquidated and returned to shareholders. The idea is that if shareholders know they will get a chance to exit at net asset value in a few years' time, it may prevent them selling out today.

Extreme volatility in markets can cause problems for mechanisms and 2008 is a good example of this.

For some investors, a stated discount control mechanism offers some reassurance that the board will be proactive when/if the discount widens significantly. But it doesn't guarantee that the gap will narrow. It may also help deter a challenge from aggressive activist investors.

DISCOUNT CONTROLS IN PRACTICE

It is now fairly routine for investment companies to adopt the power to buy back their own shares. This requires shareholder approval at a general meeting and more than two-thirds of the companies in the sector have obtained this approval. There is no doubt that many boards of investment companies are taking discount controls more seriously than in the past.

One reason is the emergence of so-called professional 'activist investors' who buy a block of shares and use that as leverage in trying to force the board of poorly performing trusts to take some action. There have been some notable examples of boards giving in to this kind of pressure in the last few years, including Alliance Trust and Electra.

However, while some boards rigorously adhere to their discount control policy, many still allow themselves a degree of wriggle room to suspend the control mechanisms they have adopted in certain circumstances. It is important to check the wording of any policy closely to see if it's a hard-and-fast rule or simply a guideline, with scope for flexibility.

While adopting a policy of controls, many trusts have not yet felt the need to exercise this power, though in any given year a fair number do so. It is open to debate how far the greater adoption of discount control mechanisms has been a factor in reducing the average level of discount across the sector.

According to Winterflood Securities, at the end of 2016 there were 51 trusts which had an explicit – as opposed to a non-specific – discount target, although these varied widely. The discount levels which these boards said they would protect ranged from 3% to 12%. Some of these targets were implemented strictly while others were only triggered if the discount exceeded the target for a specified period of time. However, of those 51 trusts, 19 had trusts which were in breach of their specified targets at the end of 2016.

Buybacks and tenders since 1996

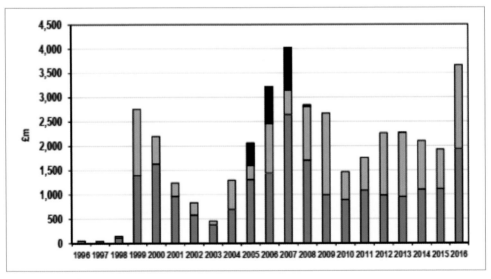

Source: Winterflood Securities, Morningstar

IPOS AND SHARE ISSUANCE

Whereas buybacks and tender offers reduce the amount of capital invested in the trust sector, in any year they will be offset by a combination of new and secondary issues by other trusts.

New issues, or IPOs (Initial Public Offerings), are the mechanism by which new trusts are launched. The number and type of new issue varies enormously from one year to the next. The IPO process involves the issue of a prospectus and significant expense in the form of legal fees and corporate finance and other professional advice.

Secondary issues can take a number of different forms. The most common are placings of new shares and so-called C-share issues. The first two mechanisms, which are less cumbersome and time-consuming than a new issue, both have the effect of allowing an existing trust to expand its capital base by growing the number of shares in issue.

Boards that have bought back their own shares also have the option of re-issuing shares that they have not yet cancelled. A number of well-known trusts whose performance or style of investing have become popular in recent years have been able to issue a steady stream of new shares at a premium to net asset value.

All issues of new shares have to be approved by existing shareholders, so as to avoid dilution of their interests. Many companies seek approval at their annual general meetings for the flexibility to issue new shares up to certain annual limits.

Investment company issuance by type 2013–2017

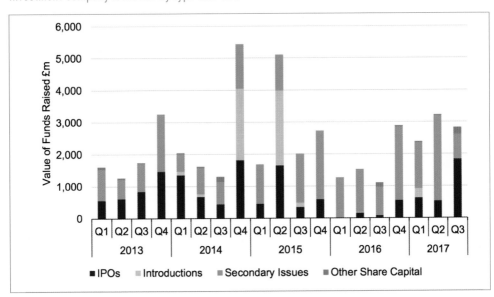

Note: Introductions represent listings of existing capital
Source: Numis Securities

Fund raising by asset class in 2014–2017 (£m year to date)

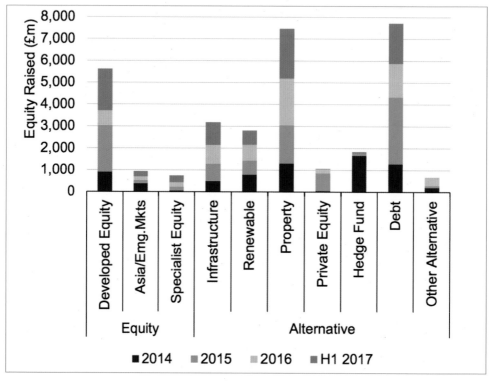

Source: Numis Securities

THE 'MYSTERY' OF DISCOUNTS

W HY DO DISCOUNTS in investment trusts exist – and why do they persist? This is a question that has confounded academic researchers whose job is to study finance for many years.

According to a recent survey, more than 100 articles about this 'mystery' have appeared in learned journals over the past 30 years. Yet no convincing, all-embracing explanation has been forthcoming.

Indeed one distinguished American academic went so far not so long ago to say that "the mysterious case" of closed-end funds poses an "irrefutable challenge" to the whole of neo-classical economic theory. Another described it as "a cause célèbre" in finance literature.

---

*   Prof Stephen Ross, Princeton lectures (2002).

So what is the mystery? It is a puzzle to academics because it flies in the face of one of the core tenets of modern financial theory: the so-called efficient market hypothesis. This says, in effect, that there are – or should be – no 'free lunches' in properly working financial markets.

If a closed-end fund like an investment trust consistently sells at a discount to its net asset value, it means that it creates an opportunity for someone smart to make a quick and easy profit. All they need to do is buy all the shares and liquidate the portfolio, banking the difference.

Yet discounts, as we know, do persist and in many cases have done so historically for many years. Those quick and easy profits remain 'on the table' for long periods of time. A related mystery is why, if this is the case, anybody buys a new closed-end fund when it is launched if they know that it is likely to go to a discount soon afterwards.

All sorts of theories have been put forward to explain this apparent paradox. They include:

- investor irrationality
- management fees
- tax effects
- liquidity issues.

There is no space to review all these different explanations. A useful round up of the academic literature can be found in 'Closed-End Funds: A Survey' (2012), by Martin Cherkes of New York's Columbia University. His conclusion: the "mystery" has not been solved.

Fortunately, the mystery is of no great importance to investors. Recent years have shown that boards of trusts can and do take effective action to eliminate the discounts on their trust, either of their own volition or in the face of threatened activist pressure.

Some professional investment trust investors, such as Peter Spiller of CG Asset Management, argue that all investment trusts should actively pursue policies to eliminate their discounts.

Others, such as Nick Greenwood – who runs Miton Global Opportunities, a fund that invests in other investment trusts – says that the opportunity to find great bargains (trusts that are selling at excessive discounts) is one of the best reasons for investing in the closed-end sector.

Simple observation shows that there is often a fairly direct link between trust performance and the discount. Look, for example, at these two charts of how the discount has moved in two of the larger sectors in the investment trust universe. In both cases the discount has narrowed significantly in recent years, having widened sharply during the big market sell-off around the time of the global financial crisis in 2007–09.

Performance (LHS) and discount (RHS) of UK Equity Income sector

Source: Thomson Reuters Datastream

Performance (LHS) and discount (RHS) of Japanese sector

Source: Thomson Reuters Datastream

Z-SCORES

A z-score is a useful statistical measure that can help to indicate whether the shares in a trust are trading at an unusual discount or premium.

They are calculated daily by brokers who follow investment trusts in order to generate interest in trading or investment opportunities.

How are z-scores calculated?

The formula is:

$$\text{Z-score} = \frac{(\text{current discount - average discount})}{\text{standard deviation of the discount}}$$

Example

Trust A is trading at a discount of 10% (minus 10%). Its average discount over the previous year has been 5% (minus 5%). The standard deviation of the discount over the same period is 2.5%.

Its z-score is therefore:

$$\frac{-10\% - (-5\%)}{2.5\%} = \frac{-10\% + 5\%}{2.5\%} = \frac{-5.0\%}{2.5\%} = \text{minus } 2.0$$

A negative z-score suggests that a trust is 'cheap' compared to its normal trading range. A positive z-score points to it being relatively 'expensive' to buy or sell at its current price.

A z-score of more than 2.0 or more (positive or negative) is particularly worthy of note and typically merits further investigation. It means that the discount (or premium) is more than two standard deviations away from its mean.

Z-scores can be calculated over any number of periods – anything from one day to one year or longer. The longer the time period, the more significant the reading may be. Short-term readings are more helpful for trading decisions.

The underlying assumption behind the calculation is that movements in discounts follow what statisticians call a normal distribution and revert to the mean over time. In practice this may well not be the case. In fact there is evidence that it is not true.[*]

INTERPRETING Z-SCORES

While they are certainly informative, therefore, z-scores always need to be treated with caution. Investors need to take into account a number of other factors which may be influencing the level at which shares are trading relative to their NAV.

Examples would be:

---

[*]   See for example an article on *Seeking Alpha* by 'Left Banker' on 17 April 2017.

- the board announcing new discount controls or buyback commitments

- changes in the shareholder register (e.g. activist stakes or overhang from a major seller)

- portfolio developments not fully reflected in the NAV (e.g. the expected realisation of an unquoted asset).

It is also possible to study how current z-scores for different sectors compare to their historic averages.

Z-scores – sector ranges, showing current sector average and sector ranges of trusts above £150m

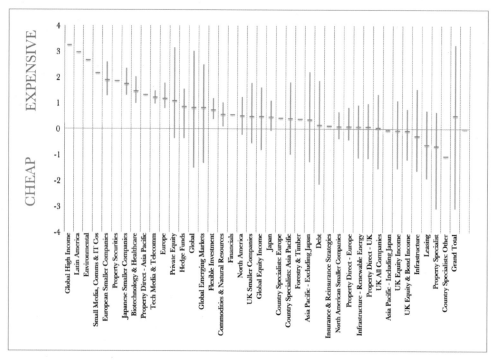

Source: Investec

The height of the bars in this chart (produced by analysts at Investec) gives an indication of which sectors have been the most and which the least volatile in this respect. Note that the majority of trusts had positive z-scores at this date.

It is not a surprise that the sectors with the widest range of z-scores are also those with the greatest volatility.

Z-scores – cheap and expensive, showing current z-score compared to their sectors range of trusts above £150m

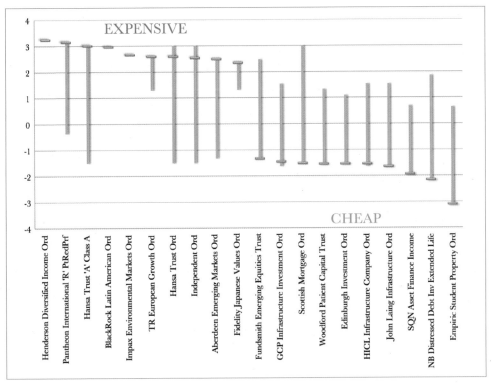

Source: Investec August 2017

This chart summarises 20 of the largest trusts with the highest and lowest z-scores (and their range) at a date we tested in August 2017. Remember that a positive z-score indicates a trust whose discount is well above its average trend while a negative z-score is the opposite. In other words, negative is often a positive from an investor's point of view!

DISCOUNT TRENDS

Discounts can vary considerably over time. A number of different factors, as already noted, can influence the level of the discount at any one time. Board policy, fund performance and market conditions can all have a bearing on the way that discounts move.

In recent years, as the impact of the global financial crisis has receded, both share and bond prices have been trending higher. While the discounts on many trusts widened sharply during the crisis, the general trend since then has been for them to have moved steadily higher on average.

For the last few years discounts on mainstream sectors have generally traded above their longer term average of around 9% (shown by the black horizontal line in the chart). It seems probable that the trend towards greater use of discount controls has been one factor in this trend, along with the general buoyancy of equity markets.

Long-term sector average discount (excl. private equity)

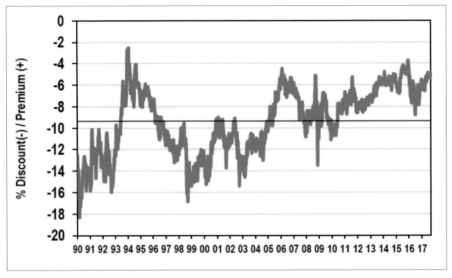

Source: Winterflood Securities, Thomson Reuters (excludes private equity, property and hedge funds)

The volatility of discounts – how far they move up and down in any given year – also varies from year to year.

Sector average discount ranges by calendar year since 2004

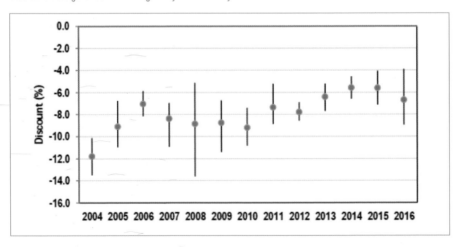

Source: Winterflood Securities

Different sectors have different experiences, though. The following chart, for example, shows how the average discount in two of the largest sectors – UK All Companies and UK Equity Income trusts – have moved over the last 20 years. The solid line shows the share price performance of the sectors (lefthand scale) and the dashed line is the average discount in the sector (righthand scale). You can see how the discount movement has diverged since the financial crisis in 2007–08, with investors placing a relatively higher value (a smaller discount) on the equity income sector for a number of years.

Two UK sectors compared – performance (LHS) and discount (RHS)

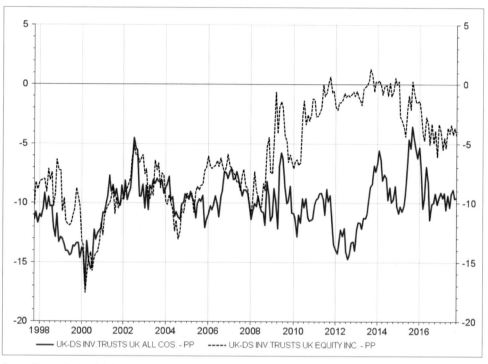

Source: Thomson Reuters Datastream

The same effect has been visible with the recent appearance of a large number of alternative asset trusts, many of which offer relatively high yields but relatively little potential for capital growth. Many of these trusts were trading at premiums in autumn 2017, reflecting investors' greater appetite for income. The discount history of this kind of trust consequently looks rather different to that of conventional trusts.

SKIN IN THE GAME

A GOOD QUESTION FOR investors to ask about any company (not just investment trusts) is the extent to which the interests of the managers of the company are aligned with the interests of the shareholders.

In an ideal world it would be comforting to know that those managing the company stand to gain or lose in the same way as those providing the capital for the business (which is what shareholders effectively do).

In the case of investment trusts, the two parties whose interests you most want to have aligned with yours as an investor are the board of directors and the individual fund managers who make the investment decisions.

In both cases it is usually a positive if they have substantial personal investments in their trusts. One exception may occur if an individual or institution holds such a large shareholding in a trust that they effectively can do what they want with it, whether sensible or not.

Directors of trusts are required to disclose at least once a year in the company's annual report and accounts the extent of their holdings in the trusts on whose boards they serve. It is also a stock exchange listing requirement they notify the market within 24 hours of any further dealings in their trust's shares. All significant shareholders must notify the market if they own more than 3% of the share capital in any trust.

While directors' interests are always available, it is less easy to discover how much the portfolio managers have invested in their trusts. They only have to disclose their shareholding if it exceeds 3% of the total issued share capital of the trust. Some choose do so voluntarily.

Alan Brierley, investment analyst at Canaccord Genuity, does the industry a service by periodically compiling a summary of the shareholdings of directors and managers (where the latter can be ascertained). His last research on this topic, based on analysing 279 trusts, was published in February 2017. Earlier reports appeared in 2014 and 2012.

These are some of his headline findings:

- The total investment by boards and managers in the 2017 report was £1.68bn. While the evolution of the closed-end industry makes comparisons of limited value, this is materially higher than the total of £1bn in 2014 and £687m in 2012.

- 61 chairmen/directors have an individual investment in excess of £1m, while 54 managers or management teams have a personal investment in excess of £1m.

- 43 investment companies, or 15% of those analysed, have chairmen or directors who all have shareholdings valued at more than one year of their director's fee.

- 15% of directors have no investment at all in their trusts (vs 16% in 2014 and 19% in 2012). Excluding those appointed in the past year, this falls to 10% (vs 12% in 2014 and 14% in 2012).

The following table highlights trusts in which the managers (or management teams) have shareholdings in excess of £10m:

Managers with a personal investment in excess of £10m at 13 February 2017

COMPANY	MANAGER	VALUE (£.000)
RIT Capital	Lord Rothschild/Hannah Rothschild	331,206
Tetragon Financial Group	Reade Griffith/Paddy Dear/management team	173,615
JZ Capital Partners	David Zalaznick/John Jordan	113,522
Pershing Square	Management team	110,037
3i Group	Simon Borrows/Julia Wilson	98,088
North Atlantic Smallers	Christopher Mills	92,456
Riverstone Energy	Management team	72,198
Scottish Mortgage	Management team	54,054
Caledonia	Will Wyatt/Jamie Cayzer Colvin	42,611
New Start Investment Trust	John Duffield	39,903
Better Capital	Jon Moulton	35,712
Aberforth Smaller Companies	Management team	32,454
HgCapital	Management team	23,200
Jupiter European	Alex Darwall	23,200
Hansa Trust	William Salomon	19,397
Value & Income	Matthew Oakeshott/Angela Lascelles	19,352
Macau Property	Management team	18,340
Independent Investment Trust	Max Ward	17,315
Syncona	Thomas Henderson	16,287
International Public Partnerships	Management team	13,206
Artemis Alpha Trust	John Dodd/Adrian PAterson	12,458
Aberforth Geared Income	Management team	12,355
Capital Gearing	Peter Spiller	11,707

BOARD COMPOSITION

The Canaccord Genuity report on board and manager shareholdings also provides some helpful data on board composition. Of the 279 trusts it analysed, 93% of the directors could be classified as independent. Women accounted for 19.1% of investment company directorships, vs 15.2% in 2014 and just 10.2% in 2012. This compares with 23.2% of FTSE 350 company directors. Notably there are 82 all-male boards vs just 12 in the FTSE 350. Given that the government has announced a voluntary target of 33% female directors by 2020, trust boards are becoming less male-dominated, but are still lagging the corporate sector generally.

MANAGEMENT FEES AND COSTS

FEW SUBJECTS HAVE aroused as much interest in the last two to three years in the fund industry as the issue of fees charged by management companies. Investment trusts, which for a long time have enjoyed a reputation for being cheap to buy and run, have found themselves under growing pressure to reduce their fees and running costs in order to stay competitive.

The competition has come from several directions.

- The growing popularity of low-cost index funds and exchange-traded funds, many of which charge much lower management fees than the average investment trust.

- The impact of the Retail Distribution Review (RDR), which since 2013 has banned unit trusts and OEICs, investment trusts' main competitors, from paying sales commission to advisors who recommended them.

- More generally greater transparency (and criticism) about the fees and costs that fund management companies have been able to charge historically.

These pressures have resulted in the investment trust industry moving towards a more standardised method of reporting cost information. The standard measure now is the ongoing charge ratio (OCR), which attempts to calculate the operating costs shareholders in trusts are paying for the privilege of having their investments managed collectively.

This figure is expressed as a percentage of the trust's NAV and is published annually by each trust. The objective is to provide shareholders with an indication of the extent to which their annual returns have been reduced by the recurring operational expenses incurred by the trust. The figure excludes, however, the cost of buying and selling securities for the investment portfolio, which can vary significantly from trust to trust and from year to year.

Even though the OCR may appear to be a relatively small figure, research has demonstrated that even a 1% increase in the annual cost of running a fund of any kind can significantly eat into the returns it delivers over time. More importantly, funds whose recurring costs exceed 1% p.a. face powerful competition from passively managed funds, some of which charge as little as 0.1% p.a.

Given that the long-term historical return from investing in equities is around 7% p.a. in real (adjusted for inflation) terms, a trust's investment performance has to be exceptionally good to overcome a 2% p.a. cost disadvantage compared to a low-cost index-tracking fund.

Historically the annual charges of investment trusts have on average been lower than those of open-ended funds, not least because trusts were not allowed to pay standard 'trail commission' to advisers, as open-ended funds were until 2013. Trail commission before RDR of 0.5% p.a. was typically passed on directly to investors in open-ended funds as part of the fund manager's annual management charge.

Now that trail commission on new sales of funds has gone, the in-built cost advantage enjoyed by trusts has eroded. A well-functioning trust board will – or should – have cost control as one of its primary areas of focus, and many have taken steps in the last few years to reduce the annual management fees paid to their external managers.

A particular focus has been on eliminating performance fees, which allow managers of trusts to receive an extra fee in the event of the trust exceeding a specified return hurdle. More than 50 trusts have taken steps to reduce or eliminate performance fees and this trend is set to continue. Fidelity recently announced plans to use a different approach – so-called 'fulcrum' fees, by which the annual management fee rises or falls according to certain performance criteria – across its whole UK fund range. This idea may also spread to investment trusts.

As can be seen from the following table, sector average ongoing charges range between 0.8% and 1.94%, but individual trust figures are considerably more variable. Some large trusts, such as Scottish Mortgage (0.44% OCR), have used the benefits of scale to cut their fee to a historically low level. The OCR figures includes not just the investment management fee but a range of other costs, including legal fees, print costs and other administrative charges.

Ongoing charges by sector

	EX PERF FEE	INC PERF FEE
Asia Pacific	1.25%	1.46%
Debt	1.17%	1.78%
Emerging Markets	1.35%	1.59%
Europe	0.97%	1.19%
Global	0.80%	0.88%
Hedge Funds	1.94%	2.17%

	EX PERF FEE	INC PERF FEE
Infrastructure	1.28%	1.32%
Japan	1.02%	1.02%
North America	0.87%	0.87%
Private Equity	1.90%	2.10%
Property	1.48%	1.90%
Sector Specialist	1.24%	1.99%
UK	0.74%	0.79%

Source: Numis Securities

The following table shows some of the trusts with the lowest OCRs – it is notable that none currently pays a performance fee. Woodford Patient Capital is the only trust which does not charge a management fee at all, but only a performance fee (which it has not yet earned). It is no surprise that most of these trusts are among the oldest and largest around.

Trusts with the lowest OCRs

	EX PERF FEE	INC PERF FEE
Woodford Patient Capital	0.18%	0.18%
Independent IT	0.34%	0.34%
Invesco Perpetual Select – Liquidity	0.40%	0.40%
Law Debenture	0.43%	0.43%
City of London	0.43%	0.43%
Scottish Mortgage	0.44%	0.44%
Mercantile	0.50%	0.50%
Bankers	0.52%	0.52%
Temple Bar	0.52%	0.52%
Alliance Trust	0.54%	0.54%
Foreign & Colonial IT	0.54%	0.54%
JPMorgan Elect – Managed Growth	0.58%	0.58%

The next table shows some of the funds with the highest management fees. Specialist, property and private equity trusts tend to have the highest annual management fees and incur more expenses, in part because they are obliged to take a more hands-on role in managing the investments. High fees may then be rewarded by exceptional performance.

Trusts with the highest management fees

	EX PERF FEE	INC PERF FEE
Cambium Global Timberland	7.95%	7.95%
Global Resources	7.56%	7.56%
Juridica Investments	7.36%	7.36%
Eastern European Property	7.32%	7.32%
Candover	7.12%	7.12%
Dolphin Capital Investors	5.20%	5.20%
St Peter Port Capital	4.68%	4.68%
Africa Opportunity	4.54%	4.54%
Athelney Trust	4.43%	4.43%
Regional REIT	4.36%	4.44%
AXA Property	4.24%	5.92%
Taliesin Property	4.11%	10.06%

CALENDAR

INTRODUCTION

THE GOOD NEWS for investment trust investors is that there is plenty of information to analyse. As listed companies all trusts have to confirm to strict reporting rules, publishing interim and final results each year, as well as a comprehensive Annual Report and Accounts which has to include a full portfolio list. Most trusts publish net asset values daily, though some that invest in less liquid assets (such as property companies) do so only weekly or monthly. Companies must also notify the market every time they issue or buy back shares. They also are required to hold an annual general meeting once a year, which provides an opportunity for shareholders to meet and question the board and managers face to face.

The bad news for active investors is that this information comes thick and fast. If you are monitoring an existing holding, or tracking a trust that you are considering buying, it is helpful to know when to expect significant announcements. Fortunately, some online platforms, and a number of investment trust websites, publish monthly factsheets and offer shareholders the opportunity to be sent email notifications when results and dividend announcements are made. Stockbroking firms will provide their professional clients with a list of forthcoming company announcement dates.

The purpose of this calendar section is to provide an advance reference guide to when trusts are likely to be making important announcements over the course of 2018. The dates are an aggregation of those provided by the trusts themselves and our own estimation based on the date of the equivalent announcement the previous year. Most trusts publish results and hold their annual meetings at more or less the same time each year (if they don't, it may be worth investigating). So even if the dates are not firm enough to be written in ink in your diary, they will not be far out. You should always check the exact dates nearer the time. You will however have a good idea in advance each month of the information coming out of the trusts you are interested in.

JANUARY

INTERIMS	W/C	FINALS	W/C	AGM	W/C
Diverse Income Trust (The)	1 Jan	Scottish Investment Trust	1 Jan	Unicorn AIM VCT	8 Jan
Invesco Perpetual Select Trust	8 Jan	JPMorgan Asian Investment Trust	1 Jan	Hargreave Hale AIM VCT 1	8 Jan
F&C Managed Portfolio Trust	15 Jan	Bankers Investment Trust	15 Jan	Funding Circle SME Income Fund Ltd	15 Jan
Henderson Smaller Companies Investment Trust	22 Jan	TwentyFour Select Monthly Income Fund Ltd	15 Jan	Majedie Investments	15 Jan
Vietnam Holding Ltd	22 Jan	Independent Investment Trust (The)	22 Jan	Redefine International	22 Jan
Aberdeen Frontier Markets Investment Company Ltd	29 Jan	JPMorgan Russian Securities	22 Jan	Standard Life Private Equity Trust	22 Jan
		River & Mercantile UK Micro Cap Investment Co Ltd	22 Jan	Lowland Investment Co	22 Jan
		Aberdeen Diversified Income & Growth Trust	22 Jan	European Investment Trust	22 Jan
		Aberforth Smaller Companies Trust	29 Jan	Edinburgh Worldwide Investment Trust	22 Jan
		BB Healthcare Trust	29 Jan	Keystone Investment Trust	22 Jan
		Drum Income Plus REIT	29 Jan	Baring Emerging Europe	22 Jan
		Aberdeen Emerging Markets Investment Company Ltd	29 Jan	Schroder AsiaPacific Fund	22 Jan
		Hazel Renewable Energy VCT 1	29 Jan	Troy Income & Growth Trust	22 Jan
		Hazel Renewable Energy VCT 2	29 Jan	Henderson Alternative Strategies Trust	22 Jan
		CC Japan Income & Growth Trust	29 Jan	Finsbury Growth & Income Trust	22 Jan
		Octopus Titan VCT	29 Jan	Residential Secure Income	29 Jan
		BlackRock Commodities Income Investment Trust	29 Jan	Jupiter Emerging & Frontier Income Trust	29 Jan

INTERIMS	W/C	FINALS	W/C	AGM	W/C
				TOC Property Backed Lending Trust	29 Jan
				Blackrock Frontiers Investment Trust	29 Jan
				Polar Capital Global Healthcare Growth & Income	29 Jan
				JPMorgan Chinese Investment Trust	29 Jan
				Schroder UK Mid & Small Cap Fund	29 Jan
				Invesco Perpetual Enhanced Income Ltd	29 Jan
				JPMorgan Indian Investment Trust	29 Jan
				Henderson European Focus Trust	29 Jan
				Dunedin Smaller Companies Investment Trust	29 Jan
				Artemis AiM VCT	29 Jan
				JPMorgan Asian Investment Trust	29 Jan

FEBRUARY

INTERIMS	W/C	FINALS	W/C	AGM	W/C
Strategic Equity Capital	5 Feb	Henderson Opportunities Trust	5 Feb	Scottish Investment Trust	5 Feb
Murray Income Trust	12 Feb	Scottish American Investment Co (The)	5 Feb	Schroder European Real Estate Investment Trust Ltd	5 Feb
City of London Investment Trust (The)	12 Feb	Blackrock Throgmorton Trust	12 Feb	Income and Growth VCT	5 Feb
Genesis Emerging Markets Fund Ltd	19 Feb	Octopus AIM VCT 2	12 Feb	MedicX Fund Ltd	5 Feb
SQN Asset Finance Income Fund Ltd	19 Feb	Brunner Investment Trust	12 Feb	GCP Infrastructure Investments Ltd	12 Feb

INTERIMS	W/C	FINALS	W/C	AGM	W/C
TR European Growth Trust	19 Feb	Foresight Solar Fund Ltd	12 Feb	F&C Capital and Income Investment Trust	12 Feb
Jupiter European Opportunities Trust	19 Feb	Primary Health Properties	12 Feb	Blackrock North American Income Trust	19 Feb
UIL Ltd	19 Feb	Temple Bar Investment Trust	19 Feb	Bankers Investment Trust	19 Feb
JPMorgan Emerging Markets Inv Trust	19 Feb	Herald Investment Trust	19 Feb	Chrysalis VCT	19 Feb
JPMorgan Global Growth & Income	19 Feb	The Renewables Infrastructure Group Ltd	19 Feb	Baronsmead Venture Trust	26 Feb
Bluefield Solar Income Fund Ltd	19 Feb	BlackRock World Mining Trust	19 Feb	Aberforth Smaller Companies Trust	26 Feb
Qatar Investment Fund	19 Feb	Henderson Diversified Income Trust	19 Feb		
AEW UK Long Lease REIT	26 Feb	Greencoat UK Wind	19 Feb		
Mid Wynd International Inv Trust	26 Feb	Mithras Investment Trust	19 Feb		
Standard Life UK Smaller Companies Trust	26 Feb	Allianz Technology Trust	19 Feb		
Target Healthcare REIT Ltd	26 Feb	Pershing Square Holdings Ltd	26 Feb		
Crown Place VCT	26 Feb	Greencoat Renewables	26 Feb		
F&C UK Real Estate Investment Ltd	26 Feb	RM Secured Direct Lending	26 Feb		
JPMorgan Mid Cap Investment Trust	26 Feb	ScotGems	26 Feb		
Pacific Horizon Investment Trust	26 Feb	NB Private Equity Partners Ltd	26 Feb		
Ruffer Investment Company Ltd	26 Feb	Kennedy Wilson Europe Real Estate	26 Feb		
Macau Property Opportunities Fund Ltd	26 Feb	Candover Investments	26 Feb		
Sanditon Investment Trust	26 Feb	CVC Credit Partners European Opportunities Ltd	26 Feb		

INTERIMS	W/C	FINALS	W/C	AGM	W/C
		Rights and Issues Inv Trust	26 Feb		
		RIT Capital Partners	26 Feb		
		Fundsmith Emerging Equities Trust	26 Feb		
		Law Debenture Corporation (The)	26 Feb		
		Symphony International Holdings Ltd	26 Feb		
		Riverstone Energy Ltd	26 Feb		
		Schroder Income Growth Fund	26 Feb		

MARCH

INTERIMS	W/C	FINALS	W/C	AGM	W/C
New Star Investment Trust	5 Mar	HgCapital Trust	5 Mar	JPMorgan Russian Securities	5 Mar
CQS New City High Yield Fund Ltd	5 Mar	APAX Global Alpha Ltd	5 Mar	Blackrock Income & Growth Investment Trust	5 Mar
Jupiter US Smaller Companies	5 Mar	Tritax Big Box REIT	5 Mar	Hazel Renewable Energy VCT 2	12 Mar
City Natural Resources High Yield Trust	12 Mar	Maven Income and Growth VCT 5	5 Mar	Hazel Renewable Energy VCT 1	12 Mar
Jupiter UK Growth Investment Trust	12 Mar	BlackRock Latin American Investment Trust	5 Mar	BlackRock Commodities Income Investment Trust	12 Mar
Pantheon International	12 Mar	Secure Income REIT	5 Mar	Henderson Opportunities Trust	12 Mar
Foresight Solar VCT	12 Mar	European Assets Trust NV	5 Mar	Brunner Investment Trust	19 Mar
JPMorgan Global Convertibles Income Fund Ltd	19 Mar	Aberdeen Smaller Companies High Income Trust	12 Mar	River & Mercantile UK Micro Cap Investment Co Ltd	19 Mar
Tiso Blackstar Group	19 Mar	EP Global Opportunities Trust	12 Mar	Blackrock Throgmorton Trust	19 Mar

INTERIMS	W/C	FINALS	W/C	AGM	W/C
JPMorgan Smaller Companies Investment Trust	19 Mar	Witan Investment Trust	12 Mar	CC Japan Income & Growth Trust	19 Mar
Alternative Liquidity Fund Ltd	19 Mar	Polar Capital Global Financials Trust	12 Mar	Independent Investment Trust (The)	19 Mar
Baillie Gifford Japan Trust (The)	26 Mar	Raven Russia Ltd	12 Mar	Octopus Titan VCT	19 Mar
GCP Student Living	26 Mar	Murray International Trust	12 Mar	Baronsmead Second Venture Trust	19 Mar
VinaCapital Vietnam Opportunity Fund Ltd	26 Mar	JPMorgan Claverhouse Investment Trust	12 Mar	Electra Private Equity	26 Mar
JPMorgan Global Emerging Markets Income Trust	26 Mar	Premier Energy and Water Trust	12 Mar	BB Healthcare Trust	26 Mar
Crystal Amber Fund Ltd	26 Mar	Fidelity European Values	12 Mar	Temple Bar Investment Trust	26 Mar
Henderson EuroTrust	26 Mar	LMS Capital	12 Mar	Aberdeen Diversified Income & Growth Trust	26 Mar
JPMorgan Private Equity Ltd	26 Mar	Princess Private Equity Holding Ltd	12 Mar	Rights and Issues Inv Trust	26 Mar
Hadrian's Wall Secured Investments Ltd	26 Mar	Baillie Gifford Shin Nippon	19 Mar	Ediston Property Investment Co	26 Mar
Vinaland Ltd	26 Mar	Asian Growth Properties Ltd	19 Mar		
Volta Finance Ltd	26 Mar	JPMorgan US Smaller Companies IT	19 Mar		
Leaf Clean Energy Company	26 Mar	Real Estate Investors	19 Mar		
		John Laing Infrastructure Fund Ltd	19 Mar		
		Dunedin Enterprise Investment Trust	19 Mar		
		Hansteen Holdings	19 Mar		
		British Smaller Companies VCT 2	19 Mar		
		Kings Arms Yard VCT	19 Mar		
		Albion Technology & General VCT	19 Mar		

INTERIMS	W/C	FINALS	W/C	AGM	W/C
		Regional REIT Ltd	19 Mar		
		Standard Life Investments Property Inc Trust Ltd	19 Mar		
		Albion Development VCT	19 Mar		
		Mobeus Income & Growth 4 VCT	19 Mar		
		North American Income Trust	26 Mar		
		Asian Total Return Investment Company	26 Mar		
		F&C Private Equity Trust	26 Mar		
		BH Macro Ltd	26 Mar		
		Maven Income and Growth VCT 3	26 Mar		
		Alliance Trust	26 Mar		
		Foreign & Colonial Investment Trust	26 Mar		
		Martin Currie Global Portfolio Trust	26 Mar		
		JPMorgan American Investment Trust	26 Mar		
		Blackrock Emerging Europe	26 Mar		
		Merchants Trust (The)	26 Mar		
		City Merchants High Yield Trust Ltd	26 Mar		
		Henderson High Income Trust	26 Mar		
		Bilfinger Berger Global Infrastructure SICAV SA	26 Mar		
		Starwood European Real Estate Finance Ltd	26 Mar		

INTERIMS	W/C	FINALS	W/C	AGM	W/C
		India Capital Growth Fund Ltd	26 Mar		
		International Public Partnership Ltd	26 Mar		
		Aberdeen Asian Income Fund Ltd	26 Mar		
		Mobeus Income & Growth VCT	26 Mar		
		Fidelity Japanese Values	26 Mar		

APRIL

INTERIMS	W/C	FINALS	W/C	AGM	W/C
Henderson International Income Trust	2 Apr	Dunedin Income Growth Inv Trust	2 Apr	CVC Credit Partners European Opportunities Ltd	2 Apr
Manchester & London Investment Trust	2 Apr	BH Global Ltd	2 Apr	Scottish American Investment Co (The)	2 Apr
Schroder Japan Growth Fund	2 Apr	EPE Special Opportunities	2 Apr	Aberdeen Emerging Markets Investment Company Ltd	9 Apr
Fidelity Asian Values	9 Apr	Highbridge Multi-Strategy Fund Ltd	2 Apr	Law Debenture Corporation (The)	9 Apr
Scottish Oriental Smaller Co's Tr (The)	9 Apr	F&C Commercial Property Trust Ltd	2 Apr	Herald Investment Trust	16 Apr
International Biotechnology Trust	23 Apr			APAX Global Alpha Ltd	16 Apr
Aberdeen Asian Smaller Companies Investment Trust	23 Apr	Globalworth Real Estate Investments Ltd	2 Apr	Allianz Technology Trust	16 Apr
BlackRock Greater Europe Investment Trust	23 Apr	Menhaden Capital	2 Apr	Octopus AIM VCT 2	16 Apr
Henderson Far East Income Ltd	23 Apr	Oakley Capital Investments Ltd	2 Apr	European Assets Trust NV	23 Apr
Edinburgh Dragon Trust	23 Apr	Pacific Assets Trust	2 Apr	JPMorgan Claverhouse Investment Trust	23 Apr
Redefine International	23 Apr	Mercantile Investment Trust (The)	2 Apr	Symphony International Holdings Ltd	23 Apr

INTERIMS	W/C	FINALS	W/C	AGM	W/C
Aberdeen Latin American Income Fund Ltd	23 Apr	NB Global Floating Rate Income Fund Ltd	2 Apr	LXB Retail Properties	23 Apr
Fidelity Special Values	23 Apr	Maven Income And Growth VCT4	9 Apr	Foreign & Colonial Investment Trust	23 Apr
JPMorgan Elect	23 Apr	Boussards & Gavaudan Holdings Ltd	9 Apr	Murray International Trust	23 Apr
Troy Income & Growth Trust	30 Apr	Baker Steel Resources Trust Ltd	9 Apr	Premier Energy and Water Trust	23 Apr
		Impax Environmental Markets	9 Apr	Maven Income and Growth VCT 5	23 Apr
		Empiric Student Property	9 Apr	Kennedy Wilson Europe Real Estate	23 Apr
		AcenciA Debt Strategies Ltd	9 Apr	Greencoat UK Wind	23 Apr
		Octopus Apollo VCT 3	9 Apr	Primary Health Properties	23 Apr
		Taliesin Property Fund Ltd	9 Apr	Polar Capital Global Financials Trust	23 Apr
		GCP Asset Backed Income Fund Ltd	9 Apr	Asian Total Return Investment Company	23 Apr
		ICG Enterprise Trust	16 Apr	Henderson Diversified Income Trust	23 Apr
		Acorn Income Fund Ltd	16 Apr	JPMorgan US Smaller Companies IT	23 Apr
		Vietnam Enterprise Investments Ltd	16 Apr	Mithras Investment Trust	23 Apr
		Aurora Investment Trust	16 Apr	Alliance Trust	23 Apr
		UK Commercial Property Trust Ltd	16 Apr	Witan Investment Trust	23 Apr
		Ashmore Global Opportunities Ltd	23 Apr	EP Global Opportunities Trust	23 Apr
		Woodford Patient Capital Trust	23 Apr	Maven Income and Growth VCT 3	23 Apr
		Foresight VCT	23 Apr	RIT Capital Partners	30 Apr
		Phaunos Timber Fund Ltd	23 Apr	Bilfinger Berger Global Infrastructure SICAV SA	30 Apr

INTERIMS	W/C	FINALS	W/C	AGM	W/C
		Kubera Cross-Border Fund Ltd	23 Apr	Greencoat Renewables	30 Apr
		ICG-Longbow Senior Secured UK Property Debt Investments Ltd	23 Apr	RM Secured Direct Lending	30 Apr
		Aberdeen New Thai Investment Trust	23 Apr	Aberdeen Smaller Companies High Income Trust	30 Apr
		Amati VCT 2 Ord 5P	23 Apr	ScotGems	30 Apr
		Phoenix Spree Deutschland Ltd	23 Apr	The Renewables Infrastructure Group Ltd	30 Apr
		Elderstreet VCT	23 Apr	BlackRock Latin American Investment Trust	30 Apr
		Witan Pacific Investment Trust	23 Apr	BlackRock World Mining Trust	30 Apr
		Weiss Korea Opportunity Fund Ltd	23 Apr		
		Invesco Perpetual UK Smaller Companies Inv Tst	23 Apr		
		Aseana Properties Ltd	23 Apr		
		Carador Income Fund	23 Apr		
		Downing Strategic Micro-Cap Investment Trust	30 Apr		
		VPC Specialty Lending Investments	30 Apr		
		Ranger Direct Lending Fund	30 Apr		
		British & American Investment Trust	30 Apr		
		P2P Global Investments	30 Apr		
		Third Point Offshore Investors Ltd	30 Apr		
		BlackRock Smaller Companies Trust	30 Apr		

INTERIMS	W/C	FINALS	W/C	AGM	W/C
		Dolphin Capital Investors Ltd	30 Apr		

MAY

INTERIMS	W/C	FINALS	W/C	AGM	W/C
Polar Capital Global Healthcare Growth & Income	7 May	3i Infrastructure Ltd	7 May	Mobeus Income & Growth 4 VCT	7 May
Finsbury Growth & Income Trust	7 May	Harbourvest Global Private Equity Ltd	14 May	Henderson High Income Trust	7 May
TwentyFour Select Monthly Income Fund Ltd	7 May	Maven Income and Growth VCT 2	14 May	HgCapital Trust	7 May
Income and Growth VCT	14 May	Scottish Mortgage Investment Trust	14 May	Aberdeen Asian Income Fund Ltd	7 May
Keystone Investment Trust	14 May	NewRiver REIT	14 May	British Smaller Companies VCT 2	7 May
Baring Emerging Europe	14 May	3i Group	14 May	Mobeus Income & Growth VCT	7 May
Henderson Alternative Strategies Trust	14 May	Amati VCT	14 May	JPMorgan American Investment Trust	7 May
Henderson European Focus Trust	21 May	JP Morgan Income & Capital Trust	14 May	Starwood European Real Estate Finance Ltd	7 May
River & Mercantile UK Micro Cap Investment Co Ltd	21 May	Octopus AIM VCT	21 May	Dunedin Enterprise Investment Trust	7 May
F&C Capital and Income Investment Trust	21 May	North Atlantic Smaller Companies Inv Trust	21 May	Fidelity European Values	14 May
Invesco Perpetual Enhanced Income Ltd	21 May	F&C UK High Income Trust	21 May	Merchants Trust (The)	14 May
Baronsmead Second Venture Trust	21 May	Assura	21 May	Impax Environmental Markets	14 May
Ediston Property Investment Co	21 May	Pacific Industrial & Logistics REIT	21 May	Real Estate Investors	14 May
European Investment Trust	21 May			Tritax Big Box REIT	14 May
Hargreave Hale AIM VCT 1	21 May			Civitas Social Housing	14 May

INTERIMS	W/C	FINALS	W/C	AGM	W/C
Majedie Investments	21 May	HICL Infrastructure Company Ltd	21 May	Menhaden Capital	14 May
Standard Life Equity Income Trust	21 May	Schroder Real Estate Investment Trust Ltd	21 May	Kings Arms Yard VCT	14 May
Blackrock Frontiers Investment Trust	21 May	TR Property Investment Trust	21 May	Maven Income And Growth VCT4	14 May
Drum Income Plus REIT	21 May	Caledonia Investments	21 May	Baillie Gifford Shin Nippon	14 May
GCP Infrastructure Investments Ltd	21 May	Martin Currie Asia Unconstrained Trust	21 May	John Laing Infrastructure Fund Ltd	21 May
JPMorgan Chinese Investment Trust	21 May	Biotech Growth Trust (The)	21 May	Asian Growth Properties Ltd	21 May
JPMorgan Japanese Investment Trust	21 May	Value & Income Trust	28 May	AcenciA Debt Strategies Ltd	21 May
Schroder European Real Estate Investment Trust Ltd	21 May	Edinburgh Investment Trust (The)	28 May	Riverstone Energy Ltd	21 May
Schroder Income Growth Fund	21 May	Londonmetric Property	28 May	Princess Private Equity Holding Ltd	21 May
British Empire Trust	28 May	Puma VCT 11	28 May	Dunedin Income Growth Inv Trust	21 May
Ecofin Global Utilities And Infrustructure Trust	28 May	Aberdeen Japan Investment Trust	28 May	GCP Asset Backed Income Fund Ltd	21 May
Electra Private Equity	28 May	Shires Income	28 May	Candover Investments	21 May
JPMorgan Asian Investment Trust	28 May	Perpetual Income & Growth Investment Trust	28 May	Foresight VCT	21 May
JPMorgan Indian Investment Trust	28 May	Capital Gearing Trust	28 May	Mercantile Investment Trust (The)	21 May
Jupiter Emerging & Frontier Income Trust	28 May	Ventus 2 VCT	28 May	Fundsmith Emerging Equities Trust	21 May
MedicX Fund Ltd	28 May	Ventus VCT	28 May	Empiric Student Property	21 May
Residential Secure Income	28 May	Pacific Alliance China Land Ltd	28 May	Regional REIT Ltd	21 May
TOC Property Backed Lending Trust	28 May	TOC Property Backed Lending Trust	28 May	F&C Private Equity Trust	21 May
Artemis AiM VCT	28 May			LMS Capital	21 May

INTERIMS	W/C	FINALS	W/C	AGM	W/C
Lowland Investment Co	28 May			Albion Development VCT	21 May
Schroder Oriental Income Fund Ltd	28 May			Pershing Square Holdings Ltd	28 May
Unicorn AIM VCT	28 May			Fidelity Japanese Values	28 May
				F&C Commercial Property Trust Ltd	28 May
				ICG-Longbow Senior Secured UK Property Debt Investments Ltd	28 May

JUNE

INTERIMS	W/C	FINALS	W/C	AGM	W/C
LXB Retail Properties	4 Jun	JPMorgan European Smaller Companies Trust	4 Jun	Vietnam Enterprise Investments Ltd	4 Jun
Candover Investments	4 Jun	Personal Assets Trust	4 Jun	Martin Currie Global Portfolio Trust	4 Jun
Standard Life Private Equity Trust	4 Jun	Maven Income and Growth VCT	4 Jun	International Public Partnership Ltd	4 Jun
Edinburgh Worldwide Investment Trust	11 Jun	Hargreave Hale AIM VCT 2	4 Jun	Secure Income REIT	4 Jun
Blackrock North American Income Trust	11 Jun	Custodian Reit	4 Jun	Standard Life Investments Property Inc Trust Ltd	4 Jun
JPMorgan Russian Securities	11 Jun	Securities Trust of Scotland	4 Jun	Albion Technology & General VCT	4 Jun
Octopus Titan VCT	11 Jun	B.P. Marsh & Partners	4 Jun	BlackRock Smaller Companies Trust	4 Jun
Dunedin Smaller Companies Investment Trust	18 Jun	ProVen Growth & Income VCT	4 Jun	Invesco Perpetual UK Smaller Companies Inv Tst	4 Jun
Henderson Opportunities Trust	18 Jun	Picton Property Income Ltd	4 Jun	Aurora Investment Trust	4 Jun
Scottish Investment Trust	18 Jun	Templeton Emerging Markets Investment Trust	4 Jun	Baker Steel Resources Trust Ltd	11 Jun
Aberdeen Diversified Income & Growth Trust	18 Jun	ProVen VCT	4 Jun	Woodford Patient Capital Trust	11 Jun

INTERIMS	W/C	FINALS	W/C	AGM	W/C
CC Japan Income & Growth Trust	18 Jun	JPMorgan Fleming Japanese Smaller Cos Inv Tr	4 Jun	Foresight Solar Fund Ltd	11 Jun
Schroder AsiaPacific Fund	18 Jun	Gresham House Strategic	11 Jun	North American Income Trust	11 Jun
Blackrock Income & Growth Investment Trust	25 Jun	Lindsell Train Investment Trust (The)	11 Jun	Hansteen Holdings	11 Jun
Aberdeen Emerging Markets Investment Company Ltd	25 Jun	Reconstruction Capital II Ltd	11 Jun	ICG Enterprise Trust	11 Jun
Hazel Renewable Energy VCT 1	25 Jun	JPMorgan European Investment Trust	11 Jun	VPC Specialty Lending Investments	11 Jun
Hazel Renewable Energy VCT 2	25 Jun	Montanaro UK Smaller Companies Inv Tr	11 Jun	NewRiver REIT	11 Jun
Northern Venture Trust	25 Jun	Fidelity China Special Situations	11 Jun	NB Global Floating Rate Income Fund Ltd	11 Jun
		Northern 2 VCT	11 Jun	Oakley Capital Investments Ltd	11 Jun
		Northern 3 VCT	11 Jun	Witan Pacific Investment Trust	11 Jun
		Seneca Global Income & Growth	11 Jun	Maven Income and Growth VCT 2	11 Jun
		Montanaro European Smaller Companies Trust	11 Jun	City Merchants High Yield Trust Ltd	11 Jun
		Aberdeen New India Investment Trust	11 Jun	Ranger Direct Lending Fund	11 Jun
		Gabelli Value Plus+ Trust	11 Jun	Globalworth Real Estate Investments Ltd	18 Jun
		Worldwide Healthcare Trust	11 Jun	Phaunos Timber Fund Ltd	18 Jun
		John Laing Environmental Assets Group Ltd	11 Jun	Blackrock Emerging Europe	18 Jun
		British Smaller Companies VCT	18 Jun	UK Commercial Property Trust Ltd	18 Jun
		Utilico Emerging Markets Ltd	18 Jun	Third Point Offshore Investors Ltd	18 Jun
		Aberdeen New Dawn Investment Trust	18 Jun	Taliesin Property Fund Ltd	18 Jun

INTERIMS	W/C	FINALS	W/C	AGM	W/C
		Sequoia Economic Infrastructure Income Fund Ltd	18 Jun	BH Macro Ltd	25 Jun
		F&C Global Smaller Companies	18 Jun	Downing Strategic Micro-Cap Investment Trust	25 Jun
		Mobeus Income & Growth 2 VCT	18 Jun	Elderstreet VCT	25 Jun
		Hansa Trust	18 Jun	BH Global Ltd	25 Jun
		Duke Royalty Ltd	18 Jun	Phoenix Spree Deutschland Ltd	25 Jun
		Real Estate Credit Investment PCC Ltd	25 Jun	North Atlantic Smaller Companies Inv Trust	25 Jun
		Monks Investment Trust (The)	25 Jun	British & American Investment Trust	25 Jun
		Aberdeen Private Equity Fund Limited	25 Jun	Aberdeen New Thai Investment Trust	25 Jun
		Sirius Real Estate Ltd	25 Jun	Amati VCT	25 Jun
		Albion Venture Capital Trust	25 Jun	Amati VCT 2 Ord 5P	25 Jun
		Terra Capital	25 Jun	3i Group	25 Jun
		Miton Global Opportunities	25 Jun	Scottish Mortgage Investment Trust	25 Jun
		Invesco Asia Trust	25 Jun	P2P Global Investments	25 Jun
		NextEnergy Solar Fund Ltd	25 Jun	Pacific Assets Trust	25 Jun
		Puma VCT 12	25 Jun	F&C UK High Income Trust	25 Jun
		Invesco Income Growth Trust	25 Jun		
		Alcentra European Floating Rate Income Fund Ltd	25 Jun		
		All Asia Asset Capital Ltd	25 Jun		

INTERIMS	W/C	FINALS	W/C	AGM	W/C
		Puma VCT 9	25 Jun		
		Puma VCT 10	25 Jun		
		Adamas Finance Asia Ltd	25 Jun		

JULY

INTERIMS	W/C	FINALS	W/C	AGM	W/C
Schroder UK Mid & Small Cap Fund	2 Jul	Better Capital PCC Ltd	2 Jul	Aseana Properties Ltd	2 Jul
Chrysalis VCT	2 Jul	Better Capital PCC Ltd Ord NPV (2009)	2 Jul	ProVen Growth & Income VCT	2 Jul
Polar Capital Global Financials Trust	9 Jul	Jupiter Green Investment Trust	2 Jul	ProVen VCT	2 Jul
Bankers Investment Trust	9 Jul	Masawara	2 Jul	Martin Currie Asia Unconstrained Trust	2 Jul
Brunner Investment Trust	16 Jul	Qannas Investments Ltd	2 Jul	Gresham House Strategic	2 Jul
Herald Investment Trust	16 Jul	Syncona Ltd	2 Jul	3i Infrastructure Ltd	2 Jul
Independent Investment Trust (The)	16 Jul	TwentyFour Income Fund Ltd	2 Jul	TwentyFour Select Monthly Income Fund Ltd	2 Jul
Allianz Technology Trust	16 Jul	Oryx International Growth Fund Ltd	9 Jul	Seneca Global Income & Growth	2 Jul
BB Healthcare Trust	16 Jul	Schroder UK Growth Fund	9 Jul	Pacific Industrial & Logistics REIT	2 Jul
Blackrock Throgmorton Trust	23 Jul	AEW UK REIT	9 Jul	Maven Income and Growth VCT	2 Jul
Temple Bar Investment Trust	23 Jul	Polar Capital Technology Trust	9 Jul	Puma VCT 11	2 Jul
Law Debenture Corporation (The)	23 Jul	Blue Planet International Financials Investment Trust	9 Jul	Value & Income Trust	9 Jul
LMS Capital	23 Jul	Albion Enterprise VCT	9 Jul	Capital Gearing Trust	9 Jul

INTERIMS	W/C	FINALS	W/C	AGM	W/C
Mithras Investment Trust	23 Jul	Chelverton Small Companies Dividend Trust	16 Jul	Aberdeen Japan Investment Trust	9 Jul
Octopus AIM VCT 2	23 Jul	Maven Income And Growth VCT 6	16 Jul	Londonmetric Property	9 Jul
Aberforth Smaller Companies Trust	23 Jul	Funding Circle SME Income Fund Ltd	16 Jul	Perpetual Income & Growth Investment Trust	9 Jul
Alliance Trust	23 Jul	Downing One VCT	16 Jul	JPMorgan European Smaller Companies Trust	9 Jul
Foreign & Colonial Investment Trust	23 Jul	JPMorgan Brazil Investment Trust	16 Jul	Shires Income	9 Jul
Greencoat UK Wind	23 Jul	Lazard World Trust Fund	16 Jul	Biotech Growth Trust (The)	9 Jul
Primary Health Properties	23 Jul	Miton UK Microcap Trust	16 Jul	Raven Russia Ltd	9 Jul
BlackRock Commodities Income Investment Trust	30 Jul	Artemis Alpha Trust	16 Jul	Octopus Apollo VCT 3	9 Jul
Rights and Issues Inv Trust	30 Jul	Draper Esprit	23 Jul	Northern 2 VCT	9 Jul
Scottish American Investment Co (The)	30 Jul	Vinaland Ltd	30 Jul	Templeton Emerging Markets Investment Trust	9 Jul
Fidelity European Values	30 Jul	Foresight 4 VCT	30 Jul	JPMorgan Fleming Japanese Smaller Cos Inv Tr	9 Jul
European Assets Trust NV	30 Jul	Pembroke VCT	30 Jul	JP Morgan Income & Capital Trust	9 Jul
Fidelity Japanese Values	30 Jul	F&C Managed Portfolio Trust	30 Jul	Northern 3 VCT	9 Jul
Henderson High Income Trust	30 Jul	Atlantis Japan Growth Fund Ltd	30 Jul	Albion Venture Capital Trust	16 Jul
Impax Environmental Markets	30 Jul	Invesco Perpetual Select Trust	30 Jul	HICL Infrastructure Company Ltd	16 Jul
Fundsmith Emerging Equities Trust	30 Jul			JPMorgan European Investment Trust	16 Jul
Premier Energy and Water Trust	30 Jul			Montanaro UK Smaller Companies Inv Tr	16 Jul
				Assura	16 Jul

INTERIMS	W/C	FINALS	W/C	AGM	W/C
				Sequoia Economic Infrastructure Income Fund Ltd	16 Jul
				Highbridge Multi-Strategy Fund Ltd	16 Jul
				Weiss Korea Opportunity Fund Ltd	16 Jul
				B.P. Marsh & Partners	16 Jul
				Ventus VCT	16 Jul
				Ventus 2 VCT	16 Jul
				Caledonia Investments	16 Jul
				Edinburgh Investment Trust (The)	16 Jul
				Harbourvest Global Private Equity Ltd	16 Jul
				Personal Assets Trust	16 Jul
				Custodian Reit	16 Jul
				Gabelli Value Plus+ Trust	16 Jul
				Ashmore Global Opportunities Ltd	16 Jul
				Octopus AIM VCT	16 Jul
				Hargreave Hale AIM VCT 2	16 Jul
				Securities Trust of Scotland	23 Jul
				TR Property Investment Trust	23 Jul
				EPE Special Opportunities	23 Jul
				Fidelity China Special Situations	23 Jul

INTERIMS	W/C	FINALS	W/C	AGM	W/C
				F&C Global Smaller Companies	23 Jul
				Boussards & Gavaudan Holdings Ltd	23 Jul
				Montanaro European Smaller Companies Trust	23 Jul
				Hansa Trust	30 Jul
				All Asia Asset Capital Ltd	30 Jul
				Carador Income Fund	30 Jul
				British Smaller Companies VCT	30 Jul
				Monks Investment Trust (The)	30 Jul
				Schroder UK Growth Fund	30 Jul

AUGUST

INTERIMS	W/C	FINALS	W/C	AGM	W/C
JPMorgan American Investment Trust	6 Aug	Diverse Income Trust (The)	6 Aug	Qannas Investments Ltd	6 Aug
Kennedy Wilson Europe Real Estate	6 Aug	Pantheon International	6 Aug	Invesco Asia Trust	6 Aug
Woodford Patient Capital Trust	6 Aug	Infrastructure India	6 Aug	Terra Capital	6 Aug
JPMorgan Claverhouse Investment Trust	6 Aug	Civitas Social Housing	6 Aug	Blue Planet International Financials Investment Trust	6 Aug
Henderson Diversified Income Trust	6 Aug	Vietnam Holding Ltd	13 Aug	Acorn Income Fund Ltd	13 Aug
Maven Income and Growth VCT 3	6 Aug	Henderson Smaller Companies Investment Trust	20 Aug	Downing One VCT	13 Aug
Maven Income and Growth VCT 5	6 Aug	Hadrian's Wall Secured Investments Ltd	27 Aug	John Laing Environmental Assets Group Ltd	13 Aug

INTERIMS	W/C	FINALS	W/C	AGM	W/C
Mobeus Income & Growth 4 VCT	6 Aug	AEW UK Long Lease REIT	27 Aug	Lazard World Trust Fund	13 Aug
Mobeus Income & Growth VCT	6 Aug	Mid Wynd International Inv Trust	27 Aug	Albion Enterprise VCT	20 Aug
Reconstruction Capital II Ltd	6 Aug	GCP Student Living	27 Aug	Puma VCT 10	20 Aug
Kubera Cross-Border Fund Ltd	6 Aug	Standard Life UK Smaller Companies Trust	27 Aug	Puma VCT 9	20 Aug
NB Private Equity Partners Ltd	6 Aug			NextEnergy Solar Fund Ltd	20 Aug
Princess Private Equity Holding Ltd	6 Aug			NB Private Equity Partners Ltd	20 Aug
Riverstone Energy Ltd	6 Aug			Puma VCT 12	27 Aug
Tritax Big Box REIT	6 Aug			Aberdeen New Dawn Investment Trust	27 Aug
British Smaller Companies VCT 2	6 Aug			Lindsell Train Investment Trust (The)	27 Aug
Taliesin Property Fund Ltd	6 Aug			Maven Income And Growth VCT 6	27 Aug
Witan Investment Trust	6 Aug			Oryx International Growth Fund Ltd	27 Aug
Foresight Solar Fund Ltd	13 Aug			Masawara	27 Aug
Aberdeen Asian Income Fund Ltd	13 Aug				
City Merchants High Yield Trust Ltd	13 Aug				
NB Global Floating Rate Income Fund Ltd	13 Aug				
APAX Global Alpha Ltd	13 Aug				
India Capital Growth Fund Ltd	13 Aug				
Murray International Trust	13 Aug				
Aurora Investment Trust	13 Aug				

INTERIMS	W/C	FINALS	W/C	AGM	W/C
Baker Steel Resources Trust Ltd	13 Aug				
JPMorgan US Smaller Companies IT	13 Aug				
UK Commercial Property Trust Ltd	13 Aug				
Asian Growth Properties Ltd	20 Aug				
Boussards & Gavaudan Holdings Ltd	20 Aug				
Symphony International Holdings Ltd	20 Aug				
Hansteen Holdings	20 Aug				
Phaunos Timber Fund Ltd	20 Aug				
Third Point Offshore Investors Ltd	20 Aug				
F&C Commercial Property Trust Ltd	20 Aug				
Starwood European Real Estate Finance Ltd	20 Aug				
AcenciA Debt Strategies Ltd	20 Aug				
BH Global Ltd	20 Aug				
BH Macro Ltd	20 Aug				
Kings Arms Yard VCT	20 Aug				
Greencoat Renewables	27 Aug				
RM Secured Direct Lending	27 Aug				
ScotGems	27 Aug				
Aseana Properties Ltd	27 Aug				

INTERIMS	W/C	FINALS	W/C	AGM	W/C
Ashmore Global Opportunities Ltd	27 Aug				
British & American Investment Trust	27 Aug				
Carador Income Fund	27 Aug				
EP Global Opportunities Trust	27 Aug				
F&C Private Equity Trust	27 Aug				
Highbridge Multi-Strategy Fund Ltd	27 Aug				
Maven Income And Growth VCT4	27 Aug				
P2P Global Investments	27 Aug				
Pershing Square Holdings Ltd	27 Aug				
The Renewables Infrastructure Group Ltd	27 Aug				
Vietnam Enterprise Investments Ltd	27 Aug				
Acorn Income Fund Ltd	27 Aug				
Raven Russia Ltd	27 Aug				
Albion Development VCT	27 Aug				
Bilfinger Berger Global Infrastructure SICAV SA	27 Aug				
BlackRock World Mining Trust	27 Aug				
Dunedin Enterprise Investment Trust	27 Aug				
Foresight VCT	27 Aug				
RIT Capital Partners	27 Aug				

SEPTEMBER

INTERIMS	W/C	FINALS	W/C	AGM	W/C
Invesco Perpetual UK Smaller Companies Inv Tst	3 Sep	JPMorgan Mid Cap Investment Trust	3 Sep	Aberdeen New India Investment Trust	3 Sep
Weiss Korea Opportunity Fund Ltd	3 Sep	Murray Income Trust	3 Sep	Draper Esprit	3 Sep
International Public Partnership Ltd	3 Sep	Aberdeen Frontier Markets Investment Company Ltd	3 Sep	Better Capital PCC Ltd	3 Sep
Standard Life Investments Property Inc Trust Ltd	3 Sep	Pacific Horizon Investment Trust	10 Sep	Jupiter Green Investment Trust	3 Sep
Aberdeen Smaller Companies High Income Trust	3 Sep	Qatar Investment Fund	10 Sep	Better Capital PCC Ltd Ord NPV (2009)	3 Sep
EPE Special Opportunities	3 Sep	Crystal Amber Fund Ltd	10 Sep	Polar Capital Technology Trust	3 Sep
Martin Currie Global Portfolio Trust	3 Sep	Bluefield Solar Income Fund Ltd	10 Sep	Chelverton Small Companies Dividend Trust	3 Sep
Qannas Investments Ltd	3 Sep	New Star Investment Trust	17 Sep	Pembroke VCT	3 Sep
Secure Income REIT	3 Sep	Ruffer Investment Company Ltd	17 Sep	Syncona Ltd	3 Sep
BlackRock Latin American Investment Trust	10 Sep	Jupiter European Opportunities Trust	17 Sep	Schroder Real Estate Investment Trust Ltd	3 Sep
HgCapital Trust	10 Sep	UIL Ltd	17 Sep	India Capital Growth Fund Ltd	3 Sep
John Laing Infrastructure Fund Ltd	10 Sep	City of London Investment Trust (The)	17 Sep	AEW UK REIT	10 Sep
Adamas Finance Asia Ltd	10 Sep	SQN Asset Finance Income Fund Ltd	17 Sep	Worldwide Healthcare Trust	10 Sep
Empiric Student Property	10 Sep	Strategic Equity Capital	17 Sep	Miton UK Microcap Trust	10 Sep
North Atlantic Smaller Companies Inv Trust	10 Sep	Jupiter UK Growth Investment Trust	17 Sep	JPMorgan Brazil Investment Trust	10 Sep
Regional REIT Ltd	10 Sep	Sanditon Investment Trust	17 Sep	Mobeus Income & Growth 2 VCT	10 Sep
Ranger Direct Lending Fund	10 Sep	JPMorgan Global Growth & Income	17 Sep	Invesco Income Growth Trust	10 Sep

INTERIMS	W/C	FINALS	W/C	AGM	W/C
All Asia Asset Capital Ltd	17 Sep	JPMorgan Global Convertibles Income Fund Ltd	24 Sep	Aberdeen Private Equity Fund Limited	10 Sep
Pacific Assets Trust	17 Sep	Jupiter US Smaller Companies	24 Sep	Vietnam Holding Ltd	10 Sep
Oakley Capital Investments Ltd	17 Sep	Macau Property Opportunities Fund Ltd	24 Sep	Utilico Emerging Markets Ltd	17 Sep
Real Estate Investors	17 Sep	Leaf Clean Energy Company	24 Sep	Miton Global Opportunities	17 Sep
Terra Capital	17 Sep	F&C UK Real Estate Investment Ltd	24 Sep	Alcentra European Floating Rate Income Fund Ltd	17 Sep
Baillie Gifford Shin Nippon	17 Sep	Target Healthcare REIT Ltd	24 Sep	Adamas Finance Asia Ltd	17 Sep
Globalworth Real Estate Investments Ltd	17 Sep			Invesco Perpetual Select Trust	17 Sep
Menhaden Capital	17 Sep			F&C Managed Portfolio Trust	17 Sep
Asian Total Return Investment Company	17 Sep			TwentyFour Income Fund Ltd	17 Sep
CVC Credit Partners European Opportunities Ltd	17 Sep			Real Estate Credit Investment PCC Ltd	24 Sep
VPC Specialty Lending Investments	17 Sep			Henderson Smaller Companies Investment Trust	24 Sep
Albion Technology & General VCT	24 Sep			Sirius Real Estate Ltd	24 Sep
Dunedin Income Growth Inv Trust	24 Sep			Duke Royalty Ltd	24 Sep
Maven Income and Growth VCT 2	24 Sep			Infrastructure India	24 Sep
Mercantile Investment Trust (The)	24 Sep			Foresight 4 VCT	24 Sep
North American Income Trust	24 Sep				
Witan Pacific Investment Trust	24 Sep				
Elderstreet VCT	24 Sep				

INTERIMS	W/C	FINALS	W/C	AGM	W/C
GCP Asset Backed Income Fund Ltd	24 Sep				
Harbourvest Global Private Equity Ltd	24 Sep				
ICG Enterprise Trust	24 Sep				
Blackrock Emerging Europe	24 Sep				
Merchants Trust (The)	24 Sep				
Pacific Alliance China Land Ltd	24 Sep				
Phoenix Spree Deutschland Ltd	24 Sep				

OCTOBER

INTERIMS	W/C	FINALS	W/C	AGM	W/C
Amati VCT 2 Ord 5P	1 Oct	City Natural Resources High Yield Trust	1 Oct	Artemis Alpha Trust	1 Oct
Dolphin Capital Investors Ltd	1 Oct	Crown Place VCT	1 Oct	Diverse Income Trust (The)	8 Oct
Masawara	1 Oct	JPMorgan Private Equity Ltd	1 Oct	Atlantis Japan Growth Fund Ltd	15 Oct
Puma VCT 10	1 Oct	Schroder Japan Growth Fund	1 Oct	JPMorgan Global Growth & Income	22 Oct
Octopus Apollo VCT 3	8 Oct	JPMorgan Emerging Markets Inv Trust	1 Oct	City of London Investment Trust (The)	22 Oct
ProVen Growth & Income VCT	8 Oct	Baillie Gifford Japan Trust (The)	1 Oct	GCP Student Living	22 Oct
ProVen VCT	8 Oct	Tiso Blackstar Group	1 Oct	Standard Life UK Smaller Companies Trust	22 Oct
Aberdeen New Thai Investment Trust	8 Oct	JPMorgan Global Emerging Markets Income Trust	8 Oct	JPMorgan Mid Cap Investment Trust	22 Oct
ICG-Longbow Senior Secured UK Property Debt Investments Ltd	15 Oct	Henderson EuroTrust	8 Oct	JPMorgan Private Equity Ltd	29 Oct

INTERIMS	W/C	FINALS	W/C	AGM	W/C
B.P. Marsh & Partners	15 Oct	TR European Growth Trust	8 Oct	Hadrian's Wall Secured Investments Ltd	29 Oct
JP Morgan Income & Capital Trust	15 Oct	Genesis Emerging Markets Fund Ltd	8 Oct	AEW UK Long Lease REIT	29 Oct
Downing Strategic Micro-Cap Investment Trust	22 Oct	Scottish Oriental Smaller Co's Tr (The)	15 Oct	Murray Income Trust	29 Oct
BlackRock Smaller Companies Trust	22 Oct	JPMorgan Smaller Companies Investment Trust	15 Oct	Jupiter European Opportunities Trust	29 Oct
Amati VCT	29 Oct	Aberdeen Latin American Income Fund Ltd	15 Oct	Schroder Japan Growth Fund	29 Oct
Maven Income and Growth VCT	29 Oct	BlackRock Greater Europe Investment Trust	15 Oct	New Star Investment Trust	29 Oct
British Smaller Companies VCT	29 Oct	Manchester & London Investment Trust	22 Oct		
Ventus 2 VCT	29 Oct	JPMorgan Elect	22 Oct		
Ventus VCT	29 Oct	Aberdeen Asian Smaller Companies Investment Trust	22 Oct		
3i Infrastructure Ltd	29 Oct	Redefine International	22 Oct		
Hargreave Hale AIM VCT 2	29 Oct	Fidelity Asian Values	22 Oct		
Octopus AIM VCT	29 Oct	Alternative Liquidity Fund Ltd	22 Oct		
		Volta Finance Ltd	29 Oct		
		VinaCapital Vietnam Opportunity Fund Ltd	29 Oct		
		Foresight Solar VCT	29 Oct		
		CQS New City High Yield Fund Ltd	29 Oct		
		Fidelity Special Values	29 Oct		
		Edinburgh Dragon Trust	29 Oct		

NOVEMBER

INTERIMS	W/C	FINALS	W/C	AGM	W/C
Capital Gearing Trust	5 Nov	Henderson International Income Trust	5 Nov	Mid Wynd International Inv Trust	5 Nov
Edinburgh Investment Trust (The)	5 Nov	Henderson Far East Income Ltd	5 Nov	Genesis Emerging Markets Fund Ltd	5 Nov
Pacific Industrial & Logistics REIT	5 Nov	LXI REIT	12 Nov	JPMorgan Emerging Markets Inv Trust	5 Nov
Pembroke VCT	5 Nov	British Empire Trust	12 Nov	Pacific Horizon Investment Trust	5 Nov
Scottish Mortgage Investment Trust	5 Nov	JPMorgan Japanese Investment Trust	12 Nov	Strategic Equity Capital	5 Nov
Worldwide Healthcare Trust	5 Nov	Standard Life Equity Income Trust	12 Nov	Jupiter UK Growth Investment Trust	5 Nov
Biotech Growth Trust (The)	5 Nov	Baronsmead Venture Trust	12 Nov	Target Healthcare REIT Ltd	5 Nov
JPMorgan Fleming Japanese Smaller Cos Inv Tr	5 Nov	European Investment Trust	19 Nov	Macau Property Opportunities Fund Ltd	12 Nov
3i Group	5 Nov	LXB Retail Properties	19 Nov	Jupiter US Smaller Companies	12 Nov
Funding Circle SME Income Fund Ltd	12 Nov	Schroder Oriental Income Fund Ltd	19 Nov	Henderson EuroTrust	12 Nov
Martin Currie Asia Unconstrained Trust	12 Nov	Blackrock Frontiers Investment Trust	19 Nov	UIL Ltd	12 Nov
Alcentra European Floating Rate Income Fund Ltd	12 Nov	Unicorn AIM VCT	19 Nov	Bluefield Solar Income Fund Ltd	12 Nov
Gabelli Value Plus+ Trust	12 Nov	Jupiter Emerging & Frontier Income Trust	26 Nov	Qatar Investment Fund	12 Nov
Northern 2 VCT	12 Nov	Residential Secure Income	26 Nov	Crown Place VCT	12 Nov
Northern 3 VCT	12 Nov	F&C Capital and Income Investment Trust	26 Nov	Crystal Amber Fund Ltd	19 Nov
HICL Infrastructure Company Ltd	12 Nov	Troy Income & Growth Trust	26 Nov	JPMorgan Global Convertibles Income Fund Ltd	19 Nov
Schroder Real Estate Investment Trust Ltd	12 Nov	Keystone Investment Trust	26 Nov	Vinaland Ltd	19 Nov

INTERIMS	W/C	FINALS	W/C	AGM	W/C
Utilico Emerging Markets Ltd	12 Nov	Northern Venture Trust	26 Nov	TR European Growth Trust	19 Nov
Duke Royalty Ltd	12 Nov	Ecofin Global Utilities And Infrustructure Trust	26 Nov	Pantheon International	19 Nov
Shires Income	12 Nov	Baronsmead Second Venture Trust	26 Nov	JPMorgan Elect	19 Nov
TwentyFour Income Fund Ltd	12 Nov	International Biotechnology Trust	26 Nov	JPMorgan Global Emerging Markets Income Trust	19 Nov
Aberdeen Japan Investment Trust	19 Nov	Invesco Perpetual Enhanced Income Ltd	26 Nov	SQN Asset Finance Income Fund Ltd	19 Nov
Aberdeen New India Investment Trust	19 Nov			Picton Property Income Ltd	26 Nov
Personal Assets Trust	19 Nov			Manchester & London Investment Trust	26 Nov
Securities Trust of Scotland	19 Nov			Aberdeen Asian Smaller Companies Investment Trust	26 Nov
Templeton Emerging Markets Investment Trust	19 Nov			Volta Finance Ltd	26 Nov
Fidelity China Special Situations	19 Nov			JPMorgan Smaller Companies Investment Trust	26 Nov
Perpetual Income & Growth Investment Trust	19 Nov			City Natural Resources High Yield Trust	26 Nov
Sequoia Economic Infrastructure Income Fund Ltd	19 Nov			Ruffer Investment Company Ltd	26 Nov
Assura	19 Nov			BlackRock Greater Europe Investment Trust	26 Nov
Custodian Reit	19 Nov			F&C UK Real Estate Investment Ltd	26 Nov
Mobeus Income & Growth 2 VCT	19 Nov				
NewRiver REIT	19 Nov				
Syncona Ltd	19 Nov				

INTERIMS	W/C	FINALS	W/C	AGM	W/C
Caledonia Investments	19 Nov				
Invesco Income Growth Trust	19 Nov				
John Laing Environmental Assets Group Ltd	19 Nov				
Lindsell Train Investment Trust (The)	19 Nov				
JPMorgan European Investment Trust	19 Nov				
JPMorgan European Smaller Companies Trust	19 Nov				
Montanaro UK Smaller Companies Inv Tr	19 Nov				
TR Property Investment Trust	19 Nov				
Albion Enterprise VCT	26 Nov				
Civitas Social Housing	26 Nov				
Gresham House Strategic	26 Nov				
LXI REIT	26 Nov				
Montanaro European Smaller Companies Trust	26 Nov				
Picton Property Income Ltd	26 Nov				
Real Estate Credit Investment PCC Ltd	26 Nov				
Value & Income Trust	26 Nov				
Draper Esprit	26 Nov				
F&C UK High Income Trust	26 Nov				

INTERIMS	W/C	FINALS	W/C	AGM	W/C
Sirius Real Estate Ltd	26 Nov				
Jupiter Green Investment Trust	26 Nov				
Lazard World Trust Fund	26 Nov				
Baronsmead Venture Trust	26 Nov				
Better Capital PCC Ltd	26 Nov				
Better Capital PCC Ltd Ord NPV (2009)	26 Nov				
Foresight 4 VCT	26 Nov				
Londonmetric Property	26 Nov				
NextEnergy Solar Fund Ltd	26 Nov				
Puma VCT 11	26 Nov				
Puma VCT 12	26 Nov				
Puma VCT 9	26 Nov				
Blue Planet International Financials Investment Trust	26 Nov				
Schroder UK Growth Fund	26 Nov				

DECEMBER

INTERIMS	W/C	FINALS	W/C	AGM	W/C
Aberdeen Private Equity Fund Limited	3 Dec	Henderson Alternative Strategies Trust	3 Dec	Baillie Gifford Japan Trust (The)	3 Dec
Hansa Trust	3 Dec	Standard Life Private Equity Trust	3 Dec	Fidelity Asian Values	3 Dec
Maven Income And Growth VCT 6	3 Dec	Majedie Investments	3 Dec	Sanditon Investment Trust	3 Dec

INTERIMS	W/C	FINALS	W/C	AGM	W/C
Seneca Global Income & Growth	3 Dec	Ediston Property Investment Co	3 Dec	Aberdeen Latin American Income Fund Ltd	3 Dec
Downing One VCT	3 Dec	Henderson European Focus Trust	3 Dec	Foresight Solar VCT	3 Dec
Monks Investment Trust (The)	3 Dec	Hargreave Hale AIM VCT 1	3 Dec	Fidelity Special Values	10 Dec
Atlantis Japan Growth Fund Ltd	3 Dec	Edinburgh Worldwide Investment Trust	10 Dec	Aberdeen Frontier Markets Investment Company Ltd	10 Dec
AEW UK REIT	10 Dec	JPMorgan Chinese Investment Trust	10 Dec	Henderson Far East Income Ltd	10 Dec
Chelverton Small Companies Dividend Trust	10 Dec	Baring Emerging Europe	10 Dec	Scottish Oriental Smaller Co's Tr (The)	10 Dec
JPMorgan Brazil Investment Trust	10 Dec	Schroder AsiaPacific Fund	10 Dec	Schroder Oriental Income Fund Ltd	10 Dec
Miton UK Microcap Trust	10 Dec	Lowland Investment Co	10 Dec	CQS New City High Yield Fund Ltd	10 Dec
Oryx International Growth Fund Ltd	10 Dec	MedicX Fund Ltd	10 Dec	Edinburgh Dragon Trust	10 Dec
Invesco Asia Trust	10 Dec	Artemis AiM VCT	10 Dec	Standard Life Equity Income Trust	10 Dec
Infrastructure India	10 Dec	GCP Infrastructure Investments Ltd	10 Dec	Tiso Blackstar Group	10 Dec
Miton Global Opportunities	17 Dec	Schroder European Real Estate Investment Trust Ltd	10 Dec	Leaf Clean Energy Company	10 Dec
Aberdeen New Dawn Investment Trust	17 Dec	Blackrock North American Income Trust	10 Dec	Alternative Liquidity Fund Ltd	10 Dec
Artemis Alpha Trust	17 Dec	JPMorgan Indian Investment Trust	10 Dec	Henderson International Income Trust	17 Dec
Albion Venture Capital Trust	24 Dec	Income and Growth VCT	10 Dec	British Empire Trust	17 Dec
F&C Global Smaller Companies	24 Dec	Polar Capital Global Healthcare Growth & Income	10 Dec	JPMorgan Japanese Investment Trust	17 Dec
Polar Capital Technology Trust	24 Dec	Dunedin Smaller Companies Investment Trust	17 Dec	Schroder Income Growth Fund	17 Dec

INTERIMS	W/C	FINALS	W/C	AGM	W/C
		Schroder UK Mid & Small Cap Fund	17 Dec	VinaCapital Vietnam Opportunity Fund Ltd	17 Dec
		Blackrock Income & Growth Investment Trust	17 Dec	Reconstruction Capital II Ltd	17 Dec
		Chrysalis VCT	17 Dec	International Biotechnology Trust	24 Dec
		Electra Private Equity	24 Dec	LXI REIT	24 Dec
		Finsbury Growth & Income Trust	24 Dec	Ecofin Global Utilities And Infrustructure Trust	24 Dec
				Northern Venture Trust	24 Dec

TRUST DIRECTORY

ABOUT THE DIRECTORY

I**T MIGHT SEEM** a simple task to compile a directory of investment trusts, but in practice it is not. Most data providers have their own distinctive criteria for deciding which trusts are – or are not – included in their lists.

The Association of Investment Companies, the industry trade body, logs aggregate industry numbers, as well as reasonably comprehensive data on the many companies in its listings pages, but not all trusts are members. With no reason to be comprehensive, stockbrokers are free to make their own lists of trusts they choose to follow. Commercial publishers and research sites have reasons to eliminate certain trusts, maybe because they are too small to be of real interest, or because the markets in their shares are too illiquid, or because the trust is controlled by a dominant family or business, or because the trust in question has not paid for a listing on that site. Some lists include venture capital trusts; others exclude them. Some include trusts that are listed or domiciled in overseas markets; others stick to UK-listed entities only.

The directory we have complied for use in this *Handbook* is based on our own arbitrary – but we believe sensible – criteria and is drawn from a number of different sources. Our aim is to provide a full but not a comprehensive list of trusts. Our directory runs to 371 trusts. We have mostly ignored trusts with multiple share classes (now a very small minority). We have looked to focus on trusts whose shares are listed either in London, on Euronext, or which are registered in the Channel Islands. We have excluded all trusts with a market capitalisation of less than £20m. We have included a number of property investment companies, mainly those which adopt a portfolio approach, but excluded some of the largest quoted property companies, even though they are classified, somewhat confusingly, as Real Estate Investment Trusts (REITs).

The choice of which data fields to include about trusts that have survived the cut is also a matter of judgement and again, by choice, not comprehensive. Our aim has been to provide a snapshot of what we believe are the most important variables investors should be interested in, recognising that this will only be a pointer to further research, not the full facts that a serious or professional analyst will want to know. We have chosen an arbitrary date of 1 September 2017 as the reference point for the data. There are many free or paid-for websites that will provide investors with real-time information on many of the most important metrics we highlight here. The AIC's own website is a good starting point, and you will find more useful links in the *Handbook*'s sources of information pages.

Our directory is ordered by sector and each entry highlights the ticker and market capitalisation (on the reference date). The aim is to give readers an easy way (a) to search for the trusts in each of the sectors and (b) to gain an impression of its size in market terms. The latter information, being determined primarily by the current share price, will clearly never be constant, as share prices ebb and flow from day to day. However, it is a starting point. Most of the other information provided in each entry is designed to fill out the snapshot, combining basic information such as the age of the trust, its investment strategy, the manager's name and vintage, its website, 10-year price performance and dividend yield, with more specialist information, such as the Sharpe ratio (a measure of return per unit of risk – a positive reading of >1.0 is noteworthy). From this base you can start the important task of comparing one trust to another and going on to further research. We also include some information on fees; these are only rough guideline figures as fee structures can be complex (i.e.difficult to encapsulate in a couple of figures), not all funds quote fees the same way, and funds occasionally change their fees.

There is an important distinction between what are often called mainstream, or conventional, investment trusts and those specialising in alternative assets. The former focus primarily on trusts that run portfolios composed, to varying degrees, of listed equities and bonds. The latter, by far the fastest growing part of the investment trust sector in recent years, invest in a wide range of other asset classes. These include trusts that invest directly in property, private equity funds, funds that buy pools of more rarefied debt securities, specialist property and infrastructure trusts (including renewable energy) and hedge funds. Many of these alternative asset trusts are primarily dedicated to providing attractive income streams in a low interest rate environment. 95% or so of the trade in these trusts, which often require specialist knowledge and skills to analyse, is carried out by professional investors, principally wealth managers, financial advisors and other private client firms.

The directory includes an index at the end, so that readers who know which trust they are looking for can find their way to the right entry. The directory can be helpfully used in conjunction with the investment calendar, which lists the expected 2018 announcement dates for many of the trusts that are listed. There is a separate listing of venture capital trust performance, which are in general smaller and more specialised than the rest of the trust world.

INVESTMENT TRUSTS BY SECTOR

For an A–Z of all investment trusts included, see page 333.

Our hunters can spot a PROFIT — no matter *where* it is on the globe.

WITH MULTIPLE Global expeditions under way, more and more of the world has become the Profit hunters' hunting ground. As they cover new territory, the hunters gain new experiences and ideas. As they share these, the collective knowledge of the whole increases. Yet the founding principles of their forebears remain unchanged. Each hunter is free to hunt in whichever way he or she sees fit. Marching boldly off the beaten track in search of their chosen target. Always prepared to go that extra mile. The value of an investment, and the income from it, can fall and rise because of stockmarket and currency movements and you may not get back the amount originally invested.

ARTEMIS
The PROFIT Hunter

ASIA PACIFIC – EXCLUDING JAPAN

ALL ASIA ASSET CAPITAL LTD

CORE INVESTMENT STRATEGY		Global buyouts		
BENCHMARK		LPX Europe		
MANAGEMENT GROUP		Apollo Alternative Assets		
FUND MANAGER		Leon Black [2006]		
WEBSITE		www.aaacap.com		

LAUNCH DATE	2006	EXCHANGE	Euronext	**SYMBOL**
DOMICILE	Guernsey	CURRENCY	USD	
STOCKBROKER	-	INDEX	-	**AAA**
GEARING	100	AVG DISCOUNT (%)	-15.8	
NAV (£M)	1,696	NET DIV YIELD (%)	-	
TURNOVER	479			
TER (%)	19.61	SHARPE RATIO	1.9	**MKT CAP (£M)**
		VOLATILITY	9.08	**1,866**
PERFORMANCE FEE	No	PERFORMANCE (10Y) (%)	207	

ABERDEEN ASIAN INCOME FUND LTD

CORE INVESTMENT STRATEGY		Asia Pacific equities (income focus)		
BENCHMARK		MSCI AC Asia Pacific (ex Jap)		
MANAGEMENT GROUP		Aberdeen AM		
FUND MANAGER		Hugh Young [2005]		
WEBSITE		www.asian-income.co.uk		

LAUNCH DATE	2005	EXCHANGE	London SE	**SYMBOL**
DOMICILE	Jersey	CURRENCY	GBP	
STOCKBROKER	Cantor Fitzgerald Europe	INDEX	FTSE Small Cap	**AAIF**
GEARING	109	AVG DISCOUNT (%)	-7.3	
NAV (£M)	431	NET DIV YIELD (%)	4.2	
TURNOVER	568			
TER (%)	1.19	SHARPE RATIO	0.3	**MKT CAP (£M)**
		VOLATILITY	1.26	**407**
PERFORMANCE FEE	No	PERFORMANCE (10Y) (%)	220	

ABERDEEN ASIAN SMALLER COMPANIES INVESTMENT TRUST PLC

CORE INVESTMENT STRATEGY		Smaller cos in Asia Pacific (ex Japan)		
BENCHMARK		MSCI AC Asia Pacific (ex Jap)		
MANAGEMENT GROUP		Aberdeen AM		
FUND MANAGER		Hugh Young [1995]		
WEBSITE		www.asian-smaller.co.uk		

LAUNCH DATE	1995	EXCHANGE	London SE	**SYMBOL**
DOMICILE	UK	CURRENCY	GBP	
STOCKBROKER	Panmure Gordon	INDEX	FTSE Small Cap	**AAS**
GEARING	111	AVG DISCOUNT (%)	-14.1	
NAV (£M)	436	NET DIV YIELD (%)	1.0	
TURNOVER	449			
TER (%)	1.76	SHARPE RATIO	0.4	**MKT CAP (£M)**
		VOLATILITY	1.44	**367**
PERFORMANCE FEE	No	PERFORMANCE (10Y) (%)	297	

ABERDEEN NEW DAWN INVESTMENT TRUST PLC

CORE INVESTMENT STRATEGY		Asia Pacific (ex Japan) equities		
BENCHMARK		MSCI AC Asia (ex Jap)		
MANAGEMENT GROUP		Aberdeen AM		
FUND MANAGER		Hugh Young [1989]		
WEBSITE		www.newdawn-trust.co.uk		

LAUNCH DATE	1989	EXCHANGE	London SE	**SYMBOL**
DOMICILE	UK	CURRENCY	GBP	
STOCKBROKER	Canaccord	INDEX	FTSE Small Cap	**ABD**
GEARING	110	AVG DISCOUNT (%)	-13.6	
NAV (£M)	305	NET DIV YIELD (%)	1.7	
TURNOVER	291			
TER (%)	0.93	SHARPE RATIO	0.6	**MKT CAP (£M)**
		VOLATILITY	1.36	**268**
PERFORMANCE FEE	No	PERFORMANCE (10Y) (%)	171	

ASIAN TOTAL RETURN INVESTMENT COMPANY PLC

CORE INVESTMENT STRATEGY		Asia Pacific (ex Japan) equities, absolute return objective		
BENCHMARK		MSCI AC Asia (ex Jap)		
MANAGEMENT GROUP		Schroder IM		
FUND MANAGER		Robin Parbrook, King Fuei Lee [2013]		
WEBSITE		www.asiantotalreturninvestmentcompany.com		

LAUNCH DATE	1987	EXCHANGE	London SE	**SYMBOL**
DOMICILE	UK	CURRENCY	GBP	
STOCKBROKER	Winterflood	INDEX	FTSE Small Cap	**ATR**
GEARING	105	AVG DISCOUNT (%)	-4.5	
NAV (£M)	262	NET DIV YIELD (%)	1.3	
TURNOVER	480			
TER (%)	1.04	SHARPE RATIO	1.3	**MKT CAP (£M)**
		VOLATILITY	1.58	**258**
PERFORMANCE FEE	Yes	PERFORMANCE (10Y) (%)	174	

EDINBURGH DRAGON TRUST PLC

CORE INVESTMENT STRATEGY	Asia Pacific (ex Japan & Aus) equities
BENCHMARK	MSCI AC Asia (ex Jap)
MANAGEMENT GROUP	Aberdeen AM
FUND MANAGER	Adrian Lim [2010]
WEBSITE	www.edinburghdragon.co.uk

LAUNCH DATE	1987	EXCHANGE	London SE	**SYMBOL**
DOMICILE	UK	CURRENCY	GBP	
STOCKBROKER	Winterflood	INDEX	FTSE Small Cap	**EFM**
GEARING	106	AVG DISCOUNT (%)	-12.7	
NAV (£M)	786	NET DIV YIELD (%)	0.9	
TURNOVER	788			
TER (%)	1.12	SHARPE RATIO	0.7	**MKT CAP (£M)**
		VOLATILITY	1.49	**690**
PERFORMANCE FEE	No	PERFORMANCE (10Y) (%)	178	

FIDELITY ASIAN VALUES PLC

CORE INVESTMENT STRATEGY	Asia Pacific (ex Japan) equities – small cap focus
BENCHMARK	MSCI AC Asia (ex Jap)
MANAGEMENT GROUP	Fidelity Investments
FUND MANAGER	Nitin Bajaj [2015]
WEBSITE	www.fidelity.co.uk/asianvalues

LAUNCH DATE	1996	EXCHANGE	London SE	**SYMBOL**
DOMICILE	UK	CURRENCY	GBP	
STOCKBROKER	Stifel	INDEX	FTSE Small Cap	**FAS**
GEARING	103	AVG DISCOUNT (%)	-6.5	
NAV (£M)	279	NET DIV YIELD (%)	1.2	
TURNOVER	709			
TER (%)	1.33	SHARPE RATIO	-	**MKT CAP (£M)**
		VOLATILITY	1.60	**261**
PERFORMANCE FEE	No	PERFORMANCE (10Y) (%)	199	

HENDERSON FAR EAST INCOME LTD

CORE INVESTMENT STRATEGY	Asia Pacific equities (income focus)
BENCHMARK	MSCI AC Asia Pacific (ex Jap)
MANAGEMENT GROUP	Janus Henderson
FUND MANAGER	Michael Kerley [2007]
WEBSITE	www.hendersonfareastincome.com

LAUNCH DATE	1905	EXCHANGE	London SE	**SYMBOL**
DOMICILE	Jersey	CURRENCY	GBP	
STOCKBROKER	Cenkos	INDEX	FTSE Small Cap	**HFEL**
GEARING	108	AVG DISCOUNT (%)	0.9	
NAV (£M)	441	NET DIV YIELD (%)	5.4	
TURNOVER	523			
TER (%)	1.18	SHARPE RATIO	0.6	**MKT CAP (£M)**
		VOLATILITY	1.29	**448**
PERFORMANCE FEE	No	PERFORMANCE (10Y) (%)	151	

INVESCO ASIA TRUST PLC

CORE INVESTMENT STRATEGY		Asia Pacific (ex Japan) equities	
BENCHMARK		MSCI AC Asia (ex Jap)	
MANAGEMENT GROUP		Invesco Perpetual	
FUND MANAGER		Ian Hargreaves [2015]	
WEBSITE		www.invescoperpetual.co.uk	

LAUNCH DATE	1995	EXCHANGE	London SE	**SYMBOL**
DOMICILE	UK	CURRENCY	GBP	**IAT**
STOCKBROKER	Investec	INDEX	FTSE Small Cap	
GEARING	100	AVG DISCOUNT (%)	-12.0	
NAV (£M)	229	NET DIV YIELD (%)	1.5	
TURNOVER	333			**MKT CAP (£M)**
TER (%)	1.02	SHARPE RATIO	1.1	**201**
		VOLATILITY	1.56	
PERFORMANCE FEE	No	PERFORMANCE (10Y) (%)	223	

JPMORGAN ASIAN INVESTMENT TRUST PLC

CORE INVESTMENT STRATEGY		Asia Pacific (ex Japan & Aus) equities	
BENCHMARK		MSCI AC Asia (ex Jap)	
MANAGEMENT GROUP		JPMorgan AM	
FUND MANAGER		Richard Titherington, Ayaz Ebrahim [2015]	
WEBSITE		www.jpmorgan.com	

LAUNCH DATE	1997	EXCHANGE	London SE	**SYMBOL**
DOMICILE	UK	CURRENCY	GBP	**JAI**
STOCKBROKER	Cenkos	INDEX	FTSE Small Cap	
GEARING	100	AVG DISCOUNT (%)	-11.5	
NAV (£M)	365	NET DIV YIELD (%)	4.3	
TURNOVER	303			**MKT CAP (£M)**
TER (%)	0.83	SHARPE RATIO	1.1	**339**
		VOLATILITY	1.53	
PERFORMANCE FEE	No	PERFORMANCE (10Y) (%)	126	

MARTIN CURRIE ASIA UNCONSTRAINED TRUST PLC

CORE INVESTMENT STRATEGY		Asia Pacific (ex Japan) equities	
BENCHMARK		MSCI AC Asia (ex Jap)	
MANAGEMENT GROUP		Martin Currie IM	
FUND MANAGER		Andrew Graham [2011]	
WEBSITE		www.martincurrie.com/uk/asia-unconstrained-trust	

LAUNCH DATE	1985	EXCHANGE	London SE	**SYMBOL**
DOMICILE	UK	CURRENCY	GBP	**MCP**
STOCKBROKER	Pell Hunt	INDEX	FTSE Small Cap	
GEARING	103	AVG DISCOUNT (%)	-14.2	
NAV (£M)	161	NET DIV YIELD (%)	2.0	
TURNOVER	179			**MKT CAP (£M)**
TER (%)	1.13	SHARPE RATIO	1.0	**142**
		VOLATILITY	1.36	
PERFORMANCE FEE	No	PERFORMANCE (10Y) (%)	77	

PACIFIC ASSETS TRUST PLC

CORE INVESTMENT STRATEGY	Asia Pacific (ex Japan & Aus) equities	
BENCHMARK	MSCI AC Asia (ex Jap)	
MANAGEMENT GROUP	First State Stewart	
FUND MANAGER	David Gait, Sashl Reddy [2010]	
WEBSITE	www.pacific-assets.co.uk	

LAUNCH DATE	1985	EXCHANGE	London SE	**SYMBOL**
DOMICILE	UK	CURRENCY	GBP	
STOCKBROKER	Canaccord	INDEX	FTSE Small Cap	**PAC**
GEARING	100	AVG DISCOUNT (%)	-1.5	
NAV (£M)	311	NET DIV YIELD (%)	1.0	
TURNOVER	520			
TER (%)	1.29	SHARPE RATIO	0.8	**MKT CAP (£M)**
		VOLATILITY	1.63	**308**
PERFORMANCE FEE	No	PERFORMANCE (10Y) (%)	133	

PACIFIC HORIZON INVESTMENT TRUST PLC

CORE INVESTMENT STRATEGY	Asia Pacific (ex Japan & Aus) equities	
BENCHMARK	MSCI AC Asia (ex Jap)	
MANAGEMENT GROUP	Baillie Gifford	
FUND MANAGER	Ewan Markson-Brown, Roderick Snell [2014]	
WEBSITE	www.pacifichorizon.co.uk	

LAUNCH DATE	1989	EXCHANGE	London SE	**SYMBOL**
DOMICILE	UK	CURRENCY	GBP	
STOCKBROKER	Cenkos	INDEX	FTSE Small Cap	**PHI**
GEARING	108	AVG DISCOUNT (%)	-10.8	
NAV (£M)	175	NET DIV YIELD (%)	0.1	
TURNOVER	133			
TER (%)	1.13	SHARPE RATIO	0.9	**MKT CAP (£M)**
		VOLATILITY	1.59	**161**
PERFORMANCE FEE	No	PERFORMANCE (10Y) (%)	102	

SCHRODER ASIAPACIFIC FUND PLC

CORE INVESTMENT STRATEGY	Asia Pacific (ex Japan) equities	
BENCHMARK	MSCI AC Asia (ex Jap)	
MANAGEMENT GROUP	Schroder IM	
FUND MANAGER	Matthew Dobbs [1995]	
WEBSITE	www.schroderasiapacificfund.com	

LAUNCH DATE	1995	EXCHANGE	London SE	**SYMBOL**
DOMICILE	UK	CURRENCY	GBP	
STOCKBROKER	Numis	INDEX	FTSE Small Cap	**SDP**
GEARING	105	AVG DISCOUNT (%)	-12.0	
NAV (£M)	825	NET DIV YIELD (%)	1.1	
TURNOVER	625			
TER (%)	1.1	SHARPE RATIO	1.2	**MKT CAP (£M)**
		VOLATILITY	1.54	**738**
PERFORMANCE FEE	No	PERFORMANCE (10Y) (%)	209	

SCHRODER ORIENTAL INCOME FUND LTD

CORE INVESTMENT STRATEGY		Asia Pacific equities (income focus)	
BENCHMARK		MSCI AC Pacific (ex Japan)	
MANAGEMENT GROUP		Schroder IM	
FUND MANAGER		Matthew Dobbs [2005]	
WEBSITE		www.schroders.co.uk	

LAUNCH DATE	2005	EXCHANGE	London SE	**SYMBOL**
DOMICILE	Guernsey	CURRENCY	GBP	
STOCKBROKER	Numis	INDEX	FTSE Small Cap	**SOI**
GEARING	107	AVG DISCOUNT (%)	-0.1	
NAV (£M)	633	NET DIV YIELD (%)	3.4	
TURNOVER	697			
TER (%)	0.89	SHARPE RATIO	0.8	**MKT CAP (£M)**
		VOLATILITY	1.44	**639**
PERFORMANCE FEE	Yes	PERFORMANCE (10Y) (%)	247	

SCOTTISH ORIENTAL SMALLER CO'S TR (THE) PLC

CORE INVESTMENT STRATEGY		Smaller cos in Asia Pacific (ex Japan & Aus)	
BENCHMARK		MSCI AC Asia Ex Jap Small Cap	
MANAGEMENT GROUP		FSS Asia	
FUND MANAGER		Vinay Agarwal [2013]	
WEBSITE		www.scottishoriental.co.uk	

LAUNCH DATE	1995	EXCHANGE	London SE	**SYMBOL**
DOMICILE	UK	CURRENCY	GBP	
STOCKBROKER	Brewin Dolphin	INDEX	FTSE Small Cap	**SST**
GEARING	100	AVG DISCOUNT (%)	-12.8	
NAV (£M)	368	NET DIV YIELD (%)	1.1	
TURNOVER	288			
TER (%)	1.04	SHARPE RATIO	0.5	**MKT CAP (£M)**
		VOLATILITY	1.30	**330**
PERFORMANCE FEE	Yes	PERFORMANCE (10Y) (%)	299	

ASIA PACIFIC – INCLUDING JAPAN

WITAN PACIFIC INVESTMENT TRUST PLC

CORE INVESTMENT STRATEGY		Asia Pacific (inc Japan & Aus) equities	
BENCHMARK		MSCI AC Asia Pacific	
MANAGEMENT GROUP		Witan Investment Services	
FUND MANAGER		Andrew Bell [2010]	
WEBSITE		www.witanpacific.com	

LAUNCH DATE	2005	EXCHANGE	London SE	
DOMICILE	UK	CURRENCY	GBP	**SYMBOL**
STOCKBROKER	JPM Cazenove	INDEX	FTSE Small Cap	**WPC**
GEARING	100	AVG DISCOUNT (%)	-13.6	
NAV (£M)	237	NET DIV YIELD (%)	1.5	
TURNOVER	133			
TER (%)	0.88	SHARPE RATIO	0.9	**MKT CAP (£M)**
		VOLATILITY	1.37	**205**
PERFORMANCE FEE	Yes	PERFORMANCE (10Y) (%)	124	

COUNTRY SPECIALISTS: ASIA PACIFIC

ABERDEEN NEW INDIA INVESTMENT TRUST PLC

CORE INVESTMENT STRATEGY		Indian equities	
BENCHMARK		MSCI India	
MANAGEMENT GROUP		Aberdeen AM	
FUND MANAGER		Hugh Young, Devan Kaloo [2004]	
WEBSITE		www.aberdeen-newindia.co.uk	

LAUNCH DATE	2004	EXCHANGE	London SE	**SYMBOL**
DOMICILE	UK	CURRENCY	GBP	
STOCKBROKER	Winterflood	INDEX	FTSE Small Cap	**ANII**
GEARING	100	AVG DISCOUNT (%)	-11.2	
NAV (£M)	312	NET DIV YIELD (%)	-	
TURNOVER	333			
TER (%)	1.3	SHARPE RATIO	1.0	**MKT CAP (£M)**
		VOLATILITY	1.54	**277**
PERFORMANCE FEE	No	PERFORMANCE (10Y) (%)	239	

ABERDEEN NEW THAI INVESTMENT TRUST PLC

CORE INVESTMENT STRATEGY		Thai equities	
BENCHMARK		Bangkok SET	
MANAGEMENT GROUP		Aberdeen AM	
FUND MANAGER		Adithep Vanabriksha [1989]	
WEBSITE		www.newthai-trust.co.uk	

LAUNCH DATE	1989	EXCHANGE	London SE	**SYMBOL**
DOMICILE	UK	CURRENCY	GBP	
STOCKBROKER	Numis	INDEX	FTSE Fledgling	**ANW**
GEARING	102	AVG DISCOUNT (%)	-15.4	
NAV (£M)	114	NET DIV YIELD (%)	1.9	
TURNOVER	131			
TER (%)	1.41	SHARPE RATIO	0.6	**MKT CAP (£M)**
		VOLATILITY	1.51	**95**
PERFORMANCE FEE	No	PERFORMANCE (10Y) (%)	279	

FIDELITY CHINA SPECIAL SITUATIONS PLC

CORE INVESTMENT STRATEGY	Investing in companies with significant interests in China or Hong Kong
BENCHMARK	MSCI China
MANAGEMENT GROUP	Fidelity Investments
FUND MANAGER	Dale Nicholls [2014]
WEBSITE	www.fidelity.co.uk/china

LAUNCH DATE	2010	EXCHANGE	London SE	SYMBOL
DOMICILE	UK	CURRENCY	GBP	**FCSS**
STOCKBROKER	Cenkos	INDEX	FTSE Mid 250	
GEARING	125	AVG DISCOUNT (%)	-13.7	
NAV (£M)	1,410	NET DIV YIELD (%)	1.1	
TURNOVER	1,681			MKT CAP (£M)
TER (%)	1.16	SHARPE RATIO	1.1	
		VOLATILITY	1.42	**1,242**
PERFORMANCE FEE	Yes*	PERFORMANCE (10Y) (%)	-	

INDIA CAPITAL GROWTH FUND LTD

CORE INVESTMENT STRATEGY	Indian small/mid-cap companies, primarily quoted
BENCHMARK	India BSE Midcap
MANAGEMENT GROUP	Ocean Dials
FUND MANAGER	David Cornell [2010]
WEBSITE	www.indiacapitalgrowth.com

LAUNCH DATE	2005	EXCHANGE	AIM	SYMBOL
DOMICILE	Guernsey	CURRENCY	GBP	**IGC**
STOCKBROKER	Stockdale	INDEX	AIM All-Share	
GEARING	100	AVG DISCOUNT (%)	-18.8	
NAV (£M)	130	NET DIV YIELD (%)	-	
TURNOVER	479			MKT CAP (£M)
TER (%)	1.79	SHARPE RATIO	1.3	
		VOLATILITY	1.60	**111**
PERFORMANCE FEE	No	PERFORMANCE (10Y) (%)	-5	

JPMORGAN INDIAN INVESTMENT TRUST PLC

CORE INVESTMENT STRATEGY	Indian equities
BENCHMARK	MSCI India
MANAGEMENT GROUP	JPMorgan AM
FUND MANAGER	Rajendra Nair, Rukhshad Shroff [2003]
WEBSITE	www.jpmindian.co.uk

LAUNCH DATE	1994	EXCHANGE	London SE	SYMBOL
DOMICILE	UK	CURRENCY	GBP	**JII**
STOCKBROKER	Numis	INDEX	FTSE Mid 250	
GEARING	108	AVG DISCOUNT (%)	-11.1	
NAV (£M)	893	NET DIV YIELD (%)	-	
TURNOVER	979			MKT CAP (£M)
TER (%)	1.22	SHARPE RATIO	1.1	
		VOLATILITY	1.75	**798**
PERFORMANCE FEE	No	PERFORMANCE (10Y) (%)	129	

*Annual performance fee of 15% of any change in NAV attributable to performance which is more than 2% above the returns on the MSCI China Index, subject to a maximum performance fee payable in any year equal to 1% of the arithmetic mean of the values of assets with valuations calculated at the end of each month during the year. Any out-performance above this cap will not be carried forward. If the Company under-performs, the under-performance must be made good before any further performance fee becomes payable. No performance fee was payable for the year ended 31 March 2017.

JPMORGAN CHINESE INVESTMENT TRUST PLC

CORE INVESTMENT STRATEGY		Chinese, HK and Taiwanese equities	
BENCHMARK		MSCI China	
MANAGEMENT GROUP		JPMorgan AM	
FUND MANAGER		Howard Wang, Emerson Yip, Shumin Huang [2006]	
WEBSITE		www.jpmchinese.co.uk	

LAUNCH DATE	1993	EXCHANGE	London SE
DOMICILE	UK	CURRENCY	GBP
STOCKBROKER	Winterflood	INDEX	FTSE Small Cap
GEARING	107	AVG DISCOUNT (%)	-14.4
NAV (£M)	232	NET DIV YIELD (%)	0.6
TURNOVER	208		
TER (%)	1.44	SHARPE RATIO	0.8
		VOLATILITY	1.80
PERFORMANCE FEE	No	PERFORMANCE (10Y) (%)	149

SYMBOL: JMC

MKT CAP (£M): 200

KUBERA CROSS-BORDER FUND LTD

CORE INVESTMENT STRATEGY		Indian companies providing services to N.America and Europe	
BENCHMARK		MSCI India	
MANAGEMENT GROUP		Kubera Partners	
FUND MANAGER		Ramanan Raghavendran [2006]	
WEBSITE		www.kuberacrossborderfund.com	

LAUNCH DATE	2006	EXCHANGE	AIM
DOMICILE	Cayman Isles	CURRENCY	USD
STOCKBROKER	Numis	INDEX	AIM All-Share
GEARING	100	AVG DISCOUNT (%)	-47.7
NAV (£M)	33	NET DIV YIELD (%)	-
TURNOVER	124		
TER (%)	1.42	SHARPE RATIO	0.1
		VOLATILITY	1.46
PERFORMANCE FEE	Yes	PERFORMANCE (10Y) (%)	-32

SYMBOL: KUBC

MKT CAP (£M): 24

MYANMAR INVESTMENTS

CORE INVESTMENT STRATEGY		Growth companies with attractive yields	
BENCHMARK		-	
MANAGEMENT GROUP		Self-Managed	
FUND MANAGER		Aung Htun [2013]	
WEBSITE		-	

LAUNCH DATE	2013	EXCHANGE	AIM
DOMICILE	British Virgin Isles	CURRENCY	USD
STOCKBROKER	Investec	INDEX	-
GEARING	-	AVG DISCOUNT (%)	48.9
NAV (£M)	25	NET DIV YIELD (%)	-
TURNOVER	5		
TER (%)	-	SHARPE RATIO	0.7
		VOLATILITY	-
PERFORMANCE FEE	-	PERFORMANCE (10Y) (%)	-

SYMBOL: MIL

MKT CAP (£M): 39

VIETNAM ENTERPRISE INVESTMENTS LTD

CORE INVESTMENT STRATEGY		Vietnam equities	
BENCHMARK		Vietnam Stock Index	
MANAGEMENT GROUP		Dragon Capital	
FUND MANAGER		Dominic Scriven, Vu Huu Dien [1995]	
WEBSITE		www.veil-dragoncapital.com	

LAUNCH DATE	1995	EXCHANGE	London SE	**SYMBOL**
DOMICILE	Cayman Isles	CURRENCY	GBP	**VEIL**
STOCKBROKER	-	INDEX	FTSE Mid 250	
GEARING	100	AVG DISCOUNT (%)	-15.0	
NAV (£M)	954	NET DIV YIELD (%)	-	
TURNOVER	1,117			**MKT CAP (£M)**
TER (%)	-	SHARPE RATIO	1.5	**867**
		VOLATILITY	0.95	
PERFORMANCE FEE	No	PERFORMANCE (10Y) (%)	-	

VIETNAM HOLDING LTD

CORE INVESTMENT STRATEGY		Former state-owned enterprises in Vietnam	
BENCHMARK		Vietnam Stock Index	
MANAGEMENT GROUP		Vietnam Holding AM	
FUND MANAGER		Vu Quang Thinh [2006]	
WEBSITE		www.vietnamholding.com	

LAUNCH DATE	2006	EXCHANGE	AIM	**SYMBOL**
DOMICILE	Cayman Isles	CURRENCY	USD	**VNH**
STOCKBROKER	Winterflood, Smith & Williamson	INDEX	AIM All-Share	
GEARING	100	AVG DISCOUNT (%)	-17.0	
NAV (£M)	153	NET DIV YIELD (%)	-	
TURNOVER	230			**MKT CAP (£M)**
TER (%)	2.85	SHARPE RATIO	-	**134**
		VOLATILITY	1.67	
PERFORMANCE FEE	Yes	PERFORMANCE (10Y) (%)	101	

VINACAPITAL VIETNAM OPPORTUNITY FUND LTD

CORE INVESTMENT STRATEGY		Vietnamese equities, private equity and property	
BENCHMARK		Vietnam Stock Index	
MANAGEMENT GROUP		VinaCapital IM	
FUND MANAGER		Andy Ho [2003]	
WEBSITE		www.vinacapital.com	

LAUNCH DATE	2003	EXCHANGE	London SE	**SYMBOL**
DOMICILE	Guernsey	CURRENCY	GBP	**VOF**
STOCKBROKER	Numis	INDEX	FTSE Small Cap	
GEARING	100	AVG DISCOUNT (%)	-20.8	
NAV (£M)	733	NET DIV YIELD (%)	1.3	
TURNOVER	1,398			**MKT CAP (£M)**
TER (%)	2.07	SHARPE RATIO	1.5	**596**
		VOLATILITY	2.06	
PERFORMANCE FEE	Yes	PERFORMANCE (10Y) (%)	94	

WEISS KOREA OPPORTUNITY FUND LTD

CORE INVESTMENT STRATEGY		Preference shares listed in South Korea	
BENCHMARK		MSCI Korea	
MANAGEMENT GROUP		Weiss Asset Management LP	
FUND MANAGER		Andrew Weiss [2013]	
WEBSITE		www.weisskoreaopportunityfund.com	

LAUNCH DATE	2013	EXCHANGE	AIM	**SYMBOL**
DOMICILE	Guernsey	CURRENCY	GBP	**WKOF**
STOCKBROKER	N+1 Singer	INDEX	AIM All-Share	
GEARING	100	AVG DISCOUNT (%)	-4.5	
NAV (£M)	151	NET DIV YIELD (%)	1.9	
TURNOVER	251			**MKT CAP (£M)**
TER (%)	1.8	SHARPE RATIO	0.6	**145**
		VOLATILITY	0.84	
PERFORMANCE FEE	No	PERFORMANCE (10Y) (%)	-	

COUNTRY SPECIALISTS: EUROPE

JPMORGAN RUSSIAN SECURITIES PLC

CORE INVESTMENT STRATEGY		Russian equities	
BENCHMARK		Russia RTS	
MANAGEMENT GROUP		JPMorgan AM	
FUND MANAGER		Oleg Biryulyov [2002]	
WEBSITE		www.jpmrussian.co.uk	

LAUNCH DATE	1994	EXCHANGE	London SE	**SYMBOL**
DOMICILE	UK	CURRENCY	GBP	**JRS**
STOCKBROKER	Numis	INDEX	FTSE Small Cap	
GEARING	102	AVG DISCOUNT (%)	-16.0	
NAV (£M)	309	NET DIV YIELD (%)	2.9	
TURNOVER	436			**MKT CAP (£M)**
TER (%)	1.4	SHARPE RATIO	0.3	**254**
		VOLATILITY	2.06	
PERFORMANCE FEE	No	PERFORMANCE (10Y) (%)	5	

COUNTRY SPECIALISTS: OTHER

MASAWARA PLC

CORE INVESTMENT STRATEGY		Companies in Zimbabwe	
BENCHMARK		MSCI Frontier Markets Africa	
MANAGEMENT GROUP		FMI Zimbabwe	
FUND MANAGER		Shingai Mutasa, Julian Vezey [2010]	
WEBSITE		www.masawara.com	

LAUNCH DATE	2010	EXCHANGE	AIM	**SYMBOL**
DOMICILE	Jersey	CURRENCY	GBP	
STOCKBROKER	Cenkos	INDEX	-	**MASA**
GEARING	107	AVG DISCOUNT (%)	-32.9	
NAV (£M)	77	NET DIV YIELD (%)	-	
TURNOVER	4			**MKT CAP (£M)**
TER (%)	14.49	SHARPE RATIO	-1.1	
		VOLATILITY	0.42	**49**
PERFORMANCE FEE	No	PERFORMANCE (10Y) (%)	-	

QATAR INVESTMENT FUND PLC

CORE INVESTMENT STRATEGY		Quoted Qatari equities	
BENCHMARK		MSCI Qatar	
MANAGEMENT GROUP		Epicure Managers Qatar	
FUND MANAGER		Leonard O'Brien, Sandeep Nanda [2007]	
WEBSITE		www.qatarinvestmentfund.com	

LAUNCH DATE	2007	EXCHANGE	London SE	**SYMBOL**
DOMICILE	Isle of Man	CURRENCY	USD	
STOCKBROKER	Panmure Gordon, FinnCap	INDEX	-	**QIF**
GEARING	100	AVG DISCOUNT (%)	-16.0	
NAV (£M)	88	NET DIV YIELD (%)	4.2	
TURNOVER	115			**MKT CAP (£M)**
TER (%)	1.74	SHARPE RATIO	0.1	
		VOLATILITY	1.81	**75**
PERFORMANCE FEE	Yes	PERFORMANCE (10Y) (%)	53	

TISO BLACKSTAR GROUP

CORE INVESTMENT STRATEGY		Invests in black economic empowerment in South Africa	
BENCHMARK		JSE All Share	
MANAGEMENT GROUP		Blackstar Investor	
FUND MANAGER		Andrew Bonamour [2006]	
WEBSITE		www.tisoblackstar.com	

LAUNCH DATE	2006	EXCHANGE	AIM	**SYMBOL**
DOMICILE	Luxembourg	CURRENCY	GBP	
STOCKBROKER	ZAI Corporate Finance	INDEX	-	**TBGR**
GEARING	102	AVG DISCOUNT (%)	-32.6	
NAV (£M)	241	NET DIV YIELD (%)	1.0	
TURNOVER	49			
TER (%)	1.88	SHARPE RATIO	-0.4	**MKT CAP (£M)**
		VOLATILITY	11.47	**142**
PERFORMANCE FEE	Yes	PERFORMANCE (10Y) (%)	-40	

EUROPE

BLACKROCK GREATER EUROPE INVESTMENT TRUST PLC

CORE INVESTMENT STRATEGY		Continental European equities, up to 20% Emg.Europe	
BENCHMARK		MSCI Europe ex UK	
MANAGEMENT GROUP		BlackRock IM	
FUND MANAGER		Stefan Gries, Sam Vecht [2008]	
WEBSITE		www.blackrock.co.uk	

LAUNCH DATE	2004	EXCHANGE	London SE	**SYMBOL**
DOMICILE	UK	CURRENCY	GBP	
STOCKBROKER	Cenkos	INDEX	FTSE Small Cap	**BRGE**
GEARING	105	AVG DISCOUNT (%)	-4.8	
NAV (£M)	330	NET DIV YIELD (%)	1.6	
TURNOVER	231			
TER (%)	1.08	SHARPE RATIO	1.0	**MKT CAP (£M)**
		VOLATILITY	1.25	**312**
PERFORMANCE FEE	No	PERFORMANCE (10Y) (%)	128	

EUROPEAN INVESTMENT TRUST PLC

CORE INVESTMENT STRATEGY		Continental European equities	
BENCHMARK		MSCI Europe ex UK	
MANAGEMENT GROUP		Edinburgh Partners	
FUND MANAGER		Craig Armour [2016]	
WEBSITE		www.theeuropeaninvestmenttrust.com	

LAUNCH DATE	1905	EXCHANGE	London SE	SYMBOL
DOMICILE	UK	CURRENCY	GBP	**EUT**
STOCKBROKER	JPM Cazenove	INDEX	FTSE Small Cap	
GEARING	100	AVG DISCOUNT (%)	-13.2	
NAV (£M)	439	NET DIV YIELD (%)	2.4	
TURNOVER	391			
TER (%)	0.63	SHARPE RATIO	0.7	MKT CAP (£M)
		VOLATILITY	1.35	**391**
PERFORMANCE FEE	No	PERFORMANCE (10Y) (%)	55	

FIDELITY EUROPEAN VALUES PLC

CORE INVESTMENT STRATEGY		Continental European equities	
BENCHMARK		FTSE World Europe ex UK	
MANAGEMENT GROUP		Fidelity Investments	
FUND MANAGER		Sam Morse [2011]	
WEBSITE		www.fidelity.co.uk/europeanvalues	

LAUNCH DATE	1991	EXCHANGE	London SE	SYMBOL
DOMICILE	UK	CURRENCY	GBP	**FEV**
STOCKBROKER	Winterflood	INDEX	FTSE Mid 250	
GEARING	106	AVG DISCOUNT (%)	-11.0	
NAV (£M)	1,017	NET DIV YIELD (%)	1.9	
TURNOVER	1,195			
TER (%)	0.99	SHARPE RATIO	1.1	MKT CAP (£M)
		VOLATILITY	1.27	**934**
PERFORMANCE FEE	No	PERFORMANCE (10Y) (%)	118	

HENDERSON EUROPEAN FOCUS TRUST PLC

CORE INVESTMENT STRATEGY		Continental European equities	
BENCHMARK		MSCI Europe ex UK	
MANAGEMENT GROUP		Janus Henderson	
FUND MANAGER		John Bennett [2010]	
WEBSITE		www.henderson.com	

LAUNCH DATE	1996	EXCHANGE	London SE	SYMBOL
DOMICILE	UK	CURRENCY	GBP	**HEFT**
STOCKBROKER	Winterflood	INDEX	FTSE Small Cap	
GEARING	110	AVG DISCOUNT (%)	-3.3	
NAV (£M)	293	NET DIV YIELD (%)	2.0	
TURNOVER	414			
TER (%)	0.9	SHARPE RATIO	0.9	MKT CAP (£M)
		VOLATILITY	1.26	**297**
PERFORMANCE FEE	Yes	PERFORMANCE (10Y) (%)	202	

HENDERSON EUROTRUST PLC

CORE INVESTMENT STRATEGY		Continental European equities	
BENCHMARK		MSCI Europe ex UK	
MANAGEMENT GROUP		Janus Henderson	
FUND MANAGER		Tim Stevenson [1992]	
WEBSITE		www.henderson.com	

LAUNCH DATE	1992	EXCHANGE	London SE	**SYMBOL**
DOMICILE	UK	CURRENCY	GBP	**HNE**
STOCKBROKER	JPM Cazenove	INDEX	FTSE Small Cap	
GEARING	101	AVG DISCOUNT (%)	-6.6	
NAV (£M)	259	NET DIV YIELD (%)	1.8	
TURNOVER	253			**MKT CAP (£M)**
TER (%)	0.88	SHARPE RATIO	1.0	**251**
		VOLATILITY	1.21	
PERFORMANCE FEE	Yes	PERFORMANCE (10Y) (%)	196	

JUPITER EUROPEAN OPPORTUNITIES TRUST PLC

CORE INVESTMENT STRATEGY		Pan-European equities	
BENCHMARK		MSCI Europe ex UK	
MANAGEMENT GROUP		Jupiter AM	
FUND MANAGER		Alex Darwall [2000]	
WEBSITE		www.jupiteram.com	

LAUNCH DATE	2000	EXCHANGE	London SE	**SYMBOL**
DOMICILE	UK	CURRENCY	GBP	**JEO**
STOCKBROKER	Cenkos	INDEX	FTSE Small Cap	
GEARING	108	AVG DISCOUNT (%)	-4.5	
NAV (£M)	819	NET DIV YIELD (%)	0.8	
TURNOVER	1,136			**MKT CAP (£M)**
TER (%)	0.98	SHARPE RATIO	1.1	**771**
		VOLATILITY	1.32	
PERFORMANCE FEE	Yes	PERFORMANCE (10Y) (%)	239	

JPMORGAN EUROPEAN INVESTMENT TRUST PLC

CORE INVESTMENT STRATEGY		Continental European equities	
BENCHMARK		MSCI Europe ex UK	
MANAGEMENT GROUP		JPMorgan AM	
FUND MANAGER		Stephen Macklow-Smith [1997]	
WEBSITE		www.jpmeuropean.co.uk	

LAUNCH DATE	1905	EXCHANGE	London SE	**SYMBOL**
DOMICILE	UK	CURRENCY	GBP	**JETG**
STOCKBROKER	Winterflood	INDEX	FTSE Small Cap	
GEARING	115	AVG DISCOUNT (%)	-10.4	
NAV (£M)	266	NET DIV YIELD (%)	2.2	
TURNOVER	212			**MKT CAP (£M)**
TER (%)	1.07	SHARPE RATIO	1.0	**241**
		VOLATILITY	1.57	
PERFORMANCE FEE	No	PERFORMANCE (10Y) (%)	95	

JPMORGAN EUROPEAN INVESTMENT TRUST PLC

CORE INVESTMENT STRATEGY	Pan-European equities, income focus
BENCHMARK	MSCI Europe ex UK
MANAGEMENT GROUP	JPMorgan AM
FUND MANAGER	Alexander Fitzalan Howard [2006]
WEBSITE	www.jpmeuropean.co.uk

LAUNCH DATE	2006	EXCHANGE	London SE
DOMICILE	UK	CURRENCY	GBP
STOCKBROKER	Winterflood	INDEX	FTSE Small Cap
GEARING	116	AVG DISCOUNT (%)	-10.3
NAV (£M)	170	NET DIV YIELD (%)	3.0
TURNOVER	207		
TER (%)	1.1	SHARPE RATIO	0.9
		VOLATILITY	1.22
PERFORMANCE FEE	No	PERFORMANCE (10Y) (%)	148

SYMBOL
JETI

MKT CAP (£M)
158

EUROPEAN EMERGING MARKETS

BARING EMERGING EUROPE PLC

CORE INVESTMENT STRATEGY	Emerging European equities
BENCHMARK	MSCI Emerging Europe 10/40
MANAGEMENT GROUP	Baring AM
FUND MANAGER	Matthias Siller [2008]
WEBSITE	www.barings.com

LAUNCH DATE	1994	EXCHANGE	London SE
DOMICILE	UK	CURRENCY	GBP
STOCKBROKER	JPM Cazenove	INDEX	FTSE Small Cap
GEARING	107	AVG DISCOUNT (%)	-13.6
NAV (£M)	127	NET DIV YIELD (%)	1.1
TURNOVER	140		
TER (%)	1.55	SHARPE RATIO	0.4
		VOLATILITY	1.94
PERFORMANCE FEE	No	PERFORMANCE (10Y) (%)	30

SYMBOL
BEE

MKT CAP (£M)
111

BLACKROCK EMERGING EUROPE PLC

CORE INVESTMENT STRATEGY		Emerging European equities, unconstrained, focused portfolio of 20-30 stocks		
BENCHMARK		MSCI Emerging Europe 10/40		
MANAGEMENT GROUP		BlackRock IM		
FUND MANAGER		Chris Colunga, Sam Vecht [2009]		
WEBSITE		www.estplc.co.uk		

LAUNCH DATE	1994	EXCHANGE	London SE	**SYMBOL**
DOMICILE	UK	CURRENCY	GBP	**BEEP**
STOCKBROKER	Winterflood	INDEX	FTSE Fledgling	
GEARING	105	AVG DISCOUNT (%)	-10.4	
NAV (£M)	136	NET DIV YIELD (%)	1.7	
TURNOVER	120			**MKT CAP (£M)**
TER (%)	1.29	SHARPE RATIO	0.5	**123**
		VOLATILITY	1.76	
PERFORMANCE FEE	No	PERFORMANCE (10Y) (%)	7	

FONDUL PROPRIETATEA GDR

CORE INVESTMENT STRATEGY		Romania companies
BENCHMARK		Romania BET
MANAGEMENT GROUP		Franklin Templeton IM
FUND MANAGER		Marius Dan [2015]
WEBSITE		-

LAUNCH DATE	2015	EXCHANGE	London SE (SFS)	**SYMBOL**
DOMICILE	Romania	CURRENCY	USD	**FP/**
STOCKBROKER	Raiffeisen Bank	INDEX	-	
GEARING	-	AVG DISCOUNT (%)	-27.7	
NAV (£M)	2,187	NET DIV YIELD (%)	5.3	
TURNOVER	825			**MKT CAP (£M)**
TER (%)	-	SHARPE RATIO	-	**1,618**
		VOLATILITY	-	
PERFORMANCE FEE	-	PERFORMANCE (10Y) (%)	-	

EUROPEAN SMALLER COMPANIES

EUROPEAN ASSETS TRUST NV

CORE INVESTMENT STRATEGY		Mid-sized cos in continental Europe		
BENCHMARK		Euromoney Sm.European Cos ex UK		
MANAGEMENT GROUP		F&C Investments		
FUND MANAGER		Sam Cosh [2011]		
WEBSITE		www.europeanassets.co.uk		

LAUNCH DATE	1905	EXCHANGE	London SE	**SYMBOL**
DOMICILE	Netherlands	CURRENCY	GBP	
STOCKBROKER	Cenkos	INDEX	-	**EAT**
GEARING	100	AVG DISCOUNT (%)	-3.8	
NAV (£M)	438	NET DIV YIELD (%)	6.1	
TURNOVER	702			**MKT CAP (£M)**
TER (%)	1.16	SHARPE RATIO	1.4	
		VOLATILITY	1.06	**444**
PERFORMANCE FEE	No	PERFORMANCE (10Y) (%)	162	

JPMORGAN EUROPEAN SMALLER COMPANIES TRUST PLC

CORE INVESTMENT STRATEGY		Smaller cos in continental Europe		
BENCHMARK		Euromoney Sm.European Cos ex UK		
MANAGEMENT GROUP		JPMorgan AM		
FUND MANAGER		Francesco Conte, Jim Campbell [1995]		
WEBSITE		www.jpmeuropeansmallercompanies.co.uk		

LAUNCH DATE	1990	EXCHANGE	London SE	**SYMBOL**
DOMICILE	UK	CURRENCY	GBP	
STOCKBROKER	Cenkos	INDEX	FTSE Small Cap	**JESC**
GEARING	103	AVG DISCOUNT (%)	-13.6	
NAV (£M)	694	NET DIV YIELD (%)	1.2	
TURNOVER	737			**MKT CAP (£M)**
TER (%)	1.13	SHARPE RATIO	1.4	
		VOLATILITY	1.39	**616**
PERFORMANCE FEE	No	PERFORMANCE (10Y) (%)	175	

MONTANARO EUROPEAN SMALLER COMPANIES TRUST PLC

CORE INVESTMENT STRATEGY		Smaller cos in continental Europe	
BENCHMARK		Euromoney Sm.European Cos ex UK	
MANAGEMENT GROUP		Montanaro IM	
FUND MANAGER		George Cooke [2006]	
WEBSITE		www.montanaro.co.uk	

LAUNCH DATE	2006	EXCHANGE	London SE	**SYMBOL**
DOMICILE	UK	CURRENCY	GBP	**MTE**
STOCKBROKER	Cantor Fitzgerald Europe	INDEX	FTSE Small Cap	
GEARING	115	AVG DISCOUNT (%)	-14.8	
NAV (£M)	153	NET DIV YIELD (%)	1.0	
TURNOVER	90			**MKT CAP (£M)**
TER (%)	1.25	SHARPE RATIO	1.1	**135**
		VOLATILITY	0.96	
PERFORMANCE FEE	No	PERFORMANCE (10Y) (%)	131	

TR EUROPEAN GROWTH TRUST PLC

CORE INVESTMENT STRATEGY		Medium/smaller cos in continental Europe	
BENCHMARK		Euromoney Sm.European Cos ex UK	
MANAGEMENT GROUP		Janus Henderson	
FUND MANAGER		Ollie Beckett [2011]	
WEBSITE		www.treuropeangrowthtrust.com	

LAUNCH DATE	1990	EXCHANGE	London SE	**SYMBOL**
DOMICILE	UK	CURRENCY	GBP	**TRG**
STOCKBROKER	Winterflood	INDEX	FTSE Small Cap	
GEARING	110	AVG DISCOUNT (%)	-11.9	
NAV (£M)	598	NET DIV YIELD (%)	0.8	
TURNOVER	985			**MKT CAP (£M)**
TER (%)	0.78	SHARPE RATIO	1.9	**578**
		VOLATILITY	1.31	
PERFORMANCE FEE	Yes	PERFORMANCE (10Y) (%)	182	

FLEXIBLE INVESTMENT

ABERDEEN DIVERSIFIED INCOME & GROWTH TRUST PLC

CORE INVESTMENT STRATEGY	Multi-asset income	
BENCHMARK	LIBOR + 5.5% pa	
MANAGEMENT GROUP	Aberdeen AM	
FUND MANAGER	Mike Brooks & Tony Foster [2017]	
WEBSITE	www.aberdeendiversified.co.uk	

LAUNCH DATE	1905	EXCHANGE	London SE	**SYMBOL**
DOMICILE	UK	CURRENCY	GBP	
STOCKBROKER	Cenkos	INDEX	FTSE Small Cap	**ADIG**
GEARING	114	AVG DISCOUNT (%)	-8.4	
NAV (£M)	415	NET DIV YIELD (%)	4.4	
TURNOVER	766			
TER (%)	0.62	SHARPE RATIO	-	**MKT CAP (£M)**
		VOLATILITY	1.27	**390**
PERFORMANCE FEE	No	PERFORMANCE (10Y) (%)	43	

CAPITAL GEARING TRUST PLC

CORE INVESTMENT STRATEGY	Closed-end funds (focus on capital preservation)	
BENCHMARK	FTSE Equity Investment Instruments	
MANAGEMENT GROUP	CG Asset Management	
FUND MANAGER	Peter Spiller, Alastair Laing [1982]	
WEBSITE	www.capitalgearingtrust.com	

LAUNCH DATE	1963	EXCHANGE	London SE	**SYMBOL**
DOMICILE	UK	CURRENCY	GBP	
STOCKBROKER	JPM Cazenove	INDEX	FTSE Small Cap	**CGT**
GEARING	100	AVG DISCOUNT (%)	1.5	
NAV (£M)	190	NET DIV YIELD (%)	0.5	
TURNOVER	219			
TER (%)	0.86	SHARPE RATIO	0.7	**MKT CAP (£M)**
		VOLATILITY	0.77	**195**
PERFORMANCE FEE	No	PERFORMANCE (10Y) (%)	109	

ESTABLISHMENT

CORE INVESTMENT STRATEGY		Global equities (bias to Asia)		
BENCHMARK		MSCI AC World		
MANAGEMENT GROUP		Blackfrairs		
FUND MANAGER		Henry Thornton [2002]		
WEBSITE		-		

LAUNCH DATE	2002	EXCHANGE	London SE	**SYMBOL**
DOMICILE	UK	CURRENCY	GBP	**ET/**
STOCKBROKER	Stockdale	INDEX	-	
GEARING	-	AVG DISCOUNT (%)	-21.0	
NAV (£M)	54	NET DIV YIELD (%)	2.6	
TURNOVER	33			
TER (%)	-	SHARPE RATIO	1.0	**MKT CAP (£M)**
		VOLATILITY	-	**44**
PERFORMANCE FEE	-	PERFORMANCE (10Y) (%)	72	

HENDERSON ALTERNATIVE STRATEGIES TRUST PLC

CORE INVESTMENT STRATEGY		Investment trusts, hedge funds and specialist funds		
BENCHMARK		MSCI World		
MANAGEMENT GROUP		Janus Henderson		
FUND MANAGER		Ian Barrass, James de Bunsen [2013]		
WEBSITE		www.henderson.com		

LAUNCH DATE	1991	EXCHANGE	London SE	**SYMBOL**
DOMICILE	UK	CURRENCY	GBP	**HAST**
STOCKBROKER	Stifel	INDEX	FTSE Small Cap	
GEARING	100	AVG DISCOUNT (%)	-16.4	
NAV (£M)	132	NET DIV YIELD (%)	1.3	
TURNOVER	187			
TER (%)	1.01	SHARPE RATIO	0.5	**MKT CAP (£M)**
		VOLATILITY	0.97	**114**
PERFORMANCE FEE	No	PERFORMANCE (10Y) (%)	-22	

MITON GLOBAL OPPORTUNITIES PLC

CORE INVESTMENT STRATEGY		Closed-end funds		
BENCHMARK		FTSE Equity Investment Instruments		
MANAGEMENT GROUP		Miton Group		
FUND MANAGER		Nick Greenwood [2004]		
WEBSITE		www.mitongroup.com		

LAUNCH DATE	2004	EXCHANGE	London SE	**SYMBOL**
DOMICILE	UK	CURRENCY	GBP	**MIGO**
STOCKBROKER	Numis	INDEX	FTSE Fledgling	
GEARING	107	AVG DISCOUNT (%)	-4.5	
NAV (£M)	67	NET DIV YIELD (%)	-	
TURNOVER	181			
TER (%)	1.34	SHARPE RATIO	1.2	**MKT CAP (£M)**
		VOLATILITY	0.54	**63**
PERFORMANCE FEE	No	PERFORMANCE (10Y) (%)	68	

NEW STAR INVESTMENT TRUST PLC

CORE INVESTMENT STRATEGY		Largely invested in funds	
BENCHMARK		MSCI AC World	
MANAGEMENT GROUP		Brompton AM	
FUND MANAGER		Gill Lakin [2010]	
WEBSITE		www.nsitplc.com	

LAUNCH DATE	2000	EXCHANGE	London SE	**SYMBOL**
DOMICILE	UK	CURRENCY	GBP	**NSI**
STOCKBROKER	None	INDEX	FTSE Fledgling	
GEARING	100	AVG DISCOUNT (%)	-30.8	
NAV (£M)	107	NET DIV YIELD (%)	0.3	
TURNOVER	19			
TER (%)	0.92	SHARPE RATIO	1.2	**MKT CAP (£M)**
		VOLATILITY	1.31	**75**
PERFORMANCE FEE	Yes	PERFORMANCE (10Y) (%)	-27	

PERSONAL ASSETS TRUST PLC

CORE INVESTMENT STRATEGY		UK & International equities (focus on capital preservation)	
BENCHMARK		FTSE All Share	
MANAGEMENT GROUP		Self-Managed	
FUND MANAGER		Sebastian Lyon [2009]	
WEBSITE		www.patplc.co.uk	

LAUNCH DATE	1983	EXCHANGE	London SE	**SYMBOL**
DOMICILE	UK	CURRENCY	GBP	**PNL**
STOCKBROKER	JPM Cazenove	INDEX	FTSE Mid 250	
GEARING	100	AVG DISCOUNT (%)	1.1	
NAV (£M)	840	NET DIV YIELD (%)	1.4	
TURNOVER	1,066			
TER (%)	0.95	SHARPE RATIO	1.3	**MKT CAP (£M)**
		VOLATILITY	0.60	**854**
PERFORMANCE FEE	No	PERFORMANCE (10Y) (%)	87	

RIT CAPITAL PARTNERS PLC

CORE INVESTMENT STRATEGY		Global multi-asset exposure	
BENCHMARK		50% MSCI AC World £, 50% MSCI AC World Local	
MANAGEMENT GROUP		J Rothschild Capital Mgmt	
FUND MANAGER		Jacob Rothschild, Francesco Goedhuis [1988]	
WEBSITE		www.ritcap.com	

LAUNCH DATE	1988	EXCHANGE	London SE	**SYMBOL**
DOMICILE	UK	CURRENCY	GBP	**RCP**
STOCKBROKER	JPM Cazenove	INDEX	FTSE Mid 250	
GEARING	115	AVG DISCOUNT (%)	5.2	
NAV (£M)	2,825	NET DIV YIELD (%)	1.7	
TURNOVER	2,861			
TER (%)	1.14	SHARPE RATIO	1.1	**MKT CAP (£M)**
		VOLATILITY	1.20	**2,998**
PERFORMANCE FEE	Yes	PERFORMANCE (10Y) (%)	98	

RUFFER INVESTMENT COMPANY LTD

CORE INVESTMENT STRATEGY		Absolute return from global equity & debt securities	
BENCHMARK		2x Bank of England base rate	
MANAGEMENT GROUP		Ruffer	
FUND MANAGER		Hamish Baillie, Steve Russell [2004]	
WEBSITE		www.ruffer.co.uk	

LAUNCH DATE	2004	EXCHANGE	London SE	**SYMBOL**
DOMICILE	Guernsey	CURRENCY	GBP	**RICA**
STOCKBROKER	Cenkos	INDEX	-	
GEARING	100	AVG DISCOUNT (%)	2.0	
NAV (£M)	381	NET DIV YIELD (%)	1.1	
TURNOVER	657			**MKT CAP (£M)**
TER (%)	1.17	SHARPE RATIO	0.8	**393**
		VOLATILITY	0.52	
PERFORMANCE FEE	No	PERFORMANCE (10Y) (%)	151	

SENECA GLOBAL INCOME & GROWTH

CORE INVESTMENT STRATEGY		UK equities & overseas/multi-asset exposure via funds	
BENCHMARK		FTSE All Share	
MANAGEMENT GROUP		Seneca Investment Managers	
FUND MANAGER		Alan Borrows, Peter Elston [2005]	
WEBSITE		www.senecaim.com	

LAUNCH DATE	2005	EXCHANGE	London SE	**SYMBOL**
DOMICILE	UK	CURRENCY	GBP	**SIGT**
STOCKBROKER	Cantor Fitzgerald Europe	INDEX	FTSE Fledgling	
GEARING	110	AVG DISCOUNT (%)	0.6	
NAV (£M)	73	NET DIV YIELD (%)	3.5	
TURNOVER	166			**MKT CAP (£M)**
TER (%)	1.59	SHARPE RATIO	2.0	**75**
		VOLATILITY	0.73	
PERFORMANCE FEE	No	PERFORMANCE (10Y) (%)	79	

SYNCONA LTD

CORE INVESTMENT STRATEGY		Switching from portfolio of funds to life sciences portfolio	
BENCHMARK		10% p.a.	
MANAGEMENT GROUP		Self-Managed	
FUND MANAGER		Tom Henderson, Martin Murphy [2012]	
WEBSITE		www.synconaltd.com	

LAUNCH DATE	2012	EXCHANGE	London SE	**SYMBOL**
DOMICILE	Guernsey	CURRENCY	GBP	**SYNC**
STOCKBROKER	Numis, JPM Cazenove	INDEX	FTSE Mid 250	
GEARING	100	AVG DISCOUNT (%)	7.9	
NAV (£M)	888	NET DIV YIELD (%)	1.4	
TURNOVER	945			**MKT CAP (£M)**
TER (%)	1.5	SHARPE RATIO	0.5	**1,113**
		VOLATILITY	0.83	
PERFORMANCE FEE	No	PERFORMANCE (10Y) (%)	-	

TETRAGON FINANCIAL GROUP LTD

CORE INVESTMENT STRATEGY		Alternative assets (CLO equity, credit, equity, real estate) and stake in management group	
BENCHMARK		12.5% p.a.	
MANAGEMENT GROUP		Tetragon Financial Management	
FUND MANAGER		Paddy Dear [2007]	
WEBSITE		www.tetragoninv.com	

LAUNCH DATE	2007	EXCHANGE	London SE (SFS), Euronext	**SYMBOL**
DOMICILE	Guernsey	CURRENCY	USD	
STOCKBROKER	Stifel, Cantor Fitzgerald Europe	INDEX	-	**TFG**
GEARING	-	AVG DISCOUNT (%)	-39.4	
NAV (£M)	1,489	NET DIV YIELD (%)	5.4	
TURNOVER	312			**MKT CAP (£M)**
TER (%)	-	SHARPE RATIO	1.6	
		VOLATILITY	1.42	**946**
PERFORMANCE FEE	-	PERFORMANCE (10Y) (%)	379	

GLOBAL

ALLIANCE TRUST PLC

CORE INVESTMENT STRATEGY	Multi-manager global equity
BENCHMARK	MSCI AC World
MANAGEMENT GROUP	Willis Towers Watson
FUND MANAGER	Craig Baker [2017]
WEBSITE	www.alliancetrust.co.uk

LAUNCH DATE	1905	EXCHANGE	London SE	**SYMBOL**
DOMICILE	UK	CURRENCY	GBP	
STOCKBROKER	Canaccord	INDEX	FTSE Mid 250	**ATST**
GEARING	109	AVG DISCOUNT (%)	-6.7	
NAV (£M)	2,692	NET DIV YIELD (%)	1.9	
TURNOVER	12,209			**MKT CAP (£M)**
TER (%)	0.54	SHARPE RATIO	1.3	
		VOLATILITY	1.13	**2,534**
PERFORMANCE FEE	No	PERFORMANCE (10Y) (%)	164	

BANKERS INVESTMENT TRUST PLC

CORE INVESTMENT STRATEGY	Global equities, typically 50% in UK
BENCHMARK	40% All Share, 60% MSCI World ex UK
MANAGEMENT GROUP	Janus Henderson
FUND MANAGER	Alex Crooke [2003]
WEBSITE	www.bankersinvestmenttrust.com

LAUNCH DATE	1905	EXCHANGE	London SE	SYMBOL
DOMICILE	UK	CURRENCY	GBP	**BNKR**
STOCKBROKER	JPM Cazenove	INDEX	FTSE Mid 250	
GEARING	106	AVG DISCOUNT (%)	-5.6	
NAV (£M)	1,050	NET DIV YIELD (%)	2.2	
TURNOVER	988			
TER (%)	0.52	SHARPE RATIO	0.9	MKT CAP (£M)
		VOLATILITY	1.21	**1,023**
PERFORMANCE FEE	No	PERFORMANCE (10Y) (%)	168	

BRITISH EMPIRE TRUST PLC

CORE INVESTMENT STRATEGY	Global stocks and funds trading at discounts
BENCHMARK	MSCI AC World ex US
MANAGEMENT GROUP	Asset Value Investors
FUND MANAGER	Joe Bauernfreund [2015]
WEBSITE	www.british-empire.co.uk

LAUNCH DATE	1905	EXCHANGE	London SE	SYMBOL
DOMICILE	UK	CURRENCY	GBP	**BTEM**
STOCKBROKER	Jefferies	INDEX	FTSE Mid 250	
GEARING	108	AVG DISCOUNT (%)	-10.4	
NAV (£M)	923	NET DIV YIELD (%)	2.0	
TURNOVER	1,821			
TER (%)	0.9	SHARPE RATIO	1.1	MKT CAP (£M)
		VOLATILITY	1.02	**830**
PERFORMANCE FEE	No	PERFORMANCE (10Y) (%)	90	

BRUNNER INVESTMENT TRUST PLC

CORE INVESTMENT STRATEGY	Global equities, typically 50% in UK
BENCHMARK	30% All Share, 70% MSCI World ex UK
MANAGEMENT GROUP	Allianz Global Investors
FUND MANAGER	Lucy MacDonald [2010]
WEBSITE	www.brunner.co.uk

LAUNCH DATE	1905	EXCHANGE	London SE	SYMBOL
DOMICILE	UK	CURRENCY	GBP	**BUT**
STOCKBROKER	Stifel	INDEX	FTSE Small Cap	
GEARING	114	AVG DISCOUNT (%)	-14.6	
NAV (£M)	355	NET DIV YIELD (%)	2.2	
TURNOVER	284			
TER (%)	0.79	SHARPE RATIO	0.9	MKT CAP (£M)
		VOLATILITY	1.06	**309**
PERFORMANCE FEE	No	PERFORMANCE (10Y) (%)	118	

CALEDONIA INVESTMENTS PLC

CORE INVESTMENT STRATEGY	Focused portfolio of long-term holdings (primarily UK)	
BENCHMARK	FTSE All Share	
MANAGEMENT GROUP	Self-Managed	
FUND MANAGER	Will Wyatt [2010]	
WEBSITE	www.caledonia.com	

LAUNCH DATE	1960	EXCHANGE	London SE	**SYMBOL**	
DOMICILE	UK	CURRENCY	GBP		
STOCKBROKER	Winterflood. JPM Cazenove	INDEX	FTSE Mid 250	**CLDN**	
GEARING	100	AVG DISCOUNT (%)	-17.4		
NAV (£M)	1,816	NET DIV YIELD (%)	2.0		
TURNOVER	1,027				
TER (%)	1.14	SHARPE RATIO	0.8	**MKT CAP (£M)**	
		VOLATILITY	1.20	**1,525**	
PERFORMANCE FEE	No	PERFORMANCE (10Y) (%)	72		

EP GLOBAL OPPORTUNITIES TRUST PLC

CORE INVESTMENT STRATEGY	Global equities (no focus on index weights)	
BENCHMARK	MSCI World	
MANAGEMENT GROUP	Edinburgh Partners	
FUND MANAGER	Sandy Nairn [2003]	
WEBSITE	www.edinburghpartners.com	

LAUNCH DATE	2003	EXCHANGE	London SE	**SYMBOL**	
DOMICILE	UK	CURRENCY	GBP		
STOCKBROKER	None	INDEX	FTSE Small Cap	**EPG**	
GEARING	100	AVG DISCOUNT (%)	-4.8		
NAV (£M)	149	NET DIV YIELD (%)	1.4		
TURNOVER	108				
TER (%)	1	SHARPE RATIO	0.8	**MKT CAP (£M)**	
		VOLATILITY	0.96	**140**	
PERFORMANCE FEE	No	PERFORMANCE (10Y) (%)	128		

EDINBURGH WORLDWIDE INVESTMENT TRUST PLC

CORE INVESTMENT STRATEGY	Global equities of smaller, less mature, companies	
BENCHMARK	S&P Citigroup Global Small Cap	
MANAGEMENT GROUP	Baillie Gifford	
FUND MANAGER	Douglas Brodie [2014]	
WEBSITE	www.bailliegifford.com	

LAUNCH DATE	1998	EXCHANGE	London SE	**SYMBOL**	
DOMICILE	UK	CURRENCY	GBP		
STOCKBROKER	Numis	INDEX	FTSE Small Cap	**EWI**	
GEARING	111	AVG DISCOUNT (%)	-9.1		
NAV (£M)	339	NET DIV YIELD (%)	-		
TURNOVER	333				
TER (%)	0.92	SHARPE RATIO	1.4	**MKT CAP (£M)**	
		VOLATILITY	1.47	**317**	
PERFORMANCE FEE	No	PERFORMANCE (10Y) (%)	182		

F&C GLOBAL SMALLER COMPANIES PLC

CORE INVESTMENT STRATEGY		UK & International smaller cos	
BENCHMARK		30% Numis SmCos ex ICs, 70% MSCI AC World ex UK Small Cap	
MANAGEMENT GROUP		F&C Investments	
FUND MANAGER		Peter Ewins [2005]	
WEBSITE		www.fandcglobalsmallers.com	

LAUNCH DATE	1905	EXCHANGE	London SE	**SYMBOL**
DOMICILE	UK	CURRENCY	GBP	
STOCKBROKER	Stifel	INDEX	FTSE Small Cap	**FCS**
GEARING	104	AVG DISCOUNT (%)	0.5	
NAV (£M)	767	NET DIV YIELD (%)	0.9	
TURNOVER	632			
TER (%)	0.61	SHARPE RATIO	1.2	**MKT CAP (£M)**
		VOLATILITY	1.04	**776**
PERFORMANCE FEE	No	PERFORMANCE (10Y) (%)	244	

F&C MANAGED PORTFOLIO TRUST PLC

CORE INVESTMENT STRATEGY		Fund of investment cos (in-house & third party)
BENCHMARK		FTSE Equity Investment Instruments
MANAGEMENT GROUP		F&C Investments
FUND MANAGER		Peter Hewitt [2008]
WEBSITE		www.fctr.co.uk

LAUNCH DATE	2008	EXCHANGE	London SE	**SYMBOL**
DOMICILE	UK	CURRENCY	GBP	
STOCKBROKER	Dickson Minto	INDEX	-	**FMPG**
GEARING	100	AVG DISCOUNT (%)	0.0	
NAV (£M)	66	NET DIV YIELD (%)	2.8	
TURNOVER	49			
TER (%)	0.95	SHARPE RATIO	1.3	**MKT CAP (£M)**
		VOLATILITY	0.95	**66**
PERFORMANCE FEE	Yes	PERFORMANCE (10Y) (%)	-	

FOREIGN & COLONIAL INVESTMENT TRUST PLC

CORE INVESTMENT STRATEGY		Global equities (target 10% private equity)
BENCHMARK		MSCI AC World
MANAGEMENT GROUP		F&C Investments
FUND MANAGER		Paul Nevin [2014]
WEBSITE		www.foreignandcolonial.com

LAUNCH DATE	1905	EXCHANGE	London SE	**SYMBOL**
DOMICILE	UK	CURRENCY	GBP	
STOCKBROKER	JPM Cazenove	INDEX	FTSE Mid 250	**FRCL**
GEARING	107	AVG DISCOUNT (%)	-8.1	
NAV (£M)	3,548	NET DIV YIELD (%)	1.6	
TURNOVER	2,381			
TER (%)	0.54	SHARPE RATIO	1.4	**MKT CAP (£M)**
		VOLATILITY	1.22	**3,355**
PERFORMANCE FEE	No	PERFORMANCE (10Y) (%)	162	

HANSA TRUST PLC

CORE INVESTMENT STRATEGY		UK Equities; Core Funds; Eclectic & Diversifying Funds; and Strategic Assets	
BENCHMARK		MSCI AC World	
MANAGEMENT GROUP		Hansa Capital	
FUND MANAGER		William Salomon, Alex Letchfield [2003]	
WEBSITE		www.hansatrust.com	

LAUNCH DATE	1905	EXCHANGE	London SE	**SYMBOL**
DOMICILE	UK	CURRENCY	GBP	**HAN**
STOCKBROKER	Winterflood	INDEX	FTSE Small Cap	
GEARING	100	AVG DISCOUNT (%)	-31.0	
NAV (£M)	108	NET DIV YIELD (%)	1.7	
TURNOVER	46			
TER (%)	1.09	SHARPE RATIO	0.0	**MKT CAP (£M)**
		VOLATILITY	1.23	**76**
PERFORMANCE FEE	No	PERFORMANCE (10Y) (%)	15	

HANSA TRUST PLC

CORE INVESTMENT STRATEGY		UK Equities; Core Funds; Eclectic & Diversifying Funds; and Strategic Assets	
BENCHMARK		MSCI AC World	
MANAGEMENT GROUP		Hansa Capital	
FUND MANAGER		William Salomon, Alex Letchfield [2003]	
WEBSITE		www.hansatrust.com	

LAUNCH DATE	1905	EXCHANGE	London SE	**SYMBOL**
DOMICILE	UK	CURRENCY	GBP	**HANA**
STOCKBROKER	Winterflood	INDEX	FTSE Small Cap	
GEARING	100	AVG DISCOUNT (%)	-32.4	
NAV (£M)	215	NET DIV YIELD (%)	1.7	
TURNOVER	156			
TER (%)	1.09	SHARPE RATIO	0.0	**MKT CAP (£M)**
		VOLATILITY	1.10	**149**
PERFORMANCE FEE	No	PERFORMANCE (10Y) (%)	16	

INDEPENDENT INVESTMENT TRUST (THE) PLC

CORE INVESTMENT STRATEGY		UK & International equities	
BENCHMARK		FTSE All Share	
MANAGEMENT GROUP		Self-Managed	
FUND MANAGER		Max Ward [2000]	
WEBSITE		www.independentinvestmenttrust.co.uk	

LAUNCH DATE	2000	EXCHANGE	London SE	**SYMBOL**
DOMICILE	UK	CURRENCY	GBP	**IIT**
STOCKBROKER	JPM Cazenove	INDEX	FTSE Small Cap	
GEARING	100	AVG DISCOUNT (%)	-4.5	
NAV (£M)	328	NET DIV YIELD (%)	1.2	
TURNOVER	94			
TER (%)	0.34	SHARPE RATIO	1.5	**MKT CAP (£M)**
		VOLATILITY	1.14	**338**
PERFORMANCE FEE	No	PERFORMANCE (10Y) (%)	174	

JPMORGAN ELECT PLC

CORE INVESTMENT STRATEGY		JPMorgan funds & other inv.trusts	
BENCHMARK		50% All Share, 50% MSCI World ex UK	
MANAGEMENT GROUP		JPMorgan AM	
FUND MANAGER		Katy Thorneycroft [2001]	
WEBSITE		www.jpmelect.co.uk	

LAUNCH DATE	1999	EXCHANGE	London SE	**SYMBOL**
DOMICILE	UK	CURRENCY	GBP	**JPE**
STOCKBROKER	Winterflood	INDEX	-	
GEARING	100	AVG DISCOUNT (%)	-2.4	
NAV (£M)	263	NET DIV YIELD (%)	1.4	
TURNOVER	113			**MKT CAP (£M)**
TER (%)	0.58	SHARPE RATIO	1.1	**258**
		VOLATILITY	0.89	
PERFORMANCE FEE	No	PERFORMANCE (10Y) (%)	130	

LINDSELL TRAIN INVESTMENT TRUST (THE) PLC

CORE INVESTMENT STRATEGY		Absolute return from equities, bonds & cash	
BENCHMARK		UK Treasury 3.5% 2068 + 0.5%	
MANAGEMENT GROUP		Lindsell Train	
FUND MANAGER		Nick Train [2001]	
WEBSITE		www.lindselltrain.com	

LAUNCH DATE	2001	EXCHANGE	London SE	**SYMBOL**
DOMICILE	UK	CURRENCY	GBP	**LTI**
STOCKBROKER	JPM Cazenove	INDEX	FTSE Small Cap	
GEARING	100	AVG DISCOUNT (%)	38.0	
NAV (£M)	136	NET DIV YIELD (%)	1.9	
TURNOVER	239			**MKT CAP (£M)**
TER (%)	0.98	SHARPE RATIO	1.3	**166**
		VOLATILITY	1.01	
PERFORMANCE FEE	Yes	PERFORMANCE (10Y) (%)	466	

LAW DEBENTURE CORPORATION (THE) PLC

CORE INVESTMENT STRATEGY		UK & International equities, with trustee business	
BENCHMARK		FTSE All Share	
MANAGEMENT GROUP		Janus Henderson	
FUND MANAGER		James Henderson, Laura Foll [2003]	
WEBSITE		www.lawdebenture.com	

LAUNCH DATE	1905	EXCHANGE	London SE	**SYMBOL**
DOMICILE	UK	CURRENCY	GBP	**LWDB**
STOCKBROKER	JPM Cazenove	INDEX	FTSE Small Cap	
GEARING	114	AVG DISCOUNT (%)	-9.7	
NAV (£M)	767	NET DIV YIELD (%)	2.8	
TURNOVER	746			**MKT CAP (£M)**
TER (%)	0.43	SHARPE RATIO	0.3	**718**
		VOLATILITY	1.18	
PERFORMANCE FEE	No	PERFORMANCE (10Y) (%)	141	

MAJEDIE INVESTMENTS PLC

CORE INVESTMENT STRATEGY	UK & International equities through Majedie funds
BENCHMARK	70% All Share, 30% MSCI World ex UK
MANAGEMENT GROUP	Majedie AM
FUND MANAGER	William Barlow [2014]
WEBSITE	www.majedie.co.uk

LAUNCH DATE	1910	EXCHANGE	London SE
DOMICILE	UK	CURRENCY	GBP
STOCKBROKER	JPM Cazenove	INDEX	FTSE Small Cap
GEARING	119	AVG DISCOUNT (%)	-10.0
NAV (£M)	172	NET DIV YIELD (%)	3.4
TURNOVER	77		
TER (%)	1.35	SHARPE RATIO	0.7
		VOLATILITY	1.25
PERFORMANCE FEE	No	PERFORMANCE (10Y) (%)	11

SYMBOL
MAJE

MKT CAP (£M)
146

MONKS INVESTMENT TRUST (THE) PLC

CORE INVESTMENT STRATEGY	Global equities
BENCHMARK	MSCI World
MANAGEMENT GROUP	Baillie Gifford
FUND MANAGER	Charles Plowden [2015]
WEBSITE	www.monksinvestmenttrust.co.uk

LAUNCH DATE	1905	EXCHANGE	London SE
DOMICILE	UK	CURRENCY	GBP
STOCKBROKER	Canaccord	INDEX	FTSE Mid 250
GEARING	107	AVG DISCOUNT (%)	-3.8
NAV (£M)	1,547	NET DIV YIELD (%)	0.2
TURNOVER	2,550		
TER (%)	0.59	SHARPE RATIO	1.6
		VOLATILITY	1.17
PERFORMANCE FEE	No	PERFORMANCE (10Y) (%)	149

SYMBOL
MNKS

MKT CAP (£M)
1,524

MARTIN CURRIE GLOBAL PORTFOLIO TRUST PLC

CORE INVESTMENT STRATEGY	UK & International equities
BENCHMARK	MSCI World
MANAGEMENT GROUP	Martin Currie IM
FUND MANAGER	Tom Walker [2000]
WEBSITE	www.martincurrieglobal.com

LAUNCH DATE	1999	EXCHANGE	London SE
DOMICILE	UK	CURRENCY	GBP
STOCKBROKER	JPM Cazenove	INDEX	FTSE Small Cap
GEARING	100	AVG DISCOUNT (%)	-0.5
NAV (£M)	228	NET DIV YIELD (%)	1.7
TURNOVER	130		
TER (%)	0.73	SHARPE RATIO	1.0
		VOLATILITY	1.17
PERFORMANCE FEE	Yes	PERFORMANCE (10Y) (%)	161

SYMBOL
MNP

MKT CAP (£M)
227

MID WYND INTERNATIONAL INV TRUST PLC

CORE INVESTMENT STRATEGY		Global equities	
BENCHMARK		MSCI AC World	
MANAGEMENT GROUP		Artemis IM	
FUND MANAGER		Simon Edelsten, Alex Illingworth, Rosanna Burcheri [2014]	
WEBSITE		www.artemisfunds.com	

LAUNCH DATE	1981	EXCHANGE	London SE	**SYMBOL**
DOMICILE	UK	CURRENCY	GBP	**MWY**
STOCKBROKER	JPM Cazenove	INDEX	FTSE Fledgling	
GEARING	104	AVG DISCOUNT (%)	0.7	
NAV (£M)	151	NET DIV YIELD (%)	1.0	
TURNOVER	116			**MKT CAP (£M)**
TER (%)	0.75	SHARPE RATIO	1.9	**152**
		VOLATILITY	0.69	
PERFORMANCE FEE	No	PERFORMANCE (10Y) (%)	233	

SCOTTISH INVESTMENT TRUST PLC

CORE INVESTMENT STRATEGY		Global equities	
BENCHMARK		MSCI AC World	
MANAGEMENT GROUP		Self-Managed	
FUND MANAGER		Alasdair McKinnon [2014]	
WEBSITE		www.thescottish.co.uk	

LAUNCH DATE	1905	EXCHANGE	London SE	**SYMBOL**
DOMICILE	UK	CURRENCY	GBP	**SCIN**
STOCKBROKER	Canaccord	INDEX	FTSE Mid 250	
GEARING	111	AVG DISCOUNT (%)	-10.1	
NAV (£M)	746	NET DIV YIELD (%)	1.7	
TURNOVER	1,803			**MKT CAP (£M)**
TER (%)	0.59	SHARPE RATIO	1.0	**678**
		VOLATILITY	1.15	
PERFORMANCE FEE	No	PERFORMANCE (10Y) (%)	114	

SCOTTISH MORTGAGE INVESTMENT TRUST PLC

CORE INVESTMENT STRATEGY		Global equities	
BENCHMARK		MSCI AC World	
MANAGEMENT GROUP		Baillie Gifford	
FUND MANAGER		James Anderson, Tom Slater [2000]	
WEBSITE		www.bailliegifford.com	

LAUNCH DATE	1905	EXCHANGE	London SE	**SYMBOL**
DOMICILE	UK	CURRENCY	GBP	**SMT**
STOCKBROKER	Cenkos, Jefferies	INDEX	FTSE 100	
GEARING	109	AVG DISCOUNT (%)	2.5	
NAV (£M)	5,922	NET DIV YIELD (%)	0.7	
TURNOVER	10,557			**MKT CAP (£M)**
TER (%)	0.44	SHARPE RATIO	1.4	**6,080**
		VOLATILITY	1.33	
PERFORMANCE FEE	No	PERFORMANCE (10Y) (%)	341	

WITAN INVESTMENT TRUST PLC

CORE INVESTMENT STRATEGY		Multi-manager global equity		
BENCHMARK		MSCI AC World		
MANAGEMENT GROUP		Self-Managed		
FUND MANAGER		Andrew Bell [2010]		
WEBSITE		www.witan.com		

LAUNCH DATE	1905	EXCHANGE	London SE	**SYMBOL**
DOMICILE	UK	CURRENCY	GBP	
STOCKBROKER	JPM Cazenove	INDEX	FTSE Mid 250	**WTAN**
GEARING	112	AVG DISCOUNT (%)	-4.3	
NAV (£M)	1,890	NET DIV YIELD (%)	1.9	
TURNOVER	2,032			**MKT CAP (£M)**
TER (%)	0.79	SHARPE RATIO	1.0	
		VOLATILITY	1.12	**1,863**
PERFORMANCE FEE	Yes	PERFORMANCE (10Y) (%)	184	

LAZARD WORLD TRUST FUND

CORE INVESTMENT STRATEGY		Global closed-end funds		
BENCHMARK		MSCI AC World ex US		
MANAGEMENT GROUP		Lazard AM		
FUND MANAGER		Kun Deng [1905]		
WEBSITE		www.lazardworldtrustfund.com		

LAUNCH DATE	1991	EXCHANGE	London SE	**SYMBOL**
DOMICILE	Luxembourg	CURRENCY	GBP	
STOCKBROKER	Cenkos	INDEX	-	**WTR**
GEARING	100	AVG DISCOUNT (%)	-12.5	
NAV (£M)	145	NET DIV YIELD (%)	3.5	
TURNOVER	369			**MKT CAP (£M)**
TER (%)	1.35	SHARPE RATIO	1.3	
		VOLATILITY	1.71	**137**
PERFORMANCE FEE	Yes	PERFORMANCE (10Y) (%)	66	

GLOBAL EMERGING MARKETS

ABERDEEN EMERGING MARKETS INVESTMENT COMPANY LTD

CORE INVESTMENT STRATEGY		Emerging market open and closed-end funds	
BENCHMARK		MSCI Emerging Markets	
MANAGEMENT GROUP		Aberdeen Emerging Capital	
FUND MANAGER		Andrew Lister, Bernard Moody [1998]	
WEBSITE		www.aberdeenemergingmarkets.co.uk	

LAUNCH DATE	1998	EXCHANGE	London SE
DOMICILE	Guernsey	CURRENCY	GBP
STOCKBROKER	Stockdale	INDEX	-
GEARING	107	AVG DISCOUNT (%)	-13.9
NAV (£M)	359	NET DIV YIELD (%)	0.8
TURNOVER	296		
TER (%)	1.1	SHARPE RATIO	0.7
		VOLATILITY	1.13
PERFORMANCE FEE	Yes	PERFORMANCE (10Y) (%)	56

SYMBOL
AEMC

MKT CAP (£M)
315

ABERDEEN FRONTIER MARKETS INVESTMENT COMPANY LTD

CORE INVESTMENT STRATEGY		Investing in companies operating in Frontier Markets	
BENCHMARK		MSCI Frontier Markets	
MANAGEMENT GROUP		Aberdeen Emerging Capital	
FUND MANAGER		Devan Kaloo, Joanne Irvine [2017]	
WEBSITE		www.aberdeenfrontiermarkets.co.uk	

LAUNCH DATE	2007	EXCHANGE	AIM
DOMICILE	Guernsey	CURRENCY	GBP
STOCKBROKER	Numis	INDEX	AIM All-Share
GEARING	100	AVG DISCOUNT (%)	-6.6
NAV (£M)	60	NET DIV YIELD (%)	3.2
TURNOVER	127		
TER (%)	1.71	SHARPE RATIO	0.4
		VOLATILITY	1.13
PERFORMANCE FEE	Yes	PERFORMANCE (10Y) (%)	39

SYMBOL
AFMC

MKT CAP (£M)
57

ASHMORE GLOBAL OPPORTUNITIES LTD

CORE INVESTMENT STRATEGY		Emerging market strategies inc. equity, debt & special situations
BENCHMARK		MSCI Emerging Markets
MANAGEMENT GROUP		Ashmore IM
FUND MANAGER		Mark Coombs, Jerome Booth, Seumas Dawes, Julian Green [2007]
WEBSITE		www.agol.com

LAUNCH DATE	2007	EXCHANGE	London SE
DOMICILE	Guernsey	CURRENCY	USD
STOCKBROKER	Jefferies	INDEX	FTSE Fledgling
GEARING	100	AVG DISCOUNT (%)	-30.6
NAV (£M)	34	NET DIV YIELD (%)	-
TURNOVER	4		
TER (%)	0.7	SHARPE RATIO	0.7
		VOLATILITY	1.26
PERFORMANCE FEE	Yes	PERFORMANCE (10Y) (%)	-

SYMBOL AGOU

MKT CAP (£M) 22

AFRICA OPPORTUNITY FUND LTD

CORE INVESTMENT STRATEGY		Value, arbitrage and special situations opportunities in Africa
BENCHMARK		MSCI Frontier Markets Africa
MANAGEMENT GROUP		Africa Opportunity Partners
FUND MANAGER		Francis Daniels, Robert Knapp [2007]
WEBSITE		-

LAUNCH DATE	2007	EXCHANGE	SFS
DOMICILE	Cayman Isles	CURRENCY	USD
STOCKBROKER	Liberum	INDEX	-
GEARING	100	AVG DISCOUNT (%)	-24.9
NAV (£M)	52	NET DIV YIELD (%)	3.3
TURNOVER	81		
TER (%)	4.54	SHARPE RATIO	-0.5
		VOLATILITY	1.16
PERFORMANCE FEE	Yes	PERFORMANCE (10Y) (%)	14

SYMBOL AOF

MKT CAP (£M) 38

APQ GLOBAL

CORE INVESTMENT STRATEGY		Emerging markets direct lending, operational control of public & private companies, acquistion of real estate & commodity companies
BENCHMARK		6% p.a.
MANAGEMENT GROUP		APQ Capital Management
FUND MANAGER		Bart Turtelboom [2016]
WEBSITE		-

LAUNCH DATE	2016	EXCHANGE	AIM
DOMICILE	Guernsey	CURRENCY	GBP
STOCKBROKER	N+1 Singer	INDEX	-
GEARING	-	AVG DISCOUNT (%)	5.2
NAV (£M)	75	NET DIV YIELD (%)	5.8
TURNOVER	62		
TER (%)	-	SHARPE RATIO	-
		VOLATILITY	-
PERFORMANCE FEE	-	PERFORMANCE (10Y) (%)	-

SYMBOL APQ

MKT CAP (£M) 80

BLACKROCK FRONTIERS INVESTMENT TRUST PLC

CORE INVESTMENT STRATEGY		Investing in companies operating in Frontier Markets	
BENCHMARK		MSCI Frontier Markets	
MANAGEMENT GROUP		BlackRock IM	
FUND MANAGER		Sam Vecht [2010]	
WEBSITE		www.blackrock.co.uk	

LAUNCH DATE	2010	EXCHANGE	London SE	**SYMBOL**
DOMICILE	UK	CURRENCY	GBP	**BRFI**
STOCKBROKER	Winterflood	INDEX	FTSE Small Cap	
GEARING	127	AVG DISCOUNT (%)	1.4	
NAV (£M)	266	NET DIV YIELD (%)	3.4	
TURNOVER	551			
TER (%)	1.37	SHARPE RATIO	0.5	**MKT CAP (£M)**
		VOLATILITY	1.29	**270**
PERFORMANCE FEE	Yes	PERFORMANCE (10Y) (%)	-	

FUNDSMITH EMERGING EQUITIES TRUST

CORE INVESTMENT STRATEGY		Emerging market equities	
BENCHMARK		MSCI Emerging Markets	
MANAGEMENT GROUP		Fundsmith	
FUND MANAGER		Terry Smith [2014]	
WEBSITE		www.feetplc.co.uk	

LAUNCH DATE	2014	EXCHANGE	London SE	**SYMBOL**
DOMICILE	UK	CURRENCY	GBP	**FEET**
STOCKBROKER	Investec	INDEX	FTSE Small Cap	
GEARING	100	AVG DISCOUNT (%)	1.3	
NAV (£M)	292	NET DIV YIELD (%)	-	
TURNOVER	630			
TER (%)	1.85	SHARPE RATIO	0.2	**MKT CAP (£M)**
		VOLATILITY	0.97	**286**
PERFORMANCE FEE	No	PERFORMANCE (10Y) (%)	-	

GENESIS EMERGING MARKETS FUND LTD

CORE INVESTMENT STRATEGY		Emerging market equities	
BENCHMARK		MSCI Emerging Markets	
MANAGEMENT GROUP		Genesis Fund Managers	
FUND MANAGER		Andrew Elder [2004]	
WEBSITE		www.giml.co.uk	

LAUNCH DATE	1989	EXCHANGE	London SE	**SYMBOL**
DOMICILE	Guernsey	CURRENCY	GBP	**GSS**
STOCKBROKER	JPM Cazenove, Smith & Williamson	INDEX	FTSE Mid 250	
GEARING	100	AVG DISCOUNT (%)	-12.7	
NAV (£M)	1,080	NET DIV YIELD (%)	-	
TURNOVER	912			
TER (%)	1.43	SHARPE RATIO	0.4	**MKT CAP (£M)**
		VOLATILITY	1.18	**945**
PERFORMANCE FEE	No	PERFORMANCE (10Y) (%)	123	

JUPITER EMERGING & FRONTIER INCOME TRUST PLC

CORE INVESTMENT STRATEGY	Emerging & Frontier markets companies	
BENCHMARK	MSCI Emerging Markets	
MANAGEMENT GROUP	Jupiter AM	
FUND MANAGER	Ross Teverson, Charlie Sunnucks [2017]	
WEBSITE	www.jupiteram.com	

LAUNCH DATE	2017	EXCHANGE	London SE	**SYMBOL**
DOMICILE	UK	CURRENCY	GBP	**JEFI**
STOCKBROKER	Peel Hunt	INDEX	-	
GEARING	114	AVG DISCOUNT (%)	1.7	
NAV (£M)	100	NET DIV YIELD (%)	3.7	
TURNOVER	190			
TER (%)	-	SHARPE RATIO	-	**MKT CAP (£M)**
		VOLATILITY	0.44	**101**
PERFORMANCE FEE	No	PERFORMANCE (10Y) (%)	-	

JPMORGAN GLOBAL EMERGING MARKETS INCOME TRUST PLC

CORE INVESTMENT STRATEGY	Predominantly listed emerging markets equities, aiming to provide dividend income and long-term capital growth	
BENCHMARK	MSCI Emerging Markets	
MANAGEMENT GROUP	JPMorgan AM	
FUND MANAGER	Jeffrey Roskell, Omar Negyal, Amit Mehta [2010]	
WEBSITE	www.jpmglobalemergingmarketsincome.co.uk	

LAUNCH DATE	2010	EXCHANGE	London SE	**SYMBOL**
DOMICILE	UK	CURRENCY	GBP	**JEMI**
STOCKBROKER	Winterflood	INDEX	FTSE Small Cap	
GEARING	109	AVG DISCOUNT (%)	-3.4	
NAV (£M)	395	NET DIV YIELD (%)	3.8	
TURNOVER	691			
TER (%)	1.35	SHARPE RATIO	0.3	**MKT CAP (£M)**
		VOLATILITY	1.11	**379**
PERFORMANCE FEE	No	PERFORMANCE (10Y) (%)	-	

JPMORGAN EMERGING MARKETS INV TRUST PLC

CORE INVESTMENT STRATEGY	Emerging market equities	
BENCHMARK	MSCI Emerging Markets	
MANAGEMENT GROUP	JPMorgan AM	
FUND MANAGER	Austin Forey [1994]	
WEBSITE	www.jpmemergingmarkets.co.uk	

LAUNCH DATE	1991	EXCHANGE	London SE	**SYMBOL**
DOMICILE	UK	CURRENCY	GBP	**JMG**
STOCKBROKER	Winterflood	INDEX	FTSE Mid 250	
GEARING	101	AVG DISCOUNT (%)	-13.1	
NAV (£M)	1,213	NET DIV YIELD (%)	1.1	
TURNOVER	1,324			
TER (%)	1.16	SHARPE RATIO	0.8	**MKT CAP (£M)**
		VOLATILITY	1.37	**1,060**
PERFORMANCE FEE	No	PERFORMANCE (10Y) (%)	130	

TERRA CAPITAL PLC

CORE INVESTMENT STRATEGY	Frontier markets, including corporate activism/value stocks
BENCHMARK	MSCI Frontier Markets
MANAGEMENT GROUP	Terra Partners AM
FUND MANAGER	Howard Golden, Filip Montfort, Yarden Mariuma [2006]
WEBSITE	www.terracapitalplc.com

LAUNCH DATE	2006	EXCHANGE	AIM	**SYMBOL**
DOMICILE	Isle of Man	CURRENCY	USD	
STOCKBROKER	Panmure Gordon	INDEX	AIM All-Share	**TCA**
GEARING	100	AVG DISCOUNT (%)	-15.4	
NAV (£M)	53	NET DIV YIELD (%)	-	
TURNOVER	256			
TER (%)	2.02	SHARPE RATIO	1.1	**MKT CAP (£M)**
		VOLATILITY	1.20	**45**
PERFORMANCE FEE	Yes	PERFORMANCE (10Y) (%)	82	

TEMPLETON EMERGING MARKETS INVESTMENT TRUST PLC

CORE INVESTMENT STRATEGY	Emerging market equities
BENCHMARK	MSCI Emerging Markets
MANAGEMENT GROUP	Franklin Templeton IM
FUND MANAGER	Carlos Hardenberg [2015]
WEBSITE	www.temit.co.uk

LAUNCH DATE	1989	EXCHANGE	London SE	**SYMBOL**
DOMICILE	UK	CURRENCY	GBP	
STOCKBROKER	Winterflood	INDEX	FTSE Mid 250	**TEM**
GEARING	105	AVG DISCOUNT (%)	-13.4	
NAV (£M)	2,403	NET DIV YIELD (%)	1.1	
TURNOVER	3,613			
TER (%)	1.21	SHARPE RATIO	0.5	**MKT CAP (£M)**
		VOLATILITY	1.46	**2,116**
PERFORMANCE FEE	No	PERFORMANCE (10Y) (%)	125	

UTILICO EMERGING MARKETS LTD

CORE INVESTMENT STRATEGY	Utility stocks in emerging markets
BENCHMARK	MSCI Emerging Markets
MANAGEMENT GROUP	ICM
FUND MANAGER	Charles Jillings [2005]
WEBSITE	www.uem.bm

LAUNCH DATE	2005	EXCHANGE	London SE	**SYMBOL**
DOMICILE	Bermuda	CURRENCY	GBP	
STOCKBROKER	Stockdale	INDEX	FTSE Small Cap	**UEM**
GEARING	125	AVG DISCOUNT (%)	-10.7	
NAV (£M)	543	NET DIV YIELD (%)	3.0	
TURNOVER	619			
TER (%)	0.93	SHARPE RATIO	0.5	**MKT CAP (£M)**
		VOLATILITY	1.15	**480**
PERFORMANCE FEE	Yes	PERFORMANCE (10Y) (%)	101	

GLOBAL EQUITY INCOME

BLUE PLANET INTERNATIONAL FINANCIALS INVESTMENT TRUST PLC

CORE INVESTMENT STRATEGY		Global financials		
BENCHMARK		MSCI World Financials		
MANAGEMENT GROUP		Blue Planet IM		
FUND MANAGER		Ken Murray [1999]		
WEBSITE		www.blueplanet.eu		

LAUNCH DATE	1999	EXCHANGE	London SE	**SYMBOL**
DOMICILE	UK	CURRENCY	GBP	
STOCKBROKER	-	INDEX	FTSE Fledgling	**BLP**
GEARING	132	AVG DISCOUNT (%)	-22.1	
NAV (£M)	27	NET DIV YIELD (%)	10.2	
TURNOVER	20			**MKT CAP (£M)**
TER (%)	3.68	SHARPE RATIO	0.7	
		VOLATILITY	2.28	**23**
PERFORMANCE FEE	No	PERFORMANCE (10Y) (%)	-	

F&C MANAGED PORTFOLIO TRUST PLC

CORE INVESTMENT STRATEGY		Fund of investment cos (in-house & third party)		
BENCHMARK		FTSE Equity Investment Instruments		
MANAGEMENT GROUP		F&C Investments		
FUND MANAGER		Peter Hewitt [2008]		
WEBSITE		www.fctr.co.uk		

LAUNCH DATE	2008	EXCHANGE	London SE	**SYMBOL**
DOMICILE	UK	CURRENCY	GBP	
STOCKBROKER	Dickson Minto	INDEX	-	**FMPI**
GEARING	109	AVG DISCOUNT (%)	0.9	
NAV (£M)	58	NET DIV YIELD (%)	3.9	
TURNOVER	51			**MKT CAP (£M)**
TER (%)	1.1	SHARPE RATIO	0.9	
		VOLATILITY	0.91	**58**
PERFORMANCE FEE	Yes	PERFORMANCE (10Y) (%)	-	

GABELLI MERGER PLUS+ TRUST PLC

CORE INVESTMENT STRATEGY		Global event merger arbitage		
BENCHMARK		HFRX Global Hedge $		
MANAGEMENT GROUP		Gabelli Funds		
FUND MANAGER		Mario Gabelli, Marc Gabelli, Douglas Jamieson [2017]		
WEBSITE		-		

LAUNCH DATE	2017	EXCHANGE	London SE (SFS)	**SYMBOL**
DOMICILE	UK	CURRENCY	USD	**GMP**
STOCKBROKER	-	INDEX	-	
GEARING	100	AVG DISCOUNT (%)	2.6	
NAV (£M)	77	NET DIV YIELD (%)	-	
TURNOVER	9			**MKT CAP (£M)**
TER (%)	-	SHARPE RATIO	-	**80**
		VOLATILITY	0.16	
PERFORMANCE FEE	Yes	PERFORMANCE (10Y) (%)	-	

HENDERSON INTERNATIONAL INCOME TRUST PLC

CORE INVESTMENT STRATEGY		Focused and internationally diversified portfolio of securities outside the UK		
BENCHMARK		MSCI World ex UK		
MANAGEMENT GROUP		Janus Henderson		
FUND MANAGER		Ben Lofthouse [2011]		
WEBSITE		www.henderson.com		

LAUNCH DATE	2011	EXCHANGE	London SE	**SYMBOL**
DOMICILE	UK	CURRENCY	GBP	**HINT**
STOCKBROKER	Panmure Gordon	INDEX	FTSE Small Cap	
GEARING	100	AVG DISCOUNT (%)	-0.3	
NAV (£M)	261	NET DIV YIELD (%)	2.9	
TURNOVER	253			**MKT CAP (£M)**
TER (%)	1.02	SHARPE RATIO	1.2	**263**
		VOLATILITY	0.74	
PERFORMANCE FEE	No	PERFORMANCE (10Y) (%)	-	

INVESCO PERPETUAL SELECT TRUST PLC

CORE INVESTMENT STRATEGY		Global equities		
BENCHMARK		MSCI World		
MANAGEMENT GROUP		Invesco Perpetual		
FUND MANAGER		Nick Mustoe [2012]		
WEBSITE		www.invescoperpetual.co.uk		

LAUNCH DATE	2006	EXCHANGE	London SE	**SYMBOL**
DOMICILE	UK	CURRENCY	GBP	**IVPG**
STOCKBROKER	Canaccord	INDEX	-	
GEARING	108	AVG DISCOUNT (%)	-1.1	
NAV (£M)	67	NET DIV YIELD (%)	3.2	
TURNOVER	40			**MKT CAP (£M)**
TER (%)	0.95	SHARPE RATIO	1.4	**66**
		VOLATILITY	0.81	
PERFORMANCE FEE	Yes	PERFORMANCE (10Y) (%)	166	

JPMORGAN GLOBAL GROWTH & INCOME PLC

CORE INVESTMENT STRATEGY		Global equities	
BENCHMARK		MSCI AC World	
MANAGEMENT GROUP		JPMorgan AM	
FUND MANAGER		Jeroen Huysinga [2008]	
WEBSITE		www.jpmoverseas.co.uk	

LAUNCH DATE	1905	EXCHANGE	London SE	**SYMBOL**
DOMICILE	UK	CURRENCY	GBP	**JPGI**
STOCKBROKER	Winterflood	INDEX	FTSE Small Cap	
GEARING	106	AVG DISCOUNT (%)	-4.8	
NAV (£M)	389	NET DIV YIELD (%)	4.9	
TURNOVER	656			**MKT CAP (£M)**
TER (%)	0.63	SHARPE RATIO	0.7	**396**
		VOLATILITY	1.14	
PERFORMANCE FEE	Yes	PERFORMANCE (10Y) (%)	219	

MURRAY INTERNATIONAL TRUST PLC

CORE INVESTMENT STRATEGY		Global equities (bias to emerging markets)	
BENCHMARK		40% All Share, 60% MSCI World ex UK	
MANAGEMENT GROUP		Aberdeen AM	
FUND MANAGER		Bruce Stout [2004]	
WEBSITE		www.murray-intl.co.uk	

LAUNCH DATE	1905	EXCHANGE	London SE	**SYMBOL**
DOMICILE	UK	CURRENCY	GBP	**MYI**
STOCKBROKER	Stifel	INDEX	FTSE Mid 250	
GEARING	112	AVG DISCOUNT (%)	0.8	
NAV (£M)	1,612	NET DIV YIELD (%)	3.7	
TURNOVER	1,873			**MKT CAP (£M)**
TER (%)	0.68	SHARPE RATIO	0.7	**1,653**
		VOLATILITY	1.16	
PERFORMANCE FEE	No	PERFORMANCE (10Y) (%)	196	

SCOTTISH AMERICAN INVESTMENT CO (THE) PLC

CORE INVESTMENT STRATEGY		Global equities plus property and bond portfolios	
BENCHMARK		MSCI AC World	
MANAGEMENT GROUP		Baillie Gifford	
FUND MANAGER		Dominic Neary [2012]	
WEBSITE		www.bailliegifford.com	

LAUNCH DATE	1905	EXCHANGE	London SE	**SYMBOL**
DOMICILE	UK	CURRENCY	GBP	**SCAM**
STOCKBROKER	Winterflood	INDEX	FTSE Small Cap	
GEARING	118	AVG DISCOUNT (%)	3.3	
NAV (£M)	465	NET DIV YIELD (%)	3.0	
TURNOVER	369			**MKT CAP (£M)**
TER (%)	0.87	SHARPE RATIO	1.2	**492**
		VOLATILITY	1.17	
PERFORMANCE FEE	No	PERFORMANCE (10Y) (%)	134	

SECURITIES TRUST OF SCOTLAND PLC

CORE INVESTMENT STRATEGY		Global equities
BENCHMARK		MSCI World
MANAGEMENT GROUP		Martin Currie IM
FUND MANAGER		Mark Whitehead [2016]
WEBSITE		www.securitiestrust.com

LAUNCH DATE	1926	EXCHANGE	London SE
DOMICILE	UK	CURRENCY	GBP
STOCKBROKER	JPM Cazenove	INDEX	FTSE Small Cap
GEARING	113	AVG DISCOUNT (%)	-5.5
NAV (£M)	203	NET DIV YIELD (%)	3.5
TURNOVER	164		
TER (%)	0.96	SHARPE RATIO	0.7
		VOLATILITY	1.25
PERFORMANCE FEE	No	PERFORMANCE (10Y) (%)	92

SYMBOL
STS

MKT CAP (£M)
189

GLOBAL HIGH INCOME

HENDERSON DIVERSIFIED INCOME TRUST PLC

CORE INVESTMENT STRATEGY		Fixed interest securities
BENCHMARK		UK£ 3 Month Libor
MANAGEMENT GROUP		Janus Henderson
FUND MANAGER		John Pattullo, Jenna Barnard [2007]
WEBSITE		www.henderson.com

LAUNCH DATE	2007	EXCHANGE	London SE
DOMICILE	Jersey	CURRENCY	GBP
STOCKBROKER	JPM Cazenove	INDEX	FTSE Small Cap
GEARING	117	AVG DISCOUNT (%)	2.7
NAV (£M)	173	NET DIV YIELD (%)	5.4
TURNOVER	339		
TER (%)	0.98	SHARPE RATIO	-
		VOLATILITY	0.91
PERFORMANCE FEE	Yes	PERFORMANCE (10Y) (%)	76

SYMBOL
HDIV

MKT CAP (£M)
179

INVESCO PERPETUAL ENHANCED INCOME LTD

CORE INVESTMENT STRATEGY		Corporate & government bonds	
BENCHMARK		UK£ 3 Month Libor	
MANAGEMENT GROUP		Invesco Perpetual	
FUND MANAGER		Paul Read, Paul Causer [2001]	
WEBSITE		www.invescoperpetual.co.uk	

LAUNCH DATE	1999	EXCHANGE	London SE	**SYMBOL**
DOMICILE	Jersey	CURRENCY	GBP	**IPE**
STOCKBROKER	Panmure Gordon	INDEX	-	
GEARING	121	AVG DISCOUNT (%)	4.3	
NAV (£M)	124	NET DIV YIELD (%)	6.2	
TURNOVER	219			
TER (%)	1.36	SHARPE RATIO	-	**MKT CAP (£M)**
		VOLATILITY	1.45	**128**
PERFORMANCE FEE	Yes	PERFORMANCE (10Y) (%)	101	

GLOBAL SMALLER COMPANIES

MARWYN VALUE INVESTORS LTD

CORE INVESTMENT STRATEGY		Smaller companies (<£500m) in UK & continental Europe	
BENCHMARK		FTSE All Share	
MANAGEMENT GROUP		Marwyn AM	
FUND MANAGER		James Corsellis, Mark Watts [2006]	
WEBSITE		-	

LAUNCH DATE	2006	EXCHANGE	London SE (SFS)	**SYMBOL**
DOMICILE	Guernsey	CURRENCY	GBP	**MVI**
STOCKBROKER	Cantor Fitzgerald Europe	INDEX	-	
GEARING	100	AVG DISCOUNT (%)	-32.1	
NAV (£M)	163	NET DIV YIELD (%)	4.9	
TURNOVER	145			
TER (%)	2.44	SHARPE RATIO	-0.5	**MKT CAP (£M)**
		VOLATILITY	2.05	**120**
PERFORMANCE FEE	Yes	PERFORMANCE (10Y) (%)	74	

ORYX INTERNATIONAL GROWTH FUND LTD

CORE INVESTMENT STRATEGY		Smaller cos, primarily in UK & US	
BENCHMARK		FTSE All Share	
MANAGEMENT GROUP		Harwood Capital	
FUND MANAGER		Chris Mills [1995]	
WEBSITE		www.oryxinternationalgrowthfund.co.uk	

LAUNCH DATE	1995	EXCHANGE	London SE	**SYMBOL**
DOMICILE	Guernsey	CURRENCY	GBP	
STOCKBROKER	Winterflood	INDEX	-	**OIG**
GEARING	100	AVG DISCOUNT (%)	-17.4	
NAV (£M)	124	NET DIV YIELD (%)	-	
TURNOVER	69			**MKT CAP (£M)**
TER (%)	1.65	SHARPE RATIO	1.4	
		VOLATILITY	0.90	**103**
PERFORMANCE FEE	No	PERFORMANCE (10Y) (%)	128	

SCOTGEMS PLC

CORE INVESTMENT STRATEGY		Global smaller companies	
BENCHMARK		MSCI World Small Cap	
MANAGEMENT GROUP		Stewart Investors	
FUND MANAGER		Ashish Swarup [2017]	
WEBSITE		www.scotgems.com	

LAUNCH DATE	2017	EXCHANGE	London SE	**SYMBOL**
DOMICILE	UK	CURRENCY	GBP	
STOCKBROKER	Dickson Minto	INDEX	-	**SGEM**
GEARING	100	AVG DISCOUNT (%)	2.8	
NAV (£M)	52	NET DIV YIELD (%)	-	
TURNOVER	81			**MKT CAP (£M)**
TER (%)	-	SHARPE RATIO	-	
		VOLATILITY	0.41	**53**
PERFORMANCE FEE	No	PERFORMANCE (10Y) (%)	-	

HEDGE FUNDS

ACENCIA DEBT STRATEGIES LTD

CORE INVESTMENT STRATEGY		Fund of hedge funds – debt strategies	
BENCHMARK		HFRX Global Hedge $	
MANAGEMENT GROUP		Saltus Partners	
FUND MANAGER		Marty Gross [2005]	
WEBSITE		www.acencia.co.uk	

LAUNCH DATE	2005	EXCHANGE	London SE	**SYMBOL**
DOMICILE	Guernsey	CURRENCY	USD	**ACD**
STOCKBROKER	Canaccord	INDEX	-	
GEARING	100	AVG DISCOUNT (%)	-6.5	
NAV (£M)	66	NET DIV YIELD (%)	3.5	
TURNOVER	63			**MKT CAP (£M)**
TER (%)	1.78	SHARPE RATIO	-	**65**
		VOLATILITY	1.49	
PERFORMANCE FEE	Yes	PERFORMANCE (10Y) (%)	-6	

ALTERNATIVE LIQUIDITY FUND LTD

CORE INVESTMENT STRATEGY		Global Illiquid assets	
BENCHMARK		HFRX Global Hedge $	
MANAGEMENT GROUP		Warana Capital	
FUND MANAGER		Tim Gardner [2015]	
WEBSITE		www.morgancreekfunds.com	

LAUNCH DATE	2015	EXCHANGE	London SE	**SYMBOL**
DOMICILE	Guernsey	CURRENCY	USD	**ALF**
STOCKBROKER	-	INDEX	-	
GEARING	100	AVG DISCOUNT (%)	-77.9	
NAV (£M)	83	NET DIV YIELD (%)	-	
TURNOVER	13			**MKT CAP (£M)**
TER (%)	1.03	SHARPE RATIO	-	**20**
		VOLATILITY	4.22	
PERFORMANCE FEE	No	PERFORMANCE (10Y) (%)	-	

BOUSSARDS & GAVAUDAN HOLDINGS LTD

CORE INVESTMENT STRATEGY		Multi-strategy hedge fund		
BENCHMARK		HFRX Global Hedge $		
MANAGEMENT GROUP		Boussard & Gavaudan AM		
FUND MANAGER		Emmanuel Gavaudan, Emmanuel Boussard [2006]		
WEBSITE		www.bgholdingltd.com		

				SYMBOL
LAUNCH DATE	2006	EXCHANGE	London SE	**BGHL**
DOMICILE	Guernsey	CURRENCY	EUR	
STOCKBROKER	Stifel	INDEX	-	
GEARING	100	AVG DISCOUNT (%)	-18.3	
NAV (£M)	629	NET DIV YIELD (%)	-	
TURNOVER	294			MKT CAP (£M)
TER (%)	1.6	SHARPE RATIO	1.4	**521**
		VOLATILITY	0.54	
PERFORMANCE FEE	Yes	PERFORMANCE (10Y) (%)	72	

BH GLOBAL LTD

CORE INVESTMENT STRATEGY		Multi-strategy hedge fund		
BENCHMARK		HFRX Global Hedge $		
MANAGEMENT GROUP		Brevan Howard		
FUND MANAGER		Alan Howard [2008]		
WEBSITE		www.bhglobal.com		

				SYMBOL
LAUNCH DATE	2008	EXCHANGE	London SE	**BHGG**
DOMICILE	Guernsey	CURRENCY	GBP	
STOCKBROKER	JPM Cazenove, Canaccord Genuity	INDEX	FTSE Small Cap	
GEARING	100	AVG DISCOUNT (%)	-10.3	
NAV (£M)	312	NET DIV YIELD (%)	-	
TURNOVER	630			MKT CAP (£M)
TER (%)	2.36	SHARPE RATIO	0.3	**282**
		VOLATILITY	0.96	
PERFORMANCE FEE	Yes	PERFORMANCE (10Y) (%)	-	

BH GLOBAL LTD

CORE INVESTMENT STRATEGY		Multi-strategy hedge fund		
BENCHMARK		HFRX Global Hedge $		
MANAGEMENT GROUP		Brevan Howard		
FUND MANAGER		Alan Howard [2008]		
WEBSITE		www.bhglobal.com		

				SYMBOL
LAUNCH DATE	2008	EXCHANGE	London SE	**BHGU**
DOMICILE	Guernsey	CURRENCY	USD	
STOCKBROKER	JPM Cazenove, Canaccord Genuity	INDEX	FTSE Small Cap	
GEARING	100	AVG DISCOUNT (%)	-9.5	
NAV (£M)	38	NET DIV YIELD (%)	-	
TURNOVER	78			MKT CAP (£M)
TER (%)	2.36	SHARPE RATIO	0.9	**34**
		VOLATILITY	1.22	
PERFORMANCE FEE	Yes	PERFORMANCE (10Y) (%)	-	

BH MACRO LTD

CORE INVESTMENT STRATEGY		Currencies & fixed interest hedge fund	
BENCHMARK		HFRX Global Hedge $	
MANAGEMENT GROUP		Brevan Howard	
FUND MANAGER		Alan Howard [2007]	
WEBSITE		www.bhmacro.com	

LAUNCH DATE	2007	EXCHANGE	London SE	**SYMBOL**
DOMICILE	Guernsey	CURRENCY	GBP	**BHMG**
STOCKBROKER	JPM Cazenove	INDEX	FTSE Small Cap	
GEARING	100	AVG DISCOUNT (%)	-7.8	
NAV (£M)	305	NET DIV YIELD (%)	-	
TURNOVER	849			**MKT CAP (£M)**
TER (%)	2.1	SHARPE RATIO	0.0	
		VOLATILITY	0.75	**278**
PERFORMANCE FEE	Yes	PERFORMANCE (10Y) (%)	71	

BH MACRO LTD

CORE INVESTMENT STRATEGY		Currencies & fixed interest hedge fund	
BENCHMARK		HFRX Global Hedge $	
MANAGEMENT GROUP		Brevan Howard	
FUND MANAGER		Alan Howard [2007]	
WEBSITE		www.bhmacro.com	

LAUNCH DATE	2007	EXCHANGE	London SE	**SYMBOL**
DOMICILE	Guernsey	CURRENCY	USD	**BHMU**
STOCKBROKER	JPM Cazenove	INDEX	FTSE Small Cap	
GEARING	100	AVG DISCOUNT (%)	-8.3	
NAV (£M)	48	NET DIV YIELD (%)	-	
TURNOVER	210			**MKT CAP (£M)**
TER (%)	2.1	SHARPE RATIO	0.8	
		VOLATILITY	0.69	**44**
PERFORMANCE FEE	Yes	PERFORMANCE (10Y) (%)	74	

HIGHBRIDGE MULTI-STRATEGY FUND LTD

CORE INVESTMENT STRATEGY		Multi-strategy hedge fund	
BENCHMARK		HFRX Global Hedge $	
MANAGEMENT GROUP		Highbridge Capital Management	
FUND MANAGER		Mark Vanacore [2016]	
WEBSITE		www.highbridgemsfltd.co.uk	

LAUNCH DATE	2006	EXCHANGE	London SE	**SYMBOL**
DOMICILE	Guernsey	CURRENCY	GBP	**HMSF**
STOCKBROKER	Peel Hunt, Fidante Capital	INDEX	FTSE Small Cap	
GEARING	100	AVG DISCOUNT (%)	-4.2	
NAV (£M)	213	NET DIV YIELD (%)	-	
TURNOVER	392			**MKT CAP (£M)**
TER (%)	0.39	SHARPE RATIO	-	
		VOLATILITY	0.61	**209**
PERFORMANCE FEE	No	PERFORMANCE (10Y) (%)	112	

PERSHING SQUARE HOLDINGS LTD

CORE INVESTMENT STRATEGY	Activist hedge fund	
BENCHMARK	HFRX Global Hedge $	
MANAGEMENT GROUP	Pershing Square CM	
FUND MANAGER	Bill Ackman [2014]	
WEBSITE	www.pershingsquareholdings.com	

LAUNCH DATE	2014	EXCHANGE	Euronext	**SYMBOL**
DOMICILE	Guernsey	CURRENCY	USD	**PSH**
STOCKBROKER	Deutsche Bank, UBS	INDEX	FTSE Mid 250	
GEARING	-	AVG DISCOUNT (%)	-17.7	
NAV (£M)	3,102	NET DIV YIELD (%)	-	
TURNOVER	2,624			
TER (%)	-	SHARPE RATIO	-	**MKT CAP (£M)**
		VOLATILITY	0.96	**2,512**
PERFORMANCE FEE	-	PERFORMANCE (10Y) (%)	-	

PERSHING SQUARE HOLDINGS £

CORE INVESTMENT STRATEGY	Activist hedge fund	
BENCHMARK	HFRX Global Hedge $	
MANAGEMENT GROUP	Pershing Square CM	
FUND MANAGER	Bill Ackman [2017]	
WEBSITE	-	

LAUNCH DATE	2017	EXCHANGE	London SE	**SYMBOL**
DOMICILE	UK	CURRENCY	GBP	**PSH £**
STOCKBROKER	Deutsche Bank, UBS	INDEX	-	
GEARING	-	AVG DISCOUNT (%)	-17.9	
NAV (£M)	3,108	NET DIV YIELD (%)	-	
TURNOVER	5,204			
TER (%)	-	SHARPE RATIO	-	**MKT CAP (£M)**
		VOLATILITY	-	**2,557**
PERFORMANCE FEE	-	PERFORMANCE (10Y) (%)	-	

THIRD POINT OFFSHORE INVESTORS LTD

CORE INVESTMENT STRATEGY	Event driven, primarily long-short equity	
BENCHMARK	HFRX Global Hedge $	
MANAGEMENT GROUP	Third Point LLC	
FUND MANAGER	Dan Loeb [2007]	
WEBSITE	www.thirdpointpublic.com	

LAUNCH DATE	2007	EXCHANGE	London SE	**SYMBOL**
DOMICILE	Guernsey	CURRENCY	GBP	**TPOG**
STOCKBROKER	Jefferies	INDEX	-	
GEARING	100	AVG DISCOUNT (%)	-16.0	
NAV (£M)	39	NET DIV YIELD (%)	4.3	
TURNOVER	48			
TER (%)	2.45	SHARPE RATIO	0.1	**MKT CAP (£M)**
		VOLATILITY	1.15	**34**
PERFORMANCE FEE	Yes	PERFORMANCE (10Y) (%)	124	

THIRD POINT OFFSHORE INVESTORS LTD

CORE INVESTMENT STRATEGY		Event driven, primarily long-short equity	
BENCHMARK		HFRX Global Hedge $	
MANAGEMENT GROUP		Third Point LLC	
FUND MANAGER		Daniel Loeb [2007]	
WEBSITE		www.thirdpointpublic.com	

LAUNCH DATE	2007	EXCHANGE	London SE	
DOMICILE	Guernsey	CURRENCY	USD	**SYMBOL**
STOCKBROKER	Jefferies	INDEX	-	**TPOU**
GEARING	100	AVG DISCOUNT (%)	-17.5	
NAV (£M)	697	NET DIV YIELD (%)	4.3	
TURNOVER	1,050			
TER (%)	2.45	SHARPE RATIO	0.6	**MKT CAP (£M)**
		VOLATILITY	1.15	**597**
PERFORMANCE FEE	Yes	PERFORMANCE (10Y) (%)	134	

JAPAN

ABERDEEN JAPAN INVESTMENT TRUST PLC

CORE INVESTMENT STRATEGY		Japanese equities	
BENCHMARK		TSE 1st Section	
MANAGEMENT GROUP		Aberdeen AM	
FUND MANAGER		Hugh Young (team managed) [2014]	
WEBSITE		www.aberdeenjapan.co.uk	

LAUNCH DATE	1998	EXCHANGE	London SE	
DOMICILE	UK	CURRENCY	GBP	**SYMBOL**
STOCKBROKER	JPM Cazenove	INDEX	FTSE Fledgling	**AJIT**
GEARING	112	AVG DISCOUNT (%)	-12.0	
NAV (£M)	96	NET DIV YIELD (%)	1.1	
TURNOVER	132			
TER (%)	1.25	SHARPE RATIO	0.8	**MKT CAP (£M)**
		VOLATILITY	1.07	**85**
PERFORMANCE FEE	No	PERFORMANCE (10Y) (%)	-	

BAILLIE GIFFORD JAPAN TRUST (THE) PLC

CORE INVESTMENT STRATEGY		Japanese equities (mid-sized companies)	
BENCHMARK		TSE 1st Section	
MANAGEMENT GROUP		Baillie Gifford	
FUND MANAGER		Sarah Whitley [1991]	
WEBSITE		www.bailliegifford.com	

LAUNCH DATE	1981	EXCHANGE	London SE	**SYMBOL**
DOMICILE	UK	CURRENCY	GBP	**BGFD**
STOCKBROKER	Canaccord	INDEX	FTSE Small Cap	
GEARING	114	AVG DISCOUNT (%)	1.4	
NAV (£M)	568	NET DIV YIELD (%)	-	
TURNOVER	1,000			
TER (%)	0.88	SHARPE RATIO	1.1	**MKT CAP (£M)**
		VOLATILITY	1.51	**598**
PERFORMANCE FEE	No	PERFORMANCE (10Y) (%)	243	

CC JAPAN INCOME & GROWTH TRUST PLC

CORE INVESTMENT STRATEGY		Japanese equities	
BENCHMARK		TSE 1st Section	
MANAGEMENT GROUP		Coupland Cardiff AM	
FUND MANAGER		Richard Ashton [2015]	
WEBSITE		www.ccjapanincomeandgrowthtrust.com	

LAUNCH DATE	2015	EXCHANGE	London SE	**SYMBOL**
DOMICILE	UK	CURRENCY	GBP	**CCJI**
STOCKBROKER	Peel Hunt	INDEX	FTSE Fledgling	
GEARING	119	AVG DISCOUNT (%)	1.1	
NAV (£M)	121	NET DIV YIELD (%)	2.2	
TURNOVER	128			
TER (%)	1.28	SHARPE RATIO	-	**MKT CAP (£M)**
		VOLATILITY	0.90	**124**
PERFORMANCE FEE	No	PERFORMANCE (10Y) (%)	-	

JPMORGAN JAPANESE INVESTMENT TRUST PLC

CORE INVESTMENT STRATEGY		Japanese equities	
BENCHMARK		TSE 1st Section	
MANAGEMENT GROUP		JPMorgan AM	
FUND MANAGER		Nicholas Weindling [2007]	
WEBSITE		www.jpmjapanese.co.uk	

LAUNCH DATE	1927	EXCHANGE	London SE	**SYMBOL**
DOMICILE	UK	CURRENCY	GBP	**JFJ**
STOCKBROKER	Canaccord	INDEX	FTSE Small Cap	
GEARING	115	AVG DISCOUNT (%)	-12.3	
NAV (£M)	687	NET DIV YIELD (%)	1.0	
TURNOVER	545			
TER (%)	0.74	SHARPE RATIO	1.0	**MKT CAP (£M)**
		VOLATILITY	1.66	**608**
PERFORMANCE FEE	No	PERFORMANCE (10Y) (%)	110	

SCHRODER JAPAN GROWTH FUND PLC

CORE INVESTMENT STRATEGY		Japanese equities	
BENCHMARK		TSE 1st Section	
MANAGEMENT GROUP		Schroder IM	
FUND MANAGER		Andrew Rose [2007]	
WEBSITE		www.schroderjapangrowthfund.com	

LAUNCH DATE	1994	EXCHANGE	London SE	**SYMBOL**
DOMICILE	UK	CURRENCY	GBP	
STOCKBROKER	Panmure Gordon	INDEX	FTSE Small Cap	**SJG**
GEARING	116	AVG DISCOUNT (%)	-9.2	
NAV (£M)	274	NET DIV YIELD (%)	1.4	
TURNOVER	341			
TER (%)	1.12	SHARPE RATIO	1.0	**MKT CAP (£M)**
		VOLATILITY	1.53	**249**
PERFORMANCE FEE	No	PERFORMANCE (10Y) (%)	116	

JAPANESE SMALLER COMPANIES

ATLANTIS JAPAN GROWTH FUND LTD

CORE INVESTMENT STRATEGY		Japanese equities (focus on smaller cos)	
BENCHMARK		Topix Small Cap	
MANAGEMENT GROUP		Tiburon Partners	
FUND MANAGER		Taeko Setaishi [2016]	
WEBSITE		www.atlantisjapangrowthfund.com	

LAUNCH DATE	1996	EXCHANGE	London SE	**SYMBOL**
DOMICILE	Guernsey	CURRENCY	GBP	
STOCKBROKER	JPM Cazenove	INDEX	FTSE Fledgling	**AJG**
GEARING	105	AVG DISCOUNT (%)	-9.2	
NAV (£M)	97	NET DIV YIELD (%)	-	
TURNOVER	265			
TER (%)	1.91	SHARPE RATIO	0.9	**MKT CAP (£M)**
		VOLATILITY	1.26	**86**
PERFORMANCE FEE	No	PERFORMANCE (10Y) (%)	91	

TESTING NAPPIES. THE LENGTHS WE'LL GO TO FOR A BETTER INVESTMENT.

LET'S TALK HOW.

It may sound odd that nappy absorption could have an impact on one of the investment trusts from our global range, but it did. When researching two manufacturers in Asia, we questioned why one of them had declining sales. Management told us it was a marketing issue, but was it something more fundamental?

We ran an independent test and found their nappy just didn't hold water, which put them out of the running. Hands-on local research helped us make a better investment decision.

Our 380 investment professionals across the globe always dig deeper by cross-checking facts, asking the difficult questions and sometimes even testing nappies. We believe this gives us stronger insights across the regions and markets our investment trusts cover.

Fidelity's range of investment trusts

- Fidelity Asian Values PLC
- Fidelity China Special Situations PLC
- Fidelity European Values PLC
- Fidelity Japanese Values PLC
- Fidelity Special Values PLC

The value of investments and the income from them can go down as well as up and you may get back less than you invest. Past performance is not a reliable indicator of future results. Overseas investments are subject to currency fluctuations. Investments in small and emerging markets can be more volatile than other overseas markets. Some funds invest more heavily than others in small companies, which can carry a higher risk because their share prices may be more volatile than those of larger companies. Resources figures reflect those of FIL Limited. Source: Fidelity International, 30 June 2017. Data is unaudited.

Let your investment benefit from our robust research. Visit fidelity.co.uk/research or speak to an adviser.

Money Observer *est* **TrustAwards 2017**
Highly Commended
Premier Group Award
Fidelity International

BAILLIE GIFFORD SHIN NIPPON PLC

CORE INVESTMENT STRATEGY		Smaller cos in Japan		
BENCHMARK		Topix Small Cap		
MANAGEMENT GROUP		Baillie Gifford		
FUND MANAGER		Praveen Kumar [2015]		
WEBSITE		www.bailliegifford.com		

LAUNCH DATE	1985	EXCHANGE	London SE	**SYMBOL**
DOMICILE	UK	CURRENCY	GBP	
STOCKBROKER	Panmure Gordon	INDEX	FTSE Small Cap	**BGS**
GEARING	112	AVG DISCOUNT (%)	3.8	
NAV (£M)	307	NET DIV YIELD (%)	-	
TURNOVER	629			
TER (%)	0.96	SHARPE RATIO	1.1	**MKT CAP (£M)**
		VOLATILITY	1.54	**326**
PERFORMANCE FEE	No	PERFORMANCE (10Y) (%)	351	

FIDELITY JAPANESE VALUES PLC

CORE INVESTMENT STRATEGY		Smaller cos in Japan		
BENCHMARK		Russell/Nomura Mid Small Cap Japan		
MANAGEMENT GROUP		Fidelity Investments		
FUND MANAGER		Nicholas Price [2015]		
WEBSITE		www.fidelity.co.uk/japanesevalues		

LAUNCH DATE	1994	EXCHANGE	London SE	**SYMBOL**
DOMICILE	UK	CURRENCY	GBP	
STOCKBROKER	Stifel	INDEX	FTSE Small Cap	**FJV**
GEARING	123	AVG DISCOUNT (%)	-15.0	
NAV (£M)	196	NET DIV YIELD (%)	-	
TURNOVER	115			
TER (%)	1.46	SHARPE RATIO	0.9	**MKT CAP (£M)**
		VOLATILITY	1.74	**169**
PERFORMANCE FEE	No	PERFORMANCE (10Y) (%)	96	

JPMORGAN FLEMING JAPANESE SMALLER COS INV TR PLC

CORE INVESTMENT STRATEGY		Smaller cos in Japan		
BENCHMARK		Topix Small Cap		
MANAGEMENT GROUP		JPMorgan AM		
FUND MANAGER		Shoichi Mizusawa, Nicholas Weindling, Eiji Saito [2012]		
WEBSITE		www.jpmjapansmallercompanies.co.uk		

LAUNCH DATE	1984	EXCHANGE	London SE	**SYMBOL**
DOMICILE	UK	CURRENCY	GBP	
STOCKBROKER	Canaccord	INDEX	FTSE Small Cap	**JPS**
GEARING	109	AVG DISCOUNT (%)	-13.6	
NAV (£M)	234	NET DIV YIELD (%)	-	
TURNOVER	250			
TER (%)	1.31	SHARPE RATIO	1.2	**MKT CAP (£M)**
		VOLATILITY	1.70	**201**
PERFORMANCE FEE	No	PERFORMANCE (10Y) (%)	68	

LATIN AMERICA

ABERDEEN LATIN AMERICAN INCOME FUND LTD

CORE INVESTMENT STRATEGY		Latin American equities and sovereign debt	
BENCHMARK		MSCI Latin America	
MANAGEMENT GROUP		Aberdeen AM	
FUND MANAGER		Devan Kaloo, Bret Diment [2010]	
WEBSITE		www.latamincome.co.uk	

LAUNCH DATE	2010	EXCHANGE	London SE	**SYMBOL**
DOMICILE	Jersey	CURRENCY	GBP	**ALAI**
STOCKBROKER	Canaccord	INDEX	-	
GEARING	112	AVG DISCOUNT (%)	-12.8	
NAV (£M)	56	NET DIV YIELD (%)	4.5	
TURNOVER	95			**MKT CAP (£M)**
TER (%)	2.04	SHARPE RATIO	0.2	**49**
		VOLATILITY	1.31	
PERFORMANCE FEE	No	PERFORMANCE (10Y) (%)	-	

BLACKROCK LATIN AMERICAN INVESTMENT TRUST PLC

CORE INVESTMENT STRATEGY		Latin American equities	
BENCHMARK		MSCI Latin America	
MANAGEMENT GROUP		BlackRock IM	
FUND MANAGER		Will Landers [2006]	
WEBSITE		www.blackrock.co.uk	

LAUNCH DATE	1990	EXCHANGE	London SE	**SYMBOL**
DOMICILE	UK	CURRENCY	GBP	**BRLA**
STOCKBROKER	Cenkos	INDEX	FTSE Small Cap	
GEARING	105	AVG DISCOUNT (%)	-14.0	
NAV (£M)	218	NET DIV YIELD (%)	2.5	
TURNOVER	220			**MKT CAP (£M)**
TER (%)	1.19	SHARPE RATIO	0.1	**188**
		VOLATILITY	1.65	
PERFORMANCE FEE	No	PERFORMANCE (10Y) (%)	43	

NORTH AMERICA

BLACKROCK NORTH AMERICAN INCOME TRUST PLC

CORE INVESTMENT STRATEGY	US equities	
BENCHMARK	S&P 500	
MANAGEMENT GROUP	BlackRock IM	
FUND MANAGER	Tony DeSpirito [2012]	
WEBSITE	www.blackrock.co.uk	

LAUNCH DATE	2012	EXCHANGE	London SE	**SYMBOL**
DOMICILE	UK	CURRENCY	GBP	
STOCKBROKER	Cenkos	INDEX	FTSE Small Cap	**BRNA**
GEARING	100	AVG DISCOUNT (%)	-5.0	
NAV (£M)	116	NET DIV YIELD (%)	3.1	
TURNOVER	192			**MKT CAP (£M)**
TER (%)	1.04	SHARPE RATIO	1.2	
		VOLATILITY	1.00	**108**
PERFORMANCE FEE	No	PERFORMANCE (10Y) (%)	-	

GABELLI VALUE PLUS+ TRUST PLC

CORE INVESTMENT STRATEGY	US equities	
BENCHMARK	S&P 500	
MANAGEMENT GROUP	Gabelli Funds	
FUND MANAGER	Mario Gabelli [2015]	
WEBSITE	www.gabelli.co.uk	

LAUNCH DATE	2015	EXCHANGE	London SE	**SYMBOL**
DOMICILE	UK	CURRENCY	GBP	
STOCKBROKER	Peel Hunt	INDEX	FTSE Fledgling	**GVP**
GEARING	100	AVG DISCOUNT (%)	-4.0	
NAV (£M)	136	NET DIV YIELD (%)	-	
TURNOVER	149			**MKT CAP (£M)**
TER (%)	1.33	SHARPE RATIO	-	
		VOLATILITY	0.71	**130**
PERFORMANCE FEE	No	PERFORMANCE (10Y) (%)	-	

JPMORGAN AMERICAN INVESTMENT TRUST PLC

CORE INVESTMENT STRATEGY		US large cap equities		
BENCHMARK		S&P 500		
MANAGEMENT GROUP		JPMorgan AM		
FUND MANAGER		Garrett Fish [2003]		
WEBSITE		www.jpmamerican.co.uk		

LAUNCH DATE	1905	EXCHANGE	London SE	**SYMBOL**
DOMICILE	UK	CURRENCY	GBP	**JAM**
STOCKBROKER	Winterflood	INDEX	FTSE Mid 250	
GEARING	111	AVG DISCOUNT (%)	-4.3	
NAV (£M)	958	NET DIV YIELD (%)	1.3	
TURNOVER	2,170			**MKT CAP (£M)**
TER (%)	0.62	SHARPE RATIO	1.1	**914**
		VOLATILITY	1.19	
PERFORMANCE FEE	Yes	PERFORMANCE (10Y) (%)	243	

MIDDLEFIELD CANADIAN INCOME TRUSTS INVESTMENT COMPANY PCC

CORE INVESTMENT STRATEGY		Canadian Income Trusts		
BENCHMARK		S&P/TSX Composite		
MANAGEMENT GROUP		Middlefield Limited		
FUND MANAGER		Andy Nasr, Dean Orrico [2006]		
WEBSITE		-		

LAUNCH DATE	2006	EXCHANGE	London SE	**SYMBOL**
DOMICILE	Jersey	CURRENCY	GBP	**MCT**
STOCKBROKER	Canaccord	INDEX	-	
GEARING	100	AVG DISCOUNT (%)	-11.3	
NAV (£M)	124	NET DIV YIELD (%)	4.9	
TURNOVER	166			**MKT CAP (£M)**
TER (%)	1.26	SHARPE RATIO	0.2	**110**
		VOLATILITY	1.30	
PERFORMANCE FEE	No	PERFORMANCE (10Y) (%)	131	

NORTH AMERICAN INCOME TRUST PLC

CORE INVESTMENT STRATEGY		S&P 500 equities		
BENCHMARK		S&P 500		
MANAGEMENT GROUP		Aberdeen AM		
FUND MANAGER		Ralph Bassett, Fran Radano [1997]		
WEBSITE		www.northamericanincome.co.uk		

LAUNCH DATE	1997	EXCHANGE	London SE	**SYMBOL**
DOMICILE	UK	CURRENCY	GBP	**NAIT**
STOCKBROKER	Winterflood	INDEX	FTSE Small Cap	
GEARING	111	AVG DISCOUNT (%)	-8.6	
NAV (£M)	376	NET DIV YIELD (%)	3.0	
TURNOVER	534			**MKT CAP (£M)**
TER (%)	1.05	SHARPE RATIO	1.3	**342**
		VOLATILITY	1.18	
PERFORMANCE FEE	No	PERFORMANCE (10Y) (%)	164	

NORTH AMERICAN SMALLER COMPANIES

JUPITER US SMALLER COMPANIES PLC

CORE INVESTMENT STRATEGY		US medium/smaller cos	
BENCHMARK		Russell 2000	
MANAGEMENT GROUP		Jupiter AM	
FUND MANAGER		Robert Siddles [2001]	
WEBSITE		www.jupiteram.com	

LAUNCH DATE	1993	EXCHANGE	London SE	**SYMBOL**
DOMICILE	UK	CURRENCY	GBP	**JUS**
STOCKBROKER	Winterflood	INDEX	FTSE Small Cap	
GEARING	100	AVG DISCOUNT (%)	-9.8	
NAV (£M)	167	NET DIV YIELD (%)	-	
TURNOVER	375			
TER (%)	1.03	SHARPE RATIO	0.6	**MKT CAP (£M)**
		VOLATILITY	1.30	**154**
PERFORMANCE FEE	Yes	PERFORMANCE (10Y) (%)	196	

JPMORGAN US SMALLER COMPANIES IT PLC

CORE INVESTMENT STRATEGY		US smaller cos	
BENCHMARK		Russell 2000	
MANAGEMENT GROUP		JPMorgan AM	
FUND MANAGER		Don San Jose [2008]	
WEBSITE		www.jpmussmallercompanies.co.uk	

LAUNCH DATE	1998	EXCHANGE	London SE	**SYMBOL**
DOMICILE	UK	CURRENCY	GBP	**JUSC**
STOCKBROKER	Numis	INDEX	FTSE Small Cap	
GEARING	111	AVG DISCOUNT (%)	-4.8	
NAV (£M)	156	NET DIV YIELD (%)	-	
TURNOVER	370			
TER (%)	1.47	SHARPE RATIO	1.3	**MKT CAP (£M)**
		VOLATILITY	0.98	**147**
PERFORMANCE FEE	No	PERFORMANCE (10Y) (%)	224	

NORTH ATLANTIC SMALLER COMPANIES INV TRUST PLC

CORE INVESTMENT STRATEGY		US & UK smaller cos		
BENCHMARK		Russell 2000		
MANAGEMENT GROUP		Harwood Capital		
FUND MANAGER		Chris Mills [1994]		
WEBSITE		www.harwoodcapital.co.uk		

LAUNCH DATE	1973	EXCHANGE	London SE	**SYMBOL**
DOMICILE	UK	CURRENCY	GBP	
STOCKBROKER	Winterflood	INDEX	FTSE Small Cap	**NAS**
GEARING	100	AVG DISCOUNT (%)	-17.6	
NAV (£M)	463	NET DIV YIELD (%)	-	
TURNOVER	170			**MKT CAP (£M)**
TER (%)	1.12	SHARPE RATIO	1.1	
		VOLATILITY	1.04	**376**
PERFORMANCE FEE	Yes	PERFORMANCE (10Y) (%)	129	

PRIVATE EQUITY

ADAMAS FINANCE ASIA LTD

CORE INVESTMENT STRATEGY		Provide credit finance to SMEs in Asia with a focus on Greater China		
BENCHMARK		MSCI China		
MANAGEMENT GROUP		Self-Managed		
FUND MANAGER		Barry Lau, Paul Heffner [2009]		
WEBSITE		www.adamasfinance.com		

LAUNCH DATE	2009	EXCHANGE	AIM	**SYMBOL**
DOMICILE	British Virgin Isles	CURRENCY	USD	
STOCKBROKER	WH Ireland	INDEX	-	**ADAM**
GEARING	100	AVG DISCOUNT (%)	1.5	
NAV (£M)	61	NET DIV YIELD (%)	-	
TURNOVER	14			**MKT CAP (£M)**
TER (%)	1.7	SHARPE RATIO	-0.1	
		VOLATILITY	25.72	**79**
PERFORMANCE FEE	Yes	PERFORMANCE (10Y) (%)	-	

APAX GLOBAL ALPHA LTD

CORE INVESTMENT STRATEGY		Apax funds & direct private and public investments	
BENCHMARK		LPX Europe	
MANAGEMENT GROUP		Apax Guernsey Managers	
FUND MANAGER		Ralf Gruss [2015]	
WEBSITE		www.apaxglobalalpha.com	

LAUNCH DATE	2015	EXCHANGE	London SE
DOMICILE	Guernsey	CURRENCY	GBP
STOCKBROKER	Jefferies	INDEX	-
GEARING	100	AVG DISCOUNT (%)	-10.6
NAV (£M)	805	NET DIV YIELD (%)	5.2
TURNOVER	361		
TER (%)	1.04	SHARPE RATIO	-
		VOLATILITY	0.85
PERFORMANCE FEE	Yes	PERFORMANCE (10Y) (%)	-

SYMBOL APAX

MKT CAP (£M) 761

ABERDEEN PRIVATE EQUITY FUND LIMITED

CORE INVESTMENT STRATEGY		Fund of private equity funds	
BENCHMARK		LPX Europe	
MANAGEMENT GROUP		Aberdeen AM	
FUND MANAGER		Alex Barr [2007]	
WEBSITE		www.aberdeenprivateequity.co.uk	

LAUNCH DATE	2007	EXCHANGE	London SE
DOMICILE	Guernsey	CURRENCY	GBP
STOCKBROKER	Liberum	INDEX	FTSE Fledgling
GEARING	100	AVG DISCOUNT (%)	-20.6
NAV (£M)	164	NET DIV YIELD (%)	3.2
TURNOVER	408		
TER (%)	1.87	SHARPE RATIO	1.8
		VOLATILITY	1.36
PERFORMANCE FEE	Yes	PERFORMANCE (10Y) (%)	47

SYMBOL APEF

MKT CAP (£M) 138

BETTER CAPITAL PCC LTD

CORE INVESTMENT STRATEGY		Distressed businesses (mainly UK)	
BENCHMARK		LPX Europe	
MANAGEMENT GROUP		Better Capital	
FUND MANAGER		Jon Moulton [2012]	
WEBSITE		www.bettercapital.gg	

LAUNCH DATE	2012	EXCHANGE	London SE
DOMICILE	Guernsey	CURRENCY	GBP
STOCKBROKER	Numis	INDEX	-
GEARING	100	AVG DISCOUNT (%)	-50.1
NAV (£M)	179	NET DIV YIELD (%)	-
TURNOVER	73		
TER (%)	0.25	SHARPE RATIO	-0.6
		VOLATILITY	1.09
PERFORMANCE FEE	No	PERFORMANCE (10Y) (%)	-

SYMBOL BC12

MKT CAP (£M) 108

BETTER CAPITAL PCC LTD ORD NPV (2009)

CORE INVESTMENT STRATEGY		Distressed businesses (mainly UK)	
BENCHMARK		LPX Europe	
MANAGEMENT GROUP		Better Capital	
FUND MANAGER		Jon Moulton [2009]	
WEBSITE		www.bettercapital.gg	

LAUNCH DATE	2009	EXCHANGE	London SE	**SYMBOL**
DOMICILE	Guernsey	CURRENCY	GBP	**BCAP**
STOCKBROKER	Numis	INDEX	-	
GEARING	100	AVG DISCOUNT (%)	-63.1	
NAV (£M)	40	NET DIV YIELD (%)	-	
TURNOVER	260			**MKT CAP (£M)**
TER (%)	0.21	SHARPE RATIO	1.3	**20**
		VOLATILITY	1.51	
PERFORMANCE FEE	No	PERFORMANCE (10Y) (%)	-	

B.P. MARSH & PARTNERS PLC

CORE INVESTMENT STRATEGY		UK financial services venture capital	
BENCHMARK		FTSE All Share	
MANAGEMENT GROUP		BP Marsh & Partners	
FUND MANAGER		Brian Marsh [2006]	
WEBSITE		www.bpmarsh.co.uk	

LAUNCH DATE	2006	EXCHANGE	AIM	**SYMBOL**
DOMICILE	UK	CURRENCY	GBP	**BPM**
STOCKBROKER	Numis	INDEX	AIM All-Share	
GEARING	100	AVG DISCOUNT (%)	-20.6	
NAV (£M)	78	NET DIV YIELD (%)	-	
TURNOVER	41			**MKT CAP (£M)**
TER (%)	3.51	SHARPE RATIO	1.0	**65**
		VOLATILITY	1.41	
PERFORMANCE FEE	No	PERFORMANCE (10Y) (%)	85	

CANDOVER INVESTMENTS PLC

CORE INVESTMENT STRATEGY		Realising portfolio of Pan-European mid/large buyouts	
BENCHMARK		LPX Europe	
MANAGEMENT GROUP		Self-managed	
FUND MANAGER		Malcolm Fallen [2009]	
WEBSITE		www.candoverinvestments.com	

LAUNCH DATE	1980	EXCHANGE	London SE	**SYMBOL**
DOMICILE	UK	CURRENCY	GBP	**CDI**
STOCKBROKER	Winterflood	INDEX	FTSE Fledgling	
GEARING	191	AVG DISCOUNT (%)	-15.9	
NAV (£M)	33	NET DIV YIELD (%)	-	
TURNOVER	37			**MKT CAP (£M)**
TER (%)	7.12	SHARPE RATIO	-1.5	**30**
		VOLATILITY	1.95	
PERFORMANCE FEE	No	PERFORMANCE (10Y) (%)	-93	

DUNEDIN ENTERPRISE INVESTMENT TRUST PLC

CORE INVESTMENT STRATEGY		UK small/mid buyouts & European buyout funds		
BENCHMARK		LPX Europe		
MANAGEMENT GROUP		Dunedin LLP		
FUND MANAGER		Shaun Middleton [2003]		
WEBSITE		www.dunedinenterprise.com		

LAUNCH DATE	1987	EXCHANGE	London SE	**SYMBOL**
DOMICILE	UK	CURRENCY	GBP	**DNE**
STOCKBROKER	Cantor Fitzgerald Europe	INDEX	FTSE Fledgling	
GEARING	100	AVG DISCOUNT (%)	-31.5	
NAV (£M)	107	NET DIV YIELD (%)	4.8	
TURNOVER	57			
TER (%)	2.66	SHARPE RATIO	-0.1	**MKT CAP (£M)**
		VOLATILITY	1.24	**75**
PERFORMANCE FEE	Yes	PERFORMANCE (10Y) (%)	13	

ELECTRA PRIVATE EQUITY PLC

CORE INVESTMENT STRATEGY		UK & European mid-market buyouts		
BENCHMARK		LPX Europe		
MANAGEMENT GROUP		Epiris		
FUND MANAGER		Alex Fortescue [2011]		
WEBSITE		www.electraequity.com		

LAUNCH DATE	1976	EXCHANGE	London SE	**SYMBOL**
DOMICILE	UK	CURRENCY	GBP	**ELTA**
STOCKBROKER	HSBC, Morgan Stanley	INDEX	FTSE Mid 250	
GEARING	100	AVG DISCOUNT (%)	-51.7	
NAV (£M)	775	NET DIV YIELD (%)	3.0	
TURNOVER	3,792			
TER (%)	0.51	SHARPE RATIO	0.6	**MKT CAP (£M)**
		VOLATILITY	1.50	**621**
PERFORMANCE FEE	Yes	PERFORMANCE (10Y) (%)	236	

EPE SPECIAL OPPORTUNITIES PLC

CORE INVESTMENT STRATEGY		UK SME financing – special situations, distressed, growth and buyout		
BENCHMARK		FTSE All Share		
MANAGEMENT GROUP		EPIC Private Equity		
FUND MANAGER		Giles Brand [2003]		
WEBSITE		www.epicprivateequity.com		

LAUNCH DATE	2003	EXCHANGE	AIM	**SYMBOL**
DOMICILE	Isle of Man	CURRENCY	GBP	**ESO**
STOCKBROKER	Numis	INDEX	AIM All-Share	
GEARING	105	AVG DISCOUNT (%)	-19.7	
NAV (£M)	120	NET DIV YIELD (%)	-	
TURNOVER	150			
TER (%)	3.27	SHARPE RATIO	1.8	**MKT CAP (£M)**
		VOLATILITY	1.45	**90**
PERFORMANCE FEE	Yes	PERFORMANCE (10Y) (%)	13	

F&C PRIVATE EQUITY TRUST PLC

CORE INVESTMENT STRATEGY	Fund of private equity funds (global focus)		
BENCHMARK	LPX Europe		
MANAGEMENT GROUP	F&C Investments		
FUND MANAGER	Hamish Mair [2001]		
WEBSITE	www.fcpet.co.uk		

LAUNCH DATE	1999	EXCHANGE	London SE	**SYMBOL**
DOMICILE	UK	CURRENCY	GBP	
STOCKBROKER	Cantor Fitzgerald Europe	INDEX	FTSE Small Cap	**FPEO**
GEARING	109	AVG DISCOUNT (%)	-5.8	
NAV (£M)	267	NET DIV YIELD (%)	4.1	
TURNOVER	317			**MKT CAP (£M)**
TER (%)	1.27	SHARPE RATIO	1.6	
		VOLATILITY	1.02	**242**
PERFORMANCE FEE	Yes	PERFORMANCE (10Y) (%)	158	

HGCAPITAL TRUST PLC

CORE INVESTMENT STRATEGY	Pan-European mid market buyouts (£50-500m)		
BENCHMARK	LPX Europe		
MANAGEMENT GROUP	HgCapital		
FUND MANAGER	Nic Humphries [1989]		
WEBSITE	www.hgcapital.com		

LAUNCH DATE	1989	EXCHANGE	London SE	**SYMBOL**
DOMICILE	UK	CURRENCY	GBP	
STOCKBROKER	Numis	INDEX	FTSE Small Cap	**HGT**
GEARING	100	AVG DISCOUNT (%)	-6.1	
NAV (£M)	673	NET DIV YIELD (%)	2.7	
TURNOVER	822			**MKT CAP (£M)**
TER (%)	1.66	SHARPE RATIO	1.6	
		VOLATILITY	0.97	**634**
PERFORMANCE FEE	Yes	PERFORMANCE (10Y) (%)	162	

HARBOURVEST GLOBAL PRIVATE EQUITY LTD

CORE INVESTMENT STRATEGY	Private equity funds (mostly primary, but also secondary funds & direct)		
BENCHMARK	LPX Europe		
MANAGEMENT GROUP	HarbourVest Partners		
FUND MANAGER	Peter Wilson, Richard Hickman [2007]		
WEBSITE	www.hvgpe.com		

LAUNCH DATE	2007	EXCHANGE	London SE, Euronext	**SYMBOL**
DOMICILE	Guernsey	CURRENCY	GBP	
STOCKBROKER	JPM Cazenove, Jefferies	INDEX	FTSE Mid 250	**HVPE**
GEARING	100	AVG DISCOUNT (%)	-17.5	
NAV (£M)	1,200	NET DIV YIELD (%)	-	
TURNOVER	1,430			**MKT CAP (£M)**
TER (%)	0.34	SHARPE RATIO	1.9	
		VOLATILITY	0.73	**990**
PERFORMANCE FEE	No	PERFORMANCE (10Y) (%)	-	

ICG ENTERPRISE TRUST PLC

CORE INVESTMENT STRATEGY		UK mid-market buyouts and private equity funds		
BENCHMARK		LPX Europe		
MANAGEMENT GROUP		Intermediate Capital Group		
FUND MANAGER		Emma Osborne [1981]		
WEBSITE		www.icg-enterprise.co.uk		

LAUNCH DATE	1981	EXCHANGE	London SE	**SYMBOL**
DOMICILE	UK	CURRENCY	GBP	**ICGT**
STOCKBROKER	Numis	INDEX	FTSE Small Cap	
GEARING	100	AVG DISCOUNT (%)	-17.0	
NAV (£M)	623	NET DIV YIELD (%)	2.7	
TURNOVER	468			
TER (%)	1.28	SHARPE RATIO	0.9	**MKT CAP (£M)**
		VOLATILITY	1.25	**517**
PERFORMANCE FEE	No	PERFORMANCE (10Y) (%)	99	

3I GROUP PLC

CORE INVESTMENT STRATEGY		Buyouts, growth capital & infrastructure (mainly pan-European)		
BENCHMARK		LPX Europe		
MANAGEMENT GROUP		Self-Managed		
FUND MANAGER		Simon Borrows [2012]		
WEBSITE		www.3i.com		

LAUNCH DATE	1945	EXCHANGE	London SE	**SYMBOL**
DOMICILE	UK	CURRENCY	GBP	**III**
STOCKBROKER	Bank of America, Barclays Capital	INDEX	FTSE 100	
GEARING	100	AVG DISCOUNT (%)	33.9	
NAV (£M)	6,277	NET DIV YIELD (%)	2.7	
TURNOVER	26,556			
TER (%)	2.15	SHARPE RATIO	1.7	**MKT CAP (£M)**
		VOLATILITY	2.12	**9,378**
PERFORMANCE FEE	Yes	PERFORMANCE (10Y) (%)	53	

JPMORGAN PRIVATE EQUITY LTD

CORE INVESTMENT STRATEGY		Fund of private equity funds (global focus)		
BENCHMARK		LPX Europe		
MANAGEMENT GROUP		Fortress Investment		
FUND MANAGER		Greg Getschow, Troy Duncan [2005]		
WEBSITE		www.jpelonline.com		

LAUNCH DATE	2005	EXCHANGE	London SE	**SYMBOL**
DOMICILE	Guernsey	CURRENCY	USD	**JPEL**
STOCKBROKER	JPM Cazenove, Liberum	INDEX	-	
GEARING	110	AVG DISCOUNT (%)	-20.6	
NAV (£M)	319	NET DIV YIELD (%)	-	
TURNOVER	284			
TER (%)	1.94	SHARPE RATIO	2.0	**MKT CAP (£M)**
		VOLATILITY	0.79	**261**
PERFORMANCE FEE	Yes	PERFORMANCE (10Y) (%)	38	

LMS CAPITAL PLC

CORE INVESTMENT STRATEGY		Private equity opportunities	
BENCHMARK		LPX Europe	
MANAGEMENT GROUP		Gresham House	
FUND MANAGER		Tony Dalwood, Graham Bird [2016]	
WEBSITE		www.lmscapital.com	

LAUNCH DATE	2006	EXCHANGE	London SE	**SYMBOL**
DOMICILE	UK	CURRENCY	GBP	**LMS**
STOCKBROKER	JPM Cazenove	INDEX	FTSE Fledgling	
GEARING	100	AVG DISCOUNT (%)	-35.3	
NAV (£M)	60	NET DIV YIELD (%)	-	
TURNOVER	85			**MKT CAP (£M)**
TER (%)	0.65	SHARPE RATIO	-0.7	**39**
		VOLATILITY	1.63	
PERFORMANCE FEE	Yes	PERFORMANCE (10Y) (%)	-32	

MITHRAS INVESTMENT TRUST PLC

CORE INVESTMENT STRATEGY		Private equity funds (LGV and other managers)	
BENCHMARK		LPX Europe	
MANAGEMENT GROUP		Mithras Capital Partners	
FUND MANAGER		Adrian Johnson [2009]	
WEBSITE		www.mithrasinvestmenttrust.com	

LAUNCH DATE	1994	EXCHANGE	London SE	**SYMBOL**
DOMICILE	UK	CURRENCY	GBP	**MTH**
STOCKBROKER	Winterflood	INDEX	FTSE Fledgling	
GEARING	100	AVG DISCOUNT (%)	-8.1	
NAV (£M)	23	NET DIV YIELD (%)	0.5	
TURNOVER	9			**MKT CAP (£M)**
TER (%)	2.41	SHARPE RATIO	1.3	**22**
		VOLATILITY	1.09	
PERFORMANCE FEE	No	PERFORMANCE (10Y) (%)	190	

NB PRIVATE EQUITY PARTNERS LTD

CORE INVESTMENT STRATEGY		Fund of global private equity LPs	
BENCHMARK		LPX Europe	
MANAGEMENT GROUP		NB Alternatives	
FUND MANAGER		Peter Von Lehe [2007]	
WEBSITE		www.nb.com	

LAUNCH DATE	2007	EXCHANGE	London SE (SFS), Euronext	**SYMBOL**
DOMICILE	Guernsey	CURRENCY	GBP	**NBPE**
STOCKBROKER	Stifel, Jefferies	INDEX	FTSE Small Cap	
GEARING	109	AVG DISCOUNT (%)	-17.9	
NAV (£M)	556	NET DIV YIELD (%)	3.8	
TURNOVER	475			**MKT CAP (£M)**
TER (%)	2.27	SHARPE RATIO	0.9	**466**
		VOLATILITY	0.94	
PERFORMANCE FEE	Yes	PERFORMANCE (10Y) (%)	-	

OAKLEY CAPITAL INVESTMENTS LTD

CORE INVESTMENT STRATEGY	Mid-market pan-European (equity investment £20-100m)
BENCHMARK	LPX Europe
MANAGEMENT GROUP	Oakley Capital
FUND MANAGER	Peter Dubens [2007]
WEBSITE	www.oakleycapitalinvestments.com

LAUNCH DATE	2007	EXCHANGE	AIM
DOMICILE	Bermuda	CURRENCY	GBP
STOCKBROKER	Liberum	INDEX	AIM 100, AIM All-Share
GEARING	100	AVG DISCOUNT (%)	-30.3
NAV (£M)	473	NET DIV YIELD (%)	2.7
TURNOVER	596		
TER (%)	0.92	SHARPE RATIO	0.2
		VOLATILITY	0.89
PERFORMANCE FEE	Yes	PERFORMANCE (10Y) (%)	66

SYMBOL **OCI**

MKT CAP (£M) **339**

PRINCESS PRIVATE EQUITY HOLDING LTD

CORE INVESTMENT STRATEGY	Private equity and private debt (focus on directs, current porfolio includes fund and secondary investments)
BENCHMARK	LPX Europe
MANAGEMENT GROUP	Partners Group
FUND MANAGER	Urs Wietlisbach [2007]
WEBSITE	www.princess-privateequity.net

LAUNCH DATE	2007	EXCHANGE	London SE
DOMICILE	Guernsey	CURRENCY	EUR
STOCKBROKER	Numis, JPM Cazenove	INDEX	-
GEARING	103	AVG DISCOUNT (%)	-10.3
NAV (£M)	677	NET DIV YIELD (%)	5.5
TURNOVER	585		
TER (%)	1.7	SHARPE RATIO	1.9
		VOLATILITY	1.38
PERFORMANCE FEE	Yes	PERFORMANCE (10Y) (%)	-

SYMBOL **PEY**

MKT CAP (£M) **629**

PANTHEON INTERNATIONAL PLC

CORE INVESTMENT STRATEGY	Fund of private equity funds (secondary bias)
BENCHMARK	LPX Europe
MANAGEMENT GROUP	Pantheon
FUND MANAGER	Andrew Lebus [1989]
WEBSITE	www.piplc.com

LAUNCH DATE	1987	EXCHANGE	London SE
DOMICILE	UK	CURRENCY	GBP
STOCKBROKER	Canaccord	INDEX	FTSE Small Cap
GEARING	100	AVG DISCOUNT (%)	-17.4
NAV (£M)	731	NET DIV YIELD (%)	-
TURNOVER	739		
TER (%)	1.13	SHARPE RATIO	1.3
		VOLATILITY	1.46
PERFORMANCE FEE	Yes	PERFORMANCE (10Y) (%)	115

SYMBOL **PIN**

MKT CAP (£M) **598**

PANTHEON INTERNATIONAL PLC

CORE INVESTMENT STRATEGY		Fund of private equity funds (secondary bias)		
BENCHMARK		LPX Europe		
MANAGEMENT GROUP		Pantheon		
FUND MANAGER		Andrew Lebus [1989]		
WEBSITE		www.piplc.com		

LAUNCH DATE	2004	EXCHANGE	London SE	**SYMBOL**
DOMICILE	UK	CURRENCY	GBP	**PINR**
STOCKBROKER	Canaccord	INDEX	FTSE Small Cap	
GEARING	100	AVG DISCOUNT (%)	-25.6	
NAV (£M)	670	NET DIV YIELD (%)	-	
TURNOVER	578			**MKT CAP (£M)**
TER (%)	1.26	SHARPE RATIO	2.0	**509**
		VOLATILITY	1.05	
PERFORMANCE FEE	Yes	PERFORMANCE (10Y) (%)	98	

PURETECH HEALTH

CORE INVESTMENT STRATEGY		Healthcare patents & research		
BENCHMARK		MSCI World		
MANAGEMENT GROUP		Self-Managed		
FUND MANAGER		- [2015]		
WEBSITE		-		

LAUNCH DATE	2015	EXCHANGE	London SE	**SYMBOL**
DOMICILE	UK	CURRENCY	GBP	**PRTC**
STOCKBROKER	Jefferies	INDEX	-	
GEARING	-	AVG DISCOUNT (%)	-	
NAV (£M)	-	NET DIV YIELD (%)	-	
TURNOVER	91			**MKT CAP (£M)**
TER (%)	-	SHARPE RATIO	-	**326**
		VOLATILITY	-	
PERFORMANCE FEE	-	PERFORMANCE (10Y) (%)	-	

QANNAS INVESTMENTS LTD

CORE INVESTMENT STRATEGY		Value investments in GCC region		
BENCHMARK		MSCI GCC Countries		
MANAGEMENT GROUP		Abu Dhabi Capital Mgt		
FUND MANAGER		Jassim Alseddiqi [2012]		
WEBSITE		www.qannasinvestments.com		

LAUNCH DATE	2012	EXCHANGE	AIM	**SYMBOL**
DOMICILE	Cayman Isles	CURRENCY	USD	**QIL**
STOCKBROKER	finnCap	INDEX	-	
GEARING	151	AVG DISCOUNT (%)	-1.8	
NAV (£M)	45	NET DIV YIELD (%)	-	
TURNOVER	1			**MKT CAP (£M)**
TER (%)	2.81	SHARPE RATIO	0.7	**46**
		VOLATILITY	0.47	
PERFORMANCE FEE	Yes	PERFORMANCE (10Y) (%)	-	

RECONSTRUCTION CAPITAL II LTD

CORE INVESTMENT STRATEGY	Companies in Romania and Bulgaria
BENCHMARK	MSCI EM Eastern Europe
MANAGEMENT GROUP	New Europe Capital
FUND MANAGER	Ion Florescu [2005]
WEBSITE	www.reconstructioncapital2.com

LAUNCH DATE	2005	EXCHANGE	AIM	**SYMBOL**
DOMICILE	Cayman Isles	CURRENCY	EUR	**RC2**
STOCKBROKER	Panmure Gordon	INDEX	-	
GEARING	100	AVG DISCOUNT (%)	-30.2	
NAV (£M)	34	NET DIV YIELD (%)	-	
TURNOVER	77			**MKT CAP (£M)**
TER (%)	4.46	SHARPE RATIO	1.0	**26**
		VOLATILITY	1.63	
PERFORMANCE FEE	Yes	PERFORMANCE (10Y) (%)	-82	

SYMPHONY INTERNATIONAL HOLDINGS LTD

CORE INVESTMENT STRATEGY	Hospitality, Healthcare & Lifestyle companies in Asia Pacific
BENCHMARK	MSCI AC Asia (ex Jap)
MANAGEMENT GROUP	Symphony Investment Managers
FUND MANAGER	Anil Thadani / Sunil Chandiramani [2007]
WEBSITE	www.symphonyasia.com

LAUNCH DATE	2007	EXCHANGE	London SE	**SYMBOL**
DOMICILE	Jersey	CURRENCY	USD	**SIHL**
STOCKBROKER	Numis	INDEX	-	
GEARING	100	AVG DISCOUNT (%)	-36.2	
NAV (£M)	472	NET DIV YIELD (%)	7.7	
TURNOVER	378			**MKT CAP (£M)**
TER (%)	2.13	SHARPE RATIO	0.7	**311**
		VOLATILITY	4.20	
PERFORMANCE FEE	No	PERFORMANCE (10Y) (%)	73	

STANDARD LIFE PRIVATE EQUITY TRUST PLC

CORE INVESTMENT STRATEGY	Fund of private equity funds (primarily European buyouts)
BENCHMARK	LPX Europe
MANAGEMENT GROUP	Standard Life Investments
FUND MANAGER	Roger Pim [2001]
WEBSITE	www.slcapital.com

LAUNCH DATE	2001	EXCHANGE	London SE	**SYMBOL**
DOMICILE	UK	CURRENCY	GBP	**SLPE**
STOCKBROKER	Winterflood	INDEX	FTSE Small Cap	
GEARING	100	AVG DISCOUNT (%)	-12.1	
NAV (£M)	585	NET DIV YIELD (%)	2.9	
TURNOVER	467			**MKT CAP (£M)**
TER (%)	0.99	SHARPE RATIO	1.1	**510**
		VOLATILITY	1.41	
PERFORMANCE FEE	Yes	PERFORMANCE (10Y) (%)	65	

PROPERTY SECURITIES

TR PROPERTY INVESTMENT TRUST PLC

CORE INVESTMENT STRATEGY	Pan-European property stocks & direct property in UK
BENCHMARK	MSCI Europe Real Estate
MANAGEMENT GROUP	F&C Investments
FUND MANAGER	Marcus Phayre-Mudge [2011]
WEBSITE	www.trproperty.com

LAUNCH DATE	1905	EXCHANGE	London SE	
DOMICILE	UK	CURRENCY	GBP	**SYMBOL**
STOCKBROKER	Cenkos, Stifel	INDEX	FTSE Mid 250	**TRY**
GEARING	120	AVG DISCOUNT (%)	-11.1	
NAV (£M)	1,239	NET DIV YIELD (%)	2.9	
TURNOVER	1,897			
TER (%)	0.77	SHARPE RATIO	0.9	**MKT CAP (£M)**
		VOLATILITY	1.29	**1,169**
PERFORMANCE FEE	Yes	PERFORMANCE (10Y) (%)	148	

PROPERTY SPECIALIST

AEW UK LONG LEASE REIT PLC

CORE INVESTMENT STRATEGY		UK alternative & specialist property	
BENCHMARK		IPD UK	
MANAGEMENT GROUP		AEW UK IM	
FUND MANAGER		Alex Short [2017]	
WEBSITE		www.aeweurope.com	

LAUNCH DATE	2017	EXCHANGE	London SE	SYMBOL
DOMICILE	UK	CURRENCY	GBP	**AEWL**
STOCKBROKER	Fidante Capital	INDEX	-	
GEARING	100	AVG DISCOUNT (%)	1.5	
NAV (£M)	79	NET DIV YIELD (%)	3.2	
TURNOVER	320			MKT CAP (£M)
TER (%)	-	SHARPE RATIO	-	**81**
		VOLATILITY	0.12	
PERFORMANCE FEE	No	PERFORMANCE (10Y) (%)	-	

TRITAX BIG BOX REIT PLC

CORE INVESTMENT STRATEGY		Commercial property in UK	
BENCHMARK		IPD UK	
MANAGEMENT GROUP		Tritax Management	
FUND MANAGER		Colin Godfrey [2013]	
WEBSITE		www.tritaxbigboxreitplc.co.uk	

LAUNCH DATE	2013	EXCHANGE	London SE	SYMBOL
DOMICILE	UK	CURRENCY	GBP	**BBOX**
STOCKBROKER	Jefferies, Akur Limited	INDEX	FTSE Mid 250	
GEARING	121	AVG DISCOUNT (%)	10.3	
NAV (£M)	1,814	NET DIV YIELD (%)	4.5	
TURNOVER	4,513			MKT CAP (£M)
TER (%)	0.93	SHARPE RATIO	1.4	**1,959**
		VOLATILITY	0.88	
PERFORMANCE FEE	No	PERFORMANCE (10Y) (%)	-	

CIVITAS SOCIAL HOUSING PLC

CORE INVESTMENT STRATEGY		UK social housing
BENCHMARK		IPD UK
MANAGEMENT GROUP		Civitas Housing Advisors
FUND MANAGER		Paul Bridge [2016]
WEBSITE		www.civitasreit.com

LAUNCH DATE	2016	EXCHANGE	London SE	**SYMBOL**
DOMICILE	UK	CURRENCY	GBP	**CSH**
STOCKBROKER	Cenkos	INDEX	FTSE Small Cap	
GEARING	100	AVG DISCOUNT (%)	7.3	
NAV (£M)	366	NET DIV YIELD (%)	2.7	
TURNOVER	759			
TER (%)	–	SHARPE RATIO	–	**MKT CAP (£M)**
		VOLATILITY	0.54	**396**
PERFORMANCE FEE	No	PERFORMANCE (10Y) (%)	–	

GCP STUDENT LIVING PLC

CORE INVESTMENT STRATEGY		Student accommodation
BENCHMARK		IPD UK
MANAGEMENT GROUP		Gravis Capital Partners
FUND MANAGER		Tom Ward [2013]
WEBSITE		www.gcpuk.com

LAUNCH DATE	2013	EXCHANGE	London SE (SFS)	**SYMBOL**
DOMICILE	UK	CURRENCY	GBP	**DIGS**
STOCKBROKER	Stifel	INDEX	FTSE Small Cap	
GEARING	141	AVG DISCOUNT (%)	6.4	
NAV (£M)	532	NET DIV YIELD (%)	3.9	
TURNOVER	904			
TER (%)	3.96	SHARPE RATIO	1.4	**MKT CAP (£M)**
		VOLATILITY	0.50	**563**
PERFORMANCE FEE	No	PERFORMANCE (10Y) (%)	–	

EMPIRIC STUDENT PROPERTY PLC

CORE INVESTMENT STRATEGY		Student accommodation
BENCHMARK		IPD UK
MANAGEMENT GROUP		London Cornwall Property Partners
FUND MANAGER		Team managed [2014]
WEBSITE		www.empiric.co.uk

LAUNCH DATE	2014	EXCHANGE	London SE	**SYMBOL**
DOMICILE	UK	CURRENCY	GBP	**ESP**
STOCKBROKER	Jefferies, Akur Ltd	INDEX	FTSE Small Cap	
GEARING	116	AVG DISCOUNT (%)	6.1	
NAV (£M)	634	NET DIV YIELD (%)	5.4	
TURNOVER	1,238			
TER (%)	1.71	SHARPE RATIO	0.8	**MKT CAP (£M)**
		VOLATILITY	0.77	**681**
PERFORMANCE FEE	No	PERFORMANCE (10Y) (%)	–	

GROUND RENTS INCOME FUND PLC

CORE INVESTMENT STRATEGY		Ground rents	
BENCHMARK		IPD UK	
MANAGEMENT GROUP		Brooks Macdonald	
FUND MANAGER		James Agar [2012]	
WEBSITE		www.groundrentsincomefund.com	

LAUNCH DATE	2012	EXCHANGE	London SE	**SYMBOL**
DOMICILE	UK	CURRENCY	GBP	
STOCKBROKER	N+1 Singer	INDEX	-	**GRIO**
GEARING	100	AVG DISCOUNT (%)	3.2	
NAV (£M)	125	NET DIV YIELD (%)	3.2	
TURNOVER	338			
TER (%)	0.85	SHARPE RATIO	1.3	**MKT CAP (£M)**
		VOLATILITY	0.49	**116**
PERFORMANCE FEE	No	PERFORMANCE (10Y) (%)	-	

IMPACT HEALTHCARE REIT PLC

CORE INVESTMENT STRATEGY		Healthcare properties in UK
BENCHMARK		FTSE 350 Real Estate
MANAGEMENT GROUP		Impact Healthcare Partners
FUND MANAGER		- [2017]
WEBSITE		-

LAUNCH DATE	2017	EXCHANGE	London SE	**SYMBOL**
DOMICILE	UK	CURRENCY	GBP	
STOCKBROKER	Winterflood	INDEX	-	**IHR**
GEARING	100	AVG DISCOUNT (%)	4.8	
NAV (£M)	158	NET DIV YIELD (%)	5.8	
TURNOVER	182			
TER (%)	-	SHARPE RATIO	-	**MKT CAP (£M)**
		VOLATILITY	0.21	**165**
PERFORMANCE FEE	No	PERFORMANCE (10Y) (%)	-	

MEDICX FUND LTD

CORE INVESTMENT STRATEGY		Healthcare properties, primarily in UK
BENCHMARK		FTSE 350 Real Estate
MANAGEMENT GROUP		MedicX Adviser
FUND MANAGER		Mike Adams [2006]
WEBSITE		www.medicxfund.com

LAUNCH DATE	2006	EXCHANGE	London SE	**SYMBOL**
DOMICILE	Guernsey	CURRENCY	GBP	
STOCKBROKER	Canaccord	INDEX	FTSE Small Cap	**MXF**
GEARING	209	AVG DISCOUNT (%)	22.0	
NAV (£M)	324	NET DIV YIELD (%)	6.7	
TURNOVER	624			
TER (%)	3.12	SHARPE RATIO	1.0	**MKT CAP (£M)**
		VOLATILITY	1.23	**384**
PERFORMANCE FEE	Yes	PERFORMANCE (10Y) (%)	94	

RESIDENTIAL SECURE INCOME PLC

CORE INVESTMENT STRATEGY		UK residential property	
BENCHMARK		IPD UK	
MANAGEMENT GROUP		ReSI Capital Management	
FUND MANAGER		- [2017]	
WEBSITE		www.resi-reit.com	

LAUNCH DATE	2017	EXCHANGE	London SE	SYMBOL
DOMICILE	UK	CURRENCY	GBP	**RESI**
STOCKBROKER	Jefferies	INDEX	-	
GEARING	100	AVG DISCOUNT (%)	2.8	
NAV (£M)	177	NET DIV YIELD (%)	3.0	
TURNOVER	442			
TER (%)	-	SHARPE RATIO	-	MKT CAP (£M)
		VOLATILITY	0.20	**183**
PERFORMANCE FEE	No	PERFORMANCE (10Y) (%)	-	

RAVEN RUSSIA LTD

CORE INVESTMENT STRATEGY		Russian property	
BENCHMARK		MSCI Russia	
MANAGEMENT GROUP		Self-Managed	
FUND MANAGER		Glyn Hirsch, Anton Bilton [2005]	
WEBSITE		www.ravenrussia.com	

LAUNCH DATE	2005	EXCHANGE	London SE	SYMBOL
DOMICILE	Guernsey	CURRENCY	GBP	**RUS**
STOCKBROKER	N+1 Singer, Barclays Bank	INDEX	FTSE Small Cap	
GEARING	192	AVG DISCOUNT (%)	-16.5	
NAV (£M)	384	NET DIV YIELD (%)	-	
TURNOVER	142			MKT CAP (£M)
TER (%)	1.87	SHARPE RATIO	-0.4	**323**
		VOLATILITY	2.28	
PERFORMANCE FEE	No	PERFORMANCE (10Y) (%)	-37	

TARGET HEALTHCARE REIT LTD

CORE INVESTMENT STRATEGY		Care homes	
BENCHMARK		UK£ 3 Month Libor	
MANAGEMENT GROUP		Target Advisers	
FUND MANAGER		Kenneth Mackenzie [2013]	
WEBSITE		www.targethealthcarereit.co.uk	

LAUNCH DATE	2013	EXCHANGE	London SE	SYMBOL
DOMICILE	Jersey	CURRENCY	GBP	**THRL**
STOCKBROKER	Stifel	INDEX	FTSE Small Cap	
GEARING	112	AVG DISCOUNT (%)	14.0	
NAV (£M)	253	NET DIV YIELD (%)	5.4	
TURNOVER	426			MKT CAP (£M)
TER (%)	1.5	SHARPE RATIO	1.0	**294**
		VOLATILITY	0.74	
PERFORMANCE FEE	Yes	PERFORMANCE (10Y) (%)	-	

PROPERTY DIRECT – ASIA SPECIFIC

ASIAN GROWTH PROPERTIES LTD

CORE INVESTMENT STRATEGY	Asia Pacific properties
BENCHMARK	MSCI AC Asia Pacific (ex Jap)
MANAGEMENT GROUP	Asian Growth Properties
FUND MANAGER	Lu Wing Chi, David Andrew Runciman [2006]
WEBSITE	www.asiangrowth.com

LAUNCH DATE	2006	EXCHANGE	AIM	**SYMBOL**
DOMICILE	British Virgin Isles	CURRENCY	GBP	**AGP**
STOCKBROKER	Panmure Gordon	INDEX	-	
GEARING	127	AVG DISCOUNT (%)	-89.7	
NAV (£M)	1,242	NET DIV YIELD (%)	-	
TURNOVER	33			**MKT CAP (£M)**
TER (%)	3.07	SHARPE RATIO	2.6	**253**
		VOLATILITY	4.44	
PERFORMANCE FEE	No	PERFORMANCE (10Y) (%)	946	

ALPHA REAL TRUST LTD

CORE INVESTMENT STRATEGY	Real estate opportunities focusd on the UK, Europe and Asia
BENCHMARK	FTSE All Share
MANAGEMENT GROUP	Alpha Real Capital
FUND MANAGER	Phillip Rose, Brad Bauman [2006]
WEBSITE	-

LAUNCH DATE	2006	EXCHANGE	London SE (SFS)	**SYMBOL**
DOMICILE	Guernsey	CURRENCY	GBP	**ARTL**
STOCKBROKER	Panmure Gordon/ Canaccord	INDEX	-	
GEARING	153	AVG DISCOUNT (%)	-27.9	
NAV (£M)	110	NET DIV YIELD (%)	1.9	
TURNOVER	23			**MKT CAP (£M)**
TER (%)	11.08	SHARPE RATIO	1.6	**87**
		VOLATILITY	1.21	
PERFORMANCE FEE	Yes	PERFORMANCE (10Y) (%)	50	

ASEANA PROPERTIES LTD

CORE INVESTMENT STRATEGY		Property in Vietnam & Malaysia		
BENCHMARK		Vietnam Stock Index		
MANAGEMENT GROUP		Ireka Development		
FUND MANAGER		Lai Voon Hon [2007]		
WEBSITE		www.aseanaproperties.com		

LAUNCH DATE	2007	EXCHANGE	AIM	**SYMBOL**
DOMICILE	Jersey	CURRENCY	USD	
STOCKBROKER	N+1 Singer	INDEX	-	**ASPL**
GEARING	247	AVG DISCOUNT (%)	-24.3	
NAV (£M)	98	NET DIV YIELD (%)	-	
TURNOVER	499			**MKT CAP (£M)**
TER (%)	18.12	SHARPE RATIO	1.0	
		VOLATILITY	1.82	**82**
PERFORMANCE FEE	Yes	PERFORMANCE (10Y) (%)	-8	

MACAU PROPERTY OPPORTUNITIES FUND LTD

CORE INVESTMENT STRATEGY		Macau property requiring refurbishment or redevelopment		
BENCHMARK		MSCI China		
MANAGEMENT GROUP		Sniper Capital Management /Heritage International		
FUND MANAGER		Martin Tacon, Tom Ashworth [2006]		
WEBSITE		www.mpofund.com		

LAUNCH DATE	2006	EXCHANGE	London SE	**SYMBOL**
DOMICILE	Guernsey	CURRENCY	GBP	
STOCKBROKER	Liberum	INDEX	FTSE Small Cap	**MPO**
GEARING	172	AVG DISCOUNT (%)	-37.4	
NAV (£M)	192	NET DIV YIELD (%)	-	
TURNOVER	100			**MKT CAP (£M)**
TER (%)	3.59	SHARPE RATIO	-0.5	
		VOLATILITY	1.42	**122**
PERFORMANCE FEE	Yes	PERFORMANCE (10Y) (%)	64	

PACIFIC ALLIANCE CHINA LAND LTD

CORE INVESTMENT STRATEGY		Residential and commercial property in China		
BENCHMARK		MSCI China		
MANAGEMENT GROUP		Pacific Alliance Real Estate		
FUND MANAGER		Patrick Boot [2007]		
WEBSITE		www.pagasia.com		

LAUNCH DATE	2007	EXCHANGE	AIM	**SYMBOL**
DOMICILE	Cayman Isles	CURRENCY	USD	
STOCKBROKER	Liberum	INDEX	-	**PACL**
GEARING	100	AVG DISCOUNT (%)	-19.2	
NAV (£M)	126	NET DIV YIELD (%)	-	
TURNOVER	152			**MKT CAP (£M)**
TER (%)	2.83	SHARPE RATIO	1.5	
		VOLATILITY	0.81	**101**
PERFORMANCE FEE	Yes	PERFORMANCE (10Y) (%)	-	

VINALAND LTD

CORE INVESTMENT STRATEGY		Vietnamese property	
BENCHMARK		Vietnam Stock Index	
MANAGEMENT GROUP		VinaCapital IM	
FUND MANAGER		David Blackhall [2007]	
WEBSITE		www.vnl-fund.com	

LAUNCH DATE	2006	EXCHANGE	AIM	SYMBOL
DOMICILE	Cayman Isles	CURRENCY	USD	**VNL**
STOCKBROKER	Numis	INDEX	AIM 100, AIM All-Share	
GEARING	132	AVG DISCOUNT (%)	-20.6	
NAV (£M)	178	NET DIV YIELD (%)	-	
TURNOVER	729			MKT CAP (£M)
TER (%)	3.93	SHARPE RATIO	1.9	**148**
		VOLATILITY	1.44	
PERFORMANCE FEE	No	PERFORMANCE (10Y) (%)	6	

PROPERTY DIRECT – EUROPE

DOLPHIN CAPITAL INVESTORS LTD

CORE INVESTMENT STRATEGY		Resort developments in south-east Europe
BENCHMARK		MSCI EM Eastern Europe
MANAGEMENT GROUP		Dolphin Capital Partners
FUND MANAGER		Andreas Papageorgiou, Miltos Kambourides, Pierre Charalambides [2005]
WEBSITE		www.dolphinci.com

LAUNCH DATE	2005	EXCHANGE	AIM	SYMBOL
DOMICILE	British Virgin Isles	CURRENCY	GBP	**DCI**
STOCKBROKER	Panmure Gordon	INDEX	AIM All-Share	
GEARING	180	AVG DISCOUNT (%)	-78.3	
NAV (£M)	243	NET DIV YIELD (%)	-	
TURNOVER	213			MKT CAP (£M)
TER (%)	5.2	SHARPE RATIO	-1.2	**62**
		VOLATILITY	1.88	
PERFORMANCE FEE	Yes	PERFORMANCE (10Y) (%)	-95	

GLOBALWORTH REAL ESTATE INVESTMENTS LTD

CORE INVESTMENT STRATEGY		Property in Romania & in the SEE & CEE region	
BENCHMARK		MSCI EM Eastern Europe	
MANAGEMENT GROUP		Globalworth Investment Advisers	
FUND MANAGER		Team managed [2013]	
WEBSITE		www.globalworth.com	

LAUNCH DATE	2013	EXCHANGE	AIM	**SYMBOL**
DOMICILE	Guernsey	CURRENCY	EUR	**GWI**
STOCKBROKER	Panmure Gordon, Jefferies	INDEX	-	
GEARING	127	AVG DISCOUNT (%)	-25.0	
NAV (£M)	689	NET DIV YIELD (%)	3.0	
TURNOVER	237			
TER (%)	2.03	SHARPE RATIO	0.7	**MKT CAP (£M)**
		VOLATILITY	13.27	**601**
PERFORMANCE FEE	No	PERFORMANCE (10Y) (%)	-	

HANSTEEN HOLDINGS PLC

CORE INVESTMENT STRATEGY		Continental European industrial property	
BENCHMARK		MSCI Europe Real Estate	
MANAGEMENT GROUP		Hansteen Holdings	
FUND MANAGER		Ian Watson and Morgan Jones [2005]	
WEBSITE		www.hansteen.co.uk	

LAUNCH DATE	2005	EXCHANGE	London SE	**SYMBOL**
DOMICILE	UK	CURRENCY	GBP	**HSTN**
STOCKBROKER	KBC Peel Hunt	INDEX	FTSE Mid 250	
GEARING	130	AVG DISCOUNT (%)	-4.8	
NAV (£M)	1,092	NET DIV YIELD (%)	4.5	
TURNOVER	2,949			
TER (%)	2.14	SHARPE RATIO	0.7	**MKT CAP (£M)**
		VOLATILITY	1.54	**1,096**
PERFORMANCE FEE	Yes	PERFORMANCE (10Y) (%)	88	

KENNEDY WILSON EUROPE REAL ESTATE PLC

CORE INVESTMENT STRATEGY		European real estate & real estate loans	
BENCHMARK		MSCI Europe Real Estate	
MANAGEMENT GROUP		KW IM	
FUND MANAGER		Team managed [2014]	
WEBSITE		www.kennedywilsoneuropeplc.com	

LAUNCH DATE	2014	EXCHANGE	London SE	**SYMBOL**
DOMICILE	Jersey	CURRENCY	GBP	**KWE**
STOCKBROKER	Deutche Bank, Bank of America, Davy	INDEX	FTSE Mid 250	
GEARING	225	AVG DISCOUNT (%)	-14.3	
NAV (£M)	1,476	NET DIV YIELD (%)	4.3	
TURNOVER	5,072			
TER (%)	1.03	SHARPE RATIO	0.3	**MKT CAP (£M)**
		VOLATILITY	1.19	**1,405**
PERFORMANCE FEE	Yes	PERFORMANCE (10Y) (%)	-	

PHOENIX SPREE DEUTSCHLAND LTD

CORE INVESTMENT STRATEGY	Residential property in Germany
BENCHMARK	9% p.a.
MANAGEMENT GROUP	PMM Partners
FUND MANAGER	Micheal Hilton, Matthew Northover, Paul Ruddle [2015]
WEBSITE	www.phoenixspree.com

LAUNCH DATE	2015	EXCHANGE	London SE	SYMBOL
DOMICILE	Jersey	CURRENCY	GBP	
STOCKBROKER	Liberum Capital, SP Angel Corporate Finance	INDEX	FTSE Small Cap	**PSDL**
GEARING	154	AVG DISCOUNT (%)	15.9	
NAV (£M)	227	NET DIV YIELD (%)	1.8	
TURNOVER	386			MKT CAP (£M)
TER (%)	6.96	SHARPE RATIO	-	
		VOLATILITY	1.33	**277**
PERFORMANCE FEE	Yes	PERFORMANCE (10Y) (%)	-	

REDEFINE INTERNATIONAL PLC

CORE INVESTMENT STRATEGY	European Government-occupied properties
BENCHMARK	FTSE 350 Real Estate
MANAGEMENT GROUP	Redefine International Property Management
FUND MANAGER	Michael Watters [2004]
WEBSITE	www.redefineinternational.com

LAUNCH DATE	2004	EXCHANGE	London SE	SYMBOL
DOMICILE	Isle of Man	CURRENCY	GBP	
STOCKBROKER	Peel Hunt, JPM Cazenove	INDEX	FTSE Mid 250	**RDI**
GEARING	193	AVG DISCOUNT (%)	-1.0	
NAV (£M)	714	NET DIV YIELD (%)	7.2	
TURNOVER	990			MKT CAP (£M)
TER (%)	2.8	SHARPE RATIO	-0.2	
		VOLATILITY	2.11	**732**
PERFORMANCE FEE	Yes	PERFORMANCE (10Y) (%)	-	

SCHRODER EUROPEAN REAL ESTATE INVESTMENT TRUST LTD

CORE INVESTMENT STRATEGY	European commercial real estate
BENCHMARK	5.5% p.a.
MANAGEMENT GROUP	Schroder IM
FUND MANAGER	Tony Smedley [2015]
WEBSITE	www.schroders.com

LAUNCH DATE	2015	EXCHANGE	London SE	SYMBOL
DOMICILE	UK	CURRENCY	GBP	
STOCKBROKER	Numis	INDEX	FTSE Small Cap	**SERE**
GEARING	100	AVG DISCOUNT (%)	-2.1	
NAV (£M)	165	NET DIV YIELD (%)	4.8	
TURNOVER	149			MKT CAP (£M)
TER (%)	3.27	SHARPE RATIO	-	
		VOLATILITY	1.44	**153**
PERFORMANCE FEE	No	PERFORMANCE (10Y) (%)	-	

SUMMIT GERMANY

CORE INVESTMENT STRATEGY		German commercial property	
BENCHMARK		S&P Germany Property	
MANAGEMENT GROUP		Summit Management Company	
FUND MANAGER		Zohar Levy [2014]	
WEBSITE		-	

LAUNCH DATE	2014	EXCHANGE	AIM	**SYMBOL**
DOMICILE	Guernsey	CURRENCY	EUR	
STOCKBROKER	Cenkos, Liberum Capital	INDEX	-	**SMTG**
GEARING	-	AVG DISCOUNT (%)	9.6	
NAV (£M)	423	NET DIV YIELD (%)	2.8	
TURNOVER	283			
TER (%)	-	SHARPE RATIO	-	**MKT CAP (£M)**
		VOLATILITY	-	**460**
PERFORMANCE FEE	-	PERFORMANCE (10Y) (%)	-	

SIRIUS REAL ESTATE LTD

CORE INVESTMENT STRATEGY		Upgrading German commercial real estate	
BENCHMARK		German DAX	
MANAGEMENT GROUP		Sirius Facilities	
FUND MANAGER		Kevin Oppenheim, Alistair Marks, Ingo Spangenberg [2007]	
WEBSITE		www.sirius-real-estate.com	

LAUNCH DATE	2007	EXCHANGE	London SE	**SYMBOL**
DOMICILE	Guernsey	CURRENCY	GBP	
STOCKBROKER	Peel Hunt, Berenberg	INDEX	-	**SRE**
GEARING	199	AVG DISCOUNT (%)	-6.3	
NAV (£M)	545	NET DIV YIELD (%)	4.2	
TURNOVER	744			
TER (%)	11.6	SHARPE RATIO	1.5	**MKT CAP (£M)**
		VOLATILITY	2.50	**558**
PERFORMANCE FEE	Yes	PERFORMANCE (10Y) (%)	14	

TALIESIN PROPERTY FUND LTD

CORE INVESTMENT STRATEGY		Berlin residential property	
BENCHMARK		S&P Germany Property	
MANAGEMENT GROUP		Taliesin Management, JJ IM	
FUND MANAGER		Mark Smith [2007]	
WEBSITE		www.taliesinberlin.com	

LAUNCH DATE	2007	EXCHANGE	AIM	**SYMBOL**
DOMICILE	Jersey	CURRENCY	GBP	
STOCKBROKER	NCB Stockbrokers	INDEX	AIM All-Share	**TPF**
GEARING	150	AVG DISCOUNT (%)	15.5	
NAV (£M)	207	NET DIV YIELD (%)	-	
TURNOVER	145			
TER (%)	4.11	SHARPE RATIO	2.0	**MKT CAP (£M)**
		VOLATILITY	0.85	**206**
PERFORMANCE FEE	Yes	PERFORMANCE (10Y) (%)	402	

PROPERTY DIRECT – UK

AEW UK REIT PLC

CORE INVESTMENT STRATEGY		UK smaller commercial property	
BENCHMARK		IPD UK	
MANAGEMENT GROUP		AEW UK IM	
FUND MANAGER		Alex Short [2015]	
WEBSITE		www.aeweurope.com	

LAUNCH DATE	2015	EXCHANGE	London SE	**SYMBOL**
DOMICILE	UK	CURRENCY	GBP	**AEWU**
STOCKBROKER	Fidante Capital	INDEX	FTSE Fledgling	
GEARING	112	AVG DISCOUNT (%)	3.8	
NAV (£M)	121	NET DIV YIELD (%)	7.8	
TURNOVER	228			
TER (%)	1.58	SHARPE RATIO	-	**MKT CAP (£M)**
		VOLATILITY	0.38	**127**
PERFORMANCE FEE	No	PERFORMANCE (10Y) (%)	-	

CUSTODIAN REIT PLC

CORE INVESTMENT STRATEGY		Commercial property in UK, focus on small lot sizes	
BENCHMARK		IPD UK	
MANAGEMENT GROUP		Custodian Capital	
FUND MANAGER		Richard Shepherd-Cross [2014]	
WEBSITE		www.custodianreit.com	

LAUNCH DATE	2014	EXCHANGE	London SE	**SYMBOL**
DOMICILE	UK	CURRENCY	GBP	**CREI**
STOCKBROKER	Numis	INDEX	FTSE Small Cap	
GEARING	117	AVG DISCOUNT (%)	8.6	
NAV (£M)	362	NET DIV YIELD (%)	5.6	
TURNOVER	790			
TER (%)	1.74	SHARPE RATIO	0.9	**MKT CAP (£M)**
		VOLATILITY	0.82	**404**
PERFORMANCE FEE	No	PERFORMANCE (10Y) (%)	-	

DRUM INCOME PLUS REIT PLC

CORE INVESTMENT STRATEGY		UK commercial property	
BENCHMARK		IPD UK	
MANAGEMENT GROUP		Drum Real Estate IM	
FUND MANAGER		Bryan Sherriff [2015]	
WEBSITE		www.dripreit.co.uk	

LAUNCH DATE	2015	EXCHANGE	London SE	**SYMBOL**
DOMICILE	UK	CURRENCY	GBP	**DRIP**
STOCKBROKER	-	INDEX	-	
GEARING	130	AVG DISCOUNT (%)	5.2	
NAV (£M)	36	NET DIV YIELD (%)	5.2	
TURNOVER	9			**MKT CAP (£M)**
TER (%)	3.11	SHARPE RATIO	-	**36**
		VOLATILITY	1.40	
PERFORMANCE FEE	No	PERFORMANCE (10Y) (%)	-	

EDISTON PROPERTY INVESTMENT CO PLC

CORE INVESTMENT STRATEGY		UK commercial property	
BENCHMARK		IPD UK	
MANAGEMENT GROUP		Ediston Real Estate	
FUND MANAGER		Danny O'Neill [2014]	
WEBSITE		www.epic-reit.com	

LAUNCH DATE	2014	EXCHANGE	London SE	**SYMBOL**
DOMICILE	UK	CURRENCY	GBP	**EPIC**
STOCKBROKER	Canaccord Genuity	INDEX	FTSE Small Cap	
GEARING	136	AVG DISCOUNT (%)	0.0	
NAV (£M)	145	NET DIV YIELD (%)	4.9	
TURNOVER	163			**MKT CAP (£M)**
TER (%)	1.64	SHARPE RATIO	-	**147**
		VOLATILITY	1.17	
PERFORMANCE FEE	No	PERFORMANCE (10Y) (%)	-	

F&C COMMERCIAL PROPERTY TRUST LTD

CORE INVESTMENT STRATEGY		Commercial property in UK	
BENCHMARK		IPD UK	
MANAGEMENT GROUP		F&C REIT	
FUND MANAGER		Richard Kirby [2005]	
WEBSITE		www.fccpt.co.uk	

LAUNCH DATE	2005	EXCHANGE	London SE	**SYMBOL**
DOMICILE	Guernsey	CURRENCY	GBP	**FCPT**
STOCKBROKER	Winterflood	INDEX	FTSE Mid 250	
GEARING	123	AVG DISCOUNT (%)	3.6	
NAV (£M)	1,114	NET DIV YIELD (%)	4.0	
TURNOVER	1,755			**MKT CAP (£M)**
TER (%)	0.96	SHARPE RATIO	0.8	**1,212**
		VOLATILITY	1.36	
PERFORMANCE FEE	No	PERFORMANCE (10Y) (%)	110	

F&C UK REAL ESTATE INVESTMENT LTD

CORE INVESTMENT STRATEGY		Commercial property in UK	
BENCHMARK		IPD UK	
MANAGEMENT GROUP		F&C REIT	
FUND MANAGER		Peter Lowe [2016]	
WEBSITE		www.fctr.co.uk	

LAUNCH DATE	2004	EXCHANGE	London SE	**SYMBOL**
DOMICILE	UK	CURRENCY	GBP	
STOCKBROKER	Cenkos	INDEX	FTSE Small Cap	**FCRE**
GEARING	145	AVG DISCOUNT (%)	3.4	
NAV (£M)	243	NET DIV YIELD (%)	4.7	
TURNOVER	284			
TER (%)	1.67	SHARPE RATIO	1.0	**MKT CAP (£M)**
		VOLATILITY	1.97	**258**
PERFORMANCE FEE	Yes	PERFORMANCE (10Y) (%)	76	

LONDONMETRIC PROPERTY PLC

CORE INVESTMENT STRATEGY		UK commercial property	
BENCHMARK		IPD UK	
MANAGEMENT GROUP		Self-Managed	
FUND MANAGER		Raymond Mould, Humphrey Price, Patrick Vaughan [2007]	
WEBSITE		www.londonmetric.com	

LAUNCH DATE	2007	EXCHANGE	London SE	**SYMBOL**
DOMICILE	Guernsey	CURRENCY	GBP	
STOCKBROKER	KBC Peel Hunt	INDEX	FTSE Mid 250	**LMP**
GEARING	147	AVG DISCOUNT (%)	8.2	
NAV (£M)	1,041	NET DIV YIELD (%)	4.5	
TURNOVER	2,636			
TER (%)	4.43	SHARPE RATIO	0.8	**MKT CAP (£M)**
		VOLATILITY	1.07	**1,154**
PERFORMANCE FEE	Yes	PERFORMANCE (10Y) (%)	-	

LXB RETAIL PROPERTIES PLC

CORE INVESTMENT STRATEGY		UK out-of-town retail properties	
BENCHMARK		IPD UK	
MANAGEMENT GROUP		LXB Manager	
FUND MANAGER		Tim Walton, Brendan O'Grady [2009]	
WEBSITE		www.lxbretailproperties.com	

LAUNCH DATE	2009	EXCHANGE	AIM	**SYMBOL**
DOMICILE	Jersey	CURRENCY	GBP	
STOCKBROKER	Stifel, JPM Cazenove	INDEX	AIM All-Share	**LXB**
GEARING	100	AVG DISCOUNT (%)	-24.6	
NAV (£M)	57	NET DIV YIELD (%)	-	
TURNOVER	90			
TER (%)	2.49	SHARPE RATIO	-0.3	**MKT CAP (£M)**
		VOLATILITY	1.92	**49**
PERFORMANCE FEE	Yes	PERFORMANCE (10Y) (%)	-	

LXI REIT PLC

CORE INVESTMENT STRATEGY		UK commercial property	
BENCHMARK		IPD UK	
MANAGEMENT GROUP		LXI REIT Advisors	
FUND MANAGER		John White, Simon Lee, Jamie Beale [2017]	
WEBSITE		www.lxireit.com	

LAUNCH DATE	2017	EXCHANGE	London SE	**SYMBOL**
DOMICILE	UK	CURRENCY	GBP	**LXI**
STOCKBROKER	Peel Hunt	INDEX	FTSE Small Cap	
GEARING	100	AVG DISCOUNT (%)	6.8	
NAV (£M)	135	NET DIV YIELD (%)	2.9	
TURNOVER	371			
TER (%)	-	SHARPE RATIO	-	**MKT CAP (£M)**
		VOLATILITY	0.77	**144**
PERFORMANCE FEE	No	PERFORMANCE (10Y) (%)	-	

NEWRIVER REIT PLC

CORE INVESTMENT STRATEGY		Retail properties in UK	
BENCHMARK		IPD UK	
MANAGEMENT GROUP		NewRiver Capital	
FUND MANAGER		David Lockhart, Alan Lockhart [2009]	
WEBSITE		www.nrr.co.uk	

LAUNCH DATE	2009	EXCHANGE	AIM	**SYMBOL**
DOMICILE	Guernsey	CURRENCY	GBP	**NRR**
STOCKBROKER	Cenkos, Morgan Stanley	INDEX	FTSE Mid 250	
GEARING	270	AVG DISCOUNT (%)	14.5	
NAV (£M)	882	NET DIV YIELD (%)	5.8	
TURNOVER	2,211			
TER (%)	5.06	SHARPE RATIO	0.7	**MKT CAP (£M)**
		VOLATILITY	0.99	**1,050**
PERFORMANCE FEE	No	PERFORMANCE (10Y) (%)	-	

PICTON PROPERTY INCOME LTD

CORE INVESTMENT STRATEGY		Commercial property in UK	
BENCHMARK		IPD UK	
MANAGEMENT GROUP		Self-Managed	
FUND MANAGER		Michael Morris [2007]	
WEBSITE		www.pictonproperty.co.uk	

LAUNCH DATE	2005	EXCHANGE	London SE	**SYMBOL**
DOMICILE	Guernsey	CURRENCY	GBP	**PCTN**
STOCKBROKER	Stifel, JPM Cazenove	INDEX	FTSE Small Cap	
GEARING	146	AVG DISCOUNT (%)	-0.8	
NAV (£M)	452	NET DIV YIELD (%)	4.0	
TURNOVER	864			
TER (%)	2.47	SHARPE RATIO	1.2	**MKT CAP (£M)**
		VOLATILITY	2.15	**462**
PERFORMANCE FEE	No	PERFORMANCE (10Y) (%)	66	

PRIMARY HEALTH PROPERTIES PLC

CORE INVESTMENT STRATEGY	Healthcare properties in UK
BENCHMARK	FTSE 350 Real Estate
MANAGEMENT GROUP	Nexus PHP
FUND MANAGER	Harry Hyman [1996]
WEBSITE	www.phpgroup.co.uk

LAUNCH DATE	1996	EXCHANGE	London SE	**SYMBOL**
DOMICILE	UK	CURRENCY	GBP	**PHP**
STOCKBROKER	Numis, KBC	INDEX	FTSE Small Cap	
GEARING	217	AVG DISCOUNT (%)	24.0	
NAV (£M)	576	NET DIV YIELD (%)	4.4	
TURNOVER	1,129			
TER (%)	1.63	SHARPE RATIO	1.3	**MKT CAP (£M)**
		VOLATILITY	1.52	**715**
PERFORMANCE FEE	Yes	PERFORMANCE (10Y) (%)	126	

PACIFIC INDUSTRIAL & LOGISTICS REIT PLC

CORE INVESTMENT STRATEGY	UK industrial & logistics property
BENCHMARK	IPD UK
MANAGEMENT GROUP	Pacifc Capital Partners
FUND MANAGER	Richard Moffitt [2017]
WEBSITE	www.pacificil.com

LAUNCH DATE	2016	EXCHANGE	AIM	**SYMBOL**
DOMICILE	UK	CURRENCY	GBP	**PILR**
STOCKBROKER	Canaccord	INDEX	-	
GEARING	9998	AVG DISCOUNT (%)	1.7	
NAV (£M)	79	NET DIV YIELD (%)	4.9	
TURNOVER	114			
TER (%)	-	SHARPE RATIO	-	**MKT CAP (£M)**
		VOLATILITY	0.50	**84**
PERFORMANCE FEE	No	PERFORMANCE (10Y) (%)	-	

PRS REIT (THE) PLC

CORE INVESTMENT STRATEGY	UK residential rental units
BENCHMARK	IPD UK
MANAGEMENT GROUP	Sigma PRS Management
FUND MANAGER	Team managed [2017]
WEBSITE	-

LAUNCH DATE	2017	EXCHANGE	London SE (SFS)	**SYMBOL**
DOMICILE	UK	CURRENCY	GBP	**PRSR**
STOCKBROKER	N+1 Singer, Stifel	INDEX	-	
GEARING	100	AVG DISCOUNT (%)	6.1	
NAV (£M)	529	NET DIV YIELD (%)	5.8	
TURNOVER	625			
TER (%)	-	SHARPE RATIO	-	**MKT CAP (£M)**
		VOLATILITY	0.29	**258**
PERFORMANCE FEE	No	PERFORMANCE (10Y) (%)	-	

REGIONAL REIT LTD

CORE INVESTMENT STRATEGY		UK commercial property	
BENCHMARK		IPD UK	
MANAGEMENT GROUP		Toscafund AM	
FUND MANAGER		Martin Hughes, Martin McKay [2015]	
WEBSITE		www.regionalreit.com	

LAUNCH DATE	2015	EXCHANGE	London SE	**SYMBOL**
DOMICILE	Guernsey	CURRENCY	GBP	**RGL**
STOCKBROKER	-	INDEX	FTSE Small Cap	
GEARING	140	AVG DISCOUNT (%)	-1.3	
NAV (£M)	309	NET DIV YIELD (%)	7.0	
TURNOVER	614			**MKT CAP (£M)**
TER (%)	4.36	SHARPE RATIO	-	**309**
		VOLATILITY	1.11	
PERFORMANCE FEE	Yes	PERFORMANCE (10Y) (%)	-	

REAL ESTATE INVESTORS PLC

CORE INVESTMENT STRATEGY		UK commercial property	
BENCHMARK		FTSE 350 Real Estate	
MANAGEMENT GROUP		Real Estate Investors	
FUND MANAGER		Paul Bassi [2004]	
WEBSITE		www.reiplc.com	

LAUNCH DATE	2004	EXCHANGE	AIM	**SYMBOL**
DOMICILE	UK	CURRENCY	GBP	**RLE**
STOCKBROKER	Liberum	INDEX	AIM All-Share	
GEARING	100	AVG DISCOUNT (%)	-8.7	
NAV (£M)	122	NET DIV YIELD (%)	4.8	
TURNOVER	86			**MKT CAP (£M)**
TER (%)	7.23	SHARPE RATIO	0.4	**106**
		VOLATILITY	1.52	
PERFORMANCE FEE	No	PERFORMANCE (10Y) (%)	-37	

SECURE INCOME REIT PLC

CORE INVESTMENT STRATEGY		UK Healthcare & Leisure property	
BENCHMARK		IPD UK	
MANAGEMENT GROUP		Prestbury Investment LLP	
FUND MANAGER		Team managed [2016]	
WEBSITE		www.secureincomereit.co.uk	

LAUNCH DATE	2014	EXCHANGE	AIM	**SYMBOL**
DOMICILE	UK	CURRENCY	GBP	**SIR**
STOCKBROKER	Stifel	INDEX		
GEARING	221	AVG DISCOUNT (%)	6.4	
NAV (£M)	723	NET DIV YIELD (%)	3.4	
TURNOVER	908			**MKT CAP (£M)**
TER (%)	1.64	SHARPE RATIO	-	**808**
		VOLATILITY	1.12	
PERFORMANCE FEE	Yes	PERFORMANCE (10Y) (%)	-	

STANDARD LIFE INVESTMENTS PROPERTY INC TRUST LTD

CORE INVESTMENT STRATEGY		Commercial property in UK	
BENCHMARK		IPD UK	
MANAGEMENT GROUP		Standard Life Investments	
FUND MANAGER		Jason Baggaley [2003]	
WEBSITE		www.standardlifeinvestments.com	

LAUNCH DATE	2003	EXCHANGE	London SE	**SYMBOL**
DOMICILE	UK	CURRENCY	GBP	**SLI**
STOCKBROKER	Winterflood	INDEX	FTSE Small Cap	
GEARING	142	AVG DISCOUNT (%)	7.8	
NAV (£M)	326	NET DIV YIELD (%)	5.3	
TURNOVER	788			
TER (%)	1.7	SHARPE RATIO	0.9	**MKT CAP (£M)**
		VOLATILITY	1.66	**353**
PERFORMANCE FEE	No	PERFORMANCE (10Y) (%)	53	

SCHRODER REAL ESTATE INVESTMENT TRUST LTD

CORE INVESTMENT STRATEGY		Commercial property in UK	
BENCHMARK		IPD UK	
MANAGEMENT GROUP		Schroder IM	
FUND MANAGER		Duncan Owen, Nick Montgomery [2004]	
WEBSITE		www.schroders.com	

LAUNCH DATE	2004	EXCHANGE	London SE	**SYMBOL**
DOMICILE	Guernsey	CURRENCY	GBP	**SREI**
STOCKBROKER	Numis, JPM Cazenove	INDEX	FTSE Small Cap	
GEARING	144	AVG DISCOUNT (%)	-3.4	
NAV (£M)	335	NET DIV YIELD (%)	4.0	
TURNOVER	414			
TER (%)	2.46	SHARPE RATIO	0.7	**MKT CAP (£M)**
		VOLATILITY	2.05	**324**
PERFORMANCE FEE	No	PERFORMANCE (10Y) (%)	12	

SUPERMARKET INCOME REIT PLC

CORE INVESTMENT STRATEGY		UK supermarket real estate	
BENCHMARK		IPD UK	
MANAGEMENT GROUP		Atrato Capital	
FUND MANAGER		- [2017]	
WEBSITE		-	

LAUNCH DATE	2017	EXCHANGE	London SE (SFS)	**SYMBOL**
DOMICILE	UK	CURRENCY	GBP	**SUPR**
STOCKBROKER	Stifel	INDEX	-	
GEARING	100	AVG DISCOUNT (%)	0.8	
NAV (£M)	98	NET DIV YIELD (%)	5.2	
TURNOVER	160			
TER (%)	-	SHARPE RATIO	-	**MKT CAP (£M)**
		VOLATILITY	0.54	**97**
PERFORMANCE FEE	No	PERFORMANCE (10Y) (%)	-	

UK COMMERCIAL PROPERTY TRUST LTD

CORE INVESTMENT STRATEGY		Commercial property in UK	
BENCHMARK		IPD UK	
MANAGEMENT GROUP		Standard Life Investments	
FUND MANAGER		Will Fulton [2006]	
WEBSITE		www.ukcpt.co.uk	

LAUNCH DATE	2006	EXCHANGE	London SE	**SYMBOL**
DOMICILE	Guernsey	CURRENCY	GBP	
STOCKBROKER	-	INDEX	FTSE Mid 250	**UKCM**
GEARING	107	AVG DISCOUNT (%)	-0.9	
NAV (£M)	1,151	NET DIV YIELD (%)	4.0	
TURNOVER	1,489			
TER (%)	1.43	SHARPE RATIO	0.6	**MKT CAP (£M)**
		VOLATILITY	1.60	**1,182**
PERFORMANCE FEE	No	PERFORMANCE (10Y) (%)	89	

SECTOR SPECIALIST: BIOTECHNOLOGY & HEALTHCARE

BB HEALTHCARE TRUST PLC

CORE INVESTMENT STRATEGY		Global healthcare stocks	
BENCHMARK		MSCI World Health Care	
MANAGEMENT GROUP		Bellevue AM	
FUND MANAGER		Daniel Koller, Paul Major [2016]	
WEBSITE		www.bbhealthcaretrust.com	

LAUNCH DATE	2016	EXCHANGE	London SE	**SYMBOL**
DOMICILE	UK	CURRENCY	GBP	
STOCKBROKER	Peel Hunt	INDEX	FTSE Small Cap	**BBH**
GEARING	104	AVG DISCOUNT (%)	2.3	
NAV (£M)	227	NET DIV YIELD (%)	3.0	
TURNOVER	505			
TER (%)	-	SHARPE RATIO	-	**MKT CAP (£M)**
		VOLATILITY	0.85	**232**
PERFORMANCE FEE	No	PERFORMANCE (10Y) (%)	-	

BIOTECH GROWTH TRUST (THE) PLC

CORE INVESTMENT STRATEGY	Major and Emerging biotechnology stocks	
BENCHMARK	Nasdaq Biotechnology	
MANAGEMENT GROUP	Frostrow Capital	
FUND MANAGER	Richard Klemm, Geoffrey Hsu [2005]	
WEBSITE	www.biotechgt.com	

LAUNCH DATE	1997	EXCHANGE	London SE	**SYMBOL**
DOMICILE	UK	CURRENCY	GBP	**BIOG**
STOCKBROKER	Winterflood	INDEX	FTSE Small Cap	
GEARING	110	AVG DISCOUNT (%)	-6.3	
NAV (£M)	510	NET DIV YIELD (%)	-	
TURNOVER	884			
TER (%)	1.1	SHARPE RATIO	0.6	**MKT CAP (£M)**
		VOLATILITY	1.75	**471**
PERFORMANCE FEE	Yes	PERFORMANCE (10Y) (%)	693	

INTERNATIONAL BIOTECHNOLOGY TRUST PLC

CORE INVESTMENT STRATEGY	Biotechnology stocks (inc. unquoteds)	
BENCHMARK	Nasdaq Biotechnology	
MANAGEMENT GROUP	SV Life Sciences	
FUND MANAGER	Carl Harald Janson [2001]	
WEBSITE	www.ibtplc.com	

LAUNCH DATE	1994	EXCHANGE	London SE	**SYMBOL**
DOMICILE	UK	CURRENCY	GBP	**IBT**
STOCKBROKER	Cenkos	INDEX	FTSE Small Cap	
GEARING	100	AVG DISCOUNT (%)	-8.6	
NAV (£M)	253	NET DIV YIELD (%)	4.0	
TURNOVER	408			
TER (%)	1.4	SHARPE RATIO	1.1	**MKT CAP (£M)**
		VOLATILITY	1.78	**236**
PERFORMANCE FEE	Yes	PERFORMANCE (10Y) (%)	368	

POLAR CAPITAL GLOBAL HEALTHCARE GROWTH & INCOME PLC

CORE INVESTMENT STRATEGY	Global healthcare and biotech stocks	
BENCHMARK	MSCI World Health Care	
MANAGEMENT GROUP	Polar Capital	
FUND MANAGER	Gareth Powell, Daniel Mahoney [2010]	
WEBSITE	www.polarcapitalhealthcaretrust.com	

LAUNCH DATE	2010	EXCHANGE	London SE	**SYMBOL**
DOMICILE	UK	CURRENCY	GBP	**PCGH**
STOCKBROKER	Panmure Gordon	INDEX	FTSE Small Cap	
GEARING	100	AVG DISCOUNT (%)	-3.1	
NAV (£M)	258	NET DIV YIELD (%)	1.5	
TURNOVER	605			
TER (%)	1.02	SHARPE RATIO	0.8	**MKT CAP (£M)**
		VOLATILITY	1.01	**260**
PERFORMANCE FEE	Yes	PERFORMANCE (10Y) (%)	-	

WORLDWIDE HEALTHCARE TRUST PLC

CORE INVESTMENT STRATEGY		Pharma & biotech stocks	
BENCHMARK		MSCI World Health Care	
MANAGEMENT GROUP		Frostrow Capital	
FUND MANAGER		Sam Isaly, Sven Borho [1995]	
WEBSITE		www.worldwidewh.com	

LAUNCH DATE	1995	EXCHANGE	London SE	**SYMBOL**
DOMICILE	UK	CURRENCY	GBP	
STOCKBROKER	Winterflood	INDEX	FTSE Mid 250	**WWH**
GEARING	112	AVG DISCOUNT (%)	-2.0	
NAV (£M)	1,212	NET DIV YIELD (%)	0.9	
TURNOVER	1,776			
TER (%)	0.91	SHARPE RATIO	1.2	**MKT CAP (£M)**
		VOLATILITY	1.35	**1,220**
PERFORMANCE FEE	Yes	PERFORMANCE (10Y) (%)	509	

SECTOR SPECIALIST: COMMODITIES & NATURAL RESOURCES

BLACKROCK COMMODITIES INCOME INVESTMENT TRUST PLC

CORE INVESTMENT STRATEGY		Mining & energy securities	
BENCHMARK		50% Euromoney Global Mining, 50% MSCI World Energy	
MANAGEMENT GROUP		BlackRock IM	
FUND MANAGER		Olivia Markham, Thomas Holl [2014]	
WEBSITE		www.blackrock.co.uk	

LAUNCH DATE	2005	EXCHANGE	London SE	**SYMBOL**
DOMICILE	UK	CURRENCY	GBP	
STOCKBROKER	Winterflood	INDEX	FTSE Fledgling	**BRCI**
GEARING	118	AVG DISCOUNT (%)	-2.9	
NAV (£M)	94	NET DIV YIELD (%)	5.5	
TURNOVER	274			
TER (%)	1.39	SHARPE RATIO	-0.3	**MKT CAP (£M)**
		VOLATILITY	1.79	**87**
PERFORMANCE FEE	No	PERFORMANCE (10Y) (%)	4	

BLACKROCK WORLD MINING TRUST PLC

CORE INVESTMENT STRATEGY	Global mining & metal equities
BENCHMARK	Euromoney Global Mining
MANAGEMENT GROUP	BlackRock IM
FUND MANAGER	Evy Hambro, Olivia Markham [2009]
WEBSITE	www.blackrock.co.uk/individual/products/investment-trust/ blackrock-world-mining-trust

LAUNCH DATE	1993	EXCHANGE	London SE	**SYMBOL**	
DOMICILE	UK	CURRENCY	GBP		
STOCKBROKER	JPM Cazenove, Winterflood	INDEX	FTSE Small Cap	**BRWM**	
GEARING	112	AVG DISCOUNT (%)	-12.5		
NAV (£M)	789	NET DIV YIELD (%)	3.1		
TURNOVER	1,740			**MKT CAP (£M)**	
TER (%)	1.1	SHARPE RATIO	-0.1		
		VOLATILITY	1.77	**686**	
PERFORMANCE FEE	No	PERFORMANCE (10Y) (%)	-3		

BAKER STEEL RESOURCES TRUST LTD

CORE INVESTMENT STRATEGY	Long term capital growth from natural resources companies
BENCHMARK	Euromoney Global Mining
MANAGEMENT GROUP	Baker Steel
FUND MANAGER	Trevor Steel, David Baker [2010]
WEBSITE	www.bakersteelresourcestrust.com

LAUNCH DATE	2010	EXCHANGE	London SE	**SYMBOL**	
DOMICILE	Guernsey	CURRENCY	GBP		
STOCKBROKER	Numis	INDEX	FTSE Fledgling	**BSRT**	
GEARING	100	AVG DISCOUNT (%)	-30.9		
NAV (£M)	61	NET DIV YIELD (%)	-		
TURNOVER	32			**MKT CAP (£M)**	
TER (%)	2.17	SHARPE RATIO	-0.1		
		VOLATILITY	2.01	**44**	
PERFORMANCE FEE	Yes	PERFORMANCE (10Y) (%)	-		

CITY NATURAL RESOURCES HIGH YIELD TRUST PLC

CORE INVESTMENT STRATEGY	Mining & resource equities & debt
BENCHMARK	Euromoney Global Mining
MANAGEMENT GROUP	CQS AM
FUND MANAGER	Ian Francis, Keith Watson, Robert Crayfourd [2010]
WEBSITE	www.ncim.co.uk

LAUNCH DATE	2003	EXCHANGE	London SE	**SYMBOL**	
DOMICILE	UK	CURRENCY	GBP		
STOCKBROKER	Cantor Fitzgerald Europe	INDEX	FTSE Fledgling	**CYN**	
GEARING	136	AVG DISCOUNT (%)	-17.3		
NAV (£M)	99	NET DIV YIELD (%)	4.8		
TURNOVER	213			**MKT CAP (£M)**	
TER (%)	1.86	SHARPE RATIO	-0.1		
		VOLATILITY	1.56	**77**	
PERFORMANCE FEE	No	PERFORMANCE (10Y) (%)	4		

DUKE ROYALTY LTD

CORE INVESTMENT STRATEGY	Global royalty financing
BENCHMARK	MSCI World
MANAGEMENT GROUP	Praetorian Resources
FUND MANAGER	Oliver Wyman [2012]
WEBSITE	www.dukeroyalty.com

LAUNCH DATE	2012	EXCHANGE	AIM	**SYMBOL**
DOMICILE	Guernsey	CURRENCY	GBP	
STOCKBROKER	Canto Fitzgerald Europe, Mirabaud	INDEX	-	**DUKE**
GEARING	100	AVG DISCOUNT (%)	81.0	
NAV (£M)	16	NET DIV YIELD (%)	4.9	
TURNOVER	10			**MKT CAP (£M)**
TER (%)	12.62	SHARPE RATIO	-0.9	
		VOLATILITY	52.77	**18**
PERFORMANCE FEE	Yes	PERFORMANCE (10Y) (%)	-	

RIVERSTONE ENERGY LTD

CORE INVESTMENT STRATEGY	Global energy
BENCHMARK	MSCI World
MANAGEMENT GROUP	Riverstone International Limited
FUND MANAGER	Team managed [2013]
WEBSITE	www.riverstonerel.com

LAUNCH DATE	2013	EXCHANGE	London SE	**SYMBOL**
DOMICILE	Guernsey	CURRENCY	GBP	
STOCKBROKER	Goldman Sachs, JPM Cazenove	INDEX	FTSE Mid 250	**RSE**
GEARING	100	AVG DISCOUNT (%)	-15.9	
NAV (£M)	1,300	NET DIV YIELD (%)	-	
TURNOVER	1,084			**MKT CAP (£M)**
TER (%)	1.76	SHARPE RATIO	0.7	
		VOLATILITY	1.43	**1,077**
PERFORMANCE FEE	Yes	PERFORMANCE (10Y) (%)	-	

SECTOR SPECIALIST: ENVIRONMENTAL

IMPAX ENVIRONMENTAL MARKETS PLC

CORE INVESTMENT STRATEGY	Waste, water & alternative energy companies
BENCHMARK	MSCI Global Enviroment Index
MANAGEMENT GROUP	Impax AM
FUND MANAGER	Jon Forster, Bruce Jenkyn-Jones [2002]
WEBSITE	www.impaxam.com

LAUNCH DATE	2002	EXCHANGE	London SE	**SYMBOL**
DOMICILE	UK	CURRENCY	GBP	
STOCKBROKER	Canaccord	INDEX	FTSE Small Cap	**IEM**
GEARING	106	AVG DISCOUNT (%)	-11.7	
NAV (£M)	491	NET DIV YIELD (%)	0.8	
TURNOVER	734			**MKT CAP (£M)**
TER (%)	1.11	SHARPE RATIO	1.4	
		VOLATILITY	1.25	**430**
PERFORMANCE FEE	No	PERFORMANCE (10Y) (%)	116	

JUPITER GREEN INVESTMENT TRUST PLC

CORE INVESTMENT STRATEGY	Companies providing environmental solutions
BENCHMARK	MSCI World
MANAGEMENT GROUP	Jupiter AM
FUND MANAGER	Charlie Thomas [2006]
WEBSITE	www.jupiteram.com

LAUNCH DATE	2006	EXCHANGE	London SE	**SYMBOL**
DOMICILE	UK	CURRENCY	GBP	
STOCKBROKER	Stifel	INDEX	FTSE Fledgling	**JGC**
GEARING	100	AVG DISCOUNT (%)	-5.6	
NAV (£M)	41	NET DIV YIELD (%)	0.7	
TURNOVER	28			**MKT CAP (£M)**
TER (%)	1.57	SHARPE RATIO	0.9	
		VOLATILITY	0.77	**38**
PERFORMANCE FEE	Yes	PERFORMANCE (10Y) (%)	59	

LEAF CLEAN ENERGY COMPANY

CORE INVESTMENT STRATEGY	Renewable energy companies and projects
BENCHMARK	MSCI World
MANAGEMENT GROUP	Energy and Climate Advisors
FUND MANAGER	Mark Lerdal, Yonatan Alemu, Matthew Fedors [2007]
WEBSITE	www.leafcleanenergy.com

LAUNCH DATE	2007	EXCHANGE	AIM	**SYMBOL**
DOMICILE	Cayman Isles	CURRENCY	GBP	**LEAF**
STOCKBROKER	Cenkos	INDEX	-	
GEARING	100	AVG DISCOUNT (%)	-42.0	
NAV (£M)	71	NET DIV YIELD (%)	-	
TURNOVER	18			**MKT CAP (£M)**
TER (%)	2.42	SHARPE RATIO	0.0	**45**
		VOLATILITY	1.22	
PERFORMANCE FEE	No	PERFORMANCE (10Y) (%)	-65	

MENHADEN CAPITAL PLC

CORE INVESTMENT STRATEGY	Energy & resource cos (quoted & unquoted)
BENCHMARK	MSCI World
MANAGEMENT GROUP	Frostrow Capital
FUND MANAGER	Ben Goldsmith, Graham Thomas, Alexander Vavalidis [2015]
WEBSITE	www.menhadencapital.com

LAUNCH DATE	2015	EXCHANGE	London SE	**SYMBOL**
DOMICILE	UK	CURRENCY	GBP	**MHN**
STOCKBROKER	Numis	INDEX	FTSE Fledgling	
GEARING	100	AVG DISCOUNT (%)	-27.3	
NAV (£M)	71	NET DIV YIELD (%)	-	
TURNOVER	98			**MKT CAP (£M)**
TER (%)	2.09	SHARPE RATIO	-	**55**
		VOLATILITY	1.07	
PERFORMANCE FEE	Yes	PERFORMANCE (10Y) (%)	-	

SECTOR SPECIALIST: FINANCIALS

POLAR CAPITAL GLOBAL FINANCIALS TRUST PLC

CORE INVESTMENT STRATEGY		Global financial companies
BENCHMARK		MSCI World Financials
MANAGEMENT GROUP		Polar Capital
FUND MANAGER		Nick Brind, John Yakes [2013]
WEBSITE		www.polarcapitalglobalfinancialstrust.com

LAUNCH DATE	2013	EXCHANGE	London SE	
DOMICILE	UK	CURRENCY	GBP	**SYMBOL**
STOCKBROKER	Panmure Gordon	INDEX	FTSE Small Cap	**PCFT**
GEARING	106	AVG DISCOUNT (%)	-6.9	
NAV (£M)	291	NET DIV YIELD (%)	2.8	
TURNOVER	679			
TER (%)	1.02	SHARPE RATIO	0.9	**MKT CAP (£M)**
		VOLATILITY	1.03	**272**
PERFORMANCE FEE	Yes	PERFORMANCE (10Y) (%)	-	

SECTOR SPECIALIST: FORESTRY

PHAUNOS TIMBER FUND LTD

CORE INVESTMENT STRATEGY		Global timber investments	
BENCHMARK		MSCI World	
MANAGEMENT GROUP		Stafford Timberland	
FUND MANAGER		Richard Bowley [2014]	
WEBSITE		www.phaunostimber.com	

LAUNCH DATE	2006	EXCHANGE	London SE	**SYMBOL**
DOMICILE	Guernsey	CURRENCY	USD	**PTF**
STOCKBROKER	VSA Capital, Winterflood	INDEX	-	
GEARING	100	AVG DISCOUNT (%)	-19.0	
NAV (£M)	225	NET DIV YIELD (%)	3.6	
TURNOVER	189			**MKT CAP (£M)**
TER (%)	1.33	SHARPE RATIO	0.6	**189**
		VOLATILITY	1.33	
PERFORMANCE FEE	Yes	PERFORMANCE (10Y) (%)	-29	

SECTOR SPECIALIST: INFRASTRUCTURE

3I INFRASTRUCTURE LTD

CORE INVESTMENT STRATEGY		Quoted & Unquoted equity & junior debt of infrastructure companies/ PPP projects (Europe, North America and Asia)	
BENCHMARK		9% p.a.	
MANAGEMENT GROUP		3i Group	
FUND MANAGER		Phil White [2009]	
WEBSITE		www.3i-infrastructure.com	

LAUNCH DATE	2007	**EXCHANGE**	London SE	**SYMBOL**
DOMICILE	Jersey	**CURRENCY**	GBP	
STOCKBROKER	JPM Cazenove, RBC	**INDEX**	FTSE Mid 250	**3IN**
GEARING	100	**AVG DISCOUNT (%)**	16.3	
NAV (£M)	1,731	**NET DIV YIELD (%)**	4.0	
TURNOVER	2,066			
TER (%)	1.29	**SHARPE RATIO**	1.6	**MKT CAP (£M)**
		VOLATILITY	1.14	**2,012**
PERFORMANCE FEE	Yes	**PERFORMANCE (10Y) (%)**	216	

BILFINGER BERGER GLOBAL INFRASTRUCTURE SICAV SA

CORE INVESTMENT STRATEGY		Equity and/or sub-ordinated debt of infrastructure PFI/ PPP projects (mostly operational) – Europe/Canada/Australia	
BENCHMARK		8% p.a.	
MANAGEMENT GROUP		Self-managed	
FUND MANAGER		Frank Schramm, Duncan Ball [2011]	
WEBSITE		www.bb-gi.com	

LAUNCH DATE	2011	**EXCHANGE**	London SE	**SYMBOL**
DOMICILE	Luxembourg	**CURRENCY**	GBP	
STOCKBROKER	Jefferies, Stifel	**INDEX**	FTSE Small Cap	**BBGI**
GEARING	107	**AVG DISCOUNT (%)**	12.1	
NAV (£M)	616	**NET DIV YIELD (%)**	4.2	
TURNOVER	782			
TER (%)	0.95	**SHARPE RATIO**	1.0	**MKT CAP (£M)**
		VOLATILITY	0.58	**715**
PERFORMANCE FEE	No	**PERFORMANCE (10Y) (%)**	-	

GCP INFRASTRUCTURE INVESTMENTS LTD

CORE INVESTMENT STRATEGY		Invests in subordinated debt instruments issued by operational UK PFI infrastructure project companies		
BENCHMARK		8% p.a.		
MANAGEMENT GROUP		Gravis Capital Partners		
FUND MANAGER		Stephen Ellis, Rollo Wright [2010]		
WEBSITE		www.gcpuk.com		

LAUNCH DATE	2010	EXCHANGE	London SE	**SYMBOL**
DOMICILE	Jersey	CURRENCY	GBP	**GCP**
STOCKBROKER	Stifel	INDEX	FTSE Mid 250	
GEARING	101	AVG DISCOUNT (%)	16.6	
NAV (£M)	861	NET DIV YIELD (%)	6.0	
TURNOVER	1,370			
TER (%)	1.22	SHARPE RATIO	0.9	**MKT CAP (£M)**
		VOLATILITY	0.57	**1,002**
PERFORMANCE FEE	No	PERFORMANCE (10Y) (%)	-	

HICL INFRASTRUCTURE COMPANY LTD

CORE INVESTMENT STRATEGY		Equity and/or sub-ordinated debt of infrastructure PFI/ PPP projects (mostly operational) – Europe/Canada		
BENCHMARK		8% p.a.		
MANAGEMENT GROUP		InfraRed Capital Partners		
FUND MANAGER		Harry Seekings [2006]		
WEBSITE		www.hicl.com		

LAUNCH DATE	2006	EXCHANGE	London SE	**SYMBOL**
DOMICILE	Guernsey	CURRENCY	GBP	**HICL**
STOCKBROKER	Canaccord	INDEX	FTSE Mid 250	
GEARING	100	AVG DISCOUNT (%)	12.4	
NAV (£M)	2,688	NET DIV YIELD (%)	4.8	
TURNOVER	6,276			
TER (%)	1.26	SHARPE RATIO	0.9	**MKT CAP (£M)**
		VOLATILITY	0.75	**2,902**
PERFORMANCE FEE	No	PERFORMANCE (10Y) (%)	160	

INFRASTRUCTURE INDIA PLC

CORE INVESTMENT STRATEGY		Indian infrastructure (focus on energy & transport)		
BENCHMARK		MSCI India		
MANAGEMENT GROUP		Guggenheim Franklin Park		
FUND MANAGER		Tom Tribone, Sonny Lulla [2011]		
WEBSITE		www.iiplc.com		

LAUNCH DATE	2008	EXCHANGE	AIM	**SYMBOL**
DOMICILE	Isle of Man	CURRENCY	GBP	**IIP**
STOCKBROKER	Smith & Williamson, Nplus1 Singer Advisory	INDEX	-	
GEARING	100	AVG DISCOUNT (%)	-85.7	
NAV (£M)	340	NET DIV YIELD (%)	-	
TURNOVER	5			
TER (%)	1.8	SHARPE RATIO	-0.9	**MKT CAP (£M)**
		VOLATILITY	2.66	**29**
PERFORMANCE FEE	Yes	PERFORMANCE (10Y) (%)	-	

INTERNATIONAL PUBLIC PARTNERSHIP LTD

CORE INVESTMENT STRATEGY		Equity and/or sub-ordinated debt of infrastructure PFI/ PPP projects (operational/construction) – Europe/Canada/Australia	
BENCHMARK		8% p.a.	
MANAGEMENT GROUP		Amber Infrastructure	
FUND MANAGER		Giles Frost [2006]	
WEBSITE		www.internationalpublicpartnerships.com	

LAUNCH DATE	2006	EXCHANGE	London SE	**SYMBOL**
DOMICILE	Guernsey	CURRENCY	GBP	**INPP**
STOCKBROKER	Numis	INDEX	FTSE Mid 250	
GEARING	100	AVG DISCOUNT (%)	10.1	
NAV (£M)	1,990	NET DIV YIELD (%)	4.2	
TURNOVER	3,280			**MKT CAP (£M)**
TER (%)	1.24	SHARPE RATIO	1.5	**2,185**
		VOLATILITY	0.95	
PERFORMANCE FEE	No	PERFORMANCE (10Y) (%)	150	

JOHN LAING INFRASTRUCTURE FUND LTD

CORE INVESTMENT STRATEGY		Equity and/or sub-ordinated debt of infrastructure PFI/ PPP projects (operational) – Europe/Canada/Australia	
BENCHMARK		8% p.a.	
MANAGEMENT GROUP		John Laing Capital Management	
FUND MANAGER		David Hardy [2010]	
WEBSITE		www.jlif.com	

LAUNCH DATE	2010	EXCHANGE	London SE	**SYMBOL**
DOMICILE	Guernsey	CURRENCY	GBP	**JLIF**
STOCKBROKER	JPM Cazenove	INDEX	FTSE Mid 250	
GEARING	100	AVG DISCOUNT (%)	11.9	
NAV (£M)	1,230	NET DIV YIELD (%)	5.1	
TURNOVER	2,155			**MKT CAP (£M)**
TER (%)	1.48	SHARPE RATIO	1.2	**1,356**
		VOLATILITY	0.49	
PERFORMANCE FEE	No	PERFORMANCE (10Y) (%)	-	

SEQUOIA ECONOMIC INFRASTRUCTURE INCOME FUND LTD

CORE INVESTMENT STRATEGY		Infrastructure Debt Investments	
BENCHMARK		8% p.a.	
MANAGEMENT GROUP		International Fund Management	
FUND MANAGER		Randall Sandstrom [2015]	
WEBSITE		www.seqifund.com	

LAUNCH DATE	2015	EXCHANGE	London SE	**SYMBOL**
DOMICILE	Guernsey	CURRENCY	GBP	**SEQI**
STOCKBROKER	Stifel	INDEX	FTSE Small Cap	
GEARING	100	AVG DISCOUNT (%)	9.0	
NAV (£M)	754	NET DIV YIELD (%)	5.2	
TURNOVER	808			**MKT CAP (£M)**
TER (%)	1.26	SHARPE RATIO	-	**851**
		VOLATILITY	0.60	
PERFORMANCE FEE	No	PERFORMANCE (10Y) (%)	-	

SECTOR SPECIALIST: INSURANCE & REINSURANCE STRATEGIES

BLUE CAPITAL ALTERNATIVE INCOME FUND LTD

CORE INVESTMENT STRATEGY		Insurance linked strategies	
BENCHMARK		UK£ 3 Month Libor + 10%	
MANAGEMENT GROUP		Blue Capital Management	
FUND MANAGER		Michael McGuire [2017]	
WEBSITE		-	

LAUNCH DATE	2012	EXCHANGE	London SE	**SYMBOL**
DOMICILE	Bermuda	CURRENCY	USD	
STOCKBROKER	Stifel	INDEX	-	**BCAI**
GEARING	100	AVG DISCOUNT (%)	-9.6	
NAV (£M)	149	NET DIV YIELD (%)	6.4	
TURNOVER	245			**MKT CAP (£M)**
TER (%)	1.64	SHARPE RATIO	1.3	
		VOLATILITY	0.40	**140**
PERFORMANCE FEE	Yes	PERFORMANCE (10Y) (%)	-	

CATCO REINSURANCE OPPORTUNITIES FUND LTD

CORE INVESTMENT STRATEGY		Catastrophe reinsurance contracts	
BENCHMARK		7.5% + US$ 3 month LIBOR	
MANAGEMENT GROUP		Markel CATCo IM	
FUND MANAGER		Tony Belisle [2010]	
WEBSITE		-	

LAUNCH DATE	2010	EXCHANGE	London SE (SFS)	**SYMBOL**
DOMICILE	Bermuda	CURRENCY	USD	
STOCKBROKER	Numis	INDEX	-	**CAT**
GEARING	100	AVG DISCOUNT (%)	0.2	
NAV (£M)	399	NET DIV YIELD (%)	5.6	
TURNOVER	534			**MKT CAP (£M)**
TER (%)	2.09	SHARPE RATIO	1.6	
		VOLATILITY	0.50	**388**
PERFORMANCE FEE	Yes	PERFORMANCE (10Y) (%)	-	

SECTOR SPECIALIST: INFRASTRUCTURE – RENEWABLE ENERGY

BLUEFIELD SOLAR INCOME FUND LTD

CORE INVESTMENT STRATEGY		UK solar energy infrastructure assets	
BENCHMARK		8% p.a.	
MANAGEMENT GROUP		Bluefield Partners LLP	
FUND MANAGER		James Armstrong [2013]	
WEBSITE		www.bluefieldsif.com	

LAUNCH DATE	2013	EXCHANGE	London SE	**SYMBOL**	
DOMICILE	Guernsey	CURRENCY	GBP	**BSIF**	
STOCKBROKER	Numis	INDEX	FTSE Small Cap		
GEARING	147	AVG DISCOUNT (%)	7.6		
NAV (£M)	386	NET DIV YIELD (%)	6.5		
TURNOVER	645			**MKT CAP (£M)**	
TER (%)	1.24	SHARPE RATIO	1.0	**410**	
		VOLATILITY	0.62		
PERFORMANCE FEE	Yes	PERFORMANCE (10Y) (%)	-		

FORESIGHT SOLAR FUND LTD

CORE INVESTMENT STRATEGY		UK ground based solar assets	
BENCHMARK		8% p.a.	
MANAGEMENT GROUP		Foresight Group CI Limited	
FUND MANAGER		Jamie Richards, Ricardo Pineiro [2013]	
WEBSITE		www.foresightgroup.eu	

LAUNCH DATE	2013	EXCHANGE	London SE	**SYMBOL**	
DOMICILE	Jersey	CURRENCY	GBP	**FSFL**	
STOCKBROKER	RBC, Stifel	INDEX	FTSE Small Cap		
GEARING	100	AVG DISCOUNT (%)	4.3		
NAV (£M)	438	NET DIV YIELD (%)	5.8		
TURNOVER	464			**MKT CAP (£M)**	
TER (%)	1.16	SHARPE RATIO	1.1	**453**	
		VOLATILITY	0.57		
PERFORMANCE FEE	No	PERFORMANCE (10Y) (%)	-		

JOHN LAING ENVIRONMENTAL ASSETS GROUP LTD

CORE INVESTMENT STRATEGY	Enviromental infrastructure
BENCHMARK	8% p.a.
MANAGEMENT GROUP	John Laing Capital Management
FUND MANAGER	Chris Tanner [2014]
WEBSITE	www.jlen.com

LAUNCH DATE	2014	EXCHANGE	London SE	**SYMBOL**
DOMICILE	Guernsey	CURRENCY	GBP	**JLEN**
STOCKBROKER	Barclays, Winterflood	INDEX	FTSE Small Cap	
GEARING	100	AVG DISCOUNT (%)	7.5	
NAV (£M)	377	NET DIV YIELD (%)	5.9	
TURNOVER	674			
TER (%)	1.46	SHARPE RATIO	0.9	**MKT CAP (£M)**
		VOLATILITY	0.63	**405**
PERFORMANCE FEE	No	PERFORMANCE (10Y) (%)	-	

GREENCOAT RENEWABLES PLC

CORE INVESTMENT STRATEGY	Eurozone renewable electricity generation assets
BENCHMARK	8% p.a.
MANAGEMENT GROUP	Greencoat Capital
FUND MANAGER	Bertrand Gautier, Stephen Lilley [2017]
WEBSITE	www.greencoat-renewables.com

LAUNCH DATE	2017	EXCHANGE	AIM	**SYMBOL**
DOMICILE	UK	CURRENCY	EUR	**GRP**
STOCKBROKER	Davy	INDEX	-	
GEARING	100	AVG DISCOUNT (%)	7.4	
NAV (£M)	242	NET DIV YIELD (%)	5.6	
TURNOVER	579			
TER (%)	-	SHARPE RATIO	-	**MKT CAP (£M)**
		VOLATILITY	0.52	**264**
PERFORMANCE FEE	No	PERFORMANCE (10Y) (%)	-	

NEXTENERGY SOLAR FUND LTD

CORE INVESTMENT STRATEGY	UK Solar PV assets
BENCHMARK	8% p.a.
MANAGEMENT GROUP	NextEnergy Capital Management
FUND MANAGER	Michael Bonte-Friedheim, Aldo Beolchini, Abid Kazim [2014]
WEBSITE	www.nextenergysolarfund.com

LAUNCH DATE	2014	EXCHANGE	London SE	**SYMBOL**
DOMICILE	Guernsey	CURRENCY	GBP	**NESF**
STOCKBROKER	Cantor Fitzgerald Europe	INDEX	FTSE Small Cap	
GEARING	100	AVG DISCOUNT (%)	7.3	
NAV (£M)	598	NET DIV YIELD (%)	5.6	
TURNOVER	481			
TER (%)	1.28	SHARPE RATIO	1.0	**MKT CAP (£M)**
		VOLATILITY	0.65	**644**
PERFORMANCE FEE	No	PERFORMANCE (10Y) (%)	-	

THE RENEWABLES INFRASTRUCTURE GROUP LTD

CORE INVESTMENT STRATEGY		Onshore/offshore wind farms & solar PV parks in UK/Europe		
BENCHMARK		8% p.a.		
MANAGEMENT GROUP		InfraRed Capital Partners		
FUND MANAGER		Richard Crawford [2013]		
WEBSITE		www.trig-ltd.com		

LAUNCH DATE	2013	EXCHANGE	London SE	**SYMBOL**
DOMICILE	Guernsey	CURRENCY	GBP	
STOCKBROKER	Canaccord, Liberum	INDEX	FTSE Mid 250	**TRIG**
GEARING	100	AVG DISCOUNT (%)	8.5	
NAV (£M)	946	NET DIV YIELD (%)	5.7	
TURNOVER	1,673			**MKT CAP (£M)**
TER (%)	1.09	SHARPE RATIO	0.8	
		VOLATILITY	0.65	**1,026**
PERFORMANCE FEE	No	PERFORMANCE (10Y) (%)	-	

GREENCOAT UK WIND PLC

CORE INVESTMENT STRATEGY		UK wind farms		
BENCHMARK		8% p.a.		
MANAGEMENT GROUP		Greencoat Capital		
FUND MANAGER		Stephen Lilley, Laurence Fumagalli [2013]		
WEBSITE		www.greencoat-ukwind.com		

LAUNCH DATE	2013	EXCHANGE	London SE	**SYMBOL**
DOMICILE	UK	CURRENCY	GBP	
STOCKBROKER	RBC	INDEX	FTSE Mid 250	**UKW**
GEARING	114	AVG DISCOUNT (%)	10.5	
NAV (£M)	807	NET DIV YIELD (%)	5.3	
TURNOVER	1,131			**MKT CAP (£M)**
TER (%)	1.37	SHARPE RATIO	1.0	
		VOLATILITY	0.73	**899**
PERFORMANCE FEE	No	PERFORMANCE (10Y) (%)	-	

SECTOR SPECIALIST: DEBT

ALCENTRA EUROPEAN FLOATING RATE INCOME FUND LTD

CORE INVESTMENT STRATEGY		European senior secured bank loans		
BENCHMARK		S&P Leveraged Loan Euro Holdings		
MANAGEMENT GROUP		Alcentra		
FUND MANAGER		Graham Rainbow [2012]		
WEBSITE		www.aefrif.com		

LAUNCH DATE	2012	EXCHANGE	London SE	**SYMBOL**
DOMICILE	Guernsey	CURRENCY	GBP	
STOCKBROKER	JPM Cazenove	INDEX	FTSE Small Cap	**AEFS**
GEARING	100	AVG DISCOUNT (%)	-3.3	
NAV (£M)	173	NET DIV YIELD (%)	5.1	
TURNOVER	424			
TER (%)	0.98	SHARPE RATIO	0.4	**MKT CAP (£M)**
		VOLATILITY	0.56	**170**
PERFORMANCE FEE	No	PERFORMANCE (10Y) (%)	-	

AXIOM EUROPEAN FINANCIAL DEBT LTD

CORE INVESTMENT STRATEGY		Regulatory capital securities of European, incl. UK, financials (e.g. AT1s)		
BENCHMARK		10% p.a.		
MANAGEMENT GROUP		Axiom Alternative Investments		
FUND MANAGER		Adrian Paturle [2015]		
WEBSITE		-		

LAUNCH DATE	2015	EXCHANGE	London SE (SFS)	**SYMBOL**
DOMICILE	Guernsey	CURRENCY	GBP	
STOCKBROKER	Liberum	INDEX	-	**AXI**
GEARING	100	AVG DISCOUNT (%)	-1.2	
NAV (£M)	61	NET DIV YIELD (%)	6.3	
TURNOVER	113			
TER (%)	1.83	SHARPE RATIO	-	**MKT CAP (£M)**
		VOLATILITY	0.31	**58**
PERFORMANCE FEE	Yes	PERFORMANCE (10Y) (%)	-	

BLACKSTONE / GSO LOAN FINANCING LTD

CORE INVESTMENT STRATEGY	Floating rate secured loans & CLO income notes
BENCHMARK	S&P Leveraged Loan Euro Holdings – GBP
MANAGEMENT GROUP	Blackstone/GSO Debt Funds Mgt
FUND MANAGER	Fiona O'Connor, Alex Leonard [2014]
WEBSITE	-

LAUNCH DATE	2014	EXCHANGE	London SE (SFS)	**SYMBOL**
DOMICILE	Jersey	CURRENCY	EUR	
STOCKBROKER	Fidante Capital, N+1 Singer	INDEX	-	**BGLF**
GEARING	100	AVG DISCOUNT (%)	1.5	
NAV (£M)	361	NET DIV YIELD (%)	9.9	
TURNOVER	915			
TER (%)	0.72	SHARPE RATIO	-	**MKT CAP (£M)**
		VOLATILITY	0.53	**374**
PERFORMANCE FEE	No	PERFORMANCE (10Y) (%)	-	

BIOPHARMA CREDIT PLC

CORE INVESTMENT STRATEGY	Debt and royalty assets in the life sciences sector
BENCHMARK	8.5% p.a.
MANAGEMENT GROUP	Pharakon Advisors LLP
FUND MANAGER	Pedro Gonzalez de Cosio, Martin Freedman [2017]
WEBSITE	-

LAUNCH DATE	2017	EXCHANGE	London SE (SFS)	**SYMBOL**
DOMICILE	Guernsey	CURRENCY	USD	
STOCKBROKER	Goldman Sachs, JPM Cazenove	INDEX	-	**BPCR**
GEARING	100	AVG DISCOUNT (%)	9.4	
NAV (£M)	583	NET DIV YIELD (%)	3.6	
TURNOVER	187			
TER (%)	-	SHARPE RATIO	-	**MKT CAP (£M)**
		VOLATILITY	0.42	**654**
PERFORMANCE FEE	Yes	PERFORMANCE (10Y) (%)	-	

CVC CREDIT PARTNERS EUROPEAN OPPORTUNITIES LTD

CORE INVESTMENT STRATEGY	Primarily senior secured loans, but also across capital structure, in Western Europe
BENCHMARK	S&P Leveraged Loan Euro Holdings
MANAGEMENT GROUP	CVC Credit Partners Investment Management
FUND MANAGER	Jonathan Bowers, Andrew Davies [2013]
WEBSITE	-

LAUNCH DATE	2013	EXCHANGE	London SE	**SYMBOL**
DOMICILE	Jersey	CURRENCY	EUR	
STOCKBROKER	Winterflood	INDEX	-	**CCPE**
GEARING	100	AVG DISCOUNT (%)	0.0	
NAV (£M)	126	NET DIV YIELD (%)	5.6	
TURNOVER	89			
TER (%)	0.19	SHARPE RATIO	1.0	**MKT CAP (£M)**
		VOLATILITY	0.58	**129**
PERFORMANCE FEE	No	PERFORMANCE (10Y) (%)	-	

CVC CREDIT PARTNERS EUROPEAN OPPORTUNITIES LTD

CORE INVESTMENT STRATEGY	Primarily senior secured loans, but also across capital structure, in Western Europe
BENCHMARK	S&P Leveraged Loan Euro Holdings
MANAGEMENT GROUP	CVC Credit Partners Investment Management
FUND MANAGER	Jonathan Bowers, Andrew Davies [2013]
WEBSITE	www.ccpeol.com

LAUNCH DATE	2013	EXCHANGE	London SE	**SYMBOL**
DOMICILE	Jersey	CURRENCY	GBP	**CCPG**
STOCKBROKER	Winterflood	INDEX	FTSE Small Cap	
GEARING	100	AVG DISCOUNT (%)	-0.7	
NAV (£M)	303	NET DIV YIELD (%)	5.5	
TURNOVER	843			**MKT CAP (£M)**
TER (%)	0.19	SHARPE RATIO	0.8	**308**
		VOLATILITY	0.80	
PERFORMANCE FEE	No	PERFORMANCE (10Y) (%)	-	

CHENAVARI CAPITAL SOLUTIONS LTD

CORE INVESTMENT STRATEGY	Regulatory capital solutions for UK & European banks, mostly primary deals
BENCHMARK	12% p.a.
MANAGEMENT GROUP	Chenavari Investment Managers
FUND MANAGER	Team managed [2013]
WEBSITE	-

LAUNCH DATE	2013	EXCHANGE	London SE (SFS)	**SYMBOL**
DOMICILE	Guernsey	CURRENCY	GBP	**CCSL**
STOCKBROKER	Fidante Capital	INDEX	-	
GEARING	100	AVG DISCOUNT (%)	0.2	
NAV (£M)	111	NET DIV YIELD (%)	7.7	
TURNOVER	125			**MKT CAP (£M)**
TER (%)	1.48	SHARPE RATIO	0.3	**106**
		VOLATILITY	0.29	
PERFORMANCE FEE	Yes	PERFORMANCE (10Y) (%)	-	

CARADOR INCOME FUND PLC

CORE INVESTMENT STRATEGY	US & European CLOs
BENCHMARK	S&P/LSTA Leveraged Loan
MANAGEMENT GROUP	Blackstone/GSO Debt Funds Mgt
FUND MANAGER	J.Richard (iDiki) Blewitt [2015]
WEBSITE	www.carador.co.uk

LAUNCH DATE	2008	EXCHANGE	London SE	**SYMBOL**
DOMICILE	Ireland	CURRENCY	USD	**CIFU**
STOCKBROKER	N+1 Singer	INDEX	-	
GEARING	100	AVG DISCOUNT (%)	-2.5	
NAV (£M)	313	NET DIV YIELD (%)	12.6	
TURNOVER	370			**MKT CAP (£M)**
TER (%)	1.82	SHARPE RATIO	0.1	**298**
		VOLATILITY	1.63	
PERFORMANCE FEE	Yes	PERFORMANCE (10Y) (%)	-	

DORIC NIMROD AIR ONE LTD

CORE INVESTMENT STRATEGY		Aircraft leasing	
BENCHMARK		9% p.a.	
MANAGEMENT GROUP		Doric Asset Finance	
FUND MANAGER		Marc Gordon [2010]	
WEBSITE		-	

LAUNCH DATE	2010	EXCHANGE	London SE (SFS)	**SYMBOL**
DOMICILE	Guernsey	CURRENCY	GBP	
STOCKBROKER	Nimrod Capital	INDEX	-	**DNA**
GEARING	205	AVG DISCOUNT (%)	32.8	
NAV (£M)	38	NET DIV YIELD (%)	7.9	
TURNOVER	27			**MKT CAP (£M)**
TER (%)	1.37	SHARPE RATIO	1.3	
		VOLATILITY	0.36	**48**
PERFORMANCE FEE	No	PERFORMANCE (10Y) (%)	-	

DORIC NIMROD AIR TWO

CORE INVESTMENT STRATEGY		Aircraft leasing	
BENCHMARK		9% p.a.	
MANAGEMENT GROUP		Doric Asset Finance	
FUND MANAGER		Marc Gordon [2011]	
WEBSITE		-	

LAUNCH DATE	2011	EXCHANGE	London SE (SFS)	**SYMBOL**
DOMICILE	Guernsey	CURRENCY	GBP	
STOCKBROKER	Nimrod Capital	INDEX	-	**DNA2**
GEARING	-	AVG DISCOUNT (%)	54.0	
NAV (£M)	240	NET DIV YIELD (%)	8.1	
TURNOVER	219			**MKT CAP (£M)**
TER (%)	-	SHARPE RATIO	0.6	
		VOLATILITY	-	**384**
PERFORMANCE FEE	-	PERFORMANCE (10Y) (%)	-	

DORIC NIMROD AIR THREE

CORE INVESTMENT STRATEGY		Aircraft leasing	
BENCHMARK		8.25% p.a.	
MANAGEMENT GROUP		Doric Asset Finance	
FUND MANAGER		Marc Gordon [2013]	
WEBSITE		-	

LAUNCH DATE	2013	EXCHANGE	London SE (SFS)	**SYMBOL**
DOMICILE	Guernsey	CURRENCY	GBP	
STOCKBROKER	Nimrod Capital	INDEX	-	**DNA3**
GEARING	-	AVG DISCOUNT (%)	71.1	
NAV (£M)	119	NET DIV YIELD (%)	8.0	
TURNOVER	112			**MKT CAP (£M)**
TER (%)	-	SHARPE RATIO	0.8	
		VOLATILITY	-	**228**
PERFORMANCE FEE	-	PERFORMANCE (10Y) (%)	-	

DP AIRCRAFT

CORE INVESTMENT STRATEGY		Aircraft leasing	
BENCHMARK		11% p.a.	
MANAGEMENT GROUP		DS Aviation GmbH & Co	
FUND MANAGER		Team managed [2013]	
WEBSITE		-	

LAUNCH DATE	2013	EXCHANGE	London SE	**SYMBOL**
DOMICILE	Guernsey	CURRENCY	USD	**DPA**
STOCKBROKER	Canaccord Genuity	INDEX	-	
GEARING	-	AVG DISCOUNT (%)	11.5	
NAV (£M)	157	NET DIV YIELD (%)	8.3	
TURNOVER	90			
TER (%)	-	SHARPE RATIO	2.0	**MKT CAP (£M)**
		VOLATILITY	-	**176**
PERFORMANCE FEE	-	PERFORMANCE (10Y) (%)	-	

FAIR OAKS INCOME LTD 2014 SHARES NPV

CORE INVESTMENT STRATEGY		US & European CLOs (capital returned from realisations)	
BENCHMARK		S&P/LSTA Leveraged Loan	
MANAGEMENT GROUP		Fair Oaks Capital	
FUND MANAGER		Miguel Ramos Fuentenebro, Roger Coyle [2017]	
WEBSITE		-	

LAUNCH DATE	2017	EXCHANGE	London SE (SFS)	**SYMBOL**
DOMICILE	Guernsey	CURRENCY	USD	**FA14**
STOCKBROKER	Numis	INDEX	-	
GEARING	100	AVG DISCOUNT (%)	3.0	
NAV (£M)	35	NET DIV YIELD (%)	13.1	
TURNOVER	41			
TER (%)	-	SHARPE RATIO	-	**MKT CAP (£M)**
		VOLATILITY	0.24	**37**
PERFORMANCE FEE	No	PERFORMANCE (10Y) (%)	-	

FAIR OAKS INCOME LTD

CORE INVESTMENT STRATEGY		US & European CLOs	
BENCHMARK		S&P/LSTA Leveraged Loan	
MANAGEMENT GROUP		Fair Oaks Capital	
FUND MANAGER		Miguel Ramos Fuentenebro, Roger Coyle [2014]	
WEBSITE		-	

LAUNCH DATE	2014	EXCHANGE	London SE (SFS)	**SYMBOL**
DOMICILE	Guernsey	CURRENCY	USD	**FAIR**
STOCKBROKER	Numis	INDEX	-	
GEARING	100	AVG DISCOUNT (%)	3.1	
NAV (£M)	252	NET DIV YIELD (%)	13.1	
TURNOVER	313			
TER (%)	0.28	SHARPE RATIO	-	**MKT CAP (£M)**
		VOLATILITY	0.66	**264**
PERFORMANCE FEE	No	PERFORMANCE (10Y) (%)	-	

FUNDING CIRCLE SME INCOME FUND LTD C NPV

CORE INVESTMENT STRATEGY		SME loans through Funding Circle's marketplaces	
BENCHMARK		8.5% p.a.	
MANAGEMENT GROUP		Self-Managed	
FUND MANAGER		Sachin Patel [2017]	
WEBSITE		-	

LAUNCH DATE	2015	EXCHANGE	London SE	**SYMBOL**
DOMICILE	Guernsey	CURRENCY	GBP	
STOCKBROKER	Numis	INDEX	-	**FCIC**
GEARING	100	AVG DISCOUNT (%)	1.9	
NAV (£M)	141	NET DIV YIELD (%)	6.2	
TURNOVER	86			
TER (%)	-	SHARPE RATIO	-	**MKT CAP (£M)**
		VOLATILITY	0.20	**145**
PERFORMANCE FEE	No	PERFORMANCE (10Y) (%)	-	

FUNDING CIRCLE SME INCOME FUND LTD

CORE INVESTMENT STRATEGY		SME loans through Funding Circle's marketplaces	
BENCHMARK		8.5% p.a.	
MANAGEMENT GROUP		Self-Managed	
FUND MANAGER		Sachin Patel [2015]	
WEBSITE		www.fcincomefund.com	

LAUNCH DATE	2015	EXCHANGE	London SE	**SYMBOL**
DOMICILE	Guernsey	CURRENCY	GBP	
STOCKBROKER	Numis	INDEX	FTSE Small Cap	**FCIF**
GEARING	100	AVG DISCOUNT (%)	2.9	
NAV (£M)	166	NET DIV YIELD (%)	6.2	
TURNOVER	158			
TER (%)	0.88	SHARPE RATIO	-	**MKT CAP (£M)**
		VOLATILITY	0.98	**172**
PERFORMANCE FEE	No	PERFORMANCE (10Y) (%)	-	

GCP ASSET BACKED INCOME FUND LTD

CORE INVESTMENT STRATEGY		UK project finance, with predictable medium term cash flows and/or physical assets	
BENCHMARK		9% p.a.	
MANAGEMENT GROUP		Gravis Capital Partners	
FUND MANAGER		David Conlon [2015]	
WEBSITE		www.gcpuk.com	

LAUNCH DATE	2015	EXCHANGE	London SE	**SYMBOL**
DOMICILE	UK	CURRENCY	GBP	
STOCKBROKER	Cenkos	INDEX	FTSE Small Cap	**GABI**
GEARING	100	AVG DISCOUNT (%)	8.8	
NAV (£M)	238	NET DIV YIELD (%)	5.7	
TURNOVER	207			
TER (%)	1.81	SHARPE RATIO	-	**MKT CAP (£M)**
		VOLATILITY	0.67	**257**
PERFORMANCE FEE	No	PERFORMANCE (10Y) (%)	-	

HONEYCOMB INVESTMENT TRUST PLC

CORE INVESTMENT STRATEGY	Consumer and SME loans
BENCHMARK	8% p.a.
MANAGEMENT GROUP	Pollen Street Capital
FUND MANAGER	Lindsey McMurray [2015]
WEBSITE	-

LAUNCH DATE	2015	EXCHANGE	London SE (SFS)	SYMBOL
DOMICILE	UK	CURRENCY	GBP	**HONY**
STOCKBROKER	Liberum	INDEX	-	
GEARING	100	AVG DISCOUNT (%)	7.8	
NAV (£M)	307	NET DIV YIELD (%)	7.6	
TURNOVER	127			MKT CAP (£M)
TER (%)	1.33	SHARPE RATIO	-	**361**
		VOLATILITY	0.30	
PERFORMANCE FEE	Yes	PERFORMANCE (10Y) (%)	-	

HADRIAN'S WALL SECURED INVESTMENTS LTD C SHARES

CORE INVESTMENT STRATEGY	Asset secured loans
BENCHMARK	8% p.a.
MANAGEMENT GROUP	International Fund Management
FUND MANAGER	Marc Bajer, Mike Schozer [2017]
WEBSITE	-

LAUNCH DATE	2017	EXCHANGE	London SE	SYMBOL
DOMICILE	Guernsey	CURRENCY	GBP	**HWSC**
STOCKBROKER	Winterflood	INDEX	-	
GEARING	100	AVG DISCOUNT (%)	4.7	
NAV (£M)	44	NET DIV YIELD (%)	5.6	
TURNOVER	113			MKT CAP (£M)
TER (%)	-	SHARPE RATIO	-	**46**
		VOLATILITY	0.35	
PERFORMANCE FEE	No	PERFORMANCE (10Y) (%)	-	

HADRIAN'S WALL SECURED INVESTMENTS LTD

CORE INVESTMENT STRATEGY	Asset secured loans
BENCHMARK	8% p.a.
MANAGEMENT GROUP	International Fund Management
FUND MANAGER	Marc Bajer, Mike Schozer [2016]
WEBSITE	www.hadrianswallcapital.com

LAUNCH DATE	2016	EXCHANGE	London SE	SYMBOL
DOMICILE	Guernsey	CURRENCY	GBP	**HWSL**
STOCKBROKER	Winterflood	INDEX	FTSE Fledgling	
GEARING	100	AVG DISCOUNT (%)	9.2	
NAV (£M)	78	NET DIV YIELD (%)	5.6	
TURNOVER	48			MKT CAP (£M)
TER (%)	-	SHARPE RATIO	-	**85**
		VOLATILITY	0.30	
PERFORMANCE FEE	No	PERFORMANCE (10Y) (%)	-	

JPMORGAN GLOBAL CONVERTIBLES INCOME FUND LTD

CORE INVESTMENT STRATEGY		Covertible securities		
BENCHMARK		MSCI World		
MANAGEMENT GROUP		JPMorgan AM		
FUND MANAGER		Antony Vallee [2013]		
WEBSITE		www.jpmconvertiblesincome.co.uk		

LAUNCH DATE	2013	EXCHANGE	London SE	**SYMBOL**
DOMICILE	Guernsey	CURRENCY	GBP	**JGCI**
STOCKBROKER	Winterflood	INDEX	FTSE Small Cap	
GEARING	109	AVG DISCOUNT (%)	-6.0	
NAV (£M)	180	NET DIV YIELD (%)	4.5	
TURNOVER	454			
TER (%)	0.85	SHARPE RATIO	-	**MKT CAP (£M)**
		VOLATILITY	0.83	**176**
PERFORMANCE FEE	No	PERFORMANCE (10Y) (%)	-	

ICG-LONGBOW SENIOR SECURED UK PROPERTY DEBT INVESTMENTS LTD

CORE INVESTMENT STRATEGY		Non-syndicated senior loans		
BENCHMARK		8% p.a.		
MANAGEMENT GROUP		Intermediate Capital Group		
FUND MANAGER		Team managed [2013]		
WEBSITE		www.icg-longbow-ssup.com		

LAUNCH DATE	2013	EXCHANGE	London SE	**SYMBOL**
DOMICILE	Guernsey	CURRENCY	GBP	**LBOW**
STOCKBROKER	Cenkos	INDEX	-	
GEARING	100	AVG DISCOUNT (%)	1.4	
NAV (£M)	105	NET DIV YIELD (%)	5.8	
TURNOVER	403			
TER (%)	1.64	SHARPE RATIO	-	**MKT CAP (£M)**
		VOLATILITY	0.50	**111**
PERFORMANCE FEE	No	PERFORMANCE (10Y) (%)	-	

DISTRESSED DEBT INVESTMENT FUND LTD

CORE INVESTMENT STRATEGY		Stressed and distressed debt secured by asset collateral		
BENCHMARK		HFRX Distressed Securities		
MANAGEMENT GROUP		Neuberger Berman Europe		
FUND MANAGER		Michael Holmberg [2010]		
WEBSITE		-		

LAUNCH DATE	2010	EXCHANGE	London SE (SFS)	**SYMBOL**
DOMICILE	Guernsey	CURRENCY	USD	**NBDD**
STOCKBROKER	Stifel, Winterflood	INDEX	-	
GEARING	100	AVG DISCOUNT (%)	-4.7	
NAV (£M)	30	NET DIV YIELD (%)	7.7	
TURNOVER	86			
TER (%)	2.48	SHARPE RATIO	0.6	**MKT CAP (£M)**
		VOLATILITY	0.33	**28**
PERFORMANCE FEE	Yes	PERFORMANCE (10Y) (%)	-	

NB DISTRESSED DEBT INVESTMENT FUND LIMITED RED ORD NPV

CORE INVESTMENT STRATEGY	Global distressed or mispriced assets
BENCHMARK	HFRX Distressed Securities
MANAGEMENT GROUP	Neuberger Berman Europe
FUND MANAGER	Michael Holmberg [2014]
WEBSITE	-

LAUNCH DATE	2014	EXCHANGE	London SE (SFS)	**SYMBOL**
DOMICILE	Guernsey	CURRENCY	GBP	**NBDG**
STOCKBROKER	Stifel, Winterflood	INDEX	-	
GEARING	100	AVG DISCOUNT (%)	-15.6	
NAV (£M)	94	NET DIV YIELD (%)	1.3	
TURNOVER	101			
TER (%)	2.48	SHARPE RATIO	-0.8	**MKT CAP (£M)**
		VOLATILITY	0.46	**78**
PERFORMANCE FEE	Yes	PERFORMANCE (10Y) (%)	-	

NB DISTRESSED DEBT INVESTMENT FUND LTD

CORE INVESTMENT STRATEGY	Stressed and distressed debt secured by asset collateral
BENCHMARK	HFRX Distressed Securities
MANAGEMENT GROUP	Neuberger Berman Europe
FUND MANAGER	Michael Holmberg [2013]
WEBSITE	-

LAUNCH DATE	2013	EXCHANGE	London SE (SFS)	**SYMBOL**
DOMICILE	Guernsey	CURRENCY	USD	**NBDX**
STOCKBROKER	Stifel, Winterflood	INDEX	-	
GEARING	100	AVG DISCOUNT (%)	-9.2	
NAV (£M)	152	NET DIV YIELD (%)	3.7	
TURNOVER	119			
TER (%)	2.48	SHARPE RATIO	-0.1	**MKT CAP (£M)**
		VOLATILITY	0.38	**131**
PERFORMANCE FEE	Yes	PERFORMANCE (10Y) (%)	-	

NB GLOBAL FLOATING RATE INCOME FUND LTD

CORE INVESTMENT STRATEGY	Senior secured bank loans, predominantly US
BENCHMARK	S&P/LSTA Leveraged Loan
MANAGEMENT GROUP	Neuberger Berman Europe
FUND MANAGER	Martin Rotheram, Joseph Lynch, Stephen Casey, [2011]
WEBSITE	www.nbgfrif.com

LAUNCH DATE	2011	EXCHANGE	London SE	**SYMBOL**
DOMICILE	Guernsey	CURRENCY	GBP	**NBLS**
STOCKBROKER	Stifel	INDEX	FTSE Mid 250	
GEARING	100	AVG DISCOUNT (%)	-0.9	
NAV (£M)	973	NET DIV YIELD (%)	4.1	
TURNOVER	1,680			
TER (%)	0.94	SHARPE RATIO	0.3	**MKT CAP (£M)**
		VOLATILITY	0.47	**952**
PERFORMANCE FEE	No	PERFORMANCE (10Y) (%)	-	

NB GLOBAL FLOATING RATE INCOME FUND LTD

CORE INVESTMENT STRATEGY		Senior secured bank loans, predominantly US	
BENCHMARK		S&P/LSTA Leveraged Loan	
MANAGEMENT GROUP		Neuberger Berman Europe	
FUND MANAGER		Martin Rotheram, Joseph Lynch, Stephen Casey, [2011]	
WEBSITE		-	

LAUNCH DATE	2011	EXCHANGE	London SE	**SYMBOL**
DOMICILE	Guernsey	CURRENCY	USD	**NBLU**
STOCKBROKER	Stifel	INDEX	-	
GEARING	100	AVG DISCOUNT (%)	0.6	
NAV (£M)	34	NET DIV YIELD (%)	4.1	
TURNOVER	68			**MKT CAP (£M)**
TER (%)	0.94	SHARPE RATIO	1.1	
		VOLATILITY	0.48	**33**
PERFORMANCE FEE	No	PERFORMANCE (10Y) (%)	-	

P2P GLOBAL INVESTMENTS PLC

CORE INVESTMENT STRATEGY		Peer to Peer lending platforms in US & Europe	
BENCHMARK		10% p.a.	
MANAGEMENT GROUP		MW Eaglewood	
FUND MANAGER		Steven Lee, Jonathon Barlow, Simon Champ [2014]	
WEBSITE		www.p2pgi.com	

LAUNCH DATE	2014	EXCHANGE	London SE	**SYMBOL**
DOMICILE	UK	CURRENCY	GBP	**P2P**
STOCKBROKER	Liberum Capital, JPM Cazenove	INDEX	FTSE Mid 250	
GEARING	100	AVG DISCOUNT (%)	-17.1	
NAV (£M)	799	NET DIV YIELD (%)	5.3	
TURNOVER	1,050			**MKT CAP (£M)**
TER (%)	1.21	SHARPE RATIO	-0.1	
		VOLATILITY	0.99	**684**
PERFORMANCE FEE	Yes	PERFORMANCE (10Y) (%)	-	

TOC PROPERTY BACKED LENDING TRUST PLC

CORE INVESTMENT STRATEGY		UK Property backed fixed rate loans	
BENCHMARK		8.5% p.a.	
MANAGEMENT GROUP		Teir One Capital	
FUND MANAGER		Steven Black, Ian McElroy [2017]	
WEBSITE		www.tocpropertybackedlendingtrust.co.uk	

LAUNCH DATE	2017	EXCHANGE	London SE	**SYMBOL**
DOMICILE	UK	CURRENCY	GBP	**PBLT**
STOCKBROKER	finncap	INDEX	FTSE Fledgling	
GEARING	100	AVG DISCOUNT (%)	5.4	
NAV (£M)	21	NET DIV YIELD (%)	6.8	
TURNOVER	258			**MKT CAP (£M)**
TER (%)	-	SHARPE RATIO	-	
		VOLATILITY	-	**23**
PERFORMANCE FEE	No	PERFORMANCE (10Y) (%)	-	

RANGER DIRECT LENDING FUND PLC

CORE INVESTMENT STRATEGY		Direct Lending Platforms	
BENCHMARK		12% p.a.	
MANAGEMENT GROUP		Ranger Alternative Management	
FUND MANAGER		Bill Kassul [2015]	
WEBSITE		www.rangerdirectlending.com	

				SYMBOL
LAUNCH DATE	2015	EXCHANGE	London SE	**RDL**
DOMICILE	UK	CURRENCY	GBP	
STOCKBROKER	Liberum Capital, Fidante Capital	INDEX	FTSE Small Cap	
GEARING	100	AVG DISCOUNT (%)	-15.8	
NAV (£M)	175	NET DIV YIELD (%)	12.0	
TURNOVER	281			MKT CAP (£M)
TER (%)	-	SHARPE RATIO	-	**124**
		VOLATILITY	1.49	
PERFORMANCE FEE	Yes	PERFORMANCE (10Y) (%)	-	

REAL ESTATE CREDIT INVESTMENT PCC LTD

CORE INVESTMENT STRATEGY		Sub-ordinated tranches of asset-backed securities	
BENCHMARK		8% p.a.	
MANAGEMENT GROUP		Cheyne Capital Management	
FUND MANAGER		Ravi Stickney, Richard Lang [2005]	
WEBSITE		www.recreditinvest.com	

				SYMBOL
LAUNCH DATE	2005	EXCHANGE	London SE	**RECI**
DOMICILE	Guernsey	CURRENCY	GBP	
STOCKBROKER	Peel Hunt, JPM Cazenove	INDEX	FTSE Small Cap	
GEARING	135	AVG DISCOUNT (%)	0.2	
NAV (£M)	165	NET DIV YIELD (%)	6.7	
TURNOVER	177			MKT CAP (£M)
TER (%)	2.34	SHARPE RATIO	-	**175**
		VOLATILITY	2.64	
PERFORMANCE FEE	Yes	PERFORMANCE (10Y) (%)	136	

RM SECURED DIRECT LENDING PLC

CORE INVESTMENT STRATEGY		UK SMEs & mid market corporates	
BENCHMARK		6.5% p.a.	
MANAGEMENT GROUP		RM Capital Markets	
FUND MANAGER		James Robson [2016]	
WEBSITE		www.rm-funds.co.uk	

				SYMBOL
LAUNCH DATE	2016	EXCHANGE	London SE	**RMDL**
DOMICILE	UK	CURRENCY	GBP	
STOCKBROKER	N+1 Singer	INDEX	FTSE Fledgling	
GEARING	100	AVG DISCOUNT (%)	4.4	
NAV (£M)	56	NET DIV YIELD (%)	3.9	
TURNOVER	48			MKT CAP (£M)
TER (%)	-	SHARPE RATIO	-	**59**
		VOLATILITY	0.14	
PERFORMANCE FEE	No	PERFORMANCE (10Y) (%)	-	

TWENTYFOUR SELECT MONTHLY INCOME FUND LTD

CORE INVESTMENT STRATEGY	Fixed income credit products	
BENCHMARK	8% p.a.	
MANAGEMENT GROUP	TwentyFour AM	
FUND MANAGER	Gary Kirk, Eoin Walsh [2014]	
WEBSITE	www.twentyfouram.com	

LAUNCH DATE	2014	EXCHANGE	London SE	**SYMBOL**	
DOMICILE	Guernsey	CURRENCY	GBP	**SMIF**	
STOCKBROKER	Numis	INDEX	FTSE Small Cap		
GEARING	100	AVG DISCOUNT (%)	2.4		
NAV (£M)	155	NET DIV YIELD (%)	6.9		
TURNOVER	453				
TER (%)	1.21	SHARPE RATIO	-	**MKT CAP (£M)**	
		VOLATILITY	0.62	**160**	
PERFORMANCE FEE	No	PERFORMANCE (10Y) (%)	-		

SQN ASSET FINANCE INCOME FUND LTD

CORE INVESTMENT STRATEGY	Business-essential, revenue producing assets	
BENCHMARK	9% p.a.	
MANAGEMENT GROUP	SQN Capital Management	
FUND MANAGER	Jeremiah Silkowski, Neil Roberts [2014]	
WEBSITE	www.sqnassetfinance.com	

LAUNCH DATE	2014	EXCHANGE	London SE	**SYMBOL**	
DOMICILE	Guernsey	CURRENCY	GBP	**SQN**	
STOCKBROKER	Winterflood	INDEX	FTSE Small Cap		
GEARING	100	AVG DISCOUNT (%)	11.4		
NAV (£M)	350	NET DIV YIELD (%)	7.3		
TURNOVER	576				
TER (%)	2.16	SHARPE RATIO	0.3	**MKT CAP (£M)**	
		VOLATILITY	0.76	**354**	
PERFORMANCE FEE	No	PERFORMANCE (10Y) (%)	-		

SQN ASSET FINANCE INCOME FUND LTD C SHARES NPV

CORE INVESTMENT STRATEGY	Business-essential, revenue producing assets	
BENCHMARK	9% p.a.	
MANAGEMENT GROUP	SQN Capital Management	
FUND MANAGER	Jeremiah Silkowski, Neil Roberts [2016]	
WEBSITE	-	

LAUNCH DATE	2016	EXCHANGE	London SE	**SYMBOL**	
DOMICILE	Guernsey	CURRENCY	GBP	**SQNX**	
STOCKBROKER	Winterflood	INDEX	-		
GEARING	100	AVG DISCOUNT (%)	5.4		
NAV (£M)	177	NET DIV YIELD (%)	7.3		
TURNOVER	295				
TER (%)	-	SHARPE RATIO	-	**MKT CAP (£M)**	
		VOLATILITY	1.02	**179**	
PERFORMANCE FEE	No	PERFORMANCE (10Y) (%)	-		

SQN SECURED INCOME FUND PLC

CORE INVESTMENT STRATEGY	SME loans originated via alternative lending platforms
BENCHMARK	8% p.a.
MANAGEMENT GROUP	SQN Capital Management
FUND MANAGER	Graham Glass [2016]
WEBSITE	-

LAUNCH DATE	2015	EXCHANGE	London SE (SFS)	**SYMBOL**
DOMICILE	UK	CURRENCY	GBP	**SSIF**
STOCKBROKER	Cantour Fitzgerald Europe	INDEX	-	
GEARING	100	AVG DISCOUNT (%)	-4.1	
NAV (£M)	52	NET DIV YIELD (%)	6.4	
TURNOVER	341			
TER (%)	1.98	SHARPE RATIO	-	**MKT CAP (£M)**
		VOLATILITY	0.37	**51**
PERFORMANCE FEE	No	PERFORMANCE (10Y) (%)	-	

STARWOOD EUROPEAN REAL ESTATE FINANCE LTD

CORE INVESTMENT STRATEGY	UK & European real estate debt
BENCHMARK	8% p.a.
MANAGEMENT GROUP	Starwood European Finance Partners
FUND MANAGER	Duncan MacPherson [2012]
WEBSITE	www.starwoodeuropeanfinance.com

LAUNCH DATE	2012	EXCHANGE	London SE	**SYMBOL**
DOMICILE	Guernsey	CURRENCY	GBP	**SWEF**
STOCKBROKER	Fidante Capital, Jefferies	INDEX	FTSE Small Cap	
GEARING	100	AVG DISCOUNT (%)	6.4	
NAV (£M)	384	NET DIV YIELD (%)	5.9	
TURNOVER	329			
TER (%)	1.01	SHARPE RATIO	-	**MKT CAP (£M)**
		VOLATILITY	0.49	**413**
PERFORMANCE FEE	No	PERFORMANCE (10Y) (%)	-	

TWENTYFOUR INCOME FUND LTD

CORE INVESTMENT STRATEGY	UK & European asset backed securities
BENCHMARK	8.5%; 7% p.a.
MANAGEMENT GROUP	TwentyFour AM
FUND MANAGER	Ben Hayward [2013]
WEBSITE	www.twentyfourincomefund.com

LAUNCH DATE	2013	EXCHANGE	London SE	**SYMBOL**
DOMICILE	Guernsey	CURRENCY	GBP	**TFIF**
STOCKBROKER	Numis	INDEX	FTSE Small Cap	
GEARING	100	AVG DISCOUNT (%)	2.8	
NAV (£M)	456	NET DIV YIELD (%)	6.0	
TURNOVER	662			
TER (%)	1.01	SHARPE RATIO	0.4	**MKT CAP (£M)**
		VOLATILITY	0.55	**460**
PERFORMANCE FEE	No	PERFORMANCE (10Y) (%)	-	

TORO LTD

CORE INVESTMENT STRATEGY	European asset backed securities, including CLO origination
BENCHMARK	13.5% p.a.
MANAGEMENT GROUP	Chenavari Investment Managers
FUND MANAGER	Team managed [2015]
WEBSITE	-

LAUNCH DATE	2015	EXCHANGE	London SE (SFS)	**SYMBOL**
DOMICILE	Guernsey	CURRENCY	EUR	**TORO**
STOCKBROKER	Fidante Capital	INDEX	-	
GEARING	100	AVG DISCOUNT (%)	-12.8	
NAV (£M)	293	NET DIV YIELD (%)	9.4	
TURNOVER	476			**MKT CAP (£M)**
TER (%)	1.46	SHARPE RATIO	-	
		VOLATILITY	0.44	**252**
PERFORMANCE FEE	Yes	PERFORMANCE (10Y) (%)	-	

UK MORTGAGES LTD

CORE INVESTMENT STRATEGY	UK residential mortgages
BENCHMARK	8% p.a.
MANAGEMENT GROUP	TwentyFour AM
FUND MANAGER	Ben Hayward, Rob Ford, Douglas Charleston, Silvia Piva [2015]
WEBSITE	-

LAUNCH DATE	2015	EXCHANGE	London SE (SFS)	**SYMBOL**
DOMICILE	Guernsey	CURRENCY	GBP	**UKML**
STOCKBROKER	Numis	INDEX	-	
GEARING	100	AVG DISCOUNT (%)	6.2	
NAV (£M)	219	NET DIV YIELD (%)	6.4	
TURNOVER	289			**MKT CAP (£M)**
TER (%)	1.3	SHARPE RATIO	-	
		VOLATILITY	0.40	**233**
PERFORMANCE FEE	No	PERFORMANCE (10Y) (%)	-	

VPC SPECIALTY LENDING INVESTMENTS PLC

CORE INVESTMENT STRATEGY	Peer to Peer lending platforms in US & Europe
BENCHMARK	10% p.a.
MANAGEMENT GROUP	Victory Park Capital Advisors
FUND MANAGER	Richard Levy [2015]
WEBSITE	vpcspecialtylending.com

LAUNCH DATE	2015	EXCHANGE	London SE	**SYMBOL**
DOMICILE	UK	CURRENCY	GBP	**VSL**
STOCKBROKER	Jefferies, Stifel	INDEX	FTSE Small Cap	
GEARING	100	AVG DISCOUNT (%)	-17.8	
NAV (£M)	344	NET DIV YIELD (%)	8.6	
TURNOVER	304			**MKT CAP (£M)**
TER (%)	3.86	SHARPE RATIO	-	
		VOLATILITY	0.85	**295**
PERFORMANCE FEE	Yes	PERFORMANCE (10Y) (%)	-	

SECTOR SPECIALIST: SMALL MEDIA, COMMS & IT COS

HERALD INVESTMENT TRUST PLC

CORE INVESTMENT STRATEGY	Smaller TMT stocks in UK, US & Europe
BENCHMARK	Dow Jones World Technology
MANAGEMENT GROUP	Herald IM
FUND MANAGER	Katie Potts [1994]
WEBSITE	www.heralduk.com

LAUNCH DATE	1994	EXCHANGE	London SE	**SYMBOL**
DOMICILE	UK	CURRENCY	GBP	**HRI**
STOCKBROKER	JPM Cazenove, N+1 Singer	INDEX	FTSE Small Cap	
GEARING	103	AVG DISCOUNT (%)	-19.3	
NAV (£M)	917	NET DIV YIELD (%)	-	
TURNOVER	950			**MKT CAP (£M)**
TER (%)	1.09	SHARPE RATIO	1.3	**765**
		VOLATILITY	1.46	
PERFORMANCE FEE	No	PERFORMANCE (10Y) (%)	181	

SECTOR SPECIALIST: TECH MEDIA & TELECOMM

ALLIANZ TECHNOLOGY TRUST PLC

CORE INVESTMENT STRATEGY		Global technology stocks	
BENCHMARK		Dow Jones World Technology	
MANAGEMENT GROUP		Allianz Global Investors	
FUND MANAGER		Walter Price [2007]	
WEBSITE		www.allianztechnologytrust.com	

LAUNCH DATE	1995	EXCHANGE	London SE	**SYMBOL**
DOMICILE	UK	CURRENCY	GBP	**ATT**
STOCKBROKER	Winterflood	INDEX	FTSE Small Cap	
GEARING	100	AVG DISCOUNT (%)	-5.4	
NAV (£M)	290	NET DIV YIELD (%)	-	
TURNOVER	466			**MKT CAP (£M)**
TER (%)	1.03	SHARPE RATIO	1.4	**273**
		VOLATILITY	1.72	
PERFORMANCE FEE	Yes	PERFORMANCE (10Y) (%)	357	

POLAR CAPITAL TECHNOLOGY TRUST PLC

CORE INVESTMENT STRATEGY		Global technology stocks	
BENCHMARK		Dow Jones World Technology	
MANAGEMENT GROUP		Polar Capital	
FUND MANAGER		Ben Rogoff [2006]	
WEBSITE		www.polarcapitaltechnologytrust.co.uk	

LAUNCH DATE	1996	EXCHANGE	London SE	**SYMBOL**
DOMICILE	UK	CURRENCY	GBP	**PCT**
STOCKBROKER	Cenkos	INDEX	FTSE Mid 250	
GEARING	103	AVG DISCOUNT (%)	-1.0	
NAV (£M)	1,406	NET DIV YIELD (%)	-	
TURNOVER	1,843			**MKT CAP (£M)**
TER (%)	1.01	SHARPE RATIO	1.6	**1,393**
		VOLATILITY	1.82	
PERFORMANCE FEE	Yes	PERFORMANCE (10Y) (%)	368	

ECOFIN GLOBAL UTILITIES AND INFRUSTRUCTURE TRUST PLC

CORE INVESTMENT STRATEGY		Global utility & infrastructure stocks
BENCHMARK		MSCI World Utilities
MANAGEMENT GROUP		Ecofin Ltd
FUND MANAGER		Jean-Hughes de Lamaze [2016]
WEBSITE		www.ecofin.co.uk

LAUNCH DATE	2016	EXCHANGE	London SE	
DOMICILE	UK	CURRENCY	GBP	
STOCKBROKER	Winterflood	INDEX	FTSE Small Cap	
GEARING	108	AVG DISCOUNT (%)	-12.3	
NAV (£M)	137	NET DIV YIELD (%)	4.8	
TURNOVER	343			
TER (%)	-	SHARPE RATIO	-	
		VOLATILITY	1.76	
PERFORMANCE FEE	No	PERFORMANCE (10Y) (%)	-	

SYMBOL

EGL

MKT CAP (£M)

122

SPLIT CAPITAL TRUSTS

ABERFORTH SPLIT LEVEL INCOME TRUST PLC

CORE INVESTMENT STRATEGY		UK smaller cos	
BENCHMARK		Numis Smaller Cos ex ICs	
MANAGEMENT GROUP		Aberforth Partners	
FUND MANAGER		Partners [2017]	
WEBSITE		-	

LAUNCH DATE	2017	EXCHANGE	London SE	**SYMBOL**
DOMICILE	UK	CURRENCY	GBP	**ASIT**
STOCKBROKER	JPM Cazenove	INDEX	-	
GEARING	125	AVG DISCOUNT (%)	-4.5	
NAV (£M)	194	NET DIV YIELD (%)	4.0	
TURNOVER	153			
TER (%)	-	SHARPE RATIO	-	**MKT CAP (£M)**
		VOLATILITY	1.43	**188**
PERFORMANCE FEE	No	PERFORMANCE (10Y) (%)	-	

JZ CAPITAL PARTNERS LTD

CORE INVESTMENT STRATEGY		US growth capital	
BENCHMARK		Russell 2000	
MANAGEMENT GROUP		Jordan-Zalaznick Advisors	
FUND MANAGER		David Zalaznick [1998]	
WEBSITE		www.jzcp.com	

LAUNCH DATE	1998	EXCHANGE	London SE (SFS)	**SYMBOL**
DOMICILE	Guernsey	CURRENCY	GBP	**JZCP**
STOCKBROKER	JPM Cazenove	INDEX	-	
GEARING	107	AVG DISCOUNT (%)	-33.4	
NAV (£M)	645	NET DIV YIELD (%)	-	
TURNOVER	141			
TER (%)	2.91	SHARPE RATIO	1.5	**MKT CAP (£M)**
		VOLATILITY	1.80	**433**
PERFORMANCE FEE	Yes	PERFORMANCE (10Y) (%)	2	

PREMIER ENERGY AND WATER TRUST PLC

CORE INVESTMENT STRATEGY		Equities of utility and regulated infrastructure cos
BENCHMARK		MSCI World Utilities
MANAGEMENT GROUP		Premier Fund Managers
FUND MANAGER		James Smith, Claire Burgess [2012]
WEBSITE		www.premierfunds.co.uk

LAUNCH DATE	2003	EXCHANGE	London SE	**SYMBOL**
DOMICILE	UK	CURRENCY	GBP	**PEW**
STOCKBROKER	N+1 Singer	INDEX	FTSE Fledgling	
GEARING	183	AVG DISCOUNT (%)	-6.7	
NAV (£M)	31	NET DIV YIELD (%)	5.0	
TURNOVER	41			**MKT CAP (£M)**
TER (%)	4.04	SHARPE RATIO	0.1	**29**
		VOLATILITY	0.77	
PERFORMANCE FEE	Yes	PERFORMANCE (10Y) (%)	66	

UIL LTD

CORE INVESTMENT STRATEGY		Investment across all sectors/markets. Previously utilities.
BENCHMARK		MSCI AC World
MANAGEMENT GROUP		ICM
FUND MANAGER		Charles Jillings, Duncan Saville [2004]
WEBSITE		www.uil.limited

LAUNCH DATE	2004	EXCHANGE	London SE	**SYMBOL**
DOMICILE	Bermuda	CURRENCY	GBP	**UTL**
STOCKBROKER	Stockdale	INDEX	-	
GEARING	218	AVG DISCOUNT (%)	-42.5	
NAV (£M)	194	NET DIV YIELD (%)	4.6	
TURNOVER	42			**MKT CAP (£M)**
TER (%)	1.24	SHARPE RATIO	0.6	**147**
		VOLATILITY	1.42	
PERFORMANCE FEE	Yes	PERFORMANCE (10Y) (%)	-5	

AURORA INVESTMENT TRUST PLC

CORE INVESTMENT STRATEGY	UK equities
BENCHMARK	FTSE All Share
MANAGEMENT GROUP	Phoenix AM
FUND MANAGER	Gary Channon [2015]
WEBSITE	www.aurorainvestmenttrust.com

LAUNCH DATE	1997	EXCHANGE	London SE	**SYMBOL**
DOMICILE	UK	CURRENCY	GBP	
STOCKBROKER	Liberum	INDEX	FTSE Fledgling	**ARR**
GEARING	100	AVG DISCOUNT (%)	1.6	
NAV (£M)	73	NET DIV YIELD (%)	1.0	
TURNOVER	55			
TER (%)	1.77	SHARPE RATIO	0.8	**MKT CAP (£M)**
		VOLATILITY	1.46	**74**
PERFORMANCE FEE	Yes	PERFORMANCE (10Y) (%)	25	

ARTEMIS ALPHA TRUST PLC

CORE INVESTMENT STRATEGY	UK equities & selected international
BENCHMARK	FTSE All Share
MANAGEMENT GROUP	Artemis IM
FUND MANAGER	John Dodd [2003] and Adrian Paterson [2009]
WEBSITE	www.artemisfunds.com

LAUNCH DATE	2003	EXCHANGE	London SE	**SYMBOL**
DOMICILE	UK	CURRENCY	GBP	
STOCKBROKER	Cantor Fitzgerald Europe	INDEX	FTSE Small Cap	**ATS**
GEARING	110	AVG DISCOUNT (%)	-21.7	
NAV (£M)	147	NET DIV YIELD (%)	1.5	
TURNOVER	121			
TER (%)	0.91	SHARPE RATIO	0.0	**MKT CAP (£M)**
		VOLATILITY	1.14	**119**
PERFORMANCE FEE	Yes	PERFORMANCE (10Y) (%)	58	

CRYSTAL AMBER FUND LTD

CORE INVESTMENT STRATEGY		Activist fund with focused portfolio of undervalued companies	
BENCHMARK		Numis Smaller Cos ex ICs	
MANAGEMENT GROUP		Crystal Amber AM	
FUND MANAGER		Richard Bernstein [2008]	
WEBSITE		www.crystalamber.com	

LAUNCH DATE	2008	EXCHANGE	AIM	**SYMBOL**
DOMICILE	Guernsey	CURRENCY	GBP	
STOCKBROKER	Numis	INDEX	AIM 100, AIM All-Share	**CRS**
GEARING	100	AVG DISCOUNT (%)	-3.9	
NAV (£M)	190	NET DIV YIELD (%)	2.7	
TURNOVER	93			**MKT CAP (£M)**
TER (%)	2.17	SHARPE RATIO	0.7	
		VOLATILITY	0.72	**184**
PERFORMANCE FEE	Yes	PERFORMANCE (10Y) (%)	-	

FIDELITY SPECIAL VALUES PLC

CORE INVESTMENT STRATEGY		UK equities	
BENCHMARK		FTSE All Share	
MANAGEMENT GROUP		Fidelity Investments	
FUND MANAGER		Alex Wright [2012]	
WEBSITE		www.fidelity.co.uk/specialvalues	

LAUNCH DATE	1994	EXCHANGE	London SE	**SYMBOL**
DOMICILE	UK	CURRENCY	GBP	
STOCKBROKER	Cenkos	INDEX	FTSE Small Cap	**FSV**
GEARING	111	AVG DISCOUNT (%)	-5.5	
NAV (£M)	674	NET DIV YIELD (%)	1.8	
TURNOVER	620			**MKT CAP (£M)**
TER (%)	1.1	SHARPE RATIO	0.9	
		VOLATILITY	1.22	**652**
PERFORMANCE FEE	No	PERFORMANCE (10Y) (%)	159	

HENDERSON OPPORTUNITIES TRUST PLC

CORE INVESTMENT STRATEGY		UK equities (unconstrained by size)	
BENCHMARK		FTSE All Share	
MANAGEMENT GROUP		Janus Henderson	
FUND MANAGER		James Henderson [2007]	
WEBSITE		www.hendersonopportunities.com	

LAUNCH DATE	2007	EXCHANGE	London SE	**SYMBOL**
DOMICILE	UK	CURRENCY	GBP	
STOCKBROKER	JPM Cazenove	INDEX	FTSE Fledgling	**HOT**
GEARING	116	AVG DISCOUNT (%)	-17.8	
NAV (£M)	95	NET DIV YIELD (%)	2.0	
TURNOVER	156			**MKT CAP (£M)**
TER (%)	0.94	SHARPE RATIO	0.1	
		VOLATILITY	1.13	**76**
PERFORMANCE FEE	Yes	PERFORMANCE (10Y) (%)	81	

INVESCO PERPETUAL SELECT TRUST PLC

CORE INVESTMENT STRATEGY	UK equities
BENCHMARK	FTSE All Share
MANAGEMENT GROUP	Invesco Perpetual
FUND MANAGER	James Goldstone [2016]
WEBSITE	www.invescoperpetual.co.uk

LAUNCH DATE	2006	EXCHANGE	London SE	SYMBOL
DOMICILE	UK	CURRENCY	GBP	
STOCKBROKER	Canaccord	INDEX	-	**IVPU**
GEARING	116	AVG DISCOUNT (%)	-1.3	
NAV (£M)	69	NET DIV YIELD (%)	3.5	
TURNOVER	50			MKT CAP (£M)
TER (%)	0.95	SHARPE RATIO	1.0	
		VOLATILITY	0.87	**67**
PERFORMANCE FEE	Yes	PERFORMANCE (10Y) (%)	183	

JPMORGAN MID CAP INVESTMENT TRUST PLC

CORE INVESTMENT STRATEGY	UK mid-cap equities
BENCHMARK	FTSE Mid Cap ex ICs
MANAGEMENT GROUP	JPMorgan AM
FUND MANAGER	Georgina Brittain, Katen Patel [2012]
WEBSITE	www.jpmmidcap.co.uk

LAUNCH DATE	1972	EXCHANGE	London SE	SYMBOL
DOMICILE	UK	CURRENCY	GBP	
STOCKBROKER	Numis	INDEX	FTSE Small Cap	**JMF**
GEARING	108	AVG DISCOUNT (%)	-10.8	
NAV (£M)	293	NET DIV YIELD (%)	2.0	
TURNOVER	335			MKT CAP (£M)
TER (%)	0.91	SHARPE RATIO	0.9	
		VOLATILITY	1.25	**255**
PERFORMANCE FEE	No	PERFORMANCE (10Y) (%)	137	

JUPITER UK GROWTH INVESTMENT TRUST PLC

CORE INVESTMENT STRATEGY	High conviction UK equity portfolio
BENCHMARK	FTSE All Share
MANAGEMENT GROUP	Jupiter AM
FUND MANAGER	Steve Davies [2016]
WEBSITE	www.jupiteram.com

LAUNCH DATE	1987	EXCHANGE	London SE	SYMBOL
DOMICILE	UK	CURRENCY	GBP	
STOCKBROKER	Numis	INDEX	FTSE Fledgling	**JUKG**
GEARING	122	AVG DISCOUNT (%)	-2.1	
NAV (£M)	45	NET DIV YIELD (%)	2.2	
TURNOVER	53			MKT CAP (£M)
TER (%)	1.13	SHARPE RATIO	0.5	
		VOLATILITY	1.13	**43**
PERFORMANCE FEE	Yes	PERFORMANCE (10Y) (%)	95	

KEYSTONE INVESTMENT TRUST PLC

CORE INVESTMENT STRATEGY		UK equities	
BENCHMARK		FTSE All Share	
MANAGEMENT GROUP		Invesco Perpetual	
FUND MANAGER		James Goldstone [2017]	
WEBSITE		www.invescoperpetual.co.uk	

LAUNCH DATE	1954	EXCHANGE	London SE	**SYMBOL**
DOMICILE	UK	CURRENCY	GBP	**KIT**
STOCKBROKER	Numis	INDEX	FTSE Small Cap	
GEARING	112	AVG DISCOUNT (%)	-10.4	
NAV (£M)	259	NET DIV YIELD (%)	3.1	
TURNOVER	293			**MKT CAP (£M)**
TER (%)	0.69	SHARPE RATIO	0.4	**229**
		VOLATILITY	1.11	
PERFORMANCE FEE	Yes	PERFORMANCE (10Y) (%)	114	

MANCHESTER & LONDON INVESTMENT TRUST PLC

CORE INVESTMENT STRATEGY		UK equities	
BENCHMARK		MSCI AC World	
MANAGEMENT GROUP		Midas IM	
FUND MANAGER		Mark Sheppard [1997]	
WEBSITE		www.manchesterandlondon.co.uk	

LAUNCH DATE	1997	EXCHANGE	London SE	**SYMBOL**
DOMICILE	UK	CURRENCY	GBP	**MNL**
STOCKBROKER	Midas IM	INDEX	FTSE Fledgling	
GEARING	109	AVG DISCOUNT (%)	-17.1	
NAV (£M)	98	NET DIV YIELD (%)	1.0	
TURNOVER	251			**MKT CAP (£M)**
TER (%)	0.88	SHARPE RATIO	0.9	**82**
		VOLATILITY	1.11	
PERFORMANCE FEE	No	PERFORMANCE (10Y) (%)	56	

MERCANTILE INVESTMENT TRUST (THE) PLC

CORE INVESTMENT STRATEGY		UK mid/small cap equities	
BENCHMARK		FTSE All Share ex FTSE 100 & ICs	
MANAGEMENT GROUP		JPMorgan AM	
FUND MANAGER		Guy Anderson [2015]	
WEBSITE		www.mercantileit.co.uk	

LAUNCH DATE	1984	EXCHANGE	London SE	**SYMBOL**
DOMICILE	UK	CURRENCY	GBP	**MRC**
STOCKBROKER	Winterflood, Cenkos	INDEX	FTSE Mid 250	
GEARING	110	AVG DISCOUNT (%)	-9.9	
NAV (£M)	1,858	NET DIV YIELD (%)	2.3	
TURNOVER	3,348			**MKT CAP (£M)**
TER (%)	0.5	SHARPE RATIO	1.1	**1,656**
		VOLATILITY	1.19	
PERFORMANCE FEE	No	PERFORMANCE (10Y) (%)	127	

SCHRODER UK MID & SMALL CAP FUND PLC

CORE INVESTMENT STRATEGY		UK mid cap equities	
BENCHMARK		FTSE Mid Cap ex ICs	
MANAGEMENT GROUP		Schroder IM	
FUND MANAGER		Andy Brough, Jean Roche [2003]	
WEBSITE		www.schroders.com	

LAUNCH DATE	2003	EXCHANGE	London SE	**SYMBOL**
DOMICILE	UK	CURRENCY	GBP	**SCP**
STOCKBROKER	Panmure Gordon	INDEX	FTSE Small Cap	
GEARING	100	AVG DISCOUNT (%)	-17.7	
NAV (£M)	222	NET DIV YIELD (%)	2.3	
TURNOVER	268			**MKT CAP (£M)**
TER (%)	0.96	SHARPE RATIO	0.4	**184**
		VOLATILITY	1.43	
PERFORMANCE FEE	No	PERFORMANCE (10Y) (%)	170	

SCHRODER UK GROWTH FUND PLC

CORE INVESTMENT STRATEGY		UK equities	
BENCHMARK		FTSE All Share	
MANAGEMENT GROUP		Schroder IM	
FUND MANAGER		Philip Matthews [2014]	
WEBSITE		www.schroders.com	

LAUNCH DATE	1994	EXCHANGE	London SE	**SYMBOL**
DOMICILE	UK	CURRENCY	GBP	**SDU**
STOCKBROKER	Winterflood	INDEX	FTSE Small Cap	
GEARING	100	AVG DISCOUNT (%)	-12.8	
NAV (£M)	302	NET DIV YIELD (%)	3.1	
TURNOVER	406			**MKT CAP (£M)**
TER (%)	0.63	SHARPE RATIO	0.3	**267**
		VOLATILITY	1.27	
PERFORMANCE FEE	No	PERFORMANCE (10Y) (%)	64	

SANDITON INVESTMENT TRUST PLC

CORE INVESTMENT STRATEGY		UK & European equities, long & short positions (20% stake in mgt co)	
BENCHMARK		FTSE All Share	
MANAGEMENT GROUP		Sanditon AM	
FUND MANAGER		Tim Russell, Chris Rice [2014]	
WEBSITE		www.sanditonam.com	

LAUNCH DATE	2014	EXCHANGE	London SE	**SYMBOL**
DOMICILE	UK	CURRENCY	GBP	**SIT**
STOCKBROKER	JPM Cazenove	INDEX	FTSE Fledgling	
GEARING	100	AVG DISCOUNT (%)	0.5	
NAV (£M)	49	NET DIV YIELD (%)	1.1	
TURNOVER	63			**MKT CAP (£M)**
TER (%)	1.25	SHARPE RATIO	-0.4	**49**
		VOLATILITY	0.49	
PERFORMANCE FEE	Yes	PERFORMANCE (10Y) (%)	-	

WOODFORD PATIENT CAPITAL TRUST PLC

CORE INVESTMENT STRATEGY		UK companies, including mid/large caps, and early stage companies
BENCHMARK		FTSE All Share
MANAGEMENT GROUP		Woodford IM
FUND MANAGER		Neil Woodford [2015]
WEBSITE		www.woodfordfunds.com

LAUNCH DATE	2015	EXCHANGE	London SE	**SYMBOL**
DOMICILE	UK	CURRENCY	GBP	**WPCT**
STOCKBROKER	Winterflood	INDEX	FTSE Mid 250	
GEARING	117	AVG DISCOUNT (%)	-3.4	
NAV (£M)	844	NET DIV YIELD (%)	-	
TURNOVER	1,566			**MKT CAP (£M)**
TER (%)	0.18	SHARPE RATIO	-	**809**
		VOLATILITY	1.17	
PERFORMANCE FEE	Yes	PERFORMANCE (10Y) (%)	-	

UK EQUITY & BOND INCOME

ACORN INCOME FUND LTD

CORE INVESTMENT STRATEGY		70% UK smaller quoted cos; 30% fixed income
BENCHMARK		Numis Smaller Cos ex ICs
MANAGEMENT GROUP		Premier AM
FUND MANAGER		Simon Moon/Fraser MacKersie (smaller cos), Paul Smith (Income) [2014]
WEBSITE		www.premierassetmanagement.co.uk

LAUNCH DATE	1999	EXCHANGE	London SE	**SYMBOL**
DOMICILE	Guernsey	CURRENCY	GBP	**AIF**
STOCKBROKER	Numis	INDEX	-	
GEARING	141	AVG DISCOUNT (%)	-8.3	
NAV (£M)	75	NET DIV YIELD (%)	3.8	
TURNOVER	106			**MKT CAP (£M)**
TER (%)	1.62	SHARPE RATIO	0.8	**71**
		VOLATILITY	0.86	
PERFORMANCE FEE	Yes	PERFORMANCE (10Y) (%)	287	

ABERDEEN SMALLER COMPANIES HIGH INCOME TRUST PLC

CORE INVESTMENT STRATEGY		UK smaller cos & fixed interest	
BENCHMARK		Numis Smaller Cos ex ICs	
MANAGEMENT GROUP		Aberdeen AM	
FUND MANAGER		Jonathan Allison [2016]	
WEBSITE		www.aberdeensmallercompanies.co.uk	

LAUNCH DATE	1992	EXCHANGE	London SE	**SYMBOL**
DOMICILE	UK	CURRENCY	GBP	**ASCI**
STOCKBROKER	Winterflood	INDEX	FTSE Fledgling	
GEARING	110	AVG DISCOUNT (%)	-21.4	
NAV (£M)	70	NET DIV YIELD (%)	2.8	
TURNOVER	78			**MKT CAP (£M)**
TER (%)	1.48	SHARPE RATIO	0.9	**56**
		VOLATILITY	0.98	
PERFORMANCE FEE	No	PERFORMANCE (10Y) (%)	75	

CITY MERCHANTS HIGH YIELD TRUST LTD

CORE INVESTMENT STRATEGY		Fixed interest securities
BENCHMARK		FTSE All Share
MANAGEMENT GROUP		Invesco Perpetual
FUND MANAGER		Paul Causer, Paul Read, Rhys Davies [2003]
WEBSITE		www.invescoperpetual.co.uk

LAUNCH DATE	1991	EXCHANGE	London SE	**SYMBOL**
DOMICILE	Jersey	CURRENCY	GBP	**CMHY**
STOCKBROKER	Winterflood	INDEX	FTSE Small Cap	
GEARING	100	AVG DISCOUNT (%)	1.6	
NAV (£M)	185	NET DIV YIELD (%)	5.0	
TURNOVER	256			**MKT CAP (£M)**
TER (%)	1.01	SHARPE RATIO	1.1	**188**
		VOLATILITY	0.92	
PERFORMANCE FEE	No	PERFORMANCE (10Y) (%)	119	

F&C UK HIGH INCOME TRUST PLC

CORE INVESTMENT STRATEGY		UK equities (FTSE 350) & corporate bonds
BENCHMARK		FTSE All Share (5% cap)
MANAGEMENT GROUP		F&C Investments
FUND MANAGER		Philip Webster [2017]
WEBSITE		www.fandcukhit.co.uk

LAUNCH DATE	2007	EXCHANGE	London SE	**SYMBOL**
DOMICILE	UK	CURRENCY	GBP	**FHI**
STOCKBROKER	Cenkos	INDEX	FTSE Fledgling	
GEARING	110	AVG DISCOUNT (%)	-6.4	
NAV (£M)	97	NET DIV YIELD (%)	4.6	
TURNOVER	38			**MKT CAP (£M)**
TER (%)	1.09	SHARPE RATIO	0.9	**90**
		VOLATILITY	0.62	
PERFORMANCE FEE	No	PERFORMANCE (10Y) (%)	90	

F&C UK HIGH INCOME TRUST PLC

CORE INVESTMENT STRATEGY	UK equities (FTSE 350) & corporate bonds	
BENCHMARK	FTSE All Share (5% cap)	
MANAGEMENT GROUP	F&C Investments	
FUND MANAGER	Philip Webster [2017]	
WEBSITE	www.fandcukhit.co.uk	

LAUNCH DATE	2007	EXCHANGE	London SE	**SYMBOL**
DOMICILE	UK	CURRENCY	GBP	**FHIB**
STOCKBROKER	Cenkos	INDEX	FTSE Fledgling	
GEARING	104	AVG DISCOUNT (%)	-6.1	
NAV (£M)	35	NET DIV YIELD (%)	-	
TURNOVER	20			**MKT CAP (£M)**
TER (%)	1.09	SHARPE RATIO	0.8	**32**
		VOLATILITY	0.70	
PERFORMANCE FEE	No	PERFORMANCE (10Y) (%)	89	

F&C UK HIGH INCOME TRUST PLC

CORE INVESTMENT STRATEGY	UK equities (FTSE 350) & corporate bonds	
BENCHMARK	FTSE All Share (5% cap)	
MANAGEMENT GROUP	F&C Investments	
FUND MANAGER	Philip Webster [2017]	
WEBSITE	www.fandcukhit.co.uk	

LAUNCH DATE	2007	EXCHANGE	London SE	**SYMBOL**
DOMICILE	UK	CURRENCY	GBP	**FHIU**
STOCKBROKER	Cenkos	INDEX	FTSE Fledgling	
GEARING	100	AVG DISCOUNT (%)	-7.5	
NAV (£M)	131	NET DIV YIELD (%)	3.4	
TURNOVER	26			**MKT CAP (£M)**
TER (%)	1.02	SHARPE RATIO	1.0	**121**
		VOLATILITY	0.50	
PERFORMANCE FEE	No	PERFORMANCE (10Y) (%)	89	

HENDERSON HIGH INCOME TRUST PLC

CORE INVESTMENT STRATEGY	UK equities & fixed interest	
BENCHMARK	FTSE All Share	
MANAGEMENT GROUP	Janus Henderson	
FUND MANAGER	David Smith [2014]	
WEBSITE	www.henderson.com	

LAUNCH DATE	1989	EXCHANGE	London SE	**SYMBOL**
DOMICILE	UK	CURRENCY	GBP	**HHI**
STOCKBROKER	JPM Cazenove	INDEX	FTSE Small Cap	
GEARING	123	AVG DISCOUNT (%)	0.9	
NAV (£M)	365	NET DIV YIELD (%)	4.8	
TURNOVER	192			**MKT CAP (£M)**
TER (%)	0.82	SHARPE RATIO	0.5	**363**
		VOLATILITY	1.17	
PERFORMANCE FEE	Yes	PERFORMANCE (10Y) (%)	106	

CQS NEW CITY HIGH YIELD FUND LTD

CORE INVESTMENT STRATEGY	Fixed interest securities	
BENCHMARK	FTSE All Share	
MANAGEMENT GROUP	CQS AM	
FUND MANAGER	Ian Francis, Keith Watson, Robert Crayfourd [2010]	
WEBSITE	www.ncim.co.uk	

LAUNCH DATE	1993	EXCHANGE	London SE	**SYMBOL**
DOMICILE	Jersey	CURRENCY	GBP	**NCYF**
STOCKBROKER	Cantor Fitzgerald Europe	INDEX	FTSE Small Cap	
GEARING	111	AVG DISCOUNT (%)	4.9	
NAV (£M)	224	NET DIV YIELD (%)	7.0	
TURNOVER	379			**MKT CAP (£M)**
TER (%)	1.24	SHARPE RATIO	0.5	**236**
		VOLATILITY	0.80	
PERFORMANCE FEE	No	PERFORMANCE (10Y) (%)	150	

CHELVERTON SMALL COMPANIES DIVIDEND TRUST PLC

CORE INVESTMENT STRATEGY	UK smaller cos (income bias)	
BENCHMARK	Numis Smaller Cos ex ICs	
MANAGEMENT GROUP	Chelverton	
FUND MANAGER	David Horner, David Taylor [1999]	
WEBSITE	www.chelvertonam.com	

LAUNCH DATE	1999	EXCHANGE	London SE	**SYMBOL**
DOMICILE	UK	CURRENCY	GBP	**SDV**
STOCKBROKER	N+1 Singer	INDEX	FTSE Fledgling	
GEARING	132	AVG DISCOUNT (%)	-4.0	
NAV (£M)	45	NET DIV YIELD (%)	3.1	
TURNOVER	86			**MKT CAP (£M)**
TER (%)	2.48	SHARPE RATIO	1.0	**44**
		VOLATILITY	1.10	
PERFORMANCE FEE	Yes	PERFORMANCE (10Y) (%)	129	

UK EQUITY INCOME

BRITISH & AMERICAN INVESTMENT TRUST PLC

CORE INVESTMENT STRATEGY		UK equities & investment trusts			
BENCHMARK		FTSE All Share			
MANAGEMENT GROUP		British & American Trust Fd Mgmt			
FUND MANAGER		Jonathan Woolf [1995]			
WEBSITE		www.baitgroup.co.uk			

LAUNCH DATE	1996	EXCHANGE	London SE	**SYMBOL**
DOMICILE	UK	CURRENCY	GBP	
STOCKBROKER	Walker Crips	INDEX	FTSE Fledgling	**BAF**
GEARING	227	AVG DISCOUNT (%)	68.9	
NAV (£M)	10	NET DIV YIELD (%)	9.3	
TURNOVER	5			**MKT CAP (£M)**
TER (%)	6.01	SHARPE RATIO	0.3	
		VOLATILITY	1.50	**23**
PERFORMANCE FEE	No	PERFORMANCE (10Y) (%)	102	

BLACKROCK INCOME & GROWTH INVESTMENT TRUST PLC

CORE INVESTMENT STRATEGY		UK equities			
BENCHMARK		FTSE All Share			
MANAGEMENT GROUP		BlackRock			
FUND MANAGER		Adam Avigdori, David Goldman [2012]			
WEBSITE		www.britishportfoliotrust.co.uk			

LAUNCH DATE	2001	EXCHANGE	London SE	**SYMBOL**
DOMICILE	UK	CURRENCY	GBP	
STOCKBROKER	JPM Cazenove	INDEX	FTSE Fledgling	**BRIG**
GEARING	104	AVG DISCOUNT (%)	-2.3	
NAV (£M)	51	NET DIV YIELD (%)	3.2	
TURNOVER	29			**MKT CAP (£M)**
TER (%)	1.02	SHARPE RATIO	0.9	
		VOLATILITY	1.13	**50**
PERFORMANCE FEE	No	PERFORMANCE (10Y) (%)	58	

CITY OF LONDON INVESTMENT TRUST (THE) PLC

CORE INVESTMENT STRATEGY		UK equities (FTSE 350)
BENCHMARK		FTSE All Share
MANAGEMENT GROUP		Janus Henderson
FUND MANAGER		Job Curtis [1991]
WEBSITE		www.cityinvestmenttrust.com

LAUNCH DATE	1905	EXCHANGE	London SE	**SYMBOL**
DOMICILE	UK	CURRENCY	GBP	**CTY**
STOCKBROKER	Cenkos	INDEX	FTSE Mid 250	
GEARING	106	AVG DISCOUNT (%)	1.6	
NAV (£M)	1,442	NET DIV YIELD (%)	3.9	
TURNOVER	2,197			**MKT CAP (£M)**
TER (%)	0.43	SHARPE RATIO	0.7	**1,464**
		VOLATILITY	1.20	
PERFORMANCE FEE	No	PERFORMANCE (10Y) (%)	123	

DUNEDIN INCOME GROWTH INV TRUST PLC

CORE INVESTMENT STRATEGY		UK equities (up to 20% overseas)
BENCHMARK		FTSE All Share
MANAGEMENT GROUP		Aberdeen AM
FUND MANAGER		Ben Ritchie [2009]
WEBSITE		www.dunedinincomegrowth.co.uk

LAUNCH DATE	1905	EXCHANGE	London SE	**SYMBOL**
DOMICILE	UK	CURRENCY	GBP	**DIG**
STOCKBROKER	JPM Cazenove	INDEX	FTSE Small Cap	
GEARING	116	AVG DISCOUNT (%)	-9.8	
NAV (£M)	432	NET DIV YIELD (%)	4.5	
TURNOVER	398			**MKT CAP (£M)**
TER (%)	0.65	SHARPE RATIO	0.3	**389**
		VOLATILITY	1.28	
PERFORMANCE FEE	No	PERFORMANCE (10Y) (%)	63	

DIVERSE INCOME TRUST (THE) PLC

CORE INVESTMENT STRATEGY		Quoted/traded UK companies with bias towards small and mid caps
BENCHMARK		FTSE All Share
MANAGEMENT GROUP		Miton Group
FUND MANAGER		Gervais Williams, Martin Turner [2011]
WEBSITE		www.mitongroup.com

LAUNCH DATE	2011	EXCHANGE	London SE	**SYMBOL**
DOMICILE	UK	CURRENCY	GBP	**DIVI**
STOCKBROKER	Cenkos	INDEX	FTSE Small Cap	
GEARING	100	AVG DISCOUNT (%)	-1.1	
NAV (£M)	394	NET DIV YIELD (%)	2.9	
TURNOVER	390			**MKT CAP (£M)**
TER (%)	1.17	SHARPE RATIO	0.7	**393**
		VOLATILITY	1.02	
PERFORMANCE FEE	No	PERFORMANCE (10Y) (%)	-	

EDINBURGH INVESTMENT TRUST (THE) PLC

CORE INVESTMENT STRATEGY	UK equities (up to 20% overseas)	
BENCHMARK	FTSE All Share	
MANAGEMENT GROUP	Invesco Perpetual	
FUND MANAGER	Mark Barnett [2014]	
WEBSITE	www.invescoperpetual.co.uk	

LAUNCH DATE	1905	EXCHANGE	London SE	SYMBOL
DOMICILE	UK	CURRENCY	GBP	**EDIN**
STOCKBROKER	Canaccord	INDEX	FTSE Mid 250	
GEARING	113	AVG DISCOUNT (%)	-4.2	
NAV (£M)	1,481	NET DIV YIELD (%)	3.6	
TURNOVER	1,882			
TER (%)	0.6	SHARPE RATIO	0.8	MKT CAP (£M)
		VOLATILITY	1.17	**1,387**
PERFORMANCE FEE	No	PERFORMANCE (10Y) (%)	134	

F&C CAPITAL AND INCOME INVESTMENT TRUST PLC

CORE INVESTMENT STRATEGY	UK equities	
BENCHMARK	FTSE All Share	
MANAGEMENT GROUP	F&C Investments	
FUND MANAGER	Julian Cane [1997]	
WEBSITE	www.fandccit.com	

LAUNCH DATE	1992	EXCHANGE	London SE	SYMBOL
DOMICILE	UK	CURRENCY	GBP	**FCI**
STOCKBROKER	JPM Cazenove	INDEX	FTSE Small Cap	
GEARING	106	AVG DISCOUNT (%)	0.4	
NAV (£M)	315	NET DIV YIELD (%)	3.2	
TURNOVER	182			
TER (%)	0.65	SHARPE RATIO	0.9	MKT CAP (£M)
		VOLATILITY	1.05	**319**
PERFORMANCE FEE	No	PERFORMANCE (10Y) (%)	102	

FINSBURY GROWTH & INCOME TRUST PLC

CORE INVESTMENT STRATEGY	UK equities (focused portfolio)	
BENCHMARK	FTSE All Share	
MANAGEMENT GROUP	Frostrow Capital	
FUND MANAGER	Nick Train [2000]	
WEBSITE	www.finsburygt.com	

LAUNCH DATE	1926	EXCHANGE	London SE	SYMBOL
DOMICILE	UK	CURRENCY	GBP	**FGT**
STOCKBROKER	Winterflood	INDEX	FTSE Mid 250	
GEARING	103	AVG DISCOUNT (%)	0.5	
NAV (£M)	1,178	NET DIV YIELD (%)	1.8	
TURNOVER	2,204			
TER (%)	0.74	SHARPE RATIO	1.2	MKT CAP (£M)
		VOLATILITY	1.02	**1,186**
PERFORMANCE FEE	No	PERFORMANCE (10Y) (%)	226	

INVESCO INCOME GROWTH TRUST PLC

CORE INVESTMENT STRATEGY		UK equities
BENCHMARK		FTSE All Share
MANAGEMENT GROUP		Invesco Perpetual
FUND MANAGER		Ciaran Mallon [2005]
WEBSITE		www.invescoperpetual.co.uk

LAUNCH DATE	1996	EXCHANGE	London SE
DOMICILE	UK	CURRENCY	GBP
STOCKBROKER	Stockdale	INDEX	FTSE Small Cap
GEARING	102	AVG DISCOUNT (%)	-10.5
NAV (£M)	194	NET DIV YIELD (%)	3.6
TURNOVER	240		
TER (%)	0.8	SHARPE RATIO	0.5
		VOLATILITY	1.10
PERFORMANCE FEE	No	PERFORMANCE (10Y) (%)	94

SYMBOL: IVI

MKT CAP (£M): 174

JPMORGAN CLAVERHOUSE INVESTMENT TRUST PLC

CORE INVESTMENT STRATEGY		UK equities
BENCHMARK		FTSE All Share
MANAGEMENT GROUP		JPMorgan AM
FUND MANAGER		William Meadon, Sarah Emly [2012]
WEBSITE		www.jpmclaverhouse.co.uk

LAUNCH DATE	1963	EXCHANGE	London SE
DOMICILE	UK	CURRENCY	GBP
STOCKBROKER	Numis	INDEX	FTSE Small Cap
GEARING	117	AVG DISCOUNT (%)	-8.7
NAV (£M)	407	NET DIV YIELD (%)	3.5
TURNOVER	352		
TER (%)	0.79	SHARPE RATIO	0.7
		VOLATILITY	1.11
PERFORMANCE FEE	No	PERFORMANCE (10Y) (%)	90

SYMBOL: JCH

MKT CAP (£M): 376

JPMORGAN ELECT PLC

CORE INVESTMENT STRATEGY		JPM funds & fixed interest
BENCHMARK		FTSE All Share
MANAGEMENT GROUP		JPMorgan AM
FUND MANAGER		Sarah Emly, John Baker [2009]
WEBSITE		www.jpmelect.co.uk

LAUNCH DATE	2000	EXCHANGE	London SE
DOMICILE	UK	CURRENCY	GBP
STOCKBROKER	Winterflood	INDEX	-
GEARING	101	AVG DISCOUNT (%)	-2.8
NAV (£M)	82	NET DIV YIELD (%)	3.7
TURNOVER	33		
TER (%)	0.73	SHARPE RATIO	0.6
		VOLATILITY	0.95
PERFORMANCE FEE	No	PERFORMANCE (10Y) (%)	63

SYMBOL: JPEI

MKT CAP (£M): 81

JP MORGAN INCOME & CAPITAL TRUST PLC

CORE INVESTMENT STRATEGY	UK equity & investment grade fixed interest
BENCHMARK	FTSE All Share
MANAGEMENT GROUP	JPMorgan AM
FUND MANAGER	John Baker, Sarah Emly [2009]
WEBSITE	www.jpmincomeandcapital.co.uk

LAUNCH DATE	2008	EXCHANGE	London SE
DOMICILE	UK	CURRENCY	GBP
STOCKBROKER	Winterflood	INDEX	FTSE Fledgling
GEARING	100	AVG DISCOUNT (%)	-6.5
NAV (£M)	135	NET DIV YIELD (%)	4.1
TURNOVER	26		
TER (%)	6.57	SHARPE RATIO	0.7
		VOLATILITY	0.61
PERFORMANCE FEE	No	PERFORMANCE (10Y) (%)	-

SYMBOL: JPIU

MKT CAP (£M): 127

LOWLAND INVESTMENT CO PLC

CORE INVESTMENT STRATEGY	UK equities (mid-cap bias)
BENCHMARK	FTSE All Share
MANAGEMENT GROUP	Janus Henderson
FUND MANAGER	James Henderson, Laura Foll [1990]
WEBSITE	www.lowlandinvestment.com

LAUNCH DATE	1966	EXCHANGE	London SE
DOMICILE	UK	CURRENCY	GBP
STOCKBROKER	JPM Cazenove	INDEX	FTSE Small Cap
GEARING	111	AVG DISCOUNT (%)	-5.9
NAV (£M)	440	NET DIV YIELD (%)	3.1
TURNOVER	357		
TER (%)	0.64	SHARPE RATIO	0.4
		VOLATILITY	1.12
PERFORMANCE FEE	Yes	PERFORMANCE (10Y) (%)	97

SYMBOL: LWI

MKT CAP (£M): 409

MERCHANTS TRUST (THE) PLC

CORE INVESTMENT STRATEGY	UK equities (FTSE 350)
BENCHMARK	FTSE All Share
MANAGEMENT GROUP	Allianz Global Investors
FUND MANAGER	Simon Gergel [2006]
WEBSITE	www.merchantstrust.co.uk

LAUNCH DATE	1905	EXCHANGE	London SE
DOMICILE	UK	CURRENCY	GBP
STOCKBROKER	JPM Cazenove	INDEX	FTSE Small Cap
GEARING	119	AVG DISCOUNT (%)	-6.1
NAV (£M)	558	NET DIV YIELD (%)	5.0
TURNOVER	693		
TER (%)	0.63	SHARPE RATIO	0.3
		VOLATILITY	1.30
PERFORMANCE FEE	No	PERFORMANCE (10Y) (%)	69

SYMBOL: MRCH

MKT CAP (£M): 532

MURRAY INCOME TRUST PLC

CORE INVESTMENT STRATEGY		UK equities
BENCHMARK		FTSE All Share
MANAGEMENT GROUP		Aberdeen AM
FUND MANAGER		Charles Luke [2006]
WEBSITE		www.murray-income.co.uk

LAUNCH DATE	1923	EXCHANGE	London SE	**SYMBOL**
DOMICILE	UK	CURRENCY	GBP	**MUT**
STOCKBROKER	Canaccord	INDEX	FTSE Small Cap	
GEARING	106	AVG DISCOUNT (%)	-8.6	
NAV (£M)	575	NET DIV YIELD (%)	4.1	
TURNOVER	565			**MKT CAP (£M)**
TER (%)	0.77	SHARPE RATIO	0.4	
		VOLATILITY	1.15	**528**
PERFORMANCE FEE	No	PERFORMANCE (10Y) (%)	76	

PERPETUAL INCOME & GROWTH INVESTMENT TRUST PLC

CORE INVESTMENT STRATEGY		UK equities (up to 10% fixed income, 20% overseas)
BENCHMARK		FTSE All Share
MANAGEMENT GROUP		Invesco Perpetual
FUND MANAGER		Mark Barnett [1999]
WEBSITE		www.invescoperpetual.co.uk

LAUNCH DATE	1996	EXCHANGE	London SE	**SYMBOL**
DOMICILE	UK	CURRENCY	GBP	**PLI**
STOCKBROKER	Winterflood	INDEX	FTSE Mid 250	
GEARING	111	AVG DISCOUNT (%)	-8.0	
NAV (£M)	996	NET DIV YIELD (%)	3.5	
TURNOVER	1,667			**MKT CAP (£M)**
TER (%)	0.65	SHARPE RATIO	0.4	
		VOLATILITY	1.26	**917**
PERFORMANCE FEE	No	PERFORMANCE (10Y) (%)	123	

SCHRODER INCOME GROWTH FUND PLC

CORE INVESTMENT STRATEGY		UK equities (FTSE 350, with up to 20% overseas)
BENCHMARK		FTSE All Share
MANAGEMENT GROUP		Schroder IM
FUND MANAGER		Sue Noflke, Jessica Ground [2010]
WEBSITE		www.schroderincomegrowthfund.com

LAUNCH DATE	1995	EXCHANGE	London SE	**SYMBOL**
DOMICILE	UK	CURRENCY	GBP	**SCF**
STOCKBROKER	Stifel	INDEX	FTSE Small Cap	
GEARING	110	AVG DISCOUNT (%)	-8.3	
NAV (£M)	216	NET DIV YIELD (%)	3.6	
TURNOVER	190			**MKT CAP (£M)**
TER (%)	1.01	SHARPE RATIO	0.5	
		VOLATILITY	1.01	**202**
PERFORMANCE FEE	No	PERFORMANCE (10Y) (%)	117	

SHIRES INCOME PLC

CORE INVESTMENT STRATEGY		UK equities	
BENCHMARK		FTSE All Share	
MANAGEMENT GROUP		Aberdeen AM	
FUND MANAGER		Ed Beal [2008]	
WEBSITE		www.shiresincome.co.uk	

LAUNCH DATE	1929	EXCHANGE	London SE	**SYMBOL**
DOMICILE	UK	CURRENCY	GBP	**SHRS**
STOCKBROKER	JPM Cazenove	INDEX	FTSE Fledgling	
GEARING	123	AVG DISCOUNT (%)	-11.0	
NAV (£M)	85	NET DIV YIELD (%)	4.7	
TURNOVER	133			**MKT CAP (£M)**
TER (%)	1.04	SHARPE RATIO	0.5	**81**
		VOLATILITY	1.27	
PERFORMANCE FEE	No	PERFORMANCE (10Y) (%)	79	

STANDARD LIFE EQUITY INCOME TRUST PLC

CORE INVESTMENT STRATEGY		UK equities	
BENCHMARK		FTSE All Share	
MANAGEMENT GROUP		Standard Life Investments	
FUND MANAGER		Tom Moore [2011]	
WEBSITE		www.standardlifeinvestments.com	

LAUNCH DATE	1991	EXCHANGE	London SE	**SYMBOL**
DOMICILE	UK	CURRENCY	GBP	**SLET**
STOCKBROKER	JPM Cazenove	INDEX	FTSE Small Cap	
GEARING	112	AVG DISCOUNT (%)	-6.4	
NAV (£M)	236	NET DIV YIELD (%)	3.6	
TURNOVER	423			**MKT CAP (£M)**
TER (%)	0.96	SHARPE RATIO	0.6	**230**
		VOLATILITY	1.05	
PERFORMANCE FEE	No	PERFORMANCE (10Y) (%)	128	

TROY INCOME & GROWTH TRUST PLC

CORE INVESTMENT STRATEGY		Predominantly UK equities to deliver attractive income yield and the prospect of income and capital growth	
BENCHMARK		FTSE All Share	
MANAGEMENT GROUP		Troy AM	
FUND MANAGER		Francis Brooke, Hugo Ure [2009]	
WEBSITE		www.tigt.co.uk	

LAUNCH DATE	1988	EXCHANGE	London SE	**SYMBOL**
DOMICILE	UK	CURRENCY	GBP	**TIGT**
STOCKBROKER	Numis	INDEX	FTSE Small Cap	
GEARING	100	AVG DISCOUNT (%)	0.7	
NAV (£M)	227	NET DIV YIELD (%)	3.2	
TURNOVER	294			**MKT CAP (£M)**
TER (%)	0.98	SHARPE RATIO	0.9	**228**
		VOLATILITY	1.18	
PERFORMANCE FEE	No	PERFORMANCE (10Y) (%)	32	

THE INVESTMENT TRUSTS HANDBOOK 2018

TEMPLE BAR INVESTMENT TRUST PLC

CORE INVESTMENT STRATEGY		UK equities (at least 50% FTSE 100)	
BENCHMARK		FTSE All Share	
MANAGEMENT GROUP		Investec IM	
FUND MANAGER		Alastair Mundy [2002]	
WEBSITE		www.templebarinvestments.co.uk	

LAUNCH DATE	1926	EXCHANGE	London SE	**SYMBOL**
DOMICILE	UK	CURRENCY	GBP	**TMPL**
STOCKBROKER	JPM Cazenove	INDEX	FTSE Mid 250	
GEARING	112	AVG DISCOUNT (%)	-5.4	
NAV (£M)	912	NET DIV YIELD (%)	3.2	
TURNOVER	1,170			**MKT CAP (£M)**
TER (%)	0.52	SHARPE RATIO	0.4	**863**
		VOLATILITY	1.19	
PERFORMANCE FEE	No	PERFORMANCE (10Y) (%)	134	

VALUE & INCOME TRUST PLC

CORE INVESTMENT STRATEGY		UK equities & commercial property	
BENCHMARK		FTSE All Share	
MANAGEMENT GROUP		OLIM	
FUND MANAGER		Matthew Oakeshott, Angela Lascelles [1981]	
WEBSITE		www.olim.co.uk	

LAUNCH DATE	1981	EXCHANGE	London SE	**SYMBOL**
DOMICILE	UK	CURRENCY	GBP	**VIN**
STOCKBROKER	None	INDEX	FTSE Small Cap	
GEARING	132	AVG DISCOUNT (%)	-16.8	
NAV (£M)	149	NET DIV YIELD (%)	4.0	
TURNOVER	108			**MKT CAP (£M)**
TER (%)	1.42	SHARPE RATIO	0.4	**125**
		VOLATILITY	1.10	
PERFORMANCE FEE	Yes	PERFORMANCE (10Y) (%)	79	

UK SMALLER COMPANIES

ABERFORTH SMALLER COMPANIES TRUST PLC

CORE INVESTMENT STRATEGY		UK smaller cos	
BENCHMARK		Numis Smaller Cos ex ICs	
MANAGEMENT GROUP		Aberforth Partners	
FUND MANAGER		Six Managers [1990]	
WEBSITE		www.aberforth.co.uk	

LAUNCH DATE	1990	EXCHANGE	London SE	**SYMBOL**
DOMICILE	UK	CURRENCY	GBP	
STOCKBROKER	None	INDEX	FTSE Mid 250	**ASL**
GEARING	100	AVG DISCOUNT (%)	-13.9	
NAV (£M)	1,401	NET DIV YIELD (%)	2.2	
TURNOVER	1,729			
TER (%)	0.8	SHARPE RATIO	0.6	**MKT CAP (£M)**
		VOLATILITY	1.16	**1,212**
PERFORMANCE FEE	No	PERFORMANCE (10Y) (%)	144	

BLACKROCK SMALLER COMPANIES TRUST PLC

CORE INVESTMENT STRATEGY		UK smaller cos	
BENCHMARK		Numis Smaller Cos ex ICs	
MANAGEMENT GROUP		BlackRock IM	
FUND MANAGER		Mike Prentis [2002]	
WEBSITE		www.blackrock.com	

LAUNCH DATE	1995	EXCHANGE	London SE	**SYMBOL**
DOMICILE	UK	CURRENCY	GBP	
STOCKBROKER	Canaccord	INDEX	FTSE Small Cap	**BRSC**
GEARING	110	AVG DISCOUNT (%)	-15.1	
NAV (£M)	691	NET DIV YIELD (%)	1.7	
TURNOVER	639			
TER (%)	0.69	SHARPE RATIO	1.1	**MKT CAP (£M)**
		VOLATILITY	1.03	**597**
PERFORMANCE FEE	Yes	PERFORMANCE (10Y) (%)	290	

DUNEDIN SMALLER COMPANIES INVESTMENT TRUST PLC

CORE INVESTMENT STRATEGY		UK smaller cos	
BENCHMARK		Numis Smaller Cos ex ICs	
MANAGEMENT GROUP		Aberdeen AM	
FUND MANAGER		Ed Beal [2006]	
WEBSITE		www.dunedinsmaller.co.uk	

LAUNCH DATE	1927	EXCHANGE	London SE	**SYMBOL**
DOMICILE	UK	CURRENCY	GBP	
STOCKBROKER	Cantor Fitzgerald Europe	INDEX	FTSE Small Cap	**DNDL**
GEARING	104	AVG DISCOUNT (%)	-18.9	
NAV (£M)	144	NET DIV YIELD (%)	2.6	
TURNOVER	78			
TER (%)	0.81	SHARPE RATIO	0.6	**MKT CAP (£M)**
		VOLATILITY	1.04	**115**
PERFORMANCE FEE	Yes	PERFORMANCE (10Y) (%)	145	

DOWNING STRATEGIC MICRO-CAP INVESTMENT TRUST PLC

CORE INVESTMENT STRATEGY		UK micro cap cos
BENCHMARK		Numis Smaller Cos inc AIM ex ICs
MANAGEMENT GROUP		Downing LLP
FUND MANAGER		Judith MacKenzie, Alyx Wood, James Lynch, Nick Hawthorne [2017]
WEBSITE		www.downing.co.uk

LAUNCH DATE	2017	EXCHANGE	London SE	**SYMBOL**
DOMICILE	UK	CURRENCY	GBP	
STOCKBROKER	Stockdale Securities	INDEX	-	**DSM**
GEARING	100	AVG DISCOUNT (%)	5.2	
NAV (£M)	53	NET DIV YIELD (%)	-	
TURNOVER	92			
TER (%)	-	SHARPE RATIO	-	**MKT CAP (£M)**
		VOLATILITY	0.63	**56**
PERFORMANCE FEE	No	PERFORMANCE (10Y) (%)	-	

GRESHAM HOUSE STRATEGIC PLC

CORE INVESTMENT STRATEGY		Significant stakes in UK smaller quoted companies
BENCHMARK		Numis Smaller Cos ex ICs
MANAGEMENT GROUP		Gresham House
FUND MANAGER		Anthony Dalwood, Graham Bird [2015]
WEBSITE		www.ghsplc.com

LAUNCH DATE	1999	EXCHANGE	AIM	**SYMBOL**
DOMICILE	UK	CURRENCY	GBP	
STOCKBROKER	Liberum, finncap	INDEX	AIM All-Share	**GHS**
GEARING	100	AVG DISCOUNT (%)	-23.5	
NAV (£M)	39	NET DIV YIELD (%)	1.8	
TURNOVER	65			
TER (%)	3.69	SHARPE RATIO	-0.1	**MKT CAP (£M)**
		VOLATILITY	2.70	**31**
PERFORMANCE FEE	Yes	PERFORMANCE (10Y) (%)	-	

HENDERSON SMALLER COMPANIES INVESTMENT TRUST PLC

CORE INVESTMENT STRATEGY	UK smaller cos	
BENCHMARK	Numis Smaller Cos ex ICs	
MANAGEMENT GROUP	Janus Henderson	
FUND MANAGER	Neil Hermon [2002]	
WEBSITE	www.hendersonsmallercompanies.com	

LAUNCH DATE	1987	EXCHANGE	London SE	**SYMBOL**
DOMICILE	UK	CURRENCY	GBP	
STOCKBROKER	Numis	INDEX	FTSE Small Cap	**HSL**
GEARING	109	AVG DISCOUNT (%)	-15.2	
NAV (£M)	699	NET DIV YIELD (%)	2.2	
TURNOVER	879			
TER (%)	0.43	SHARPE RATIO	1.1	**MKT CAP (£M)**
		VOLATILITY	1.28	**602**
PERFORMANCE FEE	Yes	PERFORMANCE (10Y) (%)	224	

INVESCO PERPETUAL UK SMALLER COMPANIES INV TST PLC

CORE INVESTMENT STRATEGY	UK smaller cos	
BENCHMARK	Numis Smaller Cos ex ICs	
MANAGEMENT GROUP	Invesco Perpetual	
FUND MANAGER	Jonathan Brown [2014]	
WEBSITE	www.invescoperpetual.co.uk	

LAUNCH DATE	1988	EXCHANGE	London SE	**SYMBOL**
DOMICILE	UK	CURRENCY	GBP	
STOCKBROKER	JPM Cazenove	INDEX	FTSE Small Cap	**IPU**
GEARING	100	AVG DISCOUNT (%)	-5.2	
NAV (£M)	172	NET DIV YIELD (%)	3.6	
TURNOVER	665			
TER (%)	0.83	SHARPE RATIO	1.4	**MKT CAP (£M)**
		VOLATILITY	1.05	**158**
PERFORMANCE FEE	Yes	PERFORMANCE (10Y) (%)	239	

JPMORGAN SMALLER COMPANIES INVESTMENT TRUST PLC

CORE INVESTMENT STRATEGY	UK smaller cos	
BENCHMARK	Numis Smaller Cos ex ICs	
MANAGEMENT GROUP	JPMorgan AM	
FUND MANAGER	Georgina Brittain, Katen Patel [2003]	
WEBSITE	www.jpmsmallercompanies.co.uk	

LAUNCH DATE	1990	EXCHANGE	London SE	**SYMBOL**
DOMICILE	UK	CURRENCY	GBP	
STOCKBROKER	Winterflood	INDEX	FTSE Small Cap	**JMI**
GEARING	114	AVG DISCOUNT (%)	-19.8	
NAV (£M)	210	NET DIV YIELD (%)	1.9	
TURNOVER	205			
TER (%)	1.16	SHARPE RATIO	0.8	**MKT CAP (£M)**
		VOLATILITY	1.00	**165**
PERFORMANCE FEE	No	PERFORMANCE (10Y) (%)	114	

MITON UK MICROCAP TRUST PLC

CORE INVESTMENT STRATEGY	UK smaller cos <£150m market cap
BENCHMARK	Numis Smaller Cos inc AIM ex ICs
MANAGEMENT GROUP	Miton Group
FUND MANAGER	Gervais Williams, Martin Turner [2015]
WEBSITE	www.mitongroup.com

LAUNCH DATE	2015	EXCHANGE	London SE
DOMICILE	UK	CURRENCY	GBP
STOCKBROKER	Peel Hunt	INDEX	FTSE Fledgling
GEARING	100	AVG DISCOUNT (%)	-3.0
NAV (£M)	110	NET DIV YIELD (%)	0.6
TURNOVER	107		
TER (%)	1.58	SHARPE RATIO	-
		VOLATILITY	0.79
PERFORMANCE FEE	No	PERFORMANCE (10Y) (%)	-

SYMBOL: MINI

MKT CAP (£M): 107

MONTANARO UK SMALLER COMPANIES INV TR PLC

CORE INVESTMENT STRATEGY	UK smaller cos
BENCHMARK	Numis Smaller Cos ex ICs
MANAGEMENT GROUP	Montanaro IM
FUND MANAGER	Charles Montanaro [2006]
WEBSITE	www.montanaro.co.uk

LAUNCH DATE	1995	EXCHANGE	London SE
DOMICILE	UK	CURRENCY	GBP
STOCKBROKER	Cenkos	INDEX	FTSE Small Cap
GEARING	109	AVG DISCOUNT (%)	-20.6
NAV (£M)	231	NET DIV YIELD (%)	1.9
TURNOVER	241		
TER (%)	1.24	SHARPE RATIO	0.6
		VOLATILITY	0.91
PERFORMANCE FEE	No	PERFORMANCE (10Y) (%)	130

SYMBOL: MTU

MKT CAP (£M): 186

RIGHTS AND ISSUES INV TRUST PLC

CORE INVESTMENT STRATEGY	UK smaller cos
BENCHMARK	Numis Smaller Cos ex ICs
MANAGEMENT GROUP	Self-Managed
FUND MANAGER	- [1969]
WEBSITE	www.maitlandgroup.com

LAUNCH DATE	1905	EXCHANGE	London SE
DOMICILE	UK	CURRENCY	GBP
STOCKBROKER	Stockdale Securities	INDEX	-
GEARING	100	AVG DISCOUNT (%)	-12.0
NAV (£M)	205	NET DIV YIELD (%)	1.4
TURNOVER	254		
TER (%)	0.59	SHARPE RATIO	1.3
		VOLATILITY	1.08
PERFORMANCE FEE	No	PERFORMANCE (10Y) (%)	203

SYMBOL: RIII

MKT CAP (£M): 183

RIVER & MERCANTILE UK MICRO CAP INVESTMENT CO LTD

CORE INVESTMENT STRATEGY	UK micro cap cos
BENCHMARK	Numis Smaller Cos inc AIM ex ICs
MANAGEMENT GROUP	River & Mercantile AM
FUND MANAGER	Philip Rodrigs [2014]
WEBSITE	microcap.riverandmercantile.com

LAUNCH DATE	2014	EXCHANGE	London SE	**SYMBOL**
DOMICILE	Guernsey	CURRENCY	GBP	**RMMC**
STOCKBROKER	Winterflood	INDEX	FTSE Fledgling	
GEARING	100	AVG DISCOUNT (%)	-4.5	
NAV (£M)	109	NET DIV YIELD (%)	-	
TURNOVER	117			**MKT CAP (£M)**
TER (%)	1.35	SHARPE RATIO	-	
		VOLATILITY	0.65	**106**
PERFORMANCE FEE	Yes	PERFORMANCE (10Y) (%)	-	

STRATEGIC EQUITY CAPITAL PLC

CORE INVESTMENT STRATEGY	Significant stakes in UK smaller quoted companies
BENCHMARK	Numis Smaller Cos inc AIM ex ICs
MANAGEMENT GROUP	GVO IM
FUND MANAGER	Jeff Harris [2017]
WEBSITE	www.strategicequitycapital.com

LAUNCH DATE	2005	EXCHANGE	London SE	**SYMBOL**
DOMICILE	UK	CURRENCY	GBP	**SEC**
STOCKBROKER	Canaccord	INDEX	FTSE Small Cap	
GEARING	100	AVG DISCOUNT (%)	-12.3	
NAV (£M)	180	NET DIV YIELD (%)	0.3	
TURNOVER	278			**MKT CAP (£M)**
TER (%)	1.42	SHARPE RATIO	0.7	
		VOLATILITY	1.48	**154**
PERFORMANCE FEE	Yes	PERFORMANCE (10Y) (%)	146	

SHERBORNE INVESTORS (GUERNSEY) B LTD

CORE INVESTMENT STRATEGY	Single position in UK company with activist approach
BENCHMARK	FTSE All Share
MANAGEMENT GROUP	Sherborne IM
FUND MANAGER	Edward Bramson [2012]
WEBSITE	-

LAUNCH DATE	2012	EXCHANGE	London SE (SFS)	**SYMBOL**
DOMICILE	Guernsey	CURRENCY	GBP	**SIGB**
STOCKBROKER	Numis	INDEX	-	
GEARING	-	AVG DISCOUNT (%)	-8.0	
NAV (£M)	143	NET DIV YIELD (%)	122.4	
TURNOVER	473			**MKT CAP (£M)**
TER (%)	-	SHARPE RATIO	0.4	
		VOLATILITY	2.13	**148**
PERFORMANCE FEE	-	PERFORMANCE (10Y) (%)	-	

SHERBORNE INVESTORS C

CORE INVESTMENT STRATEGY		Single position in UK company with activist approach	
BENCHMARK		FTSE All Share	
MANAGEMENT GROUP		Sherborne IM	
FUND MANAGER		Edward Bramson [2017]	
WEBSITE		-	

LAUNCH DATE	2017	EXCHANGE	London SE (SFS)	**SYMBOL**
DOMICILE	Guernsey	CURRENCY	GBP	
STOCKBROKER	Numis, HSBC	INDEX	-	**SIGC**
GEARING	-	AVG DISCOUNT (%)	5.6	
NAV (£M)	689	NET DIV YIELD (%)	-	
TURNOVER	228			
TER (%)	-	SHARPE RATIO	-	**MKT CAP (£M)**
		VOLATILITY	-	**739**
PERFORMANCE FEE	-	PERFORMANCE (10Y) (%)	-	

STANDARD LIFE UK SMALLER COMPANIES TRUST PLC

CORE INVESTMENT STRATEGY		UK smaller cos	
BENCHMARK		Numis Smaller Cos ex ICs	
MANAGEMENT GROUP		Standard Life Investments	
FUND MANAGER		Harry Nimmo [2003]	
WEBSITE		www.mavencp.com	

LAUNCH DATE	1993	EXCHANGE	London SE	**SYMBOL**
DOMICILE	UK	CURRENCY	GBP	
STOCKBROKER	Winterflood	INDEX	FTSE Small Cap	**SLS**
GEARING	104	AVG DISCOUNT (%)	-6.5	
NAV (£M)	327	NET DIV YIELD (%)	1.5	
TURNOVER	279			
TER (%)	1.13	SHARPE RATIO	1.1	**MKT CAP (£M)**
		VOLATILITY	1.14	**304**
PERFORMANCE FEE	No	PERFORMANCE (10Y) (%)	341	

BLACKROCK THROGMORTON TRUST PLC

CORE INVESTMENT STRATEGY		UK smaller cos (up to 30% short portfolio)	
BENCHMARK		Numis Smaller Cos ex ICs	
MANAGEMENT GROUP		BlackRock IM	
FUND MANAGER		Mike Prentis, Dan Whitestone [2008]	
WEBSITE		www.blackrock.co.uk	

LAUNCH DATE	1962	EXCHANGE	London SE	**SYMBOL**
DOMICILE	UK	CURRENCY	GBP	
STOCKBROKER	Stifel	INDEX	FTSE Small Cap	**THRG**
GEARING	126	AVG DISCOUNT (%)	-17.7	
NAV (£M)	390	NET DIV YIELD (%)	1.9	
TURNOVER	447			
TER (%)	1.06	SHARPE RATIO	1.2	**MKT CAP (£M)**
		VOLATILITY	1.09	**326**
PERFORMANCE FEE	Yes	PERFORMANCE (10Y) (%)	215	

AMEDEO AIR FOUR PLUS LTD

CORE INVESTMENT STRATEGY	Aircraft leasing
BENCHMARK	11% p.a.
MANAGEMENT GROUP	Amedeo Limited
FUND MANAGER	Mark Lapidus (Marc Gordon) [2015]
WEBSITE	-

LAUNCH DATE	2015	EXCHANGE	London SE (SFS)	**SYMBOL**
DOMICILE	Guernsey	CURRENCY	GBP	
STOCKBROKER	Nimrod Capital	INDEX	-	**AA4**
GEARING	100	AVG DISCOUNT (%)	50.0	
NAV (£M)	461	NET DIV YIELD (%)	7.7	
TURNOVER	352			
TER (%)	1.73	SHARPE RATIO	-	**MKT CAP (£M)**
		VOLATILITY	0.30	**644**
PERFORMANCE FEE	No	PERFORMANCE (10Y) (%)	-	

ASSURA PLC

CORE INVESTMENT STRATEGY	Primary care property and pharmacy businesses
BENCHMARK	FTSE 350 Real Estate
MANAGEMENT GROUP	Self-Managed
FUND MANAGER	-
WEBSITE	www.assuragroup.co.uk

LAUNCH DATE	2003	EXCHANGE	London SE	**SYMBOL**
DOMICILE	Guernsey	CURRENCY	GBP	
STOCKBROKER	Stifel, JPM Cazenove	INDEX	FTSE Mid 250	**AGR**
GEARING	-	AVG DISCOUNT (%)	25.6	
NAV (£M)	901	NET DIV YIELD (%)	3.7	
TURNOVER	1,799			
TER (%)	-	SHARPE RATIO	0.9	**MKT CAP (£M)**
		VOLATILITY	2.67	**1,201**
PERFORMANCE FEE	-	PERFORMANCE (10Y) (%)	-42	

DRAPER ESPRIT PLC

CORE INVESTMENT STRATEGY	Early stage technology companies
BENCHMARK	LPX Venture
MANAGEMENT GROUP	Self-Managed
FUND MANAGER	Simon Cook [2016]
WEBSITE	www.draperesprit.com

LAUNCH DATE	2016	EXCHANGE	AIM	**SYMBOL**	
DOMICILE	UK	CURRENCY	GBP	**GROW**	
STOCKBROKER	Numis, Goodbody	INDEX	-		
GEARING	-	AVG DISCOUNT (%)	0.5		
NAV (£M)	265	NET DIV YIELD (%)	-		
TURNOVER	107			**MKT CAP (£M)**	
TER (%)	-	SHARPE RATIO	-	**233**	
		VOLATILITY	0.41		
PERFORMANCE FEE	-	PERFORMANCE (10Y) (%)	-		

JPMORGAN BRAZIL INVESTMENT TRUST PLC

CORE INVESTMENT STRATEGY	Brazilian or Bazilian focused companies
BENCHMARK	MSCI Brazil 10/40
MANAGEMENT GROUP	JPMorgan AM
FUND MANAGER	Sophie Bosch de Hood, Luis Carrillo [2014]
WEBSITE	www.jpmbrazil.co.uk

LAUNCH DATE	2010	EXCHANGE	London SE	**SYMBOL**	
DOMICILE	UK	CURRENCY	GBP	**JPB**	
STOCKBROKER	Numis	INDEX	FTSE Fledgling		
GEARING	101	AVG DISCOUNT (%)	-13.3		
NAV (£M)	28	NET DIV YIELD (%)	1.2		
TURNOVER	91			**MKT CAP (£M)**	
TER (%)	1.99	SHARPE RATIO	-0.1	**23**	
		VOLATILITY	1.33		
PERFORMANCE FEE	Yes	PERFORMANCE (10Y) (%)	-		

VOLTA FINANCE LTD

CORE INVESTMENT STRATEGY	CLO's, corporate credits, sovereign debt, residential mortgage loans
BENCHMARK	S&P Leveraged Loan Euro Holdings – GBP
MANAGEMENT GROUP	AXA IM
FUND MANAGER	Serge Demay [2006]
WEBSITE	www.voltafinance.com

LAUNCH DATE	2006	EXCHANGE	London SE	**SYMBOL**	
DOMICILE	Guernsey	CURRENCY	EUR	**VTA**	
STOCKBROKER	Cenkos	INDEX	-		
GEARING	-	AVG DISCOUNT (%)	-11.4		
NAV (£M)	275	NET DIV YIELD (%)	8.3		
TURNOVER	116			**MKT CAP (£M)**	
TER (%)	-	SHARPE RATIO	-	**246**	
		VOLATILITY	0.62		
PERFORMANCE FEE	-	PERFORMANCE (10Y) (%)	216		

A–Z

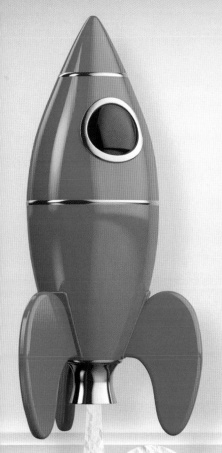

VENTURE CAPITAL TRUSTS

TOTAL RETURN		1-YEAR	3-YEAR	5-YEAR	10-YEAR	YEAR TO DATE
AIM-quoted VCTs		%	%	%	%	%
Artemis VCT	Artemis IM	47.5	122.4	256.8	190.9	19.3
Unicorn AIM VCT	Unicorn AM	8.9	27.8	114.6	109.6	9.7
Hargreave Hale AIM VCT 2	Hargreave Hale	17.7	19.9	59.8	93.0	17.2
Octopus AIM VCT	Octopus Investments	12.5	28.0	90.4	89.5	11.4
Amati VCT	Amati Global Investors	37.6	47.5	72.9	38.5	37.5
Octopus AIM VCT 2	Octopus Investments	10.8	20.5	75.8	33.9	12.1
Hargreave Hale AIM VCT 1	Hargreave Hale	13.9	19.1	72.0	30.5	11.1
Amati VCT 2	Amati Global Investors	37.7	57.4	90.2	16.3	37.3
New Century AIM VCT 2	MD Barnard	7.1	25.9	110.1	-34.0	7.1
New Century AIM VCT	MD Barnard	5.7	31.9	95.6	-36.4	5.7
Weighted average	**VCT AIM Quoted**	**18.1**	**40.6**	**111.5**	**65.0**	**15.9**

TOTAL RETURN		1-YEAR	3-YEAR	5-YEAR	10-YEAR	YEAR TO DATE
Generalist VCTs		%	%	%	%	%
Northern Venture Trust	NVM Private Equity	18.0	30.7	78.1	205.0	4.41
Maven Income and Growth VCT	Maven Capital Partners	0.5	21.0	64.7	196.3	0.89
The Income & Growth VCT	Mobeus Equity Partners	8.1	26.4	69.8	173.5	7.2
British Smaller Companies VCT 2	YFM Private Equity	-0.1	19.8	38.4	162.1	-1.79
British Smaller Companies VCT	YFM Private Equity	2.2	30.7	63.7	157.0	-7.66
Northern 3 VCT	NVM Private Equity	13.2	42.3	86.8	142.3	1.5

TOTAL RETURN		1-YEAR	3-YEAR	5-YEAR	10-YEAR	YEAR TO DATE
Northern 2 VCT	NVM Private Equity	12.5	37.4	87.6	137.7	-0.23
Mobeus Income & Growth VCT	Mobeus Equity Partners	8.8	29.1	91.9	136.3	8.08
Maven Income and Growth VCT 3	Maven Capital Partners	-0.8	25.1	58.4	117.7	1.03
Maven Income and Growth VCT 6	Maven Capital Partners	0.9	32.6	123.3	117.1	0.92
Maven Income and Growth VCT 2	Maven Capital Partners	1.5	21.5	49.2	116.4	2.6
Baronsmead Venture Trust	Living Bridge	9.4	26.6	73.0	112.0	7.27
Baronsmead Second Venture Trust	Living Bridge	6.2	24.1	66.6	105.3	7.63
Chrysalis VCT	Chrysalis VCT	7.4	39.2	127.6	96.2	10.81
ProVen VCT	Beringea	13.7	29.1	73.2	95.1	10.94
Elderstreet VCT	Elderstreet Investments	1.3	2.9	77.1	93.5	-7.32
ProVen Growth and Income VCT	Beringea	11.1	19.3	61.9	79.2	7.07
Mobeus Income & Growth 2 VCT	Mobeus Equity Partners	-2.9	10.5	112.1	74.9	-3.16
Kings Arms Yard VCT	Albion Capital	18.0	28.0	75.9	72.5	6.31
Albion Development VCT	Albion Capital	9.5	15.5	43.7	67.9	9.94
Crown Place VCT	Albion Capital	20.3	22.0	56.9	67.9	3.08
Maven Income and Growth VCT 4	Maven Capital Partners	2.7	17.9	17.9	66.9	1.55
Mobeus Income & Growth 4 VCT	Mobeus Equity Partners	-8.6	7.2	33.4	59.0	-8.62
Foresight VCT	Foresight Group	1.3	4.4	-3.5	52.8	0.67
Albion Enterprise VCT	Albion Capital	11.6	26.7	72.5	48.3	10.4
Albion VCT	Albion Capital	14.7	31.4	52.5	40.4	9.7
Albion Technology & General VCT	Albion Capital	8.7	3.9	48.3	35.8	7.02
Octopus Apollo VCT	Octopus Investments	4.5	9.2	29.7	29.5	1.15

TOTAL RETURN		1-YEAR	3-YEAR	5-YEAR	10-YEAR	YEAR TO DATE
Foresight 4 VCT	Foresight Group	29.2	16.9	-18.6	1.4	6.9
Maven Income and Growth VCT 5	Maven Capital Partners	2.6	18.7	121.7	-0.3	2.62
Downing FOUR VCT DP67 shares	Downing	-14.5	-5.6	5.7	-18.4	-12.96
Downing ONE VCT	Downing	5.2	14.9	38.2	-36.1	4.41
Downing TWO VCT D shares	Downing	164.9	185.5	216.3		164.85
Downing THREE VCT D shares	Downing	141.8	169.4	174.7		141.82
Octopus Titan VCT	Octopus Investments	4.9	23.8	106.6		5.18
Triple Point Income VCT	Triple Point IM	15.0	68.1	86.0		15
Downing FOUR VCT 2011 Structured	Downing	94.8	25.9	36.9		94.79
Downing FOUR VCT 2011 Low Carbon	Downing	39.4	14.0	25.0		39.44
Puma VCT 8	Shore Capital AM	-3.1	-3.1	-3.1		-3.08
Downing FOUR VCT D shares	Downing	-1.4	2.7	-10.9		0.78
Downing FOUR VCT B shares	Downing	0.0	-27.7	-16.2		0
Downing TWO VCT F shares	Downing	-9.4	-9.4	-24.5		-7.26
Downing FOUR VCT 2011 General	Downing	1.6	-27.4	-26.9		1.61
Downing THREE VCT F shares	Downing	-24.3	-30.2	-34.9		-22.54
Foresight VCT Planned Exit shares	Foresight Group	-42.6	-56.0	-55.4		-40.39
Weighted average	**VCT Generalist**	**6.9**	**20.9**	**58.1**	**86.8**	**3.9**

Source: The Wealth Club, from the AIC and Morningstar. Data to 30 September 2017. Minimum five-year track record.
Ranked by 10-year share price performance (total return), then by 5-year performance.

PARTNERS

ARTEMIS
The PROFIT Hunter

ABOUT ARTEMIS

Independent and owner-managed, Artemis is a leading UK-based fund manager. It manages some £26bn* of clients' money across a range of funds, two investment trusts, a venture capital trust and both pooled and segregated institutional portfolios.

Since its foundation in 1997, the firm's aim has always been to offer exemplary performance and client service. All Artemis' staff share these two precepts – and the same flair and enthusiasm for fund management.

Artemis' fund managers can only invest in their own and their colleagues' funds, which aligns their interests directly with those of Artemis' investors. Whatever markets are doing, there are opportunities for active managers to make above-average returns. Artemis' fund managers only buy a share if they think it is undervalued, and not because it represents a big proportion of the index. Artemis respects benchmarks – but is not driven by them. This produces 'high conviction' portfolios which differ markedly from those of competitors and benchmark indices.

Artemis has a history of recruiting and training fund managers with proven skills – and an excellent record of retaining fund managers. Artemis' managers have the freedom to invest without the constraints of a single house style or process. Yet Artemis' policy of co-investment gives its fund managers every reason to share their views with each other. Open, communicative and always keen to debate investment ideas, Artemis' managers immerse themselves in their markets. They do this through research (both their own and external), conferences, meetings with analysts, economists and industry experts, and with the management of companies, and also in formal and informal conversations with each other.

Artemis operates a 'knowledge management system' (called Delphi, as in the Greek oracle). Delphi stores all this information and analysis so that it can be shared across the firm.

Some of Artemis' fund managers also use proprietary stock-screening systems, which narrow down the number of stocks to be examined in more detail. This allows the managers to concentrate their time, knowledge and skills on the most promising investments.

Keeping bureaucracy to a minimum, Artemis allows its managers to concentrate on what they do best – selecting the right stocks or bonds for clients. Artemis' investment teams have a collegiate approach. Drawing on each other's experience and knowledge, sharing ideas and insights between teams, specialist units operate with support from the wider business towards a common goal.

Artemis is a Limited Liability Partnership (LLP) and currently has 30 partners who are fund managers and other key individuals at the firm. Affiliated Managers Group (AMG) and the management of Artemis own 100% of the equity of the business. This is a financial partnership: AMG takes a share of the revenues produced by Artemis, but does not get involved in the day-to-day running of the business. Artemis believes that a LLP is the ideal structure for an investment management business. It means freedom from the (often) short-term demands of shareholders; and it allows Artemis to focus entirely on trying to meet or exceed its clients' needs. The partnership enables Artemis to manage generational change, whilst also attracting new talent.

Artemis' growth has been largely organic, and the partnership is firmly committed to remaining independent. The firm's aim is likewise unchanged: superior, long-term returns for the people whose money Artemis manages.

*Source: Artemis as at 30 September 2017.

ABOUT FIDELITY INTERNATIONAL

Fidelity was established in 1969 and offers world-class investment solutions and retirement expertise. It is a privately owned, independent company with more than £300bn of assets under administration across the major asset classes.

Fidelity's model of private, independent ownership ensures it consistently acts in the best interest of its clients. It provides a long-term framework enabling heavy investment into technology and innovation to continually improve performance in supporting the goals of Fidelity's clients.

It's an approach that works: numerous awards around the globe recognise the consistent strong achievements of Fidelity's investment and client service teams. For example, Fidelity has won the Thomson Reuters Lipper 'Best Overall Group' award 42 times since 2002 in 13 countries.

FIDELITY IN THE UK

In the UK, Fidelity looks after the portfolios of 275,000 personal investors, 400,000 advised investors and 505,000 people who invest through their employer. Fidelity offers them over 700 managed funds across all sectors, regions and asset classes. These are supported by 400 investment professionals working across 12 countries.

Fidelity is continuing to develop its UK business, as demonstrated by a US$250m strategic investment into its UK platform business and infrastructure.

OUR UK INVESTMENT TRUST BUSINESS

Fidelity has over 25 years' experience managing investment companies, and manages around £3.5 billion in assets across five investment trusts. These are all focused on equity growth strategies. Fidelity won the Premier Group category in *Money Observer*'s 2015 and 2016 Investment Trust Awards and was highly commended in 2017.

As a major platform distributor, Fidelity is able to offer its own investment trusts and those managed by third parties to professional investors and retail investors alike through a range of different product wrappers. Fidelity also promotes its range of trusts directly to institutions and wealth managers through its highly experienced in-house sales teams.

octopus investments
A brighter way

ABOUT OCTOPUS INVESTMENTS

When Octopus was founded in 2000, we wanted to build an investment company that put its customers first, by solving real-life issues. We also wanted to be fully accountable, honest and upfront about how we manage investors' money. Today, Octopus is an award-winning, fast-growing UK fund management business with leading positions in tax-efficient investments, smaller company financing, renewable energy and healthcare. We manage more than £7.2bn[1] in assets for private investors and institutions. And we'll never stop trying to change the world of investments for the better, with simple, jargon-free products that do what they say they will.

Since launching our first Venture Capital Trusts (VCT) in 2002, we've become the UK's largest VCT manager, with more than £750m[2] invested on behalf of over 26,000 investors[1]. It's worth mentioning that some of the world's most innovative high-profile technology companies, such as Google, Microsoft and Amazon, have acquired businesses which have benefited from VCT funding.

VCTs work in a similar way to an investment trust, although, as an incentive for investing in early-stage smaller companies, you can claim a number of useful tax incentives, including 30% upfront income tax relief on the amount invested, tax-free capital gains and tax-free dividends. It's important to note that while a VCT offers a number of tax benefits, these will depend on your personal circumstances and may change over time. The benefits also depend on the VCT maintaining its qualifying status.

OCTOPUS HEADQUARTERS AT 33 HOLBORN, LONDON

ABOUT OCTOPUS TITAN VCT

With net assets of £425m[3] at 30 April 2017, Octopus Titan VCT plc is the UK's largest VCT. One reason why it has proven so popular is that it gives investors the opportunity to benefit from the growth of some of the UK's most exciting, early-stage businesses. We've helped several start-ups grow to become household names, specifically Zoopla Property Group, Secret Escapes and graze.com.

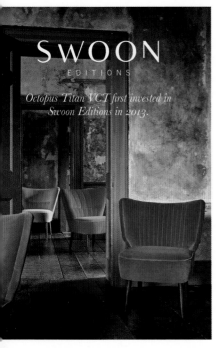

Octopus Titan VCT first invested in Swoon Editions in 2013.

Octopus Titan VCT is managed by Octopus Ventures, one of Europe's largest venture capital teams. The team, with a combined investment experience of over 150 years looks to invest in technology-enabled companies operating in a variety of different sectors. The VCT features a portfolio of around 50 established and developing early-stage companies, as well as a pipeline of exciting young businesses. For example, portfolio company myTomorrows takes an entirely new approach to how medicines should be made available, while Swoon Editions is using technology to turn the traditional world of furniture retail on its head.

KEY RISKS

VCTs are not suitable for everyone, and as we do not offer investment or tax advice, we always recommend talking to a qualified financial adviser before deciding to invest. Octopus Titan VCT is a high-risk investment designed to be held for a minimum of five years. The companies it invests in are not listed on the main market of the London Stock Exchange (LSE). They have a higher failure rate, and the shares can sharply fall or rise in value more than other shares listed on the main market of the LSE. They may also be harder to sell. Because of this, you should understand that your investment, and any income from it, could also fall as well as rise and there is no guarantee the amount you invest will be returned. Please be aware that this advertisement is not a prospectus, and you should only subscribe for shares based on information in the prospectus, which can be obtained from octopusinvestments.com/titan.

For more information about Octopus Titan VCT, please call our Client Relations team on 0800 316 2068 or visit our website. We're always happy to hear from you.

[1] Octopus Investments, August 2017

[2] Tax Efficient Review, April 2017

[3] Octopus Investments

Issued by Octopus Investments Limited, which is authorised and regulated by the Financial Conduct Authority. Registered office: 33 Holborn, London EC1N 2HT. Registered in England and Wales No. 03942880. We record telephone calls. M2-CAM05877-1710